Developmental and Educational Psychology for Teachers

Developmental and Educational Psychology for Teachers brings together a range of evidence drawn from psychology to answer a number of critical educational questions, from basic questions of readiness – for example, when is a child ready for school, through to more complex matters, such as how does a teacher understand and promote good peer relationships in their classroom? The answers to these and other questions discussed draw on the interplay between a teachers' craft expertise and their knowledge of evidence and theory from developmental and educational psychology.

Presenting a range of classic theories and contemporary research to help readers understand what the key issues are for teachers and other professionals, this book aids informed educational decisions in situations such as:

- inclusion;
- ability grouping;
- sex differences;
- developing creativity;
- home and peer influences on learning;
- and developing effective learners.

Teachers in early years, primary, and secondary settings are routinely faced with questions regarding the development of children. This not only relates to the planning and delivery of lessons, but also to the mental and physical well-being of the children and adolescents who they teach. The pedagogical features of this book are accessible and clearly presented, including question points that direct the reader's attention to key issues, activity posts that point the reader to meaningful and relevant research and show the practical applications of material covered, and extension material that gives depth to many of the topics covered.

This book aims to inform the practice of both in-service and trainee teachers, addressing issues that are relevant to their practice. With no other detailed and accessible text presenting this evidence and theory specifically for an audience of practicing and trainee teachers currently on the market, this book will be essential reading to practicing and trainee teachers for early years, primary, and secondary education and other related educational contexts such as educational psychologists, counsellors, paediatric and child doctors and nurses.

Dennis M. McInerney is honorary professor at the Australian Catholic University and an honorary professor at the Education University of Hong Kong. He is a veteran academic who has been a primary teacher, secondary teacher, teacher trainer, as well as professor specialising in educational and developmental psychology.

David W. Putwain is professor at the Liverpool John Moores University. He started his career as a teacher of psychology, sociology and personal, social and health education, and worked in a number of secondary schools and sixth form colleges in England.

Developmental and Educational Psychology for Teachers

An applied approach

Second edition

Dennis M. McInerney &
David W. Putwain

Routledge
Taylor & Francis Group

LONDON AND NEW YORK

Second edition published 2017
by Routledge
2 Park Square, Milton Park, Abingdon, Oxon OX14 4RN

and by Routledge
711 Third Avenue, New York, NY 10017

Routledge is an imprint of the Taylor & Francis Group, an informa business

© 2017 D. M. McInerney & D. W. Putwain

The right of D. M. McInerney & D.W. Putwain to be identified as authors of this work has been asserted by them in accordance with sections 77 and 78 of the Copyright, Designs and Patents Act 1988.

First edition published 2006 by Allen & Unwin.

British Library Cataloguing in Publication Data
A catalogue record for this book is available from the British Library

Library of Congress Cataloging in Publication Data
Names: McInerney, D. M. (Dennis M.), 1948- author. | Putwain, David, author.
Title: Developmental and educational psychology for teachers : an applied approach / Dennis McInerney & David Putwain.
Description: 2nd edition. | Abingdon, Oxon ; New York, NY : Routledge is an imprint of the Taylor & Francis Group, an Informa Business, [2017] | Includes bibliographical references.
Identifiers: LCCN 2016013657| ISBN 9781138947702 (hbk : alk. paper) | ISBN 9781138947726 (pbk : alk. paper) | ISBN 9781315669953 (ebk)
Subjects: LCSH: Educational psychology. | Developmental psychology.
Classification: LCC LB1051 .M398 2017 | DDC 370.15—dc23
LC record available at https://lccn.loc.gov/2016013657

ISBN: 978-1-138-94770-2 (hbk)
ISBN: 978-1-138-94772-6 (pbk)
ISBN: 978-1-315-66995-3 (ebk)

Typeset in Giovanni
by Swales & Willis Ltd, Exeter, Devon, UK
Printed and bound by CPI Group (UK) Ltd, Croydon, CR0 4YY

Contents

About the authors

Dennis M. McInerney. Dennis is a veteran academic who has been a primary teacher, secondary teacher, teacher trainer, as well as professor specialising in educational and developmental psychology. He has had senior positions in Australia, Singapore, and Hong Kong. Dennis is well published and has a number of authored and edited books including *Educational psychology: Constructing learning* (sixth edition, Pearson, Australia); *Helping kids achieve their best* (Information Age Publishing, USA), and *Publishing your psychology research: A guide to writing for journals in psychology and related fields* (Allen & Unwin and Sage, Australia and USA). He is also editor of two research monograph series, *Advances in self research* and *Research on sociocultural influences on motivation and learning* (both Information Age Publishing, USA), and publishes widely in refereed journals and book chapters. Dennis is an honorary professor at the Australian Catholic University and an honorary professor at the Education University of Hong Kong.

David W. Putwain. David started his career as a teacher of psychology, sociology and personal, social and health education, and worked in a number of secondary schools and sixth form colleges in England. Having completed a PhD, David took up a position at Edge Hill University in 2006 where he established an undergraduate programme in educational psychology, before moving to his current position at Liverpool John Moores University in 2016. David has co-authored a number of pedagogical texts, revision guides and articles on A level psychology (Taylor & Francis, Nelson-Thornes, Letts, and Philip-Allan), and has published widely on research into the psychological factors that influence learning and achievement.

Acknowledgments

We are deeply indebted to Bruce Roberts from Routledge who strongly supported this project from its beginning. We would also like to thank Roseanna Levermore, Sarah Sleath and Kristin Susser for their guidance throughout production. We would like to thank Sally Beesley for her beautiful book design, and Kelly Winter for her very thorough copyediting.

We would also like to sincerely thank Joelle Enver for her wonderful artwork that enlivens the text. Finally, we would like to thank the anonymous reviewers of an earlier draft who provided us with insights that have enriched the text.

Preface

There are many excellent developmental psychology texts available, but there are few that take teaching and learning as their specific focus.

Developmental psychology texts are often quite encyclopedic, and readers can be overwhelmed. In this text we have selected material that we believe is of most relevance to students preparing to be teachers across the broad spectrum from early childhood through to early adulthood. Our selection is based on our extensive practical experience of teaching, learning, and researching, with a clear focus on effective education.

Key themes in the text are:

- Heredity and environment, with a particular emphasis on how this information is useful for understanding normal development as well as special learning needs.
- Physical and motor development from early childhood to early adulthood, with a special emphasis on features that separate the different growth stages, and developmental health issues of relevance to teachers.
- Cognition and cognitive development from early childhood through to early adulthood, with an emphasis on contemporary approaches such as metacognition.
- Psychometric intelligence, alternative views of intelligence, and creativity.
- Contemporary views of intellectual development, particularly information processing.
- Personal, social and moral development from early childhood through to early adulthood, with particular emphasis on contemporary themes of importance.

We have developed each theme in an educational context so that the links between the information, teaching and learning are clear and explicit. We have also situated these themes within a research context so that the reader can critically evaluate research findings as well as be inspired and enthused to conduct research.

Chronological approach

No organisational structure of a developmental psychology text is ideal. One can take a topical approach or a chronological approach. We have organised the text chronologically within topics. For this reason, we ask readers to ensure that they read all chapters, even though they might be specialising in one or other level of teaching, such as early childhood, primary, secondary, or tertiary. It is essential, particularly when considering some of the big theories of development, to read the beginning, middle, and end of the theories!

Pedagogical features

We have endeavoured to write the text in clear and easy-to-understand English. We hope we have succeeded. To facilitate learning, we have included the following pedagogical features:

- An introduction to each chapter that serves as an advance organiser for the material to be covered.
- Focus questions that direct the reader's attention to key issues for elaboration.
- Practical activities that engage the reader in meaningful and relevant research and show the practical applications of material covered.
- Selected focus on extension material that gives depth to many of the topics covered.
- Captions, and drawings that illustrate key concepts covered.
- Internet references throughout.
- Glossary of key terms and a list of references.

We hope that this mix of pedagogical features helps the book to be both fun and interactive, and encourages you to deepen your understanding of themes covered.

1 Developmental psychology: themes and research

Introduction

In this book, we are concerned with *human development* from early childhood through to adulthood. What is development and what are the types of development that are of particular interest to psychologists, teachers, health care professionals, and others concerned with the healthy growth of children?

In essence, development refers to systematic, age-related changes in physical and psychological functioning. Systematic physical changes include basic biological developments that result from conception, as well as those that are the result of the interaction of biological and genetic processes and environmental influences. Systematic changes in psychological growth encompass a whole host of characteristics such as cognitive, personal, social, emotional, and moral characteristics.

Developmental changes may be qualitative, such as an infant progressing from crawling to walking, or quantitative, such as an infant becoming more and more adept at walking. Some developmental theorists, such as Piaget, believe that only qualitative changes are the real markers of development. In Piaget's stage theory of cognitive development, which is described in detail in Chapter 5, children go through four discrete cognitive stages of development each characterised by different cognitive capacities. Other psychologists, such as information processing psychologists put more emphasis on quantitative changes, such as the improved speed with which an individual can process and encode specific information. While information processing psychologists believe that qualitative changes do occur in children's thinking as they grow older, the elements of information processing are available to children at an early age and they acquire increased sophistication in their use as they grow older (see, for example, Veenman & Spaans, 2005).

 QUESTION POINT

Draw a timeline of major features of your development until adulthood. Which of the changes were qualitative in nature? Which of the changes were quantitative? Which type of change do you consider as a more significant marker of your personal development?

Another characteristic of development is continuity. Many developmental psychologists consider that once development has commenced for an individual there is a regularity and predictability about it that allows us to predict the future course of development for that individual. For example, if a child demonstrated a low academic or physical ability early in life, this will probably continue as a trend throughout the child's development. Freud's theory, which we consider later in the book is a good example of a theory that holds that personal development shows continuity based on early life experiences of the individual, which is relatively impervious to change. Of course, many other developmental psychologists argue that there is just as much evidence for discontinuity in development whereby individuals experiencing environmental interventions of various types may begin on a developmental trajectory quite different from predicted. Foremost among these psychologists were the early behavioural theorists such as John. B. Watson and Burrhus. F. Skinner who believed that an individual's behaviour was malleable depending on environmental experiences, and in particular, the reinforcing experiences an individual had for particular behaviour. Continuity in development allows prediction and intervention, however, as we have indicated, many theorists believe that a considerable number of human characteristics show discontinuity in developmental trends.

 QUESTION POINT

Consider your own development since you were a youngster. Which of your characteristics show continuity across your life? Are there characteristics that have changed? If so, what were the circumstances for the change?

Knowledge of physical and psychological development patterns and milestones, qualitative and quantitative changes, continuity and discontinuity, prepares professionals for their daily interactions with children and adolescents as they grow to maturity. Such knowledge guides teachers, social workers, nurses, psychologists, and doctors in their development of effective educational and health programmes to maximise the development of each individual. Typical patterns of development that characterise most children and adolescents allow such professionals to design programmes that may be applied generally. In contrast, knowledge of atypical patterns that vary from norms allows professionals to individualise health and educational programmes to suit the needs of particular individuals. In this book, we will consider each perspective.

Studying development

Psychology, as a discipline of science, refers to the study of human behaviour, and in particular, the study of the behaviour of individuals and groups. Psychologists study behaviour in order to understand human nature and why people do the things they do. Behaviour may be overt, as in a child demanding attention, or covert, as in a person's stomach contracting. Behaviour has both cognitive and affective elements. Much behaviour appears logical, orderly, and constructive. At other times, behaviour might appear irrational, strange, and bizarre. Behaviour might be simple or complex. Developmental psychology, as the name implies, studies, in particular, the development of human capacities such as thinking, feeling, and behaving. Developmental psychologists are interested in the various stages and elements of development, the principles of maturation, the effects of early experience and later practice on development, and a host of other issues.

In order to obtain valid and reliable information on child and adolescent development it is necessary to study development closely. Developmental psychology has had a long history of systematically obtaining, through rigorous observation and controlled studies, essential information on the regularities and exceptions to development that have guided professionals, and which forms the basis of information in books such as this one (see, for example, Hergenhahn & Henley, 2014). Two elements are important in the study of development, first, describing development, and second, explaining development. In our treatment of development throughout this book we will both describe the key elements of development over physical and psychological domains, and where appropriate, attempt to explain the nature and course of development.

There has also been centuries of theoretical and philosophical speculation on the nature of human development, and in particular, whether development is innately 'hot wired' into the system at conception, an approach often referred to as nativist or **hereditarian**, or whether development is much more malleable and subject to environmental influences, often referred to as empiricist, or **environmentalist**. This issue is often referred to as the nature–nurture debate, which we discuss in Chapter 2.

If you were to look through the history of psychology, you would also see that over the last two centuries there has been a considerable shift from identifying a few basic stages of human development such as childhood and adulthood, through to an ever-increasing identification and refinement of stages. These refined stages include not only infancy, early childhood, middle childhood, late childhood, adolescence, and adulthood, but also an entire life span approach encompassing old age as a separate developmental stage (see, for example, Santrock, 2009). In this book we divide our examination of most topics into discrete time frames such as early, middle and late childhood, and adolescence. However, you should be aware that these divisions are somewhat arbitrary and you should read across the topics in order to get a complete picture of developmental processes, their regularities, and idiosyncrasies.

There has also been an increase in interest in studying the interaction of various developmental systems (such as physical, cognitive, emotional, and social), and an increasing emphasis on the complexity of the influences (such as biological and social) that influence development. A strong exponent of this approach, Urie Bronfenbrenner, developed an ecological model of human development, which includes an ever-widening set of influences on development (Bronfenbrenner, 1979; Bronfenbrenner & Morris, 2006). While we do not specifically deal with the ecological approach in this book, it is worth your while to read up on it. Nevertheless, we do emphasise throughout the need to put development in its full context, which includes cultural and socioeconomic contexts.

While observation of human behaviour began with early philosophers such as Aristotle, St Augustine, and Jean-Jacques Rousseau, dramatists such as Shakespeare, and scientists such as Charles Darwin, careful scientific observation of human nature from which emerged great theories of human development began in the early 1900s (see, Hergenhahn & Henley, 2014). Major contributions were made by people such as, Jean Piaget, Lev Vygotsky, and Alexander Luria in the development of cognition; John Watson, Edward Thorndike, and Burrhus Skinner, in behavioural development; William James, Granville Hall, Sigmund Freud, and Carl Jung in self and personality development; Alfred Binet and James Cattell on mental testing; and Arnold Gesell on physical development. From this early systematic theorising and observational, clinical, and experimental research emerged a body of knowledge that forms the core of developmental psychology (and other branches of psychology) and from which emerged the contemporary scientific study of child and adolescent development.

Throughout the study of psychology, various research approaches have fallen in and out of favour. Many early studies were based on the **clinical method**. By the clinical method we mean a procedure whereby a psychologist probes for information by asking a respondent questions in an interview setting, and supplementing the information obtained in this manner with observations, projective techniques (such as interpreting pictures), and perhaps some activities (such as completing a relevant task). The clinical method formed the basis of the research of a whole host of early masters such as Piaget and Freud.

However, other psychologists considered such approaches too subjective, open to interpretation, and relatively non-scientific. These researchers preferred a **scientific method** based on controlled experiments in which cause and effect could be examined. Experimental approaches formed a major component of the research techniques of some early giants of psychology such as Watson, Thorndike, and Skinner.

Whether research is clinical or experimental, good research is based on theory and hypothesis testing. In other words, researchers attempt to answer questions related to development such as 'are there critical times for the development of speech?', 'is bonding with parents essential for the emotional health of children?', 'does cognitive development proceed in stages?', and 'does viewing violent television make children more violent?'. Theories, hypotheses, and research questions are essential as they drive the investigative process, and from well-designed studies is generated the information upon which psychologists, teachers, nurses, psychiatrists, and other professionals make informed judgements.

There is no right way to study child development; both the clinical method and controlled experiments allow us to discover useful information. However, it is essential that whatever method is used, is used correctly. In a later section of this chapter we discuss some common research techniques utilised by psychologists.

 QUESTION POINT

During your study at school or at university were you a participant in a research study? If so, what was the nature of the study? What were you required to do? Were you given prior information on the purpose of the study? Were you given feedback on the results of the study?

Themes in developmental psychology

What are the major themes in developmental psychology? Typically, developmental psychology examines physical development, cognitive development and cognitive processes, intelligence, personal, social, moral and emotional development, language development, as well as learning and motivational processes (see, for example, Cairns & Cairns, 2007). Biological and environmental influences on development, which include the family and peers, as well as cultural influences form a major focus of attention. In this book we consider most of these issues from the perspective of what is useful and necessary for teachers and other related professionals to know. In the following sections we give a brief overview of content to be covered in each of the subsequent chapters.

Heredity and environment

Why are we like the way we are? This question has intrigued psychologists since the beginning of the study of the development of human nature. There are two key factors involved in the development of human beings; heredity and environment. In Chapter 2, we examine the relative influence on development of heredity and environment and illustrate concepts that are important for teachers and others facilitating the development of children. Many aspects of our physical growth and motor development are canalised, that is, highly dependent on genetics such as getting bigger, walking, and talking that occur in most situations at about the same time for most children universally. It takes a significant environmental event, such as gross malnutrition or birth problems, to alter the course of canalised development (Masel & Siegal, 2009; Waddington, 1957).

Other aspects of our development, such as the development of cognition, perception, emotions, and personality, are far less canalised and more strongly under the influence of environmental influences. These lead to a range of developmental trajectories and outcomes for individual children. While the basic material of these developments is laid out in the genes of each child the environment plays an important role in moderating the effects of genes. Perhaps intelligence and temperament are two such qualities subject to considerable environmental influence. And along a continuum of human characteristics there are probably a host that are highly susceptible to environmental influences including the development of talents and skills, moral and political perspectives, and social, intrapersonal and interpersonal attributes. It is therefore essential that professionals dealing with children have a good understanding of how the environment may work to shape and mould individuals.

Chapter 2 examines the role genes play in directing the development of specific human characteristics (our genotype) as well as the role played by the interaction of genes with environment in shaping our characteristics (what is termed our phenotype). Behavioural genetics seeks to explain the potential interactions between heredity and environment and we explore this in some detail. In order to explore relative influences of heredity and environment further, the chapter also examines atypical development resulting from both genetic defects and environmental forces and draws out implications of these for teachers and other professionals.

Physical growth and motor development

In Chapters 3 and 4 we consider physical and motor development from childhood through to adolescence. Physical development refers to physical and neurological growth, and motor development refers to age-related changes in motor skills. We consider the importance of physical growth and motor development from the broadest perspectives: as part of the normal growth of individuals, to establish good life habits, and to facilitate the development of other systems (such as cognitive, social, and personal) that are intrinsically entwined with the physical development of the person.

We also look closely at cycles of physical development and the orderly and sequential nature of development, and in particular we look at cephalocaudal (head to tail development) and proximodistal (inner axis out development) growth patterns. We look specifically at motor development in the light of four key principles: maturation, motivation, experience, and practice. Significant developmental milestones are discussed and their relevance to effective education considered. Individual and sex differences in both physical growth and motor development are highlighted.

Finally, we consider a range of issues related to general physical health and safety issues from early childhood to adolescence with which teachers and other related professionals need to be familiar. An accurate picture of developmental patterns is fundamental to an understanding of children and adolescents, and knowledge of what causes variations in development is essential to an understanding of each individual.

Cognitive development

In Chapters 5 and 6 we consider cognition and cognitive development from early childhood through to early adulthood. Broadly, cognition refers to the intellectual activity of an individual, i.e. the mental processes; involving all aspects of thought and perception including imagining, reasoning, and judging. A knowledge of cognition and cognitive development is essential for teachers and related professionals. As with physical and motor growth, the growth of a child's mind shows continuity as well as change, and as the child grows older there is an increasing differentiation of cognitive capacities. Young children are emersed in learning about the world around them. Concepts such as number, time, weight, measurement, space, and existence are the everyday subjects being mastered by children through their world of experiences. As children grow older they develop more mature cognitive processes which enable them to adapt increasingly efficiently to the world around them.

In these two chapters we consider four important, and contrasting, views on cognitive development, those of Jean Piaget, Lev Vygotsky, and Jerome Bruner, and metacognition. Each believes that learning is an intentional process of constructing meaning from experience, but the means by which this knowledge construction occurs is considered differently. Three questions are raised which guides our analysis:

1 What is the best way to characterise children's intellectual functioning at various key points in their growth?
2 What is the best way to characterise the process by which children progress from one of these points to the next?
3 How can the developmental process be optimised?

Our first focus is on Piaget's theory of intellectual development. For Piaget cognitive development involves an interaction between assimilating new facts to old knowledge and accommodating old knowledge to new facts, and the maintenance of structural equilibrium. Furthermore, as children mature they develop a series of operations or thought processes through which they become increasingly able to handle inferential thinking. The first Piagetian concept discussed is structuralism, which relates to Piaget's notion that cognitive growth occurs through a series of stages: sensorimotor, preoperational, concrete-operational, and formal, each characterised by qualitatively different cognitive structures. The second Piagetian concept discussed is personal constructivism, which relates to Piaget's notion that individuals construct their own meanings through the interacting processes of assimilation, adaptation, accommodation, and equilibrium, and the extension of schemes, or ways of thinking.

Piaget's theory is quite complex, so we have selected elements to elaborate that we believe have applied significance for educators. We discuss the current status of Piaget's theory and indicate that there is presently a de-emphasis on the structuralist components and an emphasis on the constructivist components. Important cross-cultural implications of Piaget's theory are also highlighted.

The second focus is on Vygotskian theory, which presents a contrast to Piagetian theory. According to Vygotsky's theory, children are born with a wide range of perceptual, attentional, and memory capacities which are substantially transformed through socialisation and education, particularly through the use of cultural inventions such as tools, social structures, and language, to develop human cognition. While Vygotsky emphasises the active role played by the learner in constructing meaning, he focuses on the role of social factors within the external environment. In particular, his theory of social constructivism stresses the interplay between a supportive learning environment, represented by parents, teachers and peers, and the individual's cognitive manipulation of information to facilitate meaningful learning. Key elements of Vygotsky's theory, such as the zone of proximal development, holistic education, and mediated learning through social interaction, are described.

We draw contrasts between Piaget and Vygotsky regarding the nature and function of discovery in learning, the role of social interaction in learning and the relationship between language and learning.

Bruner provides another view of cognitive development. For Bruner the process of intellectual growth and learning consists in children gradually organising their environment into meaningful units by a process called conceptualisation and the formation of cognitive categories. Bruner theorised that children go through three major stages of intellectual development; enactive, iconic, and symbolic, and use two types of thinking; analytic and intuitive. We discuss elements of each of these stages and the specific characteristics of analytic and intuitive thinking, and the role of discovery learning in cognitive development.

In the final focus of these chapters, we deal with some important recent develop-ments in cognitive psychology, namely metacognition, learning strategies, and situated cognition. The ability to plan, monitor, and regulate our cognitive processes while constructing knowledge is considered by many to be essential to effective learning. This is referred to as metacognition. In order to learn effectively learners also need knowledge about how they learn, called metalearning. Many psychologists believe that metacognitive knowledge appears early and continues to develop at least throughout adolescence. We consider elements of metacognition and metalearning and some pro-grammes that may enhance the development of metacognition.

Conceptions of intelligence and creativity

In Piagetian theory a child's capacity to reason at various levels is believed to be biolog-ically linked, and the development of increasing cognitive abilities depends on natural development in an interactive, supportive environment. While Piaget would agree that there are individual differences in mental capacity, his theory emphasises the need to develop each individual's mental capacity through appropriate experiences, rather than merely identifying bright and less bright children.

Vygotsky's view emphasises the social dimension of learning and the zone of proxi-mal development. Hence, Vygotsky's focus moves beyond what the child currently knows to what is possible, and to the processes most relevant to stimulate this growth. Furthermore, because of the very strong social and cultural components of Vygotskyian thought, what is considered 'intelligent' behaviour is more broadly viewed than simply being good at school and having a lot of 'knowledge'.

In Chapter 7 we look at alternative views on intelligence and cognition. In this chap-ter we consider the psychometric approach to intelligence. The psychometric approach is quite different from Piagetian and Vygotskian perspectives as the emphasis is one of measuring the intellectual capacity of individuals relative to others of the same age. It seeks to define and quantify dimensions of intelligence, primarily through the col-lection of data on individual differences and through the construction of reliable and valid mental tests. We consider views of intelligence as a unitary construct, and as a multifaceted construct, and the valid and reliable measurement of intelligence. We deal with intelligence testing in some detail and we introduce the notions of mental age, intelligence quotient, and individual and group tests of intelligence. We describe limitations of the psychometric approach to intelligence testing, especially problems emanating from cultural differences.

We also highlight theories that describe intelligence as multifaceted, and defined by such qualities as flexibility of thought, efficient working memory, adaptability, crea-tive productivity, insight skills, **social skills**, and effective use of domain knowledge. In particular, we explore Gardner's theory of multiple intelligences and Sternberg's **triarchic theory of intelligence**. In both of these approaches one's culture and specific contexts are considered to be important determinants of intelligent behaviour as indi-viduals interact with their external world.

Intelligence tests are designed so that there is usually one and only one right answer to a question, if you answer divergently then you will not get a score on that question. But is there a place for different answers and solutions, and what is the relationship between divergent thinking and measures of intelligence that usually require convergent thinking? We look in some detail at creative and divergent thinking, its measurement, and its relationship to convergent thinking measured through conventional intelligence tests.

Cognition and information processing

Part of cognitive development is the increasing capacity for individuals to manipulate and remember information. In Chapter 8 we focus on information processing as a model for explaining human learning. We explore in detail the computer as an analogy for the learning process by examining the way in which information is attended to, encoded, processed, stored, and retrieved.

Results of information-processing research apply in three areas of learning. First, information processing research suggests that there are limits to the amount of information that learners can attend to and process effectively. If we overload our processing system, the working memory is unable to cope with the demands, and processing becomes inefficient. In Chapter 8 we present many ideas on how long and complex, or new and potentially difficult, information can be restructured so that mental demand is reduced. The second finding from information-processing research is that learners must be actively engaged in processing the information in order to transfer it from the working memory to the long-term memory. We refer to this as learning for retention and discuss a number of methods to facilitate retention of information. The third implication from information-processing research for learning is that learnt material should be encoded in such a way as to facilitate recall and facilitate transfer to new but related situations. Meaningful material is learnt more easily, retained more effectively, and recalled more efficiently than non-meaningful material. We discuss methods for enhancing meaningful learning.

Personal and social development

In Chapters 9 and 10 we consider personal and social development and, in particular, how individuals develop as people: how they relate to others and to themselves; how they develop personal goals and ambitions in life; and how they react to the many problems and challenges they meet in life. The major foci in these two chapters are on the personality theories of Freud, Erikson, Rogers, and Maslow. Each of these theorists has made a valuable contribution to our understanding of how individuals develop a sense of self.

We describe elements of Freudian theory that are of interest to educators and related professionals in order to show how perspectives from psychoanalytic theory have infused much personality psychology, and how key concepts from the theory are still useful today in our analysis of children's and adolescent's behaviour. In particular we describe and discuss defence mechanisms which are commonly used by children and adolescents.

In the description of Erikson's psychosocial theory of personality development we cover the eight stages of psychosocial development and the important process of identity formation. We emphasise, especially, the importance of caregivers, teachers, and peers in an individual's personality development. We contrast Freud and Erikson, and in particular, the continuity implied in Freud's theory in contrast to that of Erikson. We also consider the humanistic theories of Rogers and Maslow. Our major focus here is on the role that parents, caregivers, and teachers play as facilitators of children's personal and intellectual development by supplying appropriate opportunities, resources, support, and non-evaluative feedback to them.

We spend some time discussing attachment theory. It is essential that a strong, affectionate bond is established between children and caregivers and that this continues through to adulthood. Attachment theory gives a basis for considering the important and continuing role played by parents and caregivers in the personal, social, and emotional development of children. In particular, we consider the nature of family relationships and their effects on the child's self-reliance and independence. We describe three parenting styles: authoritative, authoritarian, and laissez-faire and their potential impact on children. We also consider in detail the importance of peer group interaction for personal development and group acceptance. In this context, we look at the function of groups, gangs, cliques, and friendships.

In our rapidly changing world many children and adolescents become alienated. The roots of youth alienation are very complex and may include family background, personality characteristics (such as self-esteem), and school influences. We look closely at adolescent alienation and the issue of adolescent suicide in particular. The importance of social skills to children and adolescents in order to avoid antisocial and delinquent behaviour is considered as an important element of social and personal adjustment.

Another important aspect of personal, social and emotional development is the development of a sense of self as a worthwhile human being. We consider the nature and development of the self-concept, how it is structured and formed, whether (and how) it changes over time, whether there are group differences in self-concept, and what effect it has on motivation and behaviour. We also consider the nature and importance of self-regulation and self-efficacy. Self-regulation is important because it refers to the regulation of one's own cognitive processes in order to learn effectively, and to monitor a range of other personal processes. A feeling of positive self-efficacy is essential for an adolescent's feeling of well-being because efficacy beliefs influence how they feel, think, motivate themselves, and behave.

Moral development

In all societies, a framework of rules exists to govern and control human behaviour. Many of these rules are determined to be moral obligations and moral rules can be quite complex. Given the complexity of rules, mores, and morality, how do growing children learn morality? The process of development of moral concepts arises from children's personal cognitive growth and experiences in the social world. The appreciation of the moral component of social experiences depends upon the cognitive level at which the child is functioning. In Chapter 11 we consider moral development in detail and examine closely the work of Piaget, Kohlberg (and neo-Kohlbergian approaches), Gilligan, and Turiel.

We discuss Piaget's stages of moral reasoning, together with the notions of a morality of constraint and a morality of cooperation. In line with recent thinking about Piagetian stage theory, we provide a critique of his approach to moral development. Kohlberg's stages of moral development – preconventional, conventional, and postconventional – are described and the current status of the theory is explored. In particular, we examine sex differences in moral development, the relationship between moral reasoning and moral behaviour, and cross-cultural implications. Neo-Kohlbergian developments of Kohlberg's theory are also examined. Gilligan's critique of the male bias in Kohlberg's theory is examined, as well as her call for a revision which gives greater focus to a morality of caring.

Turiel's domain theory of moral development is also described. Within domain theory a distinction is drawn between the child's developing concepts of morality, and other domains of social knowledge, such as social convention. According to domain theory, the child's concepts of morality and social convention emerge out of the child's attempts to account for qualitatively differing forms of social experience associated with these two classes of social events. Hence, there are considerable differences in perspectives between Turiel's views and the stage theories of Piaget and Kohlberg.

Throughout the book these physical, cognitive, and personal themes of developmental psychology are related to the educational experiences of the children so that you as a practitioner are better prepared to facilitate the development of children. In the next section we consider important qualities of research that provides the information on child growth and development throughout this book.

Psychology and the scientific method

Progress in many fields depends upon asking questions and seeking answers. It is no different for psychology. Why do people behave the way they do? How do people learn? How do we form emotions? What are the relative effects of heredity and environment on human development? What mechanisms are involved in walking, talking, and perceiving? In order to answer questions effectively psychological researchers must adopt scientific methods that allow for accuracy, objectivity, scepticism, and open-mindedness. Unless researchers are accurate, what store can be placed in the answers? Unless researchers are objective, how can they argue that the answers do not reflect overt and covert biases? Unless researchers are willing to be sceptical, how can their answers be challenged? Finally, unless researchers are open-minded how can they cope with answers that appear 'out of field'? (see for example, Bryman, 2012; Creswell & Clark, 2007; Robson, 2011).

To investigate questions psychologists often hypothesise effects and relationships between phenomena, and test these out through well-constructed experiments. At other times, psychologists pose questions about phenomena that allow for research approaches that are more open. When effects and relationships are found psychologists seek to discover 'why'. Most often, the 'why' is related to a theoretical perspective that underpins the research. *Theory*, rather than being something vague, is based on principles independent of observations and provides the structure for investigations, as well as a framework for analysing and interpreting data and applying findings appropriately. All good psychological research reflects theoretical principles and you will become familiar with many theories as you complete your study in psychology.

There are many under investigated research questions in developmental psychology. It is important for researchers to ascertain whether a particular research question has already been identified and answered by other researchers. It is futile to spend time and resources on a problem that has already been highly researched unless there are some puzzles still remaining. A **literature review** is conducted in a research area to find out what is already known about an issue of interest. The literature review will also suggest potential avenues for further investigation, partial solutions to the problem under consideration, and appropriate methodologies, tools, and analyses for further research. In other words, a background literature review provides researchers with a good foundation upon which to construct their studies. Research literature is also an essential resource for professionals wishing to keep abreast of their field.

When addressing a research question a researcher develops an appropriate **research design**. The research design will be comprised of the research questions, an identification of the appropriate data, the sample of participants that are needed to obtain these data, and the method for gathering these data, and the analytical tools and approaches to be used for analysing these data. Again, each of these elements must be consistent with the research aims. In addition to these components of research are associated concerns such as whether the researcher has access to the type and size of sample needed, how long will the study take, how expensive will data entry and analysis be, what special equipment is needed, and so on. For example, two basic designs used in psychological research are **cross-sectional designs** and **longitudinal designs**. Cross-sectional designs study a large number of participants at a given point in time, hence are efficient in providing much data. Longitudinal designs usually study a smaller number of participants continuously over a longer period of time that might stretch over years. However, both of these designs have strengths and limitations, and it is important to maximise the strength of a methodology so that it most clearly addresses the research issue under examination.

 QUESTION POINT

Consider cross-sectional and longitudinal research designs. What are their strengths and weaknesses? Suggest two projects, one in which it would be important to have a longitudinal approach and one in which it would be important to have a cross-sectional approach. Give reasons for your decision about the appropriateness of the research design.

In the next section we describe some common forms of research design in psychology.

Basic and applied research

Before we consider specific methodologies, it is necessary to consider **basic** and **applied research** (see, Mayer, 2008; Spiel, 2009; Stokes, 1997). It is common to make a distinction between what is called basic (sometimes called 'pure') and applied research. What is basic research? What is applied research? At its most simple level, basic research deals with the generation of new knowledge or the extension of existing knowledge. It might be an experiment examining the impact of x on y, or a study of the attitudes of individuals to a particular issue. The focus is clearly on the provision of new information without regard to immediate practical application of the knowledge. The research may even appear somewhat unrelated to 'real world' issues and the solving of specific problems. An example of this might be the tracking of eye movement in newly born children. There are many examples of basic research having a dramatic impact on our everyday lives through the clever application of new information to old problems. For example, the discovery of recency and latency effects regarding recognition and recall resulted in communication theory advocating that the delivery of information is more or less effective when given in chunks using the seven, plus or minus two, rule.

Applied research, as its name implies, is concerned with the application of knowledge to solve specific practical problems. For example, once it is discovered that x has a particular effect on y, other researchers may attempt to use this information to solve a relevant problem. Indeed the progress of much scientific practice proceeds in this way. Hence, applied research in psychology may study the effectiveness of a self-esteem programme on academic achievement. In many cases, research studies may have basic and applied components.

 QUESTION POINT

Discuss with other students some potential basic psychological experiments that relate to education. Discuss some potential applied psychological experiments that relate to education. Can you easily tell the difference between a study that has a basic focus and a study that has an applied focus?

Research methods

Below the level of basic and applied research are the research methods that researchers choose to conduct their research. We have already mentioned two designs of importance: cross-sectional and longitudinal. Research reported throughout this book will represent both types. Three methodological approaches commonly used in psychology are **experimental research**, **quasi-experimental research**, and **correlational research**. Each approach has its specific requirements and is suited to particular research questions and settings. These methods can be used with either cross-sectional or longitudinal designs.

ACTIVITY POST

Consider a range of research articles suggested by your lecturer. Can you identify the research method used in each?

Experimental research

In experimental research the researcher manipulates one or more independent variables (those chosen as important by the researcher) in order to observe their effects on one or more dependent variables (outcomes seen to be important by the researcher) (Hole, 2012; Robson, 2011). All other variables that might have a confounding effect on outcomes are controlled. Confounding refers to the situation where the researcher cannot effectively tease out what are the 'real' causes owing to the possible effects of other elements not controlled for. For example, the researcher might be interested in the effects of reaction time of individuals to blinking red and green lights. Variables that might have an impact such as sex, age, disabilities, and so on, are either built into the experiment as independent variables so that their effects may be examined, or controlled so that they do not confound the results. Control of these variables may be achieved through randomising or counterbalancing the variables, if the sample is large enough, or matching and holding them constant across groups. Extraneous elements that might also have an unwanted effect (such as time of day, room distractions, etc.) are also controlled so that the direct effect of red and green lights on reaction time is validly measured.

 QUESTION POINT

Discuss, with examples, randomising and counterbalancing in experiments. Why would a large sample be desirable for randomising and counterbalancing?

There are a number of experimental designs used by researchers. These deal with issues such as the number and arrangement of independent variables. They also deal with the way subjects are selected and assigned to conditions, how confounding variables are controlled for, and finally a description of the statistical analyses used to evaluate the results of the experimental manipulation. These elements of research design are very important for the researcher and others to establish whether the results of the experiment are generalisable to other situations, and so that other researchers can replicate the research if they want to.

Quasi-experimental research

At times, it is not possible to control all potentially confounding variables. Furthermore, the interactive effects of a whole range of variables (such as socio-economic status, educational level of parents, culture, and prior educational experiences) might not easily be controlled or manipulated in an experimental design. This is particularly the case when the researcher conducts an experiment with human participants in intact groups. In other words, the researcher has less control over matching and **randomisation**. It is common for classroom experiments to be quasi-experimental as the researcher has little control over who is in each class. For example, if a researcher wants to examine the effects of an 'old' and 'new' way of teaching by comparing the outcomes in two classes there is a more limited possibility for experimental control. Nevertheless, well-planned quasi-experimental research can have many of the hallmarks of experimental research, by incorporating as many principles of scientific control as possible given the circumstances. Well-planned quasi-experimental research can allow for pre-post comparisons when groups are tested at the beginning and end of some treatment in order to examine any differential outcomes. Any initial differences in groups owing to lack of randomisation can be partially controlled for by statistical techniques. For example, if a researcher was examining the effects of a new reading programme on an experimental classroom compared with a control classroom and there were pre-existing initial differences in intelligence and reading ability in the two classes, both prior reading ability and intelligence can be added to the statistical analyses so that these are controlled. Any residual differences remaining between the experimental and control groups can be attributed to the experimental treatment.

In other quasi-experimental research, some level of randomisation to groups, some matching, and various statistical controls over the data to eliminate variance due to extraneous features of the design and sample can be utilised. In fact, in some cases, the distinction between true experimental and quasi-experimental research is tenuous in much psychological research. Quasi-experimental research may also have greater ecological validity than experimental research when dealing with human subjects.

Correlational research

Both experimental and quasi-experimental research is concerned with demonstrating causal relationships. That is, the experimenter sets out to demonstrate that if variable x is manipulated in a particular way it will have a causal effect on what happens to variable y. Not all psychological research is amenable to such an approach, nor is all research clearly able to isolate causality. The focus of much psychological research, therefore, is to demonstrate relationships between variables, such as when variable x varies, variable y varies in some predictable way. This type of research is called correlational research.

If two variables completely covary, that is as one variable increases by one unit, the other variable also increases by one unit the coefficient of relationship is 1.0. If there is absolutely no covariation the coefficient of relationship is 0.0. If the covariation is in the same direction, that is, as one variable measure increases the other also increases, the coefficient is positive (+). If the covariation is in the opposite direction, for example, as one variable measure increases the other variable measure decreases, the coefficient is negative (−). There are statistical tests that measure whether the covariation is significant. A rule of thumb suggests that coefficients above 0.4 are generally considered meaningful relationships between variables. Much educational and developmental research is correlational in nature. There are many excellent texts around on quantitative research and you should consult some of these (see, for example, Field, 2013; Miles, 2012).

 ACTIVITY POST

Select three research articles from the journal *Child Development*, or other developmental psychology journal. Select one example of experimental, quasi-experimental, and correlational research. Write a brief overview of each article illustrating the specific qualities of the methodology that identifies it as experimental, quasi-experimental or correlational. What are the relative strengths of each approach? Can you identify three potential research questions in developmental psychology that could be answered by each approach?

 QUESTION POINT

Do you think any one method of research (experimental, quasi-experimental, correlational, qualitative) is better suited to psychological research than another? Why?

Qualitative research

The research designs we have considered so far are largely quantitative designs in which statistical analyses play a large role. One difficulty with such approaches is that they can be somewhat removed from the real world of human experience. Increasingly in psychology, researchers are using alternative methods to address questions in more naturalistic contexts. Sometimes these alternatives are used in the early stages of research to examine a problem in its 'real' or 'normal' context in order to generate plausible hypotheses, or appropriate tools (such as survey questions) for later experimental or correlational research. This research is referred to as **qualitative research** (Eatough, 2012; Robson, 2011).

Qualitative studies are also used to understand or check on findings, that is, they can be used to test hypotheses and provide information to supplement, validate, explain, illuminate, or reinterpret quantitative data. At other times, qualitative approaches are considered the essential means by which a problem can be most effectively addressed because they allow the examination of a problem holistically, taking account of real life in all its complexity and depth. In this latter case, for example, the researcher might be specifically interested in the perceptions of the participants 'from the inside' which could not be effectively addressed experimentally. In general, qualitative methods use relatively little standardised instrumentation and do not depend on extensive statistical analyses.

Qualitative research has a long and illustrious history in psychology. Many key theoretical perspectives guiding psychology were derived from qualitative analyses. We only need to mention Freud, Piaget, Vygotsky, Jung, Kohlberg, and Kuhn for you to realise the rich informative contribution made by these theoreticians to our understanding and awareness, and importantly, our view of human personality and development.

Qualitative research may be biographical involving an intense study of an individual, ethnographic involving the intensive study of groups of people, naturalistic such as observing children in classrooms and adults in shopping malls, survey based such as questionnaires and interviews, and case study based in which detailed information is gathered on particular individuals. In many cases, qualitative research is **positivistic**, that is based on a priori theorising seeking for answers to research questions. At other times qualitative research is more open and based on **grounded theory** approaches in which questions, themes and issues arise from the analysis of the data themselves.

Data may be obtained through archival records, oral histories, interviews, autobiographies, studies of individuals and their lived experiences, surveys, observations, fieldwork studies, and so on. The aim of the researcher is to reduce the data (and with qualitative research this can be quite extensive) into meaningful patterns. For each approach, therefore, there will be related data reduction and analysis techniques, such as coding, content and cluster analyses of documents and scripts. Increasingly there are computer software packages available that facilitate the coding, reduction, analysis, and interpretation of qualitative data. As with good quantitative research, the researcher needs to control extraneous variables and ensure that spurious results are not generated by faulty analyses. There are many excellent qualitative research texts around and you should consult a number of these if you are interested in conducting qualitative research (see, for example, Bannister et al., 2011; Smith, 2015; Wilig, 2013).

 QUESTION POINT

Consider a number of research issues in psychology that you believe could be studied most effectively through a qualitative approach. Why is a qualitative approach most appropriate? How would you control for the accuracy of your research in generating valid and reliable results?

Integrative reviews and meta-analyses

While you might not typically think that a literature review is a form of research, reviews that involve a secondary analysis and synthesis of data across related studies is, in fact, a very valuable form of research commonly used in psychology. All researchers depend on both **integrative reviews** and **meta-analyses** to describe what findings are already available on particular topics and how other researchers conducted their studies. An integrative review is one that primarily synthesises and interprets findings on a topic across a range of relevant research articles. It will identify themes, and may discuss the strengths and weaknesses of particular articles and the field of research as a whole. A meta-analysis goes further. It takes the primary statistical findings from a large number of research projects related to a specific topic, such as the effect of self-esteem enhancement programmes on academic achievement, and derives a measure which reflects whether, on average, results are significant or not, and positive or negative. Both forms of literature review are very useful for researchers developing a research programme. Integrative reviews and meta-analyses are routinely used by psychologists to keep abreast of recent developments in their field of expertise.

General principles of good research

Research on child growth and development is very common in Western societies. From this research much information is derived that gives norms for physical, motor, and cognitive development on which professionals and caregivers can evaluate an individual's growth, as well as guidelines for interpreting development in a whole range of areas from personal and social to moral and intellectual.

From infancy onwards, caregivers and other professionals such as nurses, doctors, social workers, teachers, and coaches weigh, measure, poke, and prod youngsters to assess whether or not they are growing and developing according to norms or other expected standards. In this sense, the process of *measurement* relates to collecting specific quantitative data which might be in centimetres, kilograms, number of erupted teeth, heart rate, or visual acuity (Fife-Shaw, 2012). *Evaluation*, on the other hand, refers to the quality, value, or worth of the information gathered (Robson, 2011). So while a child might weigh 15 kilograms (an objective measurement), they might be evaluated as being scrawny or pudgy (a subjective, 'evaluative' judgment). To make the interpretation less subjective other criteria (such as age norms) need to be applied to make the evaluation. In this context these evaluations are often referred to as *assessments* (Biesta, 2009).

Validity in measurement

We generally use the term **validity in measurement** to refer to whether we are indeed *measuring what we intend to measure*. More importantly, validity refers to the *appropriateness* of a measure for the specific inferences or decisions that result from the scores generated by the measure (Robson, 2011). Researchers need to be confident that the interpretations they make are based upon a dependable measure, do not overstate what the measure allows them to state, and are appropriate to the intentions of the measurement's use. For example, it would be inappropriate to use a measure of intellectual performance to evaluate interpersonal relationship skills for purposes of employing a person.

Various types of evidence may be accrued to support the validity of measurements (Shadish, 2002; Shadish et al., 2002). Among the evidence that may be used to support the validity of a particular measurement are **face**, **content**, **criterion**, and **construct evidence**.

Face validity evidence indicates that the task or measure in the research, at least on the surface, measures what it purports to measure (Kleine, 2000). It is a relatively low level indicator of validity, but it is, nevertheless, an important starting point. For example, a question such as 'how much is 4 times twelve' would have face validity for measuring mathematical intelligence but not for measuring emotional intelligence. Individuals completing a test or exercise should, by and large, see a link between the purposes of the task and what they are actually asked to do.

Content validity evidence is provided when the measure, such as a questionnaire or intelligence test or biological measure reflects the appropriate domain of investigation. In other words, the activity should match as closely as possible the objectives for which it was designed. In this case it would be inappropriate to test swimming ability through a paper and pencil test if the teaching consisted largely of practical swimming activities.

Criterion validity evidence is provided when the results of specific measurement such as a new intelligence or personality test converge with the results of other established measurements. For example, we might be interested in comparing individual performances on a particular aptitude test with other evidence of performance – completion of a practical activity, position in class, teacher rankings– to see if the new test is measuring the same underlying quality. In each of these cases the researcher is establishing a benchmark with which to assess how well the new measurement techniques 'measure up' (Kline, 2000; Newton & Shaw, 2014). If the data from our measurements are compared at the same time and lead to the same conclusions about the individual's performance, the evidence from each is called **concurrent validity**. When the data are able to predict a criterion outcome, such as school performance or job promotion, we can say that the measurement provides **predictive evidence** for its validity.

At times, researchers design questionnaires to measure psychological constructs such as competitiveness, self-concept, figural intelligence, creativity, or anxiety. When researchers wish to establish that the questions designed to measure a dimension such as self-concept do measure this underlying theoretical construct in a systematic way, they may use a statistical procedure called **factor analysis**. When procedures such as factor analysis are used to support the underlying dimensions being measured by a test, we speak of establishing construct validity evidence (Kline, 2000; Newton & Shaw, 2014).

Factor analysis is well beyond the scope of this book. A simpler method of establishing construct validity of tasks might be used. For example, if we design a test to measure mechanical aptitude we should be able to use the data obtained from testing individuals to classify them as either more or less mechanically able. To the extent that our classification is supported by external evidence (such as performance in mechanical tasks), we have evidence of the construct validity of the test (Newton & Shaw, 2014).

Reliability in measurement

Researchers need to be confident that any measures they use are reliable – that is, stable and consistent over time, this is referred to measurement **reliability** (Meyer, 2010). If measures are not stable and consistent over time then very little use can be made of them. For example, if a psychological measurement indicated a pathology in an individual on one testing, but not on a subsequent testing, we have no clear evidence on which to base assessment, treatment, or practice. Indeed, if a test or procedure produces unreliable results then the test or procedure can not be a valid measure of the domain under examination. There are a number of ways in which reliability is assessed, although few measures would be totally reliable. One way to evaluate reliability is to present the test or exercise to the same participants on two different occasions. If the test is reliable it should produce similar results on both occasions. This approach is referred to as **test-retest reliability**. At other times we may use two or more observers to rate a response and compare their ratings. This is referred to as **inter-rater reliability**. An illustration of this would be two raters coding responses to an open ended questionnaire, or two raters rating the incidence of aggression between two children in a playground. If the codings or observations are reliable they should be similar for the two raters. A further form of reliability referred to as **internal consistency reliability** is based on statistical techniques. If several items on a survey are used to tap into a psychological dimension such as anxiety there should be high intercorrelation between these items, and low correlation between these items and items measuring an oppositional dimension such as joy. Internal consistency reliability tests produce coefficients ranging from 1.00 which means total intercorrelation to 0.00. Usually researchers like their internal consistency measures to show a coefficient of greater than 0.7.

Ethics and research

All psychological research conducted through universities and other institutions such as schools and hospitals is controlled by ethics committees. There are ethical standards for conducting research with children and adolescents which seek to protect the participants from any intrusive or dangerous physical or psychological procedure. Ethical standards also require that participants be appropriately informed about the nature and purpose of the research, and they must give their active permission to participate. For minors, parental permission is essential. In most cases research cannot proceed until the programme of research is vetted by the appropriate committee and official sanction given. It is usual to provide some form of report to participants or organisations sponsoring or supporting the research, and in most cases reports guarantee the confidentiality of all participants.

In your careers as teachers or psychologists you may wish to conduct research, either as part of your ongoing training, or to obtain information relevant to your clients. In this instance you must ensure that you have followed all ethics provisions required in your work-place. Most professional psychological bodies such as the British Psychological Association and the British Educational Research Association have their own ethics guidelines that should be consulted. These are available at the following websites: https://bera.ac.uk/researchers-resources/resources-for-researchers and http://bps.org.uk/what-we-do/ethics-standards/ethics-standards

Internet resources

Much valuable information on developmental psychology and related topics is found on the Internet. Throughout this book, we will direct you to web addresses for further information on specific topics. Useful general websites for developmental psychology for teachers are listed below. We advise you to add these to your favourites list, as well as those you discover yourself.

- **Psychcrawler** is an excellent search engine designed by the American Psychological Association to find most things related to psychology: http://psychcrawler.com
- **Psych Web** is an excellent site that contains lots of psychology-related information for students and teachers of psychology: http://psywww.com/index.html
- **Encyclopedia of Psychology**. Type in a topic and see what you get! http://psychology.org
- **American Psychological Association (APA)**. The APA publishes many excellent journals in psychology. You will find a list of them at this website. It also has hot links to a number of useful psychology sites: http://apa.org

The following websites are for important associations in psychology or psychology in education. You should be familiar with them, as they will present many resources for your study of educational and developmental psychology.

- **American Psychological Association**. http://apa.org
- **Australian Psychological Society**. http://psychology.org.au
- **British Psychological Society**. http://bps.org.uk/index.cfm
- **The British Educational Research Association**. https://bera.ac.uk/
- **The American Educational Research Association (AERA)**. http://aera.net

The following websites will also be useful:

- **APA Style Resources**. This is a must for those writing papers in psychology: http://psywww.com/ resource/apacrib.htm
- **Journal of Educational Psychology home page**. An important journal with which you should be familiar: http://apa.org/journals/edu.html

- **Psychology Journals**. This site hot-links to major journals in psychology. It is prepared by Athabasca University in Canada: http://psych.athabascau.ca/html/aupr/journals.shtml
- **Research Digest**. Summaries of the most recent research provided by the British Psychological Society. http://digest.bps.org.uk/
- **Teaching and Learning Toolkit**. Accessible summaries of educational research. https://educationendowmentfoundation.org.uk/toolkit/
- **Guidelines for Effective Teaching**. https://teachingcommons.stanford.edu/resources/learning-resources

Heredity and environment and special learning needs

Introduction

Much of human development is set down at conception in the genetic blueprint passed on to each child by its parents. This blueprint is referred to as our genetic **heredity**. Heredity has a tendency to restrict the development of some human characteristics to just one or a few outcomes. This is called **canalisation**. There are numerous physical, motor, and cognitive developments, such as getting bigger, walking, and talking that are highly canalised, that is, occur at about the same time for most children universally, and there needs to be a major traumatic event or events to disrupt this development (Gottlieb, 1991; Masel & Siegal, 2009; Waddington, 1957). There are rhythms and peaks in these canalised developments and knowledge of particular developmental patterns including peaks in development is, therefore, of immense value to professionals involved with children. We cover a number of important developments throughout this text.

There are many other human developments that are less canalised and subject to environmental influences. These more plastic and adaptable potentials lead to a range of developmental trajectories and outcomes for individual children. While the basic material of these developments is laid out in the genes of each child, the environment plays an important role in moderating the effects of genes. Intelligence and temperament are two such qualities subject to considerable environmental influence (Asbury & Plomin, 2013). Along a continuum of human characteristics there are a host that are highly susceptible to environmental influences including the development of talents and skills, moral and political perspectives, and social, intrapersonal and interpersonal attributes. It is therefore essential that professionals dealing with children have a good understanding of how the environment may work to shape and mould individuals.

In this chapter we examine basic principles related to human development attributed to heredity and the environment and the interaction between the two. We will revisit these themes time and time again throughout the book when examining in detail the developmental trajectories of individuals.

Basis of heredity – a simplified overview

The mechanics of heredity lie within the sex cells present in the male and female gonads that hold half of the **chromosomes** present in body cells. Chromosomes are strands of DNA (deoxyribonucleic acid) molecules that carry genetic information. The sperm and ovum contain all the hereditary material of the child and this is set at conception when the union of a sperm and an egg forms a single cell. The 23 pairs of chromosomes (22 matched and the twenty-third sex chromosomes) form what is termed the person's **genotype**. About 20,000 DNA segments called **genes**, which serve as the key functional units in hereditary transmission, are carried on any one chromosome.

The possible combinations of genes in fertilisation, given the split up of chromosomes during **meiosis** (a type of cell division that results in daughter cells each with half the number of chromosomes of the parent cell), are therefore astronomical. The permutations and combinations are vast! This is why it is said that all children, apart from identical twins, are unique genetically. Because genes operate in pairs, a child has a 50% chance of inheriting a specific gene in a particular gene pair from each parent. Therefore, the genetic relatedness of parents and children is said to be 50% (Scheuerle, 2005; Weiten, 2001). Of course, despite each individual being genetically unique, all humans appear human, that is we have a head, arms and legs, circulatory system, and so on, characteristic of human beings. In fact, we are all much more similar than we are different. This is because much of the information contained in the millions of combinations of genes is redundant. For the same reason because they draw their genes from a more limited gene pool children look very much like their parents and siblings.

Dominant and recessive genes

Although children inherit their genetic material from both parents they may not, however, look very much like either the mother or the father or have any of the specific characteristics of the parents because the inherited genes may not be expressed in either of the parents. Genes are classified as **dominant** or **recessive** and an individual carries many genes that are not expressed (McKusick, 1998). The expressed genes form an individual's **phenotype,** or observable characteristics. At each gene locus, or position on the chromosome, there may be two or more alternate forms of the genes called alleles. If the alleles from both parents are the same at that point the child is said to be **homozygous** for that characteristic. If they differ the child is said to be **heterozygous**. For example, a child is homozygous for brown eyes if he has alleles from both parents for brown eyes. If brown and blue alleles are present he is heterozygous for that characteristic. In a heterozygous situation the gene that has most power in expression is called the *dominant gene* and the gene that has least power over the other is called the *recessive gene*. If dominant and recessive genes are found together three possibilities may occur. First, one allele may dominate over the other, hence brown eyes usually dominate over blue, and curly hair over straight hair. Second, the heterozygous combination of alleles may be expressed in a combination intermediate between the two alleles. So brown and blue may give hazel eyes. Short and tall may give medium height. And black and white may give brown skin colour. The third possibility is more rare, with heterozygosity being expressed in co-dominant or combined attributes carried by these alleles. For example, there are people with flecked brown and blue eyes, or in some cases one brown and one blue eye. One of the authors had a brother who had one eye blue, one eye blue with one third of the eye brown. Luckily co-dominance doesn't usually get expressed as one long and one short leg!

ACTIVITY POST

Consider your mother, father, siblings, and extended family. What strong genotypical characteristics are shared? What diverse characteristics are represented in your family group? Consider whether these diverse characteristics are more or less likely to be the result of genes, environment, or a combination.

Recessive genes only become expressed when both are present from either parent. The simplest case of this is eye colour. A recessive gene carries blue eye colour. In order to have blue eyes the blue eye gene must be present from both parents. While recessive genes carry many normal characteristics, recessive genes, can at times, create problems. One of these is **phenylketonuria** (PKU), a genetic disorder that prevents an individual from metabolising certain proteins that may lead to the build up of phenylpyruvic

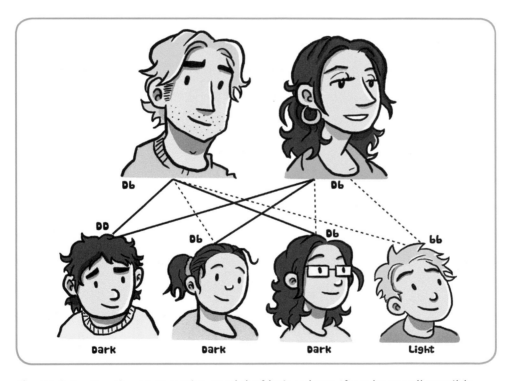

Figure 2.1   Dominant–recessive model of hair colour. If we know all possible combinations of the parents' genes for hair colour we can predict that 25% of their children are likely to inherit two dominant genes for dark hair; 50% are likely to receive one dominant gene and one recessive gene resulting in dark hair; and 25% are likely to receive two recessive genes for light hair.

acid in the body that can cause mental and physical retardation (Chelly et al., 2006; Welsh et al., 1990). Another instance is **haemophilia**. In both of these cases the recessive gene has to be present from both parents, and as this rarely happens the diseases are uncommon.

 ACTIVITY POST

Look up recessive genes on the Internet and locate information on a range of other genetic disorders that are created when recessive genes are expressed. Write a brief report describing the genetic disorder and its treatment.

 ACTIVITY POST

Consider the list of dominant and recessive genes below. Indicate which ones form part of your genotype. What environmental conditions may have interacted with your genotype to form your adult phenotype?

Dominant	Recessive
Dark hair	Blond hair
Normal hair	Pattern baldness
Curly hair	Straight hair
Non-red hair	Red hair
Facial dimples	No dimples
Normal hearing	Hearing loss
Normal vision	Short-sightedness
Farsightedness	Normal vision
Normal vision	Red-green colour blindness
Normally pigmented skin	Albinism
Double jointedness	Normal joints

(McKusick, 1998)

Figure 2.2   X-linked inheritance. The father's X chromosome is normal. The mother has one normal and one recessive allele on her X chromosomes. The possible combinations of alleles from both parents predict two normal children, one carrier and an affected male. Relate this to colour vision and haemophilia.

Personality characteristics and genes

We have indicated that many physical characteristics are determined genetically, including of course, our sex. Some dominant genes carry curly hair, dark hair, coarse body hair, and normal blood clotting. Some recessive genes carry straight hair, light hair, normal body hair, and hemophilia. You might like to look up a biology book to consider a fuller list of dominant and recessive genes.

It is also believed that genetic endowment affects a series of personality and temperamental characteristics such as intelligence, schizophrenia, mood disorders such as bipolar disorder, autism, and special talents (Bleidorn et al., 2012; Plomin & Rende, 1991). One of your major interests as a teacher will be on intellectual, as well as emotional and physical, development. Evidence that intellectual differences among individuals are partly due to genetic factors may be construed from a number of sources. There is a tendency for average correlations between the IQ scores of two groups of persons to increase with the degree of relatedness. There is a small but statistically significant correlation between the intelligences of foster children and their natural parents. The difference in intelligence between siblings in the one family, despite the environment of the home being relatively constant suggests a genetic component. And finally, the extreme difficulty of raising the mental age of some children, no matter how stimulating the environment provided is, suggests a genetic component of intelligence (see, for example, Mackintosh, 1998; Plomin, 1994a, 1994b; Plomin & Petrill, 1997; Petrill et al., 2004).

Sex-related characteristics

The X and Y chromosomes determine the sex of the child. They also contain certain genes that are not concerned with sexual characteristics. These are known as sex-linked genes since they are inherited along with the sex chromosomes. The X chromosome in particular contains many genes for which there are no homologous genes on the Y chromosome, for example, colour vision. The ability to discriminate between the colours red and green is completely dependent on a gene located only on the X chromosome. Normal colour vision is a dominant characteristic but there is also a recessive gene that causes colour blindness and can replace the normal colour vision gene on the X chromosome. As male sex chromosomes have only one X chromosome, if this contains the recessive colour vision gene the male is colour blind. Because a female has two X chromosomes both have to carry the recessive gene in order for her to be colour blind. In most cases a dominant gene carried on the alternative X chromosome masks the recessive gene. For this reason, men are more likely to be colour blind than women.

There are a number of other sex-linked characteristics such as haemophilia, so-called bleeder's disease. Persons with haemophilia are deficient in a part of blood plasma needed for normal clotting of the blood. This problem was common in the Royal families of Europe. Queen Victoria was a carrier of the recessive gene. It is interesting to follow her family tree and see who inherited the recessive gene. A beard is also an example of a sex-related trait. Women do not normally have beards, yet they carry the genes necessary to produce them. Thus a son inherits traits from both his mother and father that determine the type of beard he will grow. In fact, the dominant traits may be inherited through the mother and the beards of the father and son may be completely different!

ACTIVITY POST

Haemophilia is an example of disorders that are almost certainly directly inherited. Select two debate teams and debate: Should society try to stop people with harmful genes from passing them on to future generations? There are many Internet resources that deal with eugenics; these should be consulted when preparing your case for and against. For example, see: www.sciencemuseum.org.uk/whoami/findoutmore/yourgenes/howdoyoubecomeyou/whatiseugenics.aspx and http://uvm.edu/~eugenics/whatisf.html

Polygenetic determination

The inheritance of characteristics like albinism (lack of skin pigmentation) or haemophilia depends solely on the behaviour of a single pair of genes. When it comes to other characteristics like height or intelligence we find such a wide range that it seems that these characteristics cannot be controlled by such highly specific units as genes. Most characteristics are in fact controlled *polygenetically* (Plomin, 1990; Plomin et al., 2009).

SPOTLIGHT ON CHROMOSOMAL ABNORMALITIES

Some children are born with chromosomal abnormalities. Many countries, including the United Kingdom and Australia, practice inclusive education where developmentally challenged individuals are educated in regular schools and classrooms. The cascade model of special education allows children to be educated in the least restrictive environment suitable to their disability (see, McInerney, 2014). Therefore it is now relatively common for children with a variety of chromosomal and other abnormalities to be found in regular classrooms. However, some children with severe problems may be hospitalised.

Down syndrome is a more common genetic disability. Originally Down syndrome was regarded as a non-genetic disorder. It was attributable to the effects of physiological and biological factors on the infant while in the uterus in ageing mothers. However, Down syndrome is caused by an aberration in the pairing of the twenty-first autosome. Three chromosomes or a part of a third chromosome result instead of the usual pair. While it is generally accepted that this is passed on by the mother and is related to alterations in the chromosomes in the eggs as the woman

(continued)

(continued)

ages (Halliday et al, 1995; Meyers et al, 1997; Patterson & Costa, 2005), research has also been directed at the father as perhaps older age may lead to a breakdown of the chromosomes in the sperm cell. However, evidence for this is not strong and it appears that mutations in sperm cells occur for other reasons (Blanco et al, 1998). Children with Down syndrome are usually physically and mentally handicapped, although the severity of this can vary considerably (Hodapp, 1996). They have a specific set of physical characteristics including almond shaped eyes, protruding tongue, small nose, high foreheads, and a specific gait when walking. Increasingly over the last 30 years these children have been educated in regular schools and acquire basic reading and mathematical skills, as well as social confidence. Drug therapy is extending their life expectancy considerably (Selikowitz, 1997).

Another chromosomal abnormality is **Turner syndrome** (Kessler, 2007; Netley, 1986). This is a sex related abnormality. Normally females have an XX pairing on the twenty-third chromosome. Children with Turner syndrome have a XO structure rather than an XX structure with only 45 chromosomes. Normal sexual development does not occur during puberty but secondary sexual characteristics can be produced by the administration of estrogen, although the girls remain sterile. Even without hormone treatment girls with Turner syndrome show feminine personality characteristics and interests. These children also have a set of physical characteristics including short fingers and a pear shaped mouth.

A male sex related chromosomal abnormality is **Klinefelter syndrome** (Visootsak & Graham Jr, 2006). Instead of the usual XY pairing these children have an extra X chromosome. Consequently, while these boys have testes they do not produce sperm and normal sexual development does not occur in puberty. They have many female characteristics such as breast development, and a rounded, broad hipped female figure. There is a greater incidence of antisocial, aggressive, and delinquent behaviour among boys with Klinefelter syndrome. It is hard to conclude whether this antisocial behaviour is the result of the genetic abnormality or the social pressures to which these boys are subjected. A counterpart of Klinefelter syndrome is an abnormality where boys are born with an extra Y chromosome, that is a XYY combination. There is evidence that these males are more often found among populations of mentally handicapped people, prisoners, and men charged with violent crime. However, there is no definitive evidence to support the genetic link to behaviour here. Again it could be environmentally stimulated behaviour (see, for example, Netley, 1986; Learning about Klinefelter syndrome. National Human Genome Research Institute. http://www.genome.gov/19519068.)

There are a variety of other disorders including intersexuality where there is the presence of some of the sexual characteristics or reproductive systems of both males and females. A rare recessive gene perhaps causes this. Intersexes never have a complete set of both male and female sexual systems and in most cases they are sterile. A review of various chromosomal abnormalities might be found National Human Genome Research Institute. http://www.genome.gov/ResearchAtNHGRI/.

Diagnostic tests of the foetus

It is obviously important that genetic abnormalities are diagnosed as soon as possible so that therapeutic intervention may occur. Fortunately, today there are a number of antenatal procedures including blood tests, **amniocentesis**, **chorion biopsy**, **ultrasound**, and **fetoscopy** to examine the foetus in order to determine whether there is a genetic defect (Devers et al., 2013; Quintero et al., 1993). Blood can be taken from the umbilical cord of the developing foetus to test for a number of genetic problems. Following the discovery in 1997 that small fragments of foetal DNA are also present in the mother's blood, it is also possible to detect some disorders solely from maternal blood samples. Amniocentesis is a medical technique that involves inserting a hollow needle into a woman's abdomen during pregnancy. Amniotic fluid, which surrounds the foetus, is drawn out through the needle and is analysed to provide information on the chromosomal constitution of the foetus and for diagnosing problems with metabolism.

Chorion biopsy, often referred to as chorionic villus sampling, involves inserting a thin tube into the uterus either through the vagina or through a thin needle into the abdomen, and taking a small sample of tissue from the end of one or more chorionic villi. Again, cells are examined for genetic defects.

Ultrasound uses high frequency sound waves that are bounced off the foetus and then translated into pictures on a video screen that show the size, shape, and position of the foetus. This is a useful technique for determining foetal age, multiple pregnancies and the identification of gross abnormalities. Often ultrasound is used in combination with amniocentesis and chorionic villus sampling to guide the placement of the needle.

Fetoscopy involves inserting a small light and camera into the uterus to inspect the foetus for defects of the limbs and face. It can also allow a sample of foetal blood to be taken which can be analysed for haemophilia and sickle cell anaemia as well as neural defects.

If the risk factor for a mother is high, for example she is an older woman having her first child, or there is a history of genetic defects in the family line, one or more tests may be done to examine the status of the foetus. Some of these tests, such as chorion biopsy can be done early in the pregnancy, six to eight weeks after conception and the results are quickly available, while others, such as amniocentesis occur later, 11 to 14 weeks after conception, and the results take up to two weeks. In general, tests such as these carry their own risk factor, such as causing a spontaneous abortion, or damaging the foetus or mother, so they are not routinely done. Maternal blood tests can be taken at any time during pregnancy and are low risk as they are non-invasive to the developing foetus. Blood taken from the umbilical cord carries a risk of miscarriage.

Genetic mutations can be inherited from one's parents or be acquired due to some environmental effect. Acquired mutations can be the result of radiation, such as ultraviolet radiation from the sun, or from mistakes when DNA is copied as cells reproduce. Acquired mutations can only be passed on to the next generation if they occur in germ cells (sperm and ova). If they occur in cells in other parts of the body, such as the skin (referred to as somatic cells), they cannot be passed on. Investigations show that wearing tight trousers may cause a rise in scrotal temperature in men that has been related to infertility and mutations in sperm (Jung & Schuppe, 2007; Parazzini et al., 2008), and there is evidence that men exposed to toxic substances such as lead, benzene, paint solvents, vinyl chloride, anaesthetic gases, and radiation, have higher incidents of children with birth defects (Moline et al., 2000).

No doubt the Human Genome Project, which is mapping the human genetic blueprint, will enable researchers to examine more closely the relationship of genes and chromosomes to development, and the causes of genetic mutations and aberrations (see, for example, Plomin & Spinath, 2004; Wahlsten, 1999).

Interactions between heredity and environment

Some genotypes (one's unique genetic makeup) such as those for eye colour or curly hair may be directly expressed in phenotypes (the expression of genes in physical and behavioural characteristcis) and are very difficult to alter. However, most of our phenotypical characteristics such as intellectual, social, emotional, and personality traits are the result of extremely complex transactions between genetic and environmental factors during the course of development (Plomin, 1994a, 1994b, 2004; Rutter, 1997, 2015). The extent to which an individual's genotype is expressed in a phenotype depends on the timing, kind and amount of environmental pressures, to which the individual is exposed. In other words, it is clear that all genetically programmed effects on the development of an individual are potentially modifiable by the environment (even those that are hard to observe and may be biochemical in nature). It is also clear that all environmental effects on the development of physical and psychological characteristics involve genetic structures.

The essence of the heredity and environment issue lies in the relative importance of each of these to human development, and how environmental factors (and interpersonal and cultural factors especially) may facilitate the development of genetic potential, inhibit its development or compensate for the inherited potential of an individual. Two extreme positions are possible. On the one hand, it can be argued that individual potential is very malleable and, provided the environment is healthy and stimulating, individuals may develop many different physical and psychological skills and talents, irrespective of supposed limitations from their genetic inheritance. This is referred to as the *environmentalist* position (refer to Chapter 1). An advocate of this position was J. B. Watson (1878–1958), a famous early psychologist who argued the case for the environment when he stated that if you start with a healthy body, the right number of fingers and toes, eyes, and a few elementary movements at birth you can make that person into virtually anything from a genius to a thug!

On the other hand, it can be argued that individual development is locked in by genetic potential and that no amount of environmental engineering can alter the course of development of the individual. This is referred to as the *hereditarian* position (refer to Chapter 1). The hereditarian viewpoint was promulgated by the American Eugenics Society (founded in 1925) whose goal was to protect coming generations against individuals passing on poor biological inheritance. This group, which included some leading authorities such as Lewis M. Terman (1877–1956) and E. L. Thorndike (1874–1949), believed that undesirable traits were often inherited, rather than the result of child-rearing practices, and they recommended sterilisation of persons who are congenitally feeble-minded, epileptic or having other disabilities so that the genes would not be passed on to succeeding generations. In California, the Human Betterment Foundation promoted sterilisation from 1926 to 1942. In 1909, California became the third state to legalise the sterilisation of the then called feeble-minded and insane. Eventually, more than 30 states with similar laws sterilised about 60,000 people, one third of them in California, which repealed its laws in 1979 (Anton, 2003).

While eugenic sterilisation appears extreme today, eugenics was in the mainstream of science and politics, and it was supported by many national figures in the United States. Many doctors thought sterilisation had a therapeutic effect on mental patients. The Human Betterment Foundation also advocated the sterilisation of the blind and disabled at public expense, as well as people with other diseases, such as cancer, heart, kidney disease, and tuberculosis (Anton, 2003). Sterilisation in the United States continued until the early 1970s, by which time the link between heredity and mental illness had been discredited and other techniques for treating the mentally ill had been developed. More information on eugenics may be found in the book *Inheriting shame: The story of eugenics and racism in America* (Advances in contemporary thought series) by Stephen Selden (1999) and on the website http:// en.wikipedia.org/wiki/Eugenics

In many areas of human development the hereditarian position appears to have considerable strength. It is virtually impossible to change environmentally the development of height, eye and hair colour, and the acquisition of various motor skills such as toilet training and walking (although, of course, an impoverished environment or ill health may retard natural development). However, when we consider the vast array of behaviours that characterise human beings, it becomes problematic to argue that genetic potential alone is the primary cause of development. In accounting for intelligence, personality characteristics, creativity, physical skills, interpersonal skills and so on, we are confronted with the strong probability that the development of such skills is highly influenced by the environment.

 QUESTION POINT

Consider your own development. What aspects of your phenotype (physical or behavioural characteristics) seem to be most influenced by genetic forces and which appear to be most susceptible to environmental influences? Discuss your personal developmental profile and compare it with those of other students.
Is there general agreement on what characteristics are most likely genetically determined and which ones are environmentally determined? What problematic issues are raised by considering the relative influences of heredity and environment?

Genetic engineering

A large proportion of the evidence gathered in support of the belief that heredity is an important factor in development is based on conclusions drawn from studies of animal and plant breeding, and more recently, with advanced studies in selective breeding, genetic modification and cloning. It is possible to breed animals to determine temperamental characteristics as well as more obvious physical characteristics. Early research by Tryon (1940) at the University of California succeeded in breeding maze-bright and maze-dull rats through selective breeding, and this has been replicated many times. Clearly, all animal and plant studies suffer from the inherent difficulty of comparing humans with plants and animals. When we come to humans it is technically more difficult to selectively breed or genetically modify human genes, and human genetic science runs into considerable moral and ethical problems. However, since the refinement of in vitro fertilisation (IVF) of the human egg, and the Human Genome Project, among other scientific advances, scientific selective breeding through to cloning and genetic modification of humans may be becoming a reality.

 ACTIVITY POST

Consult the following web site for more information on the Human Genome Project: http://doegenomestolife.org/pubs/overview_screen.pdf. What are some of the positive aspects of the human genome project? What are some potential negative aspects. Discuss some of the ethical issues related to human genetic engineering.

Family studies

Prior to these more recent advanced scientific and laboratory based studies most of our knowledge about the genetic inheritance of humans and its effect on development was obtained from the study of similarities in characteristics of family members, and the interaction between heredity and environment in the production of what are called phenotypical traits. Many of these studies were conducted to discover why certain family groups are characterised by extra bright or talented people, while other family groups are characterised by mental feebleness, antisocial behaviour, and a range of genetic problems including Down syndrome, Klinefelter's syndrome and haemophilia. While many of these studies were poorly executed there is evidence that knowing the genetic history of particular groups can lead to valid predictions for the future. Indeed, **genetic counselling** is available to inform people who have a family history of particular genetic problems of the probability of a genetic defect, its likely seriousness and treatment, in order to inform their decision to have a child or not.

The closest we get to selective breeding among humans are historical examples of groups intermarrying to maximise particular characteristics such as height, strength, eye colour, intelligence, and talent. For example, through selected breeding Frederick the Great of Prussia attempted to produce tall soldiers to serve as honour guards for Prussia's noble families. Alfred Noyes (1937) encouraged Mormon polygamy to breed physically and intellectually superior people. And there were attempts in Nazi Germany during the 1930s and 1940s to produce a super race.

Twin studies

A large amount of information on the impact of genes and the environment on development has also been obtained through twin studies with **monozygotic twins**, so-called identical twins developed from the one fertilised ovum, and **dizygotic twins**, so-called fraternal twins developed from two fertilised ova (see, for example, Braungart et al., 1992). In these studies an assumption is made that monozygotic twins, who share 100% of their genes, are more similar than dizygotic twins, who share 50% of their genes, in their genetic endowment. The assumption is also made that environmental influences are similar for both types of twins, including the prenatal environment of the womb. If identical twins are much more similar with respect to a particular characteristic, trait or behaviour than fraternal twins who have different genotypes, it is assumed that the appearance of the trait is strongly influenced by genetic factors. If sets of identical and fraternal twins who have shared the same home resemble each other almost equally on a characteristic, it is assumed that this characteristic is more strongly influenced by environmental than genetic factors.

Among the characteristics examined in twin studies are physical and physiological characteristics, intellectual characteristics, and personality. In general, monozygotic twins are more similar than dizygotic twins on a variety of traits associated with physical measures and biological functioning. They are more alike in height, weight, shoulder width, and hand width. They are also more alike in facial and dental characteristics and body build. Their developmental trajectories are also more similar. The results of studies on similarities in intellectual characteristics have been very consistent. Performance on intelligence tests is heavily weighted by genetic factors (Arselan & Penke, 2015; Plomin & Spinath, 2004). The closer the genetic kinship bonds, the more similar the IQ is. The contribution of genetic factors to personality characteristics appears to be less than intellectual characteristics but there is growing evidence that a range of personality characteristics such as bipolar disorder, depression, schizophrenia, sociability, and autism are influenced by genetic factors (Plomin & Rende, 1991; Polderman et al., 2015).

The environment

What role does the environment play in the development of children? As we have said, some authorities hold that (given a normal environment of adequate food, shelter, education, and nurturance), a child's development is largely determined by the genes a child inherits at conception. Others hold that the environment is crucial to the development of children, and in fact will shape the capacities and attitudes of the child. Most psychologists hold a dual perspective where biology is accepted as fixing the range and culture or experience fixes the point within the range at which behaviour takes place.

As we have discussed above, genetic unfoldment, called our **phylogenetic development**, is best understood in processes such as seeing, walking, and talking. Our actual development as influenced by environmental factors is called our **ontogenetic development**. While physical and motor development unfolds according to a genetic schedule, the experiences a child has may facilitate or impede this development. We examine this issue in Chapters 3 and 4. There are some extreme examples of the overriding influence of the environment of the development of children and we discuss a number of these below.

 ACTIVITY POST

The abstract of an article entitled Adoption as a Natural Experiment (Haugaard & Hazan, 2003, available on-line at: http://ncbi.nlm.nih.gov/pubmed/14984132) states:

Adoption provides a unique opportunity for the study of child development. Because adopted children are raised in families in which they have no genetic relationship with their parents, and possibly none with their siblings, they provide a rare opportunity to study the relative importance of genetic, shared environmental, and non-shared environmental influences on the development of child characteristics and behaviours. Because children are adopted from a variety of circumstances and at a wide range of ages, studies of adopted children and their families provide researchers the opportunity to examine the short- and long-term influences of a wide range of environments on children's development. Because children are adopted into homes with a range of characteristics (e.g. multi-racial homes), adoption provides the opportunity to study the range of influences of these homes on child development. Adoption research that focuses on each of these areas is reviewed in this article. We present conclusions about the value of adoption in psychological research and some reasons why many psychologists ignore the opportunities presented by studying adoptive families, as well as potential useful directions for future research with adopted children and their families.

Read this article and discuss its implications for studying the relative influence of heredity and environment on development. You might also like to refer to Petrill, Lipton, Hewitt, Plomin, Cherny, Corley and DeFries (2004).

Prenatal influences

The impact of the environment on early development

We are conceived with genes that programme phylogenetic development, but from the stage of conception other factors begin to operate which lead to individualised growth and development that we call ontogenetic development. In fact, even before birth our healthy development depends upon a normal uterine environment. At its most basic the embryo must be supported by the mother's umbilical cord and placenta. Adequate nourishment is essential. The womb of the mother, and in particular, the amniotic sac must also supply a secure environment for the growing child, an environment safe from major traumatic influences.

In its extreme form, a negative prenatal environment can be fatal, so that no matter what an organism's genetic endowment, it will not survive. For example, the fertilised ovum may become implanted in the wrong place such as the fallopian tubes, which precludes development. There might be insufficient hormonal activity to stimulate proper growth such as an imbalance between the pituitary gland and ovaries. In some cases a genetic mutation might prevent proper development. Generally an embryo developing abnormally is spontaneously aborted. Statistically the number of miscarriages is very high. The processes of spontaneous abortion and stillbirth appear to be natural controls so that the number of defective children born is minimal. On some occasions a normal foetus may be aborted through emotional shock, malnutrition, or glandular disturbances. Medically performed abortions should be during the period of the embryo. After this time the process endangers the mother's health.

Teratogens

Despite the fact that the organism is programmed genetically to develop normally, the introduction of chemicals and drugs to the prenatal environment can stunt physical and mental growth so that the child is born with birth defects. Such substances are called **teratogens** (Dutta, 2015; Kopp & Kaler, 1989). In fact, while developmental irregularities may be due to defective genes they are more likely to be due to environmental influences in the uterus. The time when the teratogen is introduced rather than the teratogen itself is the important thing. The first trimester is the most significant time. We discuss some of these effects later in the chapter. Finally, even the birthing process itself can lead to deleterious after effects on growth and development. And of course, the postnatal environment has a significant impact on growth and development.

 ACTIVITY POST

Design a poster for adolescent students that dramatically emphasises the dangers of common teratogens. Why is such information important to adolescents?

Maternal diseases and disorders

As indicated above, agents that can cause malformation in the foetus are called teratogens. The effects of a teratogen vary according to the developmental stage of the embryo. Individual teratogens influence specific developmental processes and the fourth and sixth weeks of pregnancy are particularly critical. Both maternal and foetal genotypes can affect the developing organism's response to teratogenic agents and may play an important role in how much effect the teratogenic agent has. A number of diseases contracted by the mother, such as rubella, syphilis, cholera, and mumps can have very serious consequences for the embryo (Isada & Grossman, 1991; Waldorf & McAdams, 2013; White et al., 2012). Rubella and venereal diseases, for example, invade the developing embryo and remain active and may have their worst effects including cardiac disorders, cataracts, deafness, and mental disorders at later stages of development. In some cases the deleterious effects may not be apparent at birth but gradually emerge during the early years of development in the forms of juvenile paresis involving deterioration in thought processes, judgement and speech, and in a decline in motor and mental abilities, and even in eventual death.

Genital herpes and acquired immune deficiency syndrome (AIDS) are very serious diseases that may be transmitted to children either in the uterus or in the birthing process. Herpes can cause microcephaly, paralysis, deafness, blindness, and brain damage in infants and is fatal for many. Pregnant women are routinely checked for genital herpes and if there is evidence of its presence birth is usually through a caesarean section. AIDS tends to develop rapidly in infants although new drug therapies are helping considerably to alleviate the effects (Eldred & Chaisson, 1996; Goetghebuer et al., 2009).

Drugs

It is commonly known that prescription drugs used during pregnancy can cause severe developmental problems for the developing foetus (Mitchell et. al., 2011; Neibyl, 1991). The most infamous case of this is thalidomide used by pregnant women during the late 1950s and 1960s as a mild sedative to alleviate morning sickness, which when used during a critical period of development of the foetus caused severe retardation in growth of the long bones in the arms and legs of their children (Moore & Persaud, 1993). Consequently women are routinely advised to avoid all medication while pregnant except under medical advice.

Labour and delivery medication to ease pain for women in labour can also have short-term effects on newborn children. Children may show decrease in cortical activity for several days after birth, disruptions in feeding responses and general neonatal depression.

Illicit drugs such as heroin, methadone and LSD used during pregnancy can have extremely damaging effects on the newborn (Finnegan & Kandal, 1997). The newborn can exhibit symptoms of drug addiction, hyper-irritability, vomiting, trembling, shrill crying, rapid respiration, and hyperactivity which may result in the child's death in the first few days of life. Often drug addicts have difficulty in conceiving and after conception the baby is frequently spontaneously aborted.

More common problems than illicit drugs are legal drugs such as tobacco and alcohol (Finnegan & Kandal, 1997). Smoking influences the cardiovascular system of the foetus, which frequently, but not invariably, increases the foetal heart rate (Chavkin, 1995) and is linked to birth defects, slow physical and psychological development, and the development of illness later in life (Hackshaw et al., 2011; Knopik et al., 2012). Women who are long-term smokers have premature infants twice as often as non-smokers with the rate of prematurity directly related to the amount of maternal smoking. Generally infants of non-smokers are heavier than infants of smokers at birth. Excessive consumption of alcohol during pregnancy can lead to Foetal Alcohol Syndrome (FAS) which includes distinctive facial features, mental disability, impairment of motor coordination, attention, memory and language, as well as overactivity, and slow physical growth. Among other terms used to describe the influence of alcohol on the developing foetus are Foetal Alcohol Effects (FAE), Alcohol Related Neurodevelopmental Disorders (ARND), and Alcohol Related Birth Defects (ARBD).

 ACTIVITY POST

Using each of these descriptors (Foetal Alcohol Syndrome, Foetal Alcohol Effects, Alcohol Related Neurodevelopmental Disorders and Alcohol Related Birth Defects) complete an Internet search and investigate the potential ill effects of alcohol on foetal development. Write a brief report outlining your findings. Prepare a poster for adolescents illustrating the effects of consumption of alcohol during pregnancy.

Maternal diet

A poor maternal diet is often symptomatic of an impoverished environment generally, including such things as inferior sanitation and housing, inadequate medical care, poor education, and so on. It is therefore difficult to separate the factors that might impact on prenatal development (Black et al., 2008; Worthington-Roberts & Klerman, 1990). Studies on a variety of populations have shown that gross dietary deficiencies, especially in some vitamins and in protein are related to increased rates of spontaneous abortions, prematurity, stillbirths, infant mortality, and physical and neural defects in infants (Bhutta et al., 2013; Rosenblith, 1992). Babies of malnourished mothers are smaller in length and weight. As we mentioned earlier, it is hard to tease out what is causing what in impoverished situations. For example, studies show that the more disadvantaged the group the higher is the rate of infant mortality (Katz et al., 2013). Malnutrition of the child can impede the development of the nervous system and **myelinisation** (the development of the insulating fatty sheath around nerves which facilitates the speed with which neural impulses are sent) prenatally and postnatally. Gross malnutrition can also lead to the development of smaller brains. A detailed UK government report detailed the effects of foetal and maternal nutrition can be found at: https://gov.uk/government/uploads/system/uploads/attachment_data/file/339325/SACN_Early_Life_Nutrition_Report.pdf

Parental age

There is evidence that the incidence of congenital abnormalities increases in mothers over 35 years of age, particularly if the mother is bearing her first child (Cleary-Goldman et al., 2005; Halliday et al., 1995). As the father's age increases, genetic mutations are more likely to occur that have been linked with an increased likelihood of miscarriage (Sharma et al., 2015) and neurodevelopmental disorders, such as autistic spectrum disorder (Torellio & Meck, 2008).

Birth factors and development

A poor birthing can have deleterious effects on children. Prolonged labour, breech births (buttocks presented first), prolapsed umbilical cord, development of the placenta in the lower portion of the uterus so that it blocks the uterine opening, and instrument births can lead to neurological damage through pressure, or haemorrhage in the brain, or through anoxia (lack of oxygen to the brain). The effects of this may be mental disability, cerebral palsy, paralysis, motor coordination problems, sensory defects, and even death of the new born (Rosenberg, 1991).

Deprived postnatal environments

There is evidence that a significantly deprived postnatal environment can have deleterious effects on the development of children. Such things as malnutrition, unhygienic living conditions, extremes of climate, and lack of a caregiver or a caring environment can all have quite marked effects on development and the opportunities for learning special skills. Investigations of institutionalised children tend to support the view that a lack of a caring environment can lead to a drop off in intellectual, social and physical functioning (Hodges & Tizard, 1989; Kiernan & Huerta, 2008). Gross neglect of children after birth, both emotionally and physically (such as malnourishment) may lead to a condition called **infant marasmus**, where there is a marked breakdown in the normal development of the child, illustrated by poor physical growth and intellectual impairment.

Malnourishment is particularly insidious for the young child as poor nutrition can lead to mental disability (Black et al., 2008). We need to be careful here in defining what we mean by a deprived environment. Just because an environment is different from the norm or appears squalid does not mean that it does not provide the support for normal developmental growth for children. Furthermore, there is considerable evidence that developmentally deprived children can make significant gains in development and be put back on a normal trajectory once given an enriched environment (Pollit et al., 1993; Pollit, 1994). This is called **catch-growth** where the physical growth returns to its genetically determined path after being delayed by environmental factors (Van IJzendoorn et al., 2007).

We have been illustrating above how important a healthy environment is for the atypical child, but a stimulating environment is essential for all children. Opportunities should be provided for all children to practise language, to develop social skills, to explore, and to solve problems. It is important for parents and other caregivers to design their living areas so that they are safe and inviting for young children to play in and explore. Parents and caregivers should assist, enthuse, sooth and consult with children,

SPOTLIGHT ON ENVIRONMENT COMPENSATING FOR GENETICS

There are a number of interesting examples of the environment compensating for a faulty set of genes. In about 1 in 40,000 births a child is born with *phenylketonuria* (PKU), a digestive disorder that makes it impossible for a child to metabolise the amino acid phenylalanine that is commonly in milk products. This inability to metabolise leads to a build up of a toxic substance, phenylpyruvic acid that can lead to mental retardation. As with a number of genetic and viral disorders, PKU is routinely tested for at birth, and with a careful control of the baby's eating of protein later mental and physical retardation can be avoided (Marcason, 2014; see also About phenylketonuria (PKU). National Human Genome Research Institute. http://www.genome.gov/25020037).

A stimulating and challenging environment provided for Down syndrome children can lead to unprecedented development among children who were thought to have very limited potential. Children with cerebral palsy make similar advances when the environment provided them is stimulating and supportive. Other genetic problems may be controlled by drug therapy.

It is essential that the interaction with children with disabilities is enriched rather than impoverished. Unfortunately, it is often difficult for parents to interact with a child who is different mentally or physically, and hence normal interactions, which characterise mother and child, may be lessened, rather than heightened for the child with disabilities, with the consequence that development is further impeded.

In order to enhance the early environment of deprived children there has been a development of education and support programmes in various countries. In the United Kingdom, Sure Start centres in deprived areas for children under the age of four years (and their parents) were opened in 1998. Unfortunately many have subsequently closed due to cuts in funding. Head Start is a project funded through the National Lottery launched in 2013 that aims to build life skills and resilience in 10 to 14 year olds in deprived areas. There is also a well-development programme in the United States called Head Start as well as others including Follow Through and Homestart, in which children are given enrichment programmes to stimulate development. There has also been a development of home intervention programmes that train mothers to stimulate and encourage their children in daily interactions around the house. Many schools such as the Bereiter-Engelman and Montessori schools are also based upon the theory that early stimulating educational experiences will enhance the development of children.

Use the Internet to discover more information on well-established intervention programmes such as Sure Start or Head Start (the US version). What are the aims and characteristics of each programme? What is the research evidence that they are effective?

and use a lot of rich language. Parents and caregivers should also set clear limits and be authoritative. We talk about authoritative parenting in Chapter 9.

> ## Developmental problems in childhood and educational implications

Among the common disabilities that children may have are learning disabilities, such as **Attention Deficit Hyperactivity Disorder** (ADHD), intellectual disabilities, autistic spectrum disorder, and organic brain diseases, for example, birth trauma, infection, and head injury (refer to Diagnostic and Statistical Manual of Mental Disorders [DSM-5-American Psychiatric Association, 2013) and International Classification of Diseases [ICD-10] National Center for Health Statistics for Disease Control and Prevention, 2010). Others suffer from behavioural, physical, hearing, and visual disabilities. Although individuals with 'disorders' need to be categorised for purposes of effective diagnosis, treatment, and research, given our limited knowledge of the aetiology of particular problems, we should not forget to take a holistic approach, that is, individuals should not be defined and bound by their disabilities. For purposes of description, we give a brief survey of a few of the identifiable characteristics of a number of these disabilities that are relevant to teachers.

Attention deficit hyperactivity disorder (ADHD)

Among the student disabilities that teachers are most likely to encounter in the regular classroom is attention deficit hyperactivity disorder. The title of the disorder aptly sums up the symptoms – namely, children characterised by low attention to task and high physical activity levels inconsistent with the level of development of the child or adolescent (Diagnostic and Statistical Manual of Mental Disorders [DSM-5]-American Psychiatric Association, 2013). The International Classification of Mental and Behavioural Disorders – ICD-10 medical classification system refers to ADHD as HKD, a term widely used in Europe and included in European clinical guidelines developed with the European Network for Hyperkinetic Disorders (EUNETHYDIS). This classification system defines HKD as a persistent and severe impairment of psychological development, characterised by 'early onset; a combination of overactive, poorly modulated behaviour with marked inattention and lack of persistent task involvement; and pervasiveness over situations and persistence over time of these behavioural characteristics'. See more at: http://adhd-institute.com/assessment-diagnosis/diagnosis/#sthash.IAdTzQQu.dpuf

ADHD has three cardinal symptoms: inattention, impulsivity, and hyperactivity. The most common manifestations of inattention for children and adolescents are failure to finish assigned tasks, short concentration spans, inability to meet academic demands, fluctuation in moods, and being incommunicative. The most common manifestations of impulsivity include poor self-control, verbal indiscretion, and engaging in risky sexual activities. The most common manifestations of hyperactivity are excessive fidgeting and talking, and internal feelings of restlessness. Hyperactive children often make unusual vocal noises and they generally talk excessively, commenting and vocalising during quiet play and work activities (Antrop et al., 2005; Barkley, 1998; Pellegrini & Horvat, 1995). During free play, children with ADHD spend less time playing with one toy and more time moving from one toy to another than a child of the same age (ADHD/HKD Diagnosis and Management 2010). Children with high rather than low physical activity levels are typically low achievers at school and often experience such social problems as peer rejection and teasing. Inattention to task has obvious implications for academic achievement. When these characteristics occur together they can cause profound problems for the children concerned.

ADHD is a significant educational problem in the UK and elsewhere. Prevalence of ADHD has been found to range from 1–4% although many persons are not diagnosed (Ford et al., 2003). The onset of ADHD appears to occur in the first year of school and remains relatively stable after that. Symptoms of what appears to be ADHD in a range of settings, including school, are assessed using a diagnostic manual.

The causes of ADHD are uncertain. There is strong evidence that there is a genetic component of ADHD, supported by evidence that ADHD is more common in biological relatives of children with ADHD than non-biological relatives. First-degree relatives of male subjects are five times more likely to be diagnosed with ADHD than relatives of normal controls (Thapar et al., 1999, see also ADHD/HKD Diagnosis and Management 2010). It is also supported by evidence from twin studies. The success of treating ADHD with dopamine agonists further suggests the strong likelihood that there is an underlying biochemical pathology of the disease (Barkley, 1998; Winsberg & Comings, 1999). While biology might explain the initial occurrence of ADHD, later social experiences within the home and school probably contribute to its maintenance and development (Bailey 1993; Purdie et al., 2002). In this instance parents might not identify and seek appropriate treatment for the condition, and teachers and peers might inadvertently reinforce the ADHD behaviours (Bailey, 1992; Purdie et al., 2002; Saltmarsh et al., 2005).

 QUESTION POINT

How might home and school experiences contribute to the maintenance of ADHD? What is the evidence for and against drug therapy for ADHD? You should consult the following websites for information on this topic: http://livingwithadhd.co.uk/ and https://nice.org.uk/guidance/cg72

Students diagnosed with ADHD can be particularly difficult for teachers to handle, although behaviour modification programme and an increasing use of drug therapy have helped to alleviate their symptoms (Castle et al., 2008; Purdie et al., 2002). Among the burdens in school are poor classroom behaviour, poor academic performance, the necessity for special education requirements, and increased incidence of school exclusion. Among the cognitive aspects are reduced intellectual capacity and increased learning difficulties, problems with verbal and non-verbal memory, motivation, and productivity. They may also have language problems, such as impairment in speech and excessive talking, problems with verbal reasoning and an impaired ability to express ideas and emotions, which correlates with delinquency and substance abuse (Barkley, 1998). Some would argue that it is possible that a better matching of students' temperaments to educational experiences may alleviate the problem for many students (see DuPaul et al., 2011; Pellegrini & Horvat, 1995). Others believe that ADHD may be related to the unpreparedness of some students for particular learning activities and advocate further learning experiences to improve these inaptitudes (see Gureasko-Moore et al., 2007).

More can be read on ADHD in the United Kingdom by consulting *Attention deficit hyperactivity disorder: Diagnosis and management of ADHD in children, young people and adults*, from the National Institute of Clinical Excellence available at: http://nice.org.uk/guidance/cg72/resources/guidance-attention-deficit-hyperactivity-disorder-pdf

Intellectual disability

Intellectual disability is a very broad term encompassing a wide range of disabilities within two basic categories: mild intellectual disability and moderate to severe disability. Two criteria are usually employed to classify individuals as intellectually disabled: first, their intellectual functioning must be significantly below average and, second, their adaptive behaviour (i.e. their ability to be personally and socially independent) must be severely impaired.

Research has consistently shown that either changing environmental conditions or increasing environmental stimulation for the individuals with intellectual disabilities enhances development, in some cases quite dramatically (Balla & Zigler, 1975; Dennis, 1973; Verdonschot et al., 2009). Individuals with intellectual disabilities also show behavioural disorders, which create further management difficulties for teachers and parents, and limit the placement of such individuals in regular school settings. However, there is sufficient evidence to indicate that individuals with intellectual disabilities benefit from normal activities, even though the stresses on the caregiver may be high.

Autism

Autism is within a spectrum of pervasive developmental disorders and is a condition that usually appears in infancy or early childhood. It is characterised by severe deficit in social responsiveness and interpersonal relationships; abnormal speech and language development; behavioural peculiarities such as ritualised, repetitive, or stereotyped behaviours; rigidity; and poverty of age-typical interests and activities (DSM-5; Jones, 1988; Matson et al., 2012). As autism occurs early in life it is essential to diagnose the condition early. Symptoms are deficits in reciprocal social interactions, imitative play and delay in language development. Children often display peculiar interests; bizarre responses to sensory stimuli; and repetitive, stereotyped motor behaviours such as twirling and hand flapping (Prater & Zylstra, 2002). Parents and caregivers should be on the alert for these symptoms. While autism is uncommon, teachers in special schools will have the opportunity to work with such children. How educable these individuals are depends on the severity of the symptoms as well as their level of intelligence. When severity is less and the individual has a reasonable level of intelligence, parental and educational interventions can enhance the child's development so that they become able to socialise and engage in productive work (Tobin et al., 2014). Asperger syndrome is a condition that has some of the characteristics of autism but fails to meet all the diagnostic criteria of autism in terms of severity, clinical profile, and age of onset. Recent studies show that this syndrome is comparatively more common than autism and teachers may come across this condition more often. Its later and more insidious onset means that teachers in early childhood settings may be the first to systematically identify the symptoms. However, teachers may overlook these symptoms and attribute them to personal characteristics such as laziness and naughtiness. Early detection of the condition and prompt referral is essential for facilitating appropriate intervention.

Cerebral palsy

Cerebral palsy is a form of paralysis resulting from brain injury. In addition to the motor dysfunction caused by the paralysis, cerebral palsy may also include learning difficulties, psychological problems, sensory defects, convulsions, and behavioural disorders (Smithers-Sheedy et al., 2014). As with the other disabilities we have discussed, there is a great range in severity and manifestation.

While intellectual disability may be associated with cerebral palsy, not all cerebral palsied individuals have intellectual disability (indeed, some are in the higher levels of intellectual functioning). Furthermore, it is not certain whether some who are classified as intellectually disabled really are, or whether the tests used to measure level of intellectual functioning have been inadequate to assess their true potential (Dalvand et al., 2012). Due to the neurological damage, even people with cerebral palsy and normal intelligence suffer significant difficulties with perceptual and language disorders, poor manual control and visual-motor ability, distractability and lessened physical vitality. Associated emotional and behavioural problems together with absenteeism further exacerbate their educational problems (Sentenac et al., 2013).

Visual impairment and hearing impairment

Two common disabilities are visual impairment and hearing impairment. As much of the early learning of a child is sensorimotor-oriented children who are visually impaired from birth may have limited opportunity to test themselves out in the physical world (parents may be hesitant to allow the visually impaired child to explore in case they hurt themselves). Consequently, the gross and fine motor skills, perception and perceptual-motor integration, which are so important for development, may not be acquired. Furthermore, such restricted experiences ultimately limit cognitive development. Visually impaired children may also develop mannerisms such as rocking or tilting the head which can be disturbing to parents and other people, such as teachers.

A general term, hearing impairment, is often used to describe individuals with all levels of hearing loss. However, there is great diversity within this group related to the degree and nature of the hearing loss, the age of onset of the loss (e.g. prelingual or later), existence of other disabilities, the nature of the infant care, and socialising experiences of the child (among a host of other things). To highlight one of the complexities here, some hearing-impaired individuals might not learn to speak as a result of intellectual disability that is also manifested in hearing impairment, while in other cases they may fail to speak simply because they have never heard the spoken word.

In general, individuals with hearing impairment with no other disability have essentially the same distribution of intelligence as hearing individuals. The use of hearing aids and knowledge of speech reading help many of these individuals to develop well (McKee et al., 2014). There is some debate as to whether signing should be taught or whether children should be taught speech reading exclusively. However, today the trend is to teach sign and speech reading as part of a total programme that also includes gestures and facial expressions (Pérez-Pereira & Conti-Ramsden, 2013).

Other disabilities

There are many students in regular classrooms who experience a range of other disabilities that have an impact on their learning and motivation. For example, you may teach students who have *behaviour problems*, *speech disorders* (such as poor articulation, stuttering, and delayed language development), *motivation* and *attention* problems, and psychological problems such as excessive *fear* and *anxiety disorders* e.g. test anxiety and school phobia). Increasingly, individuals with even severe physical impairments, such as being restricted to a wheelchair or walking with the aid of callipers, are being included in regular classrooms as part of the move towards inclusive education (Morley et al., 2005; Peters, 2007).

SPOTLIGHT ON BEHAVIOURAL GENETICS

As we have seen earlier in the chapter there is a strong interaction between the hereditary potential of children and the environment (see, for example, Belsky et al., 2007; Belsky, & Pluess, 2009). This interaction explains the marked variations in the patterns of development of different children. If human development were due to maturation alone, as in some animal species, there would be no such thing as individuality.

A specialised area of psychology, **behavioural genetics**, explores the interaction of environment and heredity (see, Asbury & Plomin, 2013; Plomin, 2004; Plomin & Rende,

1991). For behavioural geneticists the question is not whether genes or environments are operating, but how much impact genes and environments have on human development. Behavioural geneticists have designed complex research using identical and fraternal twins, and unrelated people, to examine this. Genetic research also examines DNA sequences to identify the genes that are associated with cognitive ability and achievement. As we have discussed earlier, genes influence intelligence and other personality characteristics, such as emotional stability, with estimates of gene influence averaging around 50% when combined across all available twin and adoption studies. However, environmental influences play a significant role as well.

Behavioural geneticists have developed models to explain how the interaction between genes and environment might occur in influencing intelligence and achievement. Scarr and McCartney (1983) outline three types of gene–environment interactions. The first of these is passive interaction where both genes and environments derive from the same source, the parents. In this case if parents are cognitively able they might provide their children with more books than other children normally receive, or if they are good musicians they might provide a more musically oriented environment. Hence, because the parents provide both the genes and the environment, the child's environment is indirectly correlated with their genes and as a result are likely to become good readers or musicians.

In the second model genes directly influence the type of environment the child experiences. This is called reactive or evocative interaction. Some children may be more social because of traits passed on through genes which then evokes more sociability from others. This in turn reinforces their sociability.

Finally, a third model posits active interaction, when a child's genes make them more likely to seek out certain environments. In this case it may be that more academically oriented children seek out more academically enriched environments and musically oriented children seek out musical environments and hence increase their performance as a result. The tendency to actively choose environments that complement our heredity is called **niche-picking** (Scarr & McCartney, 1983). Niche-picking begins to predominate as children grow older. Younger children do not have much choice as most situations are provided by their parents, however, older children and adolescents actively seek social, physical, and intellectual environments that suit themselves. The concept of niche-picking helps explain why identical twins separated and reared apart during childhood and then reunited later in life are surprised by the number of interests they share in common. The point behind this analysis is to indicate that genes may be influential in mediating the extent to which children seek out academically related environments or have more or less enriched environments provided for them. However, as with many areas of inquiry, this is still in its infancy.

Consider the notion of niche-picking. Draw a developmental timeline of some key aspects of your personal, social, intellectual, and physical behaviour. Is there any evidence here of you choosing a niche that reflects your genetic inheritance?

Streaming and ability grouping

Inclusion and teaching

Many educators believe that the environment is particularly powerful in shaping human development and therefore emphasise the need for *all* children to experience a range of enriched environments to maximise individual development. Educational environments based on this belief have parallel classrooms, and children with assessed developmental or learning difficulties are included so that they may benefit from the enriched environment of the regular classroom.

The alternative view is that students with disabilities should be educated in separate environments in which special resources are used to maximise their learning and development. This position is strongly argued for children who have moderate to severe disabilities. Such a position that streamed classrooms, special resource rooms, and, at times, special and separate facilities provide a better educational environment for these children. It is argued that without such special resources children with disabilities may be neglected and fall further behind in regular classrooms (see, for example, Brantlinger, 1997; Frederickson et al., 2004; Terzi, 2005).

 QUESTION POINT

We have discussed the issue of inclusion and selective education. Discuss the strengths and weaknesses of both approaches to educating for diversity. If a parent of a child with an intellectual disability asked you for advice regarding the placement of his or her child what would you advise? If a parent of a child with sporting or intellectual prowess asked for your advice what would you advise?

The importance of early intervention

Because inclusion has become established in educational policy there will be, from time to time, students in your classroom with various kinds of disabilities. There will also be students in your classroom with mild forms of disabilities which may not have been identified in the home. As a teacher you should take note of unusual behaviour of individuals, such as holding books too close to the eyes or turning one ear in the direction of the teacher, and refer any student suspected of having an undiagnosed disability to a health specialist. Early attention, even at this stage, will help avoid more severe problems developing and may have positive consequences for behavioural and learning outcomes (see, for example, Blachman, 2011; Nicholson et al., 1999; Rapee et al., 2005).

The early identification and treatment of problems may be hampered in a number of ways. For example, children of migrant parents who speak little or no English may have disabilities which are not diagnosed before the child begins school owing to the parents' lack of awareness and lack of information on sources of health monitoring (Sullivan, 2011). When at school the problems may continue to be undetected for a period because of the child's lack of English. At other times, parents may fail to acknowledge that their child has a disability, hence delaying and frustrating attempts by other caregivers to assist their child. This can be made worse if parents spend little time with their young children and don't want to acknowledge 'problems'. Such situations occur if both parents work and leave the child for long periods in the care of untrained caregivers rather than family members or leave them by themselves. It is important to note that qualified early childhood caregivers are trained to take note of developmental anomalies in young children.

 ACTIVITY POST

There are many issues to be developed later in this text that should be considered from the perspective of heredity and environment as these are reflected in social and cultural practices. In each of the subsequent chapters you should consider the environmental (which includes sociocultural) forces which impact on children's development. These will include the quality and amount of food available, the climate, the population density, racial and blood ties, the occurrence of epidemiological factors such as diseases and toxins, and the occurrence of catastrophes such as wars and natural disasters. Consider each of these and, in advance of reading subsequent chapters, have a go at projecting what might be some of the impacts of cultural and environmental factors on physical, motor, personal, social, emotional, intellectual, and moral development. We will revisit these as we develop these topics throughout the book.

Physical and motor development: infancy to late childhood

Introduction

This book is concerned with human development, particularly over the years of schooling. What do we mean by human development? By human development we specifically refer to systematic, age-related changes in physical and psychological functioning. In the following two chapters we focus on physical and motor development as children grow from infancy to adulthood. **Physical development** refers to physical and neurological growth and **motor development** refers to age-related changes in motor skills. In later chapters we deal with psychological development.

Teachers, parents, and other professionals such as paediatric doctors and nurses involved in child care and development, need to know the characteristics of physical and motor development including:

- when there are physical growth spurts;
- when growth slows down;
- what are the norms of physical and motor growth;
- are girls and boys, and individuals from different genetic backgrounds similar in their developmental trajectories;
- how to support optimal development and remediate slow development;
- what part diet and parenting (home background) play in development;
- how physical and motor development relates to the development of learning capacities.

 ACTIVITY POST

Consider your physical and motor development over time. A good way to remember key elements of your physical and motor development is by looking through family photograph albums. Collate a series of photos that record your physical development, place them in a timeline, and annotate them with principles of development covered in this and the next chapter. Compare your timeline and notes with the timeline and notes of other students. What are some of the common features of development? What are some individual features?

For educators, the sequence of physical and motor development and its relationship to the development of learning capacities have important implications for the design of academic and non-academic curricula. Such information is useful to evaluate the development of individuals and groups of children in order to match educational programmes effectively to the specific needs of children. Many of our school programmes, both academic and non-academic, relate closely to what we know of the developmental stages of children.

 QUESTION POINT

Before you read this chapter consider some of the elements of physical and motor development that you think are of most importance to you as a trainee or qualified teacher. List these and compare them with those of other students. Why did you include these elements? Are they different from the elements listed by other students?

Principles of development

Orderly and sequential development

Children all over the world appear to develop physical and motor capacities in an orderly and sequential way unless there is some traumatic event, such as birthing problems, infant disease, or malnutrition (refer to Chapter 2). This regularity or continuity in development, driven by genetic forces, is often referred to as *canalisation* which we described in Chapter 2. While particular individuals and groups develop more quickly or slowly than others, and become taller or heavier, shorter or lighter, in general, the overall pattern of development across individuals and groups is one of sequence and regularity. Within this orderly sequence there are periods of rapid growth and development interspersed with slower periods of growth (Blair & Raver, 2012; Cameron & Bogin, 2012; Hermanussen et al., 2001).

There may also be changes in individual growth and maturation caused by the interaction between genetic and environmental forces that influence development. For example, malnutrition in childhood can slow growth, delay development, and slow the end of adolescence (Evans, 2006; Georgieff, 2007). In order to evaluate individual development, professionals consult **growth charts**. Growth charts are graphs representing chronological norms of development for height, weight, skeletal structure, muscles, internal organs, the brain, and the sexual system.

Growth norms present information on:

1 Periods of peak human physical development. This is important information for matching diet, rest, and exercise to the needs of children and adolescents at peak times. Teachers of children and adolescents can be prepared for particular behavioural symptoms of rapid growth.

2   The order in which physical systems become operational. For teachers this is particularly important for scheduling curriculum activities so that they are presented at an optimal time in terms of students' development.
3   Comparisons between the sexes in their growth to physical maturity. This allows questions to be answered about such issues as the appropriateness of particular physical activities for both sexes, the presentation of sex education courses, and the need for personal health and dietary information.
4   Children and adolescents in relation to the general developmental level of others their age and the ability and readiness to learn of the individual. This is important for teachers to identify children with developmental issues that may be addressed through intervention and remedial programmes.

(Borghi et al., 2006; Hasbrouck & Tindal, 2006; Onis, 2006)

 QUESTION POINT

Why is knowledge of growth lines of development so important to teachers? How should teachers be sensitive to individual and cultural differences in timing and rates of development?

Developmental milestones

There are developmental milestones that mark children's physical and motor development. In early childhood (2–6 years of age) there are slower gains in weight and height than in toddlerhood. Physical milestones include increasing abilities in motor skills such as balance, walking, running and skipping, throwing a ball, building block towers, and using scissors. Children in early childhood show an increasing competence in basic self-care and personal hygiene. During middle childhood (6–10 years of age) children become more physically coordinated and their body shape proportions become similar to adults. First permanent teeth erupt. Children become more adept at complex motor skills such as riding a bike and integrating complex motor movements such as tying shoelaces. We discuss these features of development in greater detail below.

Cephalocaudal and proximodistal growth

We have indicated that physical growth is regular. Two components of this regular pattern of growth are what are known as cephalocaudal and proximodistal trends. **Cephalocaudal growth** refers to the development of physical and motor systems from the head down, while **proximodistal growth** refers to growth from the central axis of the body outward.

Newly born children have disproportionately large heads and smaller extremities such as arms and legs. As children age their heads become smaller in proportion to the rest of their body. A rough estimate is that in infancy heads are about one quarter of a person's body length while at adulthood heads are about one eighth of a person's body

Height-for-age GIRLS
5 to 19 years (percentiles)

Height (cm)

Age (completed months and years)

Months
Years

97th
85th
50th
15th
3rd

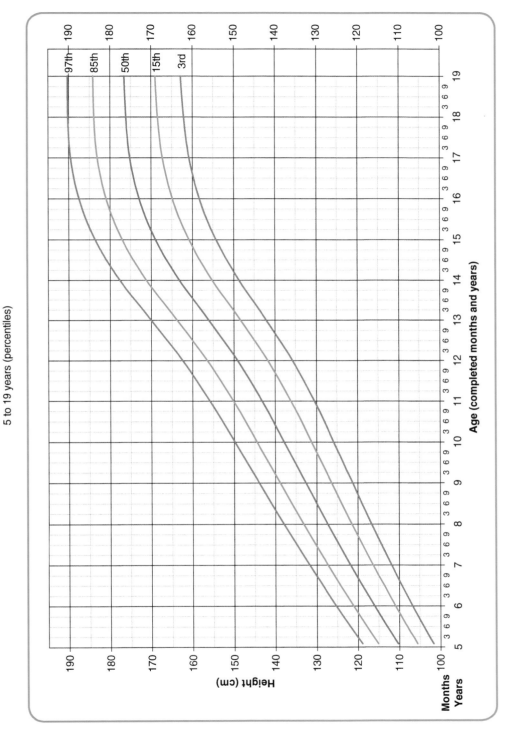

Height-for-age BOYS
5 to 19 years (percentiles)

Figure 3.1 Examples of growth charts for girls and boys aged 5 to 19 years from the World Health Organisation. Those individuals at the 3rd percentile are short, compared to a typically developing person, and those at the 97th percentile are tall compared to a typically developing person.

Table 3.1	Age norms for various gross motor skills
5 years	Walk backward, heel to toes
4 years	Catch bounced ball
3 years	Balance on one foot for 5 seconds
24 months	Pedal tricycle
22 months	Jump in one place
20 months	Kick ball
18 months	Walk-up steps
16 months	Run
14 months	Walk smoothly
12 months	Stand alone without support
8 months	Crawl
6 months	Sit without support
4 months	Lift chest, supporting with arms
2 months	Rollover
6 weeks	Lift head and hold head steady

Based on Onis (2006) and Van Haastert, De Vries, Helders, and Jongmans (2006).

Table 3.2	Age norms for various fine motor skills
5 years	Draw a person with six or more parts
3.5 years	Copy drawing of a cross
3 years	Copy drawing of a circle
2 years	Build a tower with six blocks
22 months	Draw a vertical line imitating an adult
18 months	Build a tower out of four blocks
15 months	Scribble, imitating an adult
11 months	Pincer grasp of a raisin
6 months	Pass a block from hand to hand
5 months	Reach for an object
4 months	Grasp a rattle

Based on Grissmer, Grimm, Aiyer, Murrah, and Steele (2010) and Payne and Isaacs (2012).

length. Young infants have considerable control of their head and shoulders before they gain control of their arms and legs. Furthermore, the internal organs of the body, such as the heart and lungs, are in fine working order before more peripheral systems

Figure 3.2   Cephalocaudal and proximodistal development.

such as the musculature controlling outward movement and fine motor movements (for example, pincer grips with thumb and forefinger).

As we have noted above, the human head (including brain and sensory receptors) is one of the earliest systems to become functional. The human trunk is next in overall rate of growth, followed by the legs. Motor skills involving the use of the upper body develop before those using the lower body. Infants are capable of lifting their heads before they can lift their trunks, and then sit up and walk. This progression in physical and motor growth continues from conception to young adulthood and is called **cephalocaudal development**. Can you think of other examples?

The internal organs of the body, such as heart and lungs, develop and become operational before the development of the long limbs of the body, the fingers, and toes. This is called **proximodistal development**. Infants, children, and adolescents are capable of mastering skills requiring gross motor movements of the body before those requiring the use of fine, or peripheral, motor movement. **Gross motor skills** refer to large movements of the body that allow movement around the environment, such as walking. **Fine motor skills** refer to small precise movements of the body, especially the hands and fingers, such as in using scissors, or writing. Typically, we master the movement of shoulders and trunk before we master the use of hands and fingers.

These ages are only approximate, as many children are ahead of or behind norms. But these categories give us a systematic way of looking at general trends of development as children grow older. In this chapter, we take a brief look at each of the physical and motor developments that characterise development from infancy to the end of childhood and draw out the implications for parents and teachers. In the next chapter, we look at key elements of physical development during adolescence. Many other developmental systems, such as the cognitive, emotional, and personal developmental systems, develop hand-in-hand with the physical and motor systems, and we will examine these in later chapters. Indeed, all developmental systems interact to such a degree that a separate examination of each is only useful as a schema around which to organise our ideas. A full picture of the growing person requires us to see the systems acting interactively

 QUESTION POINT

Each of these developmental trends has implications for parents and educators. From your perspective what might some of these implications be? Cephalocaudal and proximodistal growth continues into adolescence. What are some of the implications of this for planning school lessons and other activities (such as outdoor play)?

Overview of developmental stages

Growth patterns are frequently described in the following stages:

- prenatal development and the newborn;
- infancy: 2 months to 2 years;
- early childhood: 2 years to 6 years;
- middle and later childhood: 7 years to puberty;
- adolescence: puberty to 18 years;
- adulthood.

These ages are only approximate as many children are ahead or behind norms. But these categories give us a systemaic way of looking at general trends of development as children grow older. In this chapter we will take a brief look at each of the physical and motor developments that characterise development from infancy to the end of childhood and draw out the implications for parents and teachers. In the next chapter we look at key elements of physical development during adolescence. Many other developmental systems, such as the cognitive, emotional, and personal developmental systems, develop hand-in-hand with the physical and motor systems and we will examine these in later chapters. Indeed, all developmental systems interact to such a degree that a separate examination of each is only useful as a schema around which to organise our ideas. A full picture of the growing person requires us to see the systems acting interactively (Davis et al., 2011; Paus, 2005; Piek et al., 2008; Steinberg, 2005). As you read, ask yourself, *what do I need to keep in mind about this stage of development from my perspective as a caregiver and educator?*

Prenatal development and the newborn

The prenatal and neonatal periods are characterised by very rapid growth. Within four weeks of conception the organism has grown 10,000 times larger than the original fertilised egg, and internal organs assume nearly adult positions by the fifth week. During the 280-day gestation period the human infant rapidly progresses from a fertilised egg engaged in cell division (often called the ovum or germinal period) to an *embryo* with organ systems developing, and then to a *foetus* which increasingly resembles a human being (Gluckman & Hanson, 2005; Malas et al., 2006).

The support systems necessary for life – heart, lungs, brain, nervous system, and muscles – are sufficiently developed after 26 weeks (out of 40) for the foetus to survive outside the womb. There are many cases of premature babies from about 26 weeks (and sometimes even earlier) surviving and growing normally once their development is back on track. Very low birth rate babies have similar problems to premature babies, and almost all very low birth rate children are preterm. Extensive research confirms that low birth weight children are at greater risk for cognitive and school performance problems than are their normal birth weight peers, and that the risk for adverse outcomes increases as birth weight decreases (further information on this can be obtained from the following website: http://childtrends.org/?indicators=low-and-very-low-birthweight-infants).

At birth, the baby, referred to as a neonate, is born with a series of reflexes, such as the sucking and breathing reflexes, that are essential for the child's survival (the newborn attaches to the mother's breast and sucks with great energy only hours after birth). Other reflexes such as the moro, grasping, stepping, and Babinski reflexes signal the effective

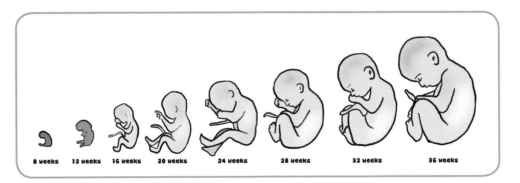

8 weeks   12 weeks   16 weeks   20 weeks   24 weeks   28 weeks   32 weeks   36 weeks

Figure 3.3   **The development of the body during the prenatal period.**

operation of the child's nervous system. These reflexes are used by paediatricians to assess the physiological development of the child and form the basis for later motor development. Indeed, the child's responses to environmental stimulation facilitates further neurological development (Nithianantharajah & Hannan, 2006; Sale et al., 2009). A number of these reflexes disappear as a normal course of development as the neonate ages. The persistence of a reflex might indicate a neurological problem. It is also important that the reflexes are symmetric, meaning that they are the same on both sides of the body. An asymmetric moro reflex, for example, might mean that your baby has weakness on one side of his or her body.

As we discussed in Chapter 2, genetic or environmental influences during the prenatal and neonatal period may cause developmental problems for the baby which become manifest in delaying or limiting physical, motor, and intellectual development. In particular, a range of *genetic diseases* (such as cystic fibrosis and phenylketonuria), *chromosomal abnormalities* (such as Down syndrome and Klinefelter syndrome), *birth complications* (such as oxygen deprivation – called anoxia), **drugs** taken by the mother during pregnancy (such as alcohol, nicotine, cocaine, or heroin), maternal diseases passed on to the infant (such as AIDS), and malnourishment of the foetus and newborn have been shown to be related to later developmental problems such as cerebral palsy and infant foetus alcohol syndrome (FAS).

 ACTIVITY POST

Do an Internet search on each of the influences on development covered above. List their major characteristics and their potential effects in a table to be used by parents, teachers, and other professionals involved in child development.

Infancy

Significant physical and motor development occurs during infancy which lasts for about two years. Following a proximodistal direction there is a lengthening of the lower limbs and, in general, body proportions become more adult-like. In the period between two months and two years, children gain on average about 9 kilograms in weight and 40 centimetres in height. Females achieve approximately half their adult height by two years of age. By two and a half years, males have reached about half their adult height.

Many motor skills are developed during infancy. Infants learn to eat liquid and solid foods, to control the neck and shoulders, and to sit, reach, and walk. They also develop some fine muscle movements and the ability to grasp and hold with the fingers.

While many infant boys and girls are provided with different play and socialising opportunities, different toys, and different clothing, the difference between boys and girls in growth rate and body proportions, strength, agility, and innate interest in particular activities, is of no practical significance during infancy. Consequently, there is no justification for why girls and boys should be treated differently simply because they are a boy or a girl. In most societies, however, they are treated differently. Sex stereotyping occurs in most societies from a very early age (Burn, 2005). We return to this theme a number of times throughout the text. The age of infancy comes to an end when the child becomes more mobile, communicative, and social.

 ACTIVITY POST

At your school, or when on a school placement, observe the types of games that children play during break time. Are there any observable differences between groups of girls and groups of boys? Also observe the interaction of adults with children during break time. Do boys and girls get different attention and encouragement from their teachers or parent(s) to engage in different activities? If you observe any differences ask the adults about their attitudes towards what is appropriate or not appropriate physical activities and games for boys and girls and if they think boys and girls should be treated differently.

Early childhood

The next period of development is referred to as the period of early childhood. While the rate of growth during early childhood is slower than during infancy, the considerable changes that take place are nevertheless very significant and very important for teachers, parents, and other professionals to note. Developing muscle systems, beginning with the *broader muscle systems* and then the *finer muscle systems* replace fatty tissue which characterised the bouncing baby and infant. The trunk and legs grow rapidly and the skeletal system becomes more developed; new bone is established with the conversion of cartilage into bone and the growth of existing bones. By about three years most children have a complete set of baby teeth. Children's height increases by 6 centimetres and weight increases by 2–3 kilograms on average each year.

While cranial growth is slower during this period by the age of five the brain has reached 75% of its adult weight and, within another year, 90%. In line with this cranial growth is a very significant period of cognitive development, as we will see when we examine theories of children's cognition in Chapter 4. The nervous system also develops during this time and the sheathing of the nerve fibres in the brain and nervous system is substantially completed by the end of this period (de Graaf-Peters & Hadders-Algra, 2006; Deoni et al., 2011; Paus, 2005). This process is called *myelinisation* the growth of an insulating fatty sheath (called myelin) around neurons that improves the efficiency of message transfer. Myelinisation is responsible for the rapid gain in overall size of the brain at this time. Myelinisation continues over a period of years, with neurons involved in basic survival skills beginning in the pre-natal period and those involving motor skills and higher thinking processes coming later (Haynes et al., 2006). Even at this early age, females tend to mature faster than males. It is essential during this time that children avoid malnutrition and serious brain trauma as these can lead to serious brain and physiological damage. In contrast to earlier beliefs it is now believed that the brain continues to develop throughout adulthood. Recent research has suggested that important forebrain regions, such as the hippocampus (involved in establishing memory for facts and relationships), continue to receive new nerve cells into adulthood in humans and that lifelong enrichment experiences cause brain development in adulthood. Further information on myelinisation and brain development may be found at the following website: http://main.zerotothree.org/site/PageServer?pagename=ter_key_brainFAQ

Is there a 'critical period' for brain development?

By six years of age children have assumed the body proportions they will have as adults. During early childhood children increasingly learn to coordinate their body movements and, in particular, learn many important gross motor skills such as run-ning, skipping, hopping, catching, and balancing, and fine motor skills such as writing and drawing. It is very important for teachers and parents to support these develop-ments by providing appropriate physical and motor activities. This is also a time when healthy children begin to form concepts of social and physical reality and are intensely curious about the world around them. We will examine some of these features of social development in Chapter 9.

Because of the development and coordination of gross muscle systems, energetic physical activity is typical of this age. Children should be given the opportunity to exercise gross motor skills in both directed and undirected settings such as formal physical activity programmes and unstructured play activities. Along with the gross motor development is fine motor development.

A short list of common fine motor activities, roughly in developmental order, include:

- grasping and (just as important) letting go;
- turning objects around in his or her hand;
- picking up smaller and smaller things;
- stacking blocks, threading beads;
- holding a crayon and drawing;
- using snaps, buttons, and zippers;
- cutting with scissors;
- tying shoelaces.

Opportunities for engaging in fine motor activies are provided through numerous home and school activies such as dressing and undressing, pouring drinks, drawing, writing, and craft activities. Pride in doing these things is important to foster, as is encouragement to copy and be involved in adult activities.

ACTIVITY POST

Consider a primary school's programme for physical activities, structured, and unstructured play activities. What opportunities are provided for fine and gross motor development? Do you think enough time is made available within the school day for these activities? Survey a group of teachers and parents and find out what they think. Write a brief report on your findings and compare them with other students. Are activities and opportunities made available at the secondary school level for fine and gross motor development and refinement?

 ACTIVITY POST

If you have the opportunity to observe some children in an early years setting, first do an Internet search for 'fine motor skills' and 'getting ready for school'. Observe children engaged in a range of the activities suggested in the various webpages. What do your observations tell you about fine motor development in young children?

 SPOTLIGHT ON SEX-TYPING ACTIVITIES

There is very little difference between the size of boys and girls during early childhood and they have very much the same body proportions. While boys develop more muscle tissue, and girls tend to retain more fat than boys, their coordination skills are the same. There is, therefore, little justification for different physical education, sport, or health programmes for boys and girls at this age. Any apparent differences in performance which appear are likely to be the result of differing social expectations and the opportunities presented to girls and boys (Änggård, 2011; Cherney & London, 2006; Miller & Kuhaneck, 2008;

Sandberg & Pramling-Samuelsson, 2005; Venetsanou & Kambas, 2010).

It is not uncommon for children, from an early age, to be encouraged by parents, siblings, and peers to engage in different physical activities that are sex stereotyped. For example, fathers might play ball games less frequently with their daughters than with their sons. Cricket bats and footballs are purchased for sons, while skipping ropes are purchased for daughters. As children get older, differences in motor skills between girls and boys increase. It is likely that this reflects the social pressures on boys to be active and physically skilled and girls

(continued)

(continued)

to be more passive and skilled at fine motor activities rather than true differences emerging because of genetic differences between the sexes. If we wish boys and girls to have similar physical skills during childhood it is important that girls and boys are given opportunities to engage in similar physical activities and are not limited to those that might be considered sex appropriate. Increasingly, childcare settings and schools are encouraging young children to participate equally in physical activities such as dancing, skipping, and team ball games, and fine motor skills such as sewing and knitting and a variety of arts and crafts. These activities are presented as a means of developing physical fitness, motor coordination, and team cooperation that are appropriate to all.

As a consequence of non-sexist educational programmes, a number of these features of

sexist conditioning of motor skills are changing slowly. Many schools are introducing cross-sex and mixed-sex sporting and health programmes, and craft activities such as woodwork; sewing and knitting are being taught to both females and males. Many schools resist coeducational classes, however, because of the perceived differences in ability between females and males, the desire to allow females to participate free of the domination of males and the restrictions imposed by single-sex sporting organisations and competitions.

How important do you think these arguments are for continuing to segregate boys and girls in physical and motor activities?

Why do you think sex-stereotyping is so entrenched in our society that, despite many initiatives to eliminate it, it persists? What further initiatives might be taken to alleviate it?

Middle and late childhood to puberty

During middle childhood growth is steady and children's bodies gradually approach adult dimensions. If well nourished, children grow 4.4 to 6.6 centimetres in height and gain from 2 to 2.75 kilograms per year. By 12 years of age, children have reached approximately 90% of their adult height. Significant advances are made in gross and fine motor skills coordination. While younger children run and jump for the sheer pleasure, older children use these skills in organised games and sports. They intensify their development of these gross motor skills and put much practice into perfecting them. Children at this age also improve their fine motor skills. They begin to draw more complex drawings (Cherney et al., 2006) and their handwriting becomes smaller, smoother, and more even (Feder & Majnemer, 2007). Their activities also become more complex with them becoming more adept at activities such as sewing, model building, and various arts and crafts. However, at this time gross motor skills are more developed than fine motor skills and hand–eye and foot–eye coordination continue to develop. In fact, many fine skills do not come to full maturity until adolescence. Because children in early primary grades are in perpetual motion running, chasing, and climbing they are easily susceptible to injury and fatigue.

Some body parts grow at different rates relative to other body parts during middle to late childhood and some awkwardness and lankiness may characterise children's appearance and coordination. The growth of the skeleton, for example, is frequently more rapid than the growth of the muscles and ligaments. **Asynchrony** is the term used to describe this differential development. Children at this age become more concerned about their physical appearance. Because attitudes towards self are important in developing a healthy outlook on life it is important for parents and teachers to give sensitive support to children as they come to understand their physical appearance. It is very important for teachers not to favour children who are stereotypically more attractive and physically poised than other children.

During early childhood the first teeth begin to fall out and permanent teeth begin to appear. As speech, appearance and body image are all affected by the health of teeth, sound oral hygiene and dental care must be encouraged by parents and teachers.

In line with their growing maturity children in the early grades can be very individualistic, curious, imaginative, creative, and dramatic. They often display a desire to please and excel, and to assume leadership and responsibility. Nevertheless, they seek to establish this independence in a secure environment.

By about nine, children are quite aware that they are 'growing up', and feel that they are too big for little ones (Year 1, or Primary 1 in Scottish schools) and too little for the big ones (Year 6, or Primary 6 in Scottish schools). By 10 or 11 many children go through another period of rapid physical growth with a further development of muscular strength and bone length. These developments give further capacity to develop motor skills and more fine coordination. Teachers usually provide extensive opportunities for children to practice more sophisticated physical and motor skills for older children particularly in individual activities such as group sports and craft activities. Increasingly, as well as individual development of skills such as dancing, gymnastics, and swimming, there is a growing emphasis on team sports such as netball, basketball, and football, which not only facilitate the development of physical and motor skills, but also social interaction and the learning of rules, which are very important at this age. Luckily, most children in Years 4–6 (Primary 4–6 in Scottish schools) enjoy vigorous physical activities, and are increasingly interested in competitive activities and organised games. During these games they are very concerned with game rules and their correct application. This attitude is generalised to an interest in ethics and values, and the desire to make fair judgments. You can see here the interaction of cognitive, social, and moral development.

During late childhood there are considerable differences in rates of development and children may show increasing interest in growth patterns, comparing who is the smallest and who is the tallest. As girls tend to mature earlier than boys, the development of sexual characteristics may become noticeable among girls at this age.

 QUESTION POINT

Given that there is a relationship between physical, cognitive, social, and moral development how would you ensure that your planning for physical or outdoor activities took this in to account at various age groupings during primary school?

Many children at this time also begin to display independent behaviour demonstrated in some forms of rebellion against teachers and parents. It is also a period of strong peer allegiance and hero worship.

In summary, during this period children develop and refine physical skills for games and academic purposes, and acquire a healthy concept of self. Social skills in dealing with peers, appropriate social and sex roles, and aspects of personal independence also develop along with intellectual capacity, which we deal with in detail in a later chapter. Within this context, children learn many moral and social concepts required for daily living, including conscience, morality, and values.

Principles of motor development

The development of an individual's motor coordination runs parallel to physical growth. Motor development continues throughout childhood and adolescence and into adulthood, following a predictable sequence. As we have suggested earlier each of the systems of development we are examining such as physical, motor, cognitive, and social development should be seen as part of the holistic development of the individual and all systems are interactive (Piek et al., 2008; Stodden et al., 2008; Yeates et al., 2007).

During childhood motor capacities develop gradually from a set of reflex actions to a complex set of motor abilities. Considerable research has been done on the sequence of motor development and its relationship to physical development which informs practitioners of the major milestones of development (Onis, 2006; Van Haastert et al., 2006; World Health Organisation & de Onis, 2006). While it does not appear that motor development can be accelerated, there is evidence that physical and motor development can be retarded under the impact of poor environmental conditions such as sickness, accident, or gross physical neglect. We have considered a number of these factors in Chapter 2.

There are two related processes involved in motor development: differentiation and integration. **Differentiation** refers to the gradual separation of children's motor movements from gross movement patterns into more refined and functional movements as they mature. **Integration** refers to children bringing various opposing muscle and sensory systems into coordinated interaction with one another (Serrien et al., 2006; Sober & Sabes, 2005; Taube, 2007). Differentiation and integration of motoric systems allows the child to become increasingly able to manipulate body movements in complex motor movements such as holding a glass, moving it to the mouth, and drinking from it. Consider a range of motor movements that you do each day and what processes of differentiation and integration are involved. Most of these motor movements become automated so that we do not consciously have to think about doing them. However, consider a new motor movement you have learnt or are learning, such as driving a manual car and the motor movements involved in coordinating clutch, brake, accelerator, and steering wheel! We are sure you will then appreciate what we are referring to. Furthermore, you might also get an inkling of what we mean when we say that all systems: intellectual, emotional, social, and cognitive, as well as physical, need to be seen as integrated and holistic.

There are four key principles of motor development: maturation, motivation, experience, and practice (Hadders-Algra, 2010; Martin, 2005; Taube, 2007; Ulrich, 2007). These elements are not hierarchical but mutually interdependent (Diamond, 2007; Piek et al., 2008; Stodden et al., 2008).

Maturation

The brain is the command centre of human functioning. The brain regulates and coordinates the activities of complex bodily systems through the interactions of neurons (Lewis & Todd, 2007). Not all centres of the brain are operational at birth – many brain centres that control movement develop over time (Lebel et al., 2008). This is referred to as *neurological maturation*. By approximately five years of age, however, the brain is capable of stimulating and controlling the wide range of motor activities in which children engage. Doing actions in physical space requires an appreciation of depth, height, velocity, and so on. Therefore, *growth in perceptual capacities* is very important to the development of motor skills (Iverson, 2010).

As we have indicated in the discussion of physical development, maturation of the physical systems develops progressively. Larger muscle systems, controlling gross body movements such as walking and running, develop before the striated muscle systems, which control finer movements such as the manipulation of fingers on a keyboard or the use of a pair of scissors. These striated muscles are not really fully developed until adolescence, and so there are motor movements beyond children's capacity until after puberty. Nevertheless, children are generally capable of a full range of differentiated motor movements that are later integrated into performing complex motor skills by middle childhood. For example, while children of five can hop, skip, and jump, they later develop the coordination skills necessary to combine these fluently into one action – hop–skip–jump.

Each muscle has its own special name. They are also, however, described by their function: Muscles that bend a limb are *flexors*; those which straighten a limb are *extensors* (e.g. elbow flexors and elbow extensors.) Muscles which move a limb to the side, away from the body, are *abductors*; those which move a limb sideways toward the body are *adductors* (e.g. hip abductors and hip adductors.) Other functional groups are *elevators*, *depressors*, *rotators*, *doriflexors*, *planar flexors*, and *palmar flexors*. The following webpage contains lots of information about muscle types and function: http://livescience.com/26854-muscular-system-facts-functions-diseases.html

 QUESTION POINT

Consider various motor activities that characterise children such as playing complex sports, engaging in individual skilled activities such as gymnastics, writing, and learning the piano. Why is an understanding of developmentally appropriate activities essential for parents and teachers? You might also like to consider whether motor development can be accelerated through enrichment programmes.

Table 3.3 Motor development milestones

First year
- Good head balance
- Reaches for an object
- Transfers objects from hand to hand
- Sitting at 6 months
- Pulls to standing at 9–10 months
- Cruises furniture
- Takes first steps

18–24 months
- Opens a small box
- Marks with a pencil
- Seats self in a small chair
- Points
- Feeds self with a spoon
- Places square and circle in a formboard
- Builds a 3 block tower

24–36 months
- Turns pages of a book
- Scribbles with a pencil
- Makes a tower of 7 blocks
- Completes 3 piece of formboard
- Kicks a ball
- Walks and runs fairly well
- Toilet training, with assistance

3–4 years
- Imitates drawings of circle and cross
- Builds a 10 block tower
- Imitates building of a 4 block train
- Imitates a 3 block bridge
- Achieving toilet independence
- Hand dominance
- Stands on one foot momentarily

4 years
- Stands heel to toe for 15 seconds, eyes closed
- Performs finger to nose well, eyes closed
- Can hop on both feet for up to 7 seconds

5 years
- Balances on tiptoes for 10 seconds
- Hops 15 feet on one foot
- Parts lips and clenches teeth

6 years
- Balances on one foot for 10 seconds
- Hits target (10 square inches) with a ball from 5 feet
- Jumps over a rope 8 inches high

7 years
- Balances on tiptoes for 10 seconds, bending at hips
- Walks in a straight line, heel to toe for 6 feet

8 years
- Maintains crouched position on tiptoes for 10 seconds, arms extended and eyes closed
- Touches fingertips of one hand successively with thumb, starting with little finger and repeating in reverse order

Class notes for UNCG's CSD 500 Diagnostic Procedures: Inquiry, Observation and Measurement: 'Cognitive and Motor Development Screening' with permission from Mariana Newton, Instructor.

Motivation

Motivation is the driving force behind children acquiring motor skills rather than pre-specified genetic instructions (Martin et al., 2009). Children appear to be innately interested in learning a wide range of motor skills in order to achieve goals such as putting a toy in the mouth or crossing the room. Even tasks as ordinary as undoing buttons and tying shoelaces, which signify some independence from adults, can motivate children to acquire important motor skills through practice. At particular times, the acquisition of motor skills become the focus of much voluntary activity and children spend endless time learning to skip, play with a yo-yo, or master elaborate string games in order to demonstrate skills comparable with their peers. Almost as quickly the preoccupation with the skill will disappear. Motivation is essential to the development of motor skills throughout the lifespan.

Experience

Experience is essential for the development of motor skills (Clark, 2007). Children should be provided with frequent opportunities to run, hop, climb, jump, and engage in a wide range of physical activities in a safe and supportive environment. Equipment and toys provided should be developmentally appropriate. It is quite hazardous if toys and play equipment are wrongly sized. It is also problematic if the social climate surrounding the practice of motor skills is overly competitive, restrictive, or demanding. In these cases the enthusiasm of children to acquire the skills can be dampened. It is very important that children develop gross motor skills at an early age as limited competence in motor skills can negatively affect future performance in physical and motor activities (Haga, 2008; Stodden et al., 2008). The lack of motor skills can impact negatively on self-concept. If children are not encouraged to engage in appropriate physical and motor activities when they are interested, motivation may dissipate and later attempts to learn particular skills may be more difficult. However, even after the optimal age, motor skills may still be learnt, although the earlier a skill is learnt the better, because children are more supple, adventurous, agreeable to repetition, and have more time to practise. Children who fail to develop motor skills appropriate for their age participate less in organised sports and other physical programmes. This has significant consequences for their individual well-being.

Practice

It is essential that children *practise* motor skills in order to perfect them (Sullivan et al., 2008). Some motoric systems such as bowel and bladder control mature without much practice; other skills based on muscle control, such as skipping, need extensive practice. When children show a readiness to learn particular motor skills, they are also willing to put endless hours into practising the skill. Practice does not appear to bore children. Whether it is learning to click one's fingers, whistle, or roller skate, the activity often appears quite compulsive to children until it is mastered. As we get older, such dedication to acquiring new motor skills begins to wane.

Individual differences in motor development

While motor development follows a predictable pattern in the acquisition of basic skills there are individual differences which teachers need to allow for. For most motor skills there are individual differences, particularly in fine motor skills. For example, research indicates that girls are better at some fine motor skills, such as writing, than boys (Junaid & Fellowes, 2006). These individual differences are more dramatic when we consider children who might have some disability such as Down syndrome (Vicari, 2006). While instruction and practice can help children improve their fine motor skills it is inevitable that some differences will persist.

What are the reason for these individual differences in motor development? It is obvious that genetic influences are very important in the development of motor skills, both as related to the physical structures of the body, as well as to muscle coordination. However, it is also most likely that the child's experiential background significantly influences the development of motor skills. Some children are encouraged and stimulated in their efforts and exposed to a wide range of models demonstrating diverse motor skills. Older brothers and sisters, as well as early experiences in local playgrounds, give children opportunities to observe and practice what others can do. In other cases, children may not be exposed to models or encouraged to be much more than couch potatoes and so do not have the experiences necessary to develop their skills. Demanding, critical, or overprotective parents may inhibit the development of confidence, while limited experiences and a deprived environment may impede growth.

Motor development norms

For all of these variations in individual development, there exist general age-related norms for the development of common motor skills. If a child does not reach a given level of development within these norms an abnormality may be present. The delayed development may be the result of a poorly maturing physiological system, the absence of relevant experiences, or some trauma. Teachers and other professionals should always be on the look-out for developmentally delayed individuals so that they may assess the cause of the delay and introduce interventions to maximise development.

Children go through stages when motor skills are occasionally insufficiently developed for body maturation which leads to an appearance of awkwardness. This is referred to as motor development asynchrony. A pathology should only be suspected when children's control over body movements fall well below age norms (Polatajko & Cantin, 2005; Wuang et al., 2008). Children vary in their awkwardness, and at every age more children tend to fall below the norm in **motor coordination** than above it. While an individual may be awkward at some activities it is likely that he or she is coordinated at others. It is important for teachers to put children in situations where they can demonstrate their coordination as this gives them confidence to extend their experiences to other areas in which they might be less coordinated. The early detection of motor problems and the start of appropriate intervention programmes is very important to eliminate or minimise many physical and related emotional problems that may impact on the child's learning (Glascoe, 2005; Sugden, 2007).

Sex differences in motor development

Are there inherent differences in the growth of motor skills between the sexes prior to puberty? Physiologically, there seems to be no reason why males and females shouldn't develop the same motor skills. However, males and females develop different motor skills that are seen as sex-'appropriate'. Males are generally expected to learn skills that require daring, strength, and endurance such as skate board riding, while females are expected to learn skills that require precision, dexterity, and patience, such as sewing and knitting. Is this the result of cultural conditioning? It certainly appears that it is still strongly entrenched in Western societies that boys and girls are given different opportunities to develop motor skills. Take a survey of any local toy and sports stores and you will quickly evaluate that even in the twenty-first century there is a clear demarkation between what is considered appropriate activities and purchases for boys and girls.

As a consequence of *non-sexist educational programmes* a number of these features of sexist conditioning of motor skills are changing slowly. Many schools are introducing cross-sex and mixed-sex sporting and health programmes, and craft activities, such as woodwork, sewing, and knitting, are being taught to both females and males. Many schools resist co-educational classes, however, because of the perceived differences in ability between females and males, the desire to allow females to participate free of the domination of males and the restrictions imposed by single-sex sporting organisations and competitions. How important do you think these arguments are for continuing to segregate boys and girls in physical and motor activities?

SPOTLIGHT ON RECESS TIMING AND CHILDREN'S PLAYGROUND AND CLASSROOM BEHAVIOURS

Childhood is a time when physical activity is very important for physical and motor development. It is also a period when social skills are developed and practised. In some ways classrooms are quite artificial environments for children as they require students to be sedentary for relatively long periods of time doing classwork and, in general, not interacting with their peers socially. These classwork periods are punctuated by relatively small periods of free physical and social activity at recess and lunch breaks. Some schools have one morning break of about 15 minutes, followed by a longer 45-minute lunch break, and then an afternoon break of about 15 minutes. Other schools have more frequent short breaks. Other schools internationally, such as in the United States, have dispensed with breaks altogether.

What are the effects of frequency and length of break on students' playground and classroom behaviours? It's probable that frequent breaks are advantageous for students as they alleviate the potential for tiredness and boredom – in other words students learn best when their efforts are broken-up across tasks (Pellegrini & Bohn, 2005; Ramstetter et al., 2010). Furthermore, the timing and length of the break may have implications for children's behaviour when they return to the classroom. It's likely that students will return to the classroom after these breaks refreshed and motivated once more to engage in cognitive tasks. There is some evidence for this although it might take some time for boisterous out of classroom behaviour to subside and for the students to settle back into classwork. Of course,

(continued)

(continued)

for the positive effects of playground activity to occur, students would need to be returning to interesting and relevant activities. If they return to boring, repetitive activities no amount of breaks are likely to improve their attention to the task.

Theory suggests that there will be greater levels of social and physical behaviour the longer the period of deprivation from those behaviours. This is called the deprivation-rebound hypothesis (Pellegrini & Bohn-Gettler, 2013). In other words, if students have long periods of deprivation from physical and social activity prior to recess they are more likely to be very active when recess comes. As we have indicated above, in the context of physical and motor development, there may be differences in level of activity at recess depending on the sex of the students and their age, with males being more physically active than females. Research also shows that level and type of activity depends upon the climate and the venue (inside or outside). Schools should look carefully at their recess policies to ensure that they are getting best value for the time students spend in recess. Perhaps distributed recess would be more effective. What do you think?

 QUESTION POINT

In order to be effective teachers in a multicultural society we should consider physical and motor development from a cross cultural perspective. Among the issues that should be considered are:

- The impact of culture and genetics on physical size and patterns of growth.
- The availability of growth and development opportunities and diet across cultural groups.
- The valued physical and motor characteristics and activities across cultural groups.
- The parental and societal expectations for physical and motor development and the presentation of appropriate experiences for development.
- The norms for healthy living and mores associated with health and hygiene.

Consider a range of cultural groups with which you are familiar. These could include persons of Indian, Pakistani, Bangladeshi, Chinese, Polish, or Romanian heritage. Discuss the application of each of the points above. How does this exercise sensitise you to the necessity of taking a cultural perspective on the physical growth and motor development of children?

In Chapter 4, we consider physical and motor development during adolescence and some health issues that apply across the developmental span during which children are at school.

Physical and motor development: puberty to adulthood and developmental health issues

Introduction

Puberty and adolescence is a period of tremendous physical, cognitive, and social change, and perhaps a period of stress for adolescents. Whether it is actually a period of stress for most adolescents is hotly debated. As we have indicated in Chapter 2, most physiological changes are canalised and programmed genetically at birth, and this includes the changes that occur during adolescence. These changes involve important physiological differences between males and females related to average developmental rates, disposition of muscle and fat tissue, rate of skeletal ossification, overall strength and size, and sexual development (Hermanussen et al., 2001; Patton & Viner, 2007; Proos & Gustafsson, 2012). In this chapter we will examine the physical changes that occur during adolescence as well as some developmental health issues from childhood through to adolescence.

Puberty and adolescence

Pubescence (derived from the Latin 'to grow hairy'!) refers to changes that occur in individuals that result in sexual maturity. The onset of puberty comes with the physiological development of the sexual system. This leads into the longer period of physical development called **adolescence**. In boys, these changes include the enlargement of the testes and penis; growth of pubic, underarm, and facial hair; changes in the voice; and the production of and ability to ejaculate semen. Each of these developments has a very significant impact on the development of a sense of self for the maturing boy.

In girls, pubescence is characterised by rapid physical growth, particularly of the uterus, vagina and fallopian tubes. Other changes include the occurrence of the first menstrual cycle (menarche or period); a slight lowering of the voice; an enlargement and development of the breasts; rounding of the pelvic area; and growth of pubic and underarm hair (Brooks-Gunn & Peterson, 2013; Christie & Viner, 2005; Pinyerd & Zipf, 2005). As with boys, each of these developments has a very significant impact on the development of a sense of self for the maturing girl. Further information on pubertal development, particularly aimed at teens can be found on the Childline website. They have a separate page for girls https://childline.org.uk/Explore/puberty/Pages/PubertyGirls. aspx and boys https://childline.org.uk/Explore/puberty/Pages/PubertyGirls.aspx. There is also information on the NHS website available at: http://nhs.uk/conditions/Puberty/ Pages/Introduction.aspx

Growth spurts and interpersonal comparisons

The biological system and the ability to procreate matures relatively early in this period. However, significant physical changes continue for a number of years. At times these changes occur so rapidly that they are called *growth spurts*. On average, girls develop faster than boys and dramatic physical growth begins between the ages of eight and a half and ten and a half and reaches its peak around 12. Boys growth spurt, on average, occurs between the ages of ten and a half and 12 and a half and reaches peak rates of increase at about 14 or 15. In general, boys begin the pubertal growth spurt after girls, but it lasts three to four years longer than that of girls. Because of this, girls are initially taller and heavier than boys in the age range 11 to 14+ but boys end up, on average, significantly taller and heavier than girls.

During adolescence there is a lot of comparison within the same sex with both boys and girls comparing themselves with others – am I as tall, am I getting breasts, am I getting facial hair, am I menstruating, is my penis as large as others, and so on. While maybe not a time of stress and strain, adolescence is certainly a time of emotions and self-reflections for adolescents. Associated with this development, of course, and as we will elaborate on further in later chapters, are issues of personal, intellectual, social, and moral development. During adolescence, perhaps more than at any other stage, these various systems become inextricably entwined.

Differences in physical growth, muscle growth, and motor development

We earlier noted that during early to late childhood there are few physical differences in growth rates and little effective differences in children in muscle growth and motor development. During adolescence however there are considerable differences in physical development between the sexes. Muscle growth is greater for boys than for girls, and is more marked in the arm than in the calf. Hence adolescent males are, on average, stronger than adolescent females. Males usually develop larger hearts and lungs, together with a greater capacity for absorbing oxygen in the blood and for eliminating the biochemical products of exercise. Males also develop wider shoulders. This makes particular forms of physical activity more suited to males than females. Females develop a wider pelvis and store more fat in their tissues than boys and develop as a consequence a more rounded shape. Most males develop deeper voices than females. The overall average size and strength difference between males and females after puberty is due to the longer pre-adolescent growth period of males prior to the onset of puberty.

Implications for education

Because of the differences in physical development during adolescence there is some justification for differentiated sporting and health programmes for males and females. However, both sexes are capable of vigorous physical activity. Traditionally, schools often provided different types of sports activities for boys and girls and more opportunities for vigorous physical activity for males than for female (Hills, 2006; Klomsten et al., 2005). Nowadays many sports that were once reserved for males (e.g. football) are now open to both girls and boys. There is also a considerable number of both sexes who do not engage in any substantial physical activity which is essential to the development of good health and vitality. It is important that any pre-conceived notions of what sports activities may be more appropriate for boys or girls are put to oneside. Although there may be physical differences in strength and coordination between adolscent males and females (Smoll & Schutz, 1990; Thomas & French, 1985) it is important that a lack of opportunity for physical development in school PE lessons is not a contributory factor.

As teachers and parents we should ensure that all males and females receive appropriate fitness and endurance training, and provide opportunities for the development of physical and motor skills including vigorous physical activity for girls (Bailey, 2006; Giles-Corti et al., 2009). Over the last decade schools have increasingly encouraged females to participate in a wide range of male sex-stereotyped sports, such as cricket, touch football, and golf. The number of females engaged in such vigorous sports has substantially improved due to initiatives such as Kwick Cricket by the English and Wales Cricket Board, and the Girls' England Talent Pathway by the Football Association.

 QUESTION POINT

Consider when you were in secondary school. What was your school's policy towards physical education and activity for males and females? What were the strengths of the policy and programmes based on it? What were the weaknesses?

Multicultural issues

In the United Kingdon, like many other other countries including the United States and Australia there are significant differences in the onset of puberty and the growth spurt related to racial differences (Slyper, 2006; Wardle et al., 2006). Certain groups develop earlier and growth norms may vary from group to group. Therefore, norms for height and weight derived from Western groups may not be representative of other non-Western groups (e.g. children from a number of racial groups are typically lighter and shorter at each level of development, while others are typically heavier). Care should be used, therefore, when applying norms in ethnically and racially diverse societies.

SPOTLIGHT ON ASYNCHRONY DURING ADOLESCENCE

Asynchrony refers to the differential rate at which different body parts grow. Although asynchronous development occurs in late childhood, individuals appear to be blissfully unaware of their gawkiness. Asynchronous development, however, seems to cause distress for some adolescents. There are two types of asynchrony: interpersonal, where development varies from individual to individual, and intrapersonal, where there is an uneven progression of development within an individual (Dorn & Biro, 2011).

The onset of development can vary quite markedly within any cohort of age peers, so that in any Year 6 grade there might be prepubescent, pubescent, and adolescent children, with some children early developers and others late developers. This is a case of interpersonal asynchrony. To further complicate this there will be differences between individuals in the sequencing of their development. Not all boys will start to grow facial hair, nor girls breasts in the same sequence with other developments as is occurring with other children. While most boys acquire pubic hair before the height spurt, and most girls' breasts have nearly finished growing before menarche, some individuals deviate from this sequential pattern. This can be a source of serious worry for them. Personal development and health programmes in schools generally address this issue and demonstrate how there is a wide variety of developmental patterns as children mature through adolescence.

Intrapersonal asynchrony refers to the apparent out of sequence development within an individual which can also cause concern. The nose, for example, develops to full size very early and may appear disproportionately large on a youngster's face. Ears, limbs, and fingers may also give an appearance of gawkiness to this age group. The sebaceous (oil-producing) glands of the skin can develop more quickly than the ducts, causing the blockages and infections known as acne. Shoulders and hips may grow out of sequence for girls, giving them an overly masculine appearance or an exaggerated 'pear' shape.

Both intrapersonal and interpersonal asynchrony have an effect on boys' and girls' self-concept and self-confidence. Teachers, in particular, need to be aware of, and alleviate, potential problems in sensible and sensitive ways. For example, the custom of students changing clothing publicly for sport can be embarrassing for many children, and teachers should be vigilant for when students are embarrassing or bullying each other over their appearance. Asynchronous development can have an effect on the poise and balance of children so that they may appear ungainly and poorly coordinated. While adolescents become less coordinated in particular tasks from time to time because muscle movement might be outstripped by physical growth, Malina (1990) found no point in the adolescent growth process at which individuals become consistently less coordinated or skilful on physical tasks.

Developmental trajectories: early and late maturation

As we have mentioned before, one form of interpersonal asynchrony is the age of onset of pubertal development. Some individuals develop early, while others develop relatively late. The effects of early and late maturation on males and females have been carefully studied (Christie & Viner, 2005; Forbes & Dahl, 2010; Michaud et al., 2006; Negriff & Susman, 2011). Questions asked include; what are the general effects of being an early or late maturer on emotional, intellectual, and social development, and are these effects similar for males and females?

Early maturing males

Research indicates that early maturing males appear more self-assured, more relaxed, more masculine, better groomed, and more poised and handsome than both the late and average group. Late maturers apparently stand out for their restless attention seeking, tense manner, boyish eagerness, and social awkwardness. Early maturers appear more popular with their male peers than the late maturers and are chosen in preference to both late and average maturers in contests for leadership. The late maturers are judged by adults to be less responsible and less mature than other males their age in their relationships with females. Late maturers emerged at a disadvantage to early maturers in virtually all areas of behaviour and adjustment during adolescence. While in later life the physical differences between these groups have been shown to disappear, personality differences may persist (Branje et al., 2007; Mendle, 2014; Mendle & Ferrero, 2012).

 QUESTION POINT

Think back to when you were an adolescent. Were you aware of differences in patterns of growth among your peers? Were you concerned about what you perceived as out of sequence development personally? How did you handle any concerns you had? Discuss your thoughts with others in your group. Were there common concerns? Were there concerns that appear to be specific to particular individuals?

Among the reasons given for the apparent advantage early maturing boys have over late developing boys is that because of their size, early maturing males are expected by parents and teachers to be more competent than less developed peers and therefore may be given more responsibilities and opportunities to develop personality characteristics such as independence and responsibility. Any difference between early and late maturers could therefore be the result of socialisation.

Because individuals are physically underdeveloped does not mean that they are simultaneously cognitively, emotionally, or socially immature. Many physically underdeveloped males are sufficiently cognitively, socially, and emotionally developed to benefit from the responsibilities and opportunities given to their more physically developed peers, but are often denied them. Such a situation may breed resentment and poor adjustment in youth who feel they are being denied appropriate opportunities. Being physically developed does not mean that one is necessarily also cognitively, socially, and emotionally developed, so some physically advanced males may not be cognitively and emotionally prepared for the responsibilities they are expected to assume because of their physical size and appearance. It is therefore important that a range of developmental criteria be assessed when providing age appropriate opportunities for children, such as increasing physical independence and growing opportunities to make decisions and control one's life.

Early maturing females

There appear to be very few differences between early and late maturing females. This is quite a contrast to the situation with males. Among the reasons given for this difference are the relatively shorter pubertal period for females, and the fact that late maturing females still have males of the same age who are less developed physically and sexually than they are. However, early developing females sometimes experience emotional and social difficulties that may be reflected in lack of popularity, withdrawal, and low self-confidence (Christie & Viner, 2005; Mendle et al., 2007). Menstruating is a significant physical event for pubescent girls which is emotionally demanding. Early maturers' psychological preparedness may be inadequate to cope with the physical stress of menstruating or the added responsibilities that they might be expected to assume, such as putting up with pain, attention to cleanliness, ability to handle 'accidents', appropriate levels of communication, and privacy over such an intimate event.

Some early developing girls may become rebellious in an attempt to assume more personal freedom which they think is appropriate because of their physical maturity, and in line with many models, real and media, they observe. Considerable conflict may ensue with parents because their parents may become more restrictive in an attempt to protect them from potential sexual dangers. This stands in marked contrast to the way that early maturing males may be treated, with many actively encouraged to be more independent as they physically mature. Early maturing girls may also be at increased risk of peer victimisation via malicious rumours and gossip. Finally, early maturing females may feel isolated from their peer group and not have an effective group with which to socialise (Haynie, 2003; Reynolds & Juvonen, 2011).

 ACTIVITY POST

Refer back to the section of the chapter dealing with early and late maturing adolescents. Research suggests that the timing of puberty can influence personality adjustment in adolescence. Personality profiles have been drawn for both the early and later maturer, e.g. the girl who appears conspicuous physically may be developing an interest in boys, but may not be capable of handling emotional relationships with an older boy.

The physical status of adolescents influences the way adults and peers react to them. Thus the social environment to which later maturers are exposed may be significantly different from that of their early maturing peers. This exercise will help you review some of the characteristics and problems of late maturing boys.

For this activity you will need to obtain the permission of the school, parents, and student before you start. Identify two adolescent boys who appear to be late maturers. Late-maturing boys typically display some of the following characteristics: delayed muscle development, minimal beard growth and bodily hair, short stature. Observe each boy's interactions with the teacher and with other students both in a classroom and playground setting.

Interview each student individually about his social relationships. Include questions about whether he prefers younger or older friends, whether or not he belongs to social clubs and which ones, whether he is active in sports, whether he has a steady girlfriend, whether he has a part-time job, etc. You may add a number of other questions which will tap some of the features of late-maturing adolescents talked about in the literature.

Write a brief report that summarises your findings. Compare your findings with those of other students.

In order to investigate whether any of the effects of early and late maturing remained throughout adulthood, longitudinal studies have been conducted. These studies indicate that several aspects of adolescent adjustment may remain evident into middle adulthood. In one study the social skills of early maturing males were still in evidence at age 38, while the late maturing adolescents remained more impulsive and assertive over the years. There can be some interesting reversals, however. For example, many late maturing males and early maturing females, who initially lacked self-assurance, developed into very self-assured and contented adults (Johansson & Ritzén, 2005). In contrast, many confident and self-assured early maturing males and late maturing females became somewhat discontented adults (Posner, 2006). These findings show that earlier social experiences can have differential effects on the long-term development of early and late maturers. Perhaps as a result of the 'deviant' timing of their development, late maturing males and early maturing females encounter more adjustment problems which give them superior skills for dealing with the stresses of adult life. What might some of these skills be?

 ACTIVITY POST

We have discussed a number of the potential effects of early and late maturation on individuals. Do an Internet search to investigate this issue further. What other effects are there? What are the speculative causes? What programmes may schools adopt to alleviate any of the stresses associated with maturational issues? Write a report documenting your findings and compare your findings with those of other students.

SPOTLIGHT ON SECULAR TREND IN PHYSICAL DEVELOPMENT

There has been a trend towards accelerated maturation in height and weight among males and females over the last century. The age of sexual maturation and the onset of puberty are also occuring at an earlier age than before. Such developments are not thought to be the result of any alterations in the genetic constitution of populations, but rather result from changes in the environment in which growth takes place (Castilho & Lahr 2001; Parent et al., 2003). This has impacted on clothing sizes, bed sizes (now the king single is common), sporting, social, and sexual activities. This effect has been termed the **secular trend** towards earlier growth (Frisch, 1983; Garn, 1980; Tanner, 1990). It appears that the age for the onset of puberty has decreased by about four months per decade in Western Europe over the past 120 years (Ong et al., 2006). There are a number of possible explanations for this which we consider.

The first potential explanation relates to diet. There is no doubt that in the Western world and much of the Eastern and developing worlds there has be an improvement in living and nutritional standards with higher protein diets being common. Better nutrition, scientists argue, may lead to accelerated maturation (Cole, 2003; Eveleth & Tanner, 1990). In many non-Western countries for example, Japan, where there has been a swing towards a more Western diet the average height and weight of children and adolescents have increased steadily (Günther et al., 2010; Murata, 2000).

A second explanation relates to good health (Cole, 2003; Gluckman & Hanson, 2006). Over the last century there has been a marked decline in many major childhood illnesses, through eradication programmes (such as eradicating malaria sources) and immunisation programmes (such as measles innoculation). Better health is also associated with earlier maturation. Fewer children experience significant childhood illnesses today. Childhood diseases that were endemic in earlier years were responsible for potential growth deficiencies. Most of these childhood diseases are now under control.

A third explanation relates to the multiethnic diversity which characterises many societies today. It is suggested that intermarriage among a wider genetic pool, the result of increased world travel, and immigration, may be implicated. For example, people from warmer climates and certain races appear to mature earlier (Kaplowitz, 2006). Hence when these early maturing groups marry later maturing groups there is a potential effect on growth norms.

Finally there is also a suggestion that our present Western culture's emphasis on sexuality might be hastening puberty for modern adolescents although this is a controversial view (Roberts, 2013). In other words, psychological factors could be having an effect on the purely physiological process. The media is full of images of very mature looking adolescents engaging in physical and sexual activities that were considered inappropriate in earlier ages. It is certainly true that children and adolescents today have much greater exposure to sexually explicit material and models than children did decades ago.

Each of these propositions gives us much food for thought. Current research indicates that the secular trend ceases to have an impact when a nation's (or cultural/social group's) health and nutritional standards reach an optimal level.

 QUESTION POINT

Consider each of these explanations of the secular trend in physical development. Which of them appear to be most plausible? Are there other reasons for the secular trend? A quick search on the Internet will locate some interesting sources. What impact may the secular trend have had on educational processes over the last 50 years?

Adolescents and body image

During adolescence, looks and popularity become a major preoccupation for many adolescents. The peers one mixes with, the social environment one experiences, mass media, and product management have a strong influence on what are considered appropriate sexual attitudes and behaviour for each gender. The mass media in particular portrays what is the 'ideal' body type for males and females, and this ideal may lead those who vary from such types to feel negative towards themselves (Clay et al., 2005; Tiggemann, 2005). Most adolescents are concerned that their physical appearance is in line with norms of appropriateness, and that they have the right mix of sexually appropriate characteristics. Because of these concerns with meeting desirable standards of appearance some adolescents experience considerable anxiety over issues such as weight, strength, and attractiveness.

When rating photographs of various male body types, males between the ages of ten and 20 clearly prefer strong athletic types on dimensions such as leadership, popularity, and ability to endure pain. Stereotypes associated with the other physical types, such as skinny and fat, are generally negative. Thus adolescents who perceive their bodies as fat or skinny probably feel bad about themselves and believe that their peer group dislikes them (Davison & McCabe, 2006; Gerner & Wilson, 2005). Positive self-concept is related to a higher degree of satisfaction with one's own bodily characteristics for both men and women (Marsh & Craven, 1997).

> ## (?) QUESTION POINT
>
> ### Sexual development education
>
> What role should the school play in sexual development education? In particular consider the psychological aspects of
>
> 1 sexual awareness;
> 2 menstruation;
> 3 erection, ejaculation, and nocturnal emission;
> 4 birth control;
> 5 early and late maturation;
> 6 eating disorders.

Eating disorders

As we have indicated above, many adolescents these days are preoccupied with the way they look. Any dissatisfaction is the product of complex societal forces such as the influence of the peer group, adult models, and the mass media. This preoccupation has resulted in many of them, particularly females, engaging in unwise dieting practices. Crash diets and unhealthy eating habits are having a negative effect on good health. Body dissatisfaction appears to increase with age, with the onset beginning for many children in late childhood (Clark & Tiggemann, 2006; Paxton et al., 2006). Newspaper reports indicate that girls as young as eight are dieting, some to the point of starvation, because they wish to grow up to be supermodels (Pulter, 2010). It is not uncommon for young children concerned with their weight to refuse to eat regular meals and snacks at a time when they are entering a growth spurt and need the nutrition. Children who starve themselves become lethargic, unable to concentrate during lessons or take part in sport. They may also become very moody and difficult to handle. Damage can also be long term.

At a time when the mass media (and especially television and magazine advertisements for fashion, diet foods, and entertainment) seem to promote the ideal that to be attractive and popular one needs to be slim, adolescents are going through a growth spurt that leads to normal weight gain! Many adolescent girls confuse obesity with the normal weight gain that occurs with the pubertal growth of bones, muscles, breasts and hips. As a consequence of this, many adolescent girls wish they were thinner (Bearman et al., 2006; Westerberg-Jacobson et al., 2010). Peer and parental influence may also contribute to these unhealthy attitudes and behaviours of adolescents in regard to weight, body shape, and eating. Adolescent girls whose friends are preccupied with their looks and weight and who encourage dieting are more likely to diet themselves (Dohnt & Tiggemann, 2005; Eisenberg et al., 2005). On the other hand, girls who belong to friendship cliques that do not emphasise calorie counting and dieting are less likely to be involved in dieting.

A recent UK government report (Burrowes, 2013) concluded that at 9–10 years of age 8% of boys and 14% of girls had a negative body image with 3% of boys and 7% of girls, in the normal weight range, describing themselves as 'too fat'. By adolescence, 9% of boys and 28% of girls aged 13–14 years, in the normal weight range, describe themselves as 'too fat'. It is believed that men's body image dissatisfaction has tripled in the previous 25 years from 15% to 45% of all Western men (Frederick et al., 2007).

Bulimia nervosa and anorexia nervosa

In some cases this preoccupation with dieting leads to a severe eating disorder called **bulimia nervosa**. Adolescents with this disorder engage in uncontrollable binge eating followed by a combination of purging of the stomach contents through laxatives, diuretics, self-induced vomiting, strict fasting, and strenuous exercise (Grilo, 2006; Herpertz-Dahlmann, 2009). Cycles of binge eating, followed by purging and severe dieting, can cause physical and psychological health problems that can be life-threatening (Arcelus et al., 2011; Crow et al., 2009). Recent UK studies estimate very few children show early onset bulima, aged 13 years or younger, (Nichols et al., 2011). Only three persons out of a sample of 100,000 met the clinical criteria for bulima, and other types of eating disorder, such an anorexia and excessive dieting, were more common.

Bulimia nervosa can lead to the development of the most serious eating disorder – **anorexia nervosa** and one teenager in 1,000 is anorexic. Anorexic individuals restrict their eating to such an extent that they become painfully thin, and the malnutrition that accompanies the illness leads to additional side effects such as brittle, discoloured nails, pale skin, fine dark hairs appearing all over the body, and extreme sensitivity to cold. Menstrual periods also cease (Grilo, 2006; Strumia, 2005). Anorexia is a severe disorder for which proper medical help must be obtained. While adolescent girls seem to be most susceptible to both bulimia nervosa and anorexia nervosa, boys and adults of both sexes are also affected. A recent survey of UK adolescents revealed that 25.5% of females and 14.5% of males were restricting their food intake a little or often (Micali et al., 2013).

There are many explanations of the causes of dieting and eating disorders such as bulimia nervosa and anorexia nervosa, including cultural, familial, and psychological conditions and a range of treatments exist which are beyond the scope of this book (Grilo, 2006; Waller & Sheffield, 2008). Early identification of anorexic students is very important in order to permit treatment before the development of irreversible medical complications – 5% of anorexic individuals die as a result of the severity of this problem (Arcelus et al., 2011). Where it becomes apparent that a particular student may be bulimic or anorexic, professional help and guidance should be obtained.

Body shape and personality

It is likely that one's body shape influences one's attitudes to, and involvement in, a variety of activities. It might also be the case that body shape and personality have some links. According to William Sheldon (1940, 1970; Sheldon & Stevens 1942; Sinclair 1989), body type gives a clue to personality characteristics. Sheldon's *Atlas of Man* contains over a thousand carefully posed photos of college aged men depicting various body types. From his analysis of body type and temperament Sheldon developed two descriptive typologies, one dealing with temperament, with three major classifications – viscerotonia, somatonia, and cerebrotonia – and one dealing with physique, with three major classifications – endomorphs, ectomorphs, and mesomorphs. His research showed a very high level of relationship between temperament and physique. Large, round people, known as **endomorphs**, were more likely to be sociable, jolly, happy, placid, and slow-moving (viscerotonia). Muscular, solid people, known as **mesomorphs**, were more likely to be forceful, aggressive, unsympathetic, loud, direct, and action oriented (somatonia). Skinny, angular people, known as **ectomorphs**, were more likely to be non-sociable, intense, shy, and intellectual (cerebrotonia). Figure 4.1 presents a diagram and characteristics of stylised examples of each body type. More detail on Sheldon's typology may be found at: http://innerexplorations.com/psytext/3.htm and http://kheper.net/topics/typology/somatotypes.html

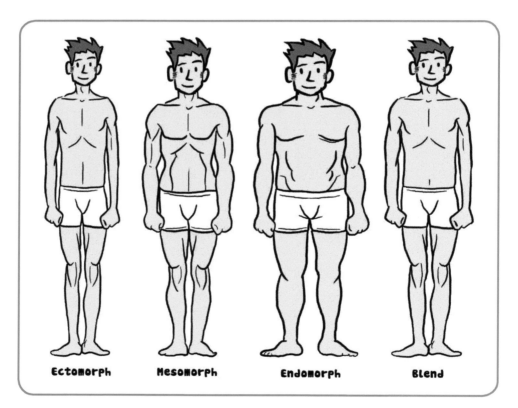

Figure 4.1   Sheldon's body types.

Nobody belongs exclusively to only one of these types. According to Sheldon, each of us has elements of all three, and in measuring a person's physique Sheldon assigned a score of 1 to 7 on each of them, which is known as the person's somatotype or body type.

A number of reasons have been suggested for the striking relationship between predominant body type, abilities, and personality. First, an individual's body type may limit the range of activities engaged in or, conversely, present particular opportunities for the individual to develop in specific ways. Second, it is believed that the relation between physique and temperament may be a product of stereotyping and the social expectations that individuals incorporate into their behaviour. Third, the environmental factors that influence the development of physique may be the same ones that influence the development of personality. For example, parents who are determined to make their children great athletes may not only encourage the training and development of the body through exercise and continuous practice, but develop the mind as well to cope with the discipline such training demands. The rate at which infants physically develop may also influence how people react to them and their subsequent personality development (Buss, 2009). For instance, a larger child may learn to influence their environment though being dominant and aggressive whereas their smaller counterparts may have to learn to be more agreeable and conciliatory. And finally, it is thought that the genes that lead to the development of body type may also be influential in the development of personality. In any event, a large number of studies have indicated a relationship between physique and temperament (although not to the level found in Sheldon's work) (Ellis et al., 2008; Fontana, 1986).

Educational implications of body shape

Although Sheldon's work is still discussed, and there are a number of good websites dealing with his theory, little new research has been carried out in recent years, which means we are still unable to draw firm conclusions from it, although it appears to have some well-founded support (Fontana, 1986; Wells, 1983).

Sheldon's theory has made a valuable contribution in alerting us to the fact that our body shape may influence our view of self. How we and others view our body shape becomes incorporated into our self-concept. Indeed, most recent self-concept scales include a subscale for physical self-concept (Hau et al., 2005; Marsh, 2002; Marsh et al., 1997). Research (Cohane & Pope, 2001; Staffieri, 1967) has shown that from early childhood through to adolescence the preferred body shape is mesomorphic. In children's stories the mesomorph is described as brave, attractive, strong, and intelligent. Less favourable adjectives are reserved for the ectomorph and endomorph. Furthermore, mesomorphs appear to be more popular in the classroom than either of the other body types (Staffieri, 1967).

Clearly, educators need to avoid stereotyping children on the basis of their physique. There are several potential dangers in doing so. We might, for example, expect muscular-looking children (mesomorphs) to be mainly, or perhaps exclusively, interested in sport and consequently supply little encouragement for their talents in music or dance. We might expect thin, angular children (ectomorphs) to be only good at, and interested in, intellectual activities, and fail to provide the opportunities and encouragement for them to become involved in physical activities. Finally, fatter children (endomorphs) may be consigned to passive activities, with no great physical challenges being made available. Furthermore, educators may inadvertently contribute to children's negative self-images by choosing the more stereotypically attractive for public roles such as presentations and demonstrations.

The fact that attitudes to body types are socially conditioned is very easily demonstrated cross-culturally. In Fiji and a number of other Pacific islander communities, body bulk is considered highly desirable and, instead of starving before their wedding (which is often the norm in Western societies) brides-to-be eat up to ensure good rounded proportions! In these cultures size is associated with fertility, fecundity, and sexuality. Some Western research also suggests that men prefer rounded women to thin women (once model types are discounted!). Other information on cultural differences in attitude to body shape may be investigated at: http://findarticles.com/p/articles/mi_m2294/is_2001_Dec/ai_89239000

Related research into teachers' expectations, impressions, and judgments of physically attractive students indicates that these students are usually judged more favourably by teachers in a number of dimensions including intelligence, academic potential, grades, and various social skills (Jackson et al., 1995; Ritts et al., 1992). It appears that teachers expect physically attractive students to be more intelligent and to attain a higher level of education than less physically attractive students. Furthermore, physically attractive students are rated by teachers as more friendly, more attentive, more popular, and more outgoing (Ritts et al., 1992). When judged in terms of committing a serious misconduct, physically less attractive students are considered to be more chronically antisocial than more attractive students, for whom the behaviour is considered an aberration (Langlois et al., 2000).

The basis of these expectations is not clear. However, it behoves us as teachers to take care not to hold unwarranted assumptions about students because of physical appearance.

Health issues and the school environment

Potential health problems

In the last two chapters we have discussed issues related to the physical and motor development of children from early childhood through to the end of adolescence. It is important to note that some children attending school will have physical problems related to their development that need to be addressed in order to provide them with the most appropriate educational experiences. From time to time, physical problems that go unnoticed in the home become apparent in school, particularly through the primary years, although some health problems only become apparent in adolescence. Difficulties with sight and hearing, for example, can impede the effective learning of students at school. Routine testing of sight and hearing when children begin school is an important means of minimising difficulties. Vigilant teachers can alert parents to seek medical attention in minor cases. At other times students may require special school facilities.

Hearing and sight

Some children may undergo periods of temporary deafness as a result of ear infections, particularly in the infant grades. Apart from hearing difficulties affecting learning and motivation, continued absences, as a result of ineffective treatment of the problem, will cause students to fall further and further behind in their work. This will also have repercussions in terms of self-esteem and self-confidence. Most vision problems can easily be corrected by the use of eyeglasses. Temporary eye disorders such as conjunctivitis, which can be caused by children rubbing their eyes with dirty hands, can have deleterious effects on vision if left untreated leading to serious eye problems such as scarring of the cornea (McMonnies, 2009). This problem is usually easily treated with antibiotics.

Dietary deficiencies – undernourishment and obesity

Dietary deficiencies are often responsible for abnormal growth patterns. As we have indicated earlier in this chapter unhealthy dieting of young people is becoming an increasing phenomenon in many countries. Sometimes children arrive at school undernourished because they have not been fed well enough at home. Some schools, particularly in less affluent areas have introduced breakfast and snack programmes so that children can have a good meal prior to commencing the school day. Hungry students can not apply themselves to schooling effectively. Many schools in the UK run a breakfast club to ensure that students receive a proper breafast in the morning before starting lessons. A Children's Food Trust report examined breakfast clubs in London primary schools finding that it improved SATs results at the end of Year 6 (http://childrensfoodtrust.org.uk/assets/research-reports/sft_breakfast_club_findings_dec08.pdf). You might like to look up the following website (http://mpshu.on.ca/ChildHealth/B4L%20main.htm) which deals with a programme entitled Muskoka Food For Learning Programme which details a breakfast programme in 17 schools in Canada. In these schools students are able to pick up healthy breakfasts and snacks as they arrive at school. The programme is based on the belief that food is a learning tool and that children who eat proper, healthy meals do better in school, in many ways. Breakfast or snack programmes provide a healthy beginning to the school day and enhance students' concentration, behaviour, energy level, and attendance, as well as having the following effects:

- test performance and standardised test scores improve;
- violence in the schoolyard decreases;
- eating habits and social skills are improved;
- students start their days with a positive social experience.

Counterpointing undernourishment is the problem of *obesity*. Obesity occurs when a person eats more calories than the body burns up. Many children and adolescents are obese, which reduces their ability to exercise the physical and motor structures in their body essential for healthy development. The causes of obesity are complex and include genetic, biological, behavioural, and cultural factors (Crothers et al., 2009; Wright & Aronne, 2012). If one parent is obese, there is a 50% chance that their children will also be obese. However, when both parents are obese, the children have an 80% chance of being obese. Although certain medical disorders can cause obesity, less than 1% of all obesity is caused by physical problems. Obesity in childhood and adolescence can be related to:

- poor eating habits;
- overeating or binging;
- lack of exercise (i.e. couch potato kids);
- family history of obesity;
- medical illnesses (endocrine, neurological problems);
- medications (steroids, some psychiatric medications);
- stressful life events or changes (separations, divorce, housing moves, deaths, abuse);
- family and peer problems;
- low self-esteem;
- depression or other emotional problems.

(http://aacap.org/AACAP/Families_and_Youth/Facts_
for_Families/FActs_for_Families_Pages/Obesity_
In_Children_And_Teens_79.aspx)

As indicated above some obesity may be genetically linked, but many overweight children and adolescents become so through a poor diet that includes too much food and empty calories for their level of activity and laziness, with too much time spent in front of the television predisposing them to little exercise and endless snacking on the wrong kinds of food.

In part, poor eating habits are set up in the home through parental feeding practices, such as rewarding children with high-calorie foods and snacks. At other times, poor eating may be associated with stress reduction or traumatic events such as divorce or death (Torres & Nowson, 2007). Again, while teachers and schools are not responsible in the first instance for children's obesity, a school's health programme should be designed to educate children and adolescents in good eating and exercise habits. The 2013–2014 National Child Measurement Programme Survey by Public Health England found 33.5% of children in Year 6 (aged 10–11 years) were obese or overweight (Health and Social Care Information Centre, 2014). The American Academy of Child and Adolescent Psychiatry (http://aacap.org/AACAP/ Families_and_Youth/Facts_for_Families/FActs_for_Families_Pages/Obesity_In_ Children_And_Teens_79.aspx) recommend the following techniques to manage obesity in children and adolescents:

- start a weight-management programme;
- change eating habits (eat slowly, develop a routine);
- plan meals and make better food selections (eat less fatty foods, avoid junk and fast foods);

- control portions and consume less calories;
- increase physical activity (especially walking) and have a more active lifestyle;
- know what your child eats at school;
- eat meals as a family instead of while watching television or at the computer;
- do not use food as a reward;
- limit snacking;
- attend a support group (e.g. Weight Watchers, Overeaters Anonymous).

 QUESTION POINT

How common do you think the problem of undernourishment is in the United Kingdom? What course of action may schools take to address this problem? Are there any breakfast programmes in UK schools with which you are familiar?

 QUESTION POINT

Are there cultural differences in the prevalence and onset of eating disorders? Are there differences between cultures for which food is a more or less central aspect of socialising within the family and community? Do children who come from ethnic backgrounds that emphasise healthy and plentiful eating become socialised into the pursuit of thinness, and defy family and cultural expectations regarding food in their quest for the 'ideal' body shape? You might like to consider this issue and discuss it with friends from different cultural groups. A quick surf of the Internet will provide some interesting data. You might like to look up the following website http://b-eat.co.uk/ or http://eating-disorders.org.uk/, websites on eating disorders and http://findarticles.com/p/articles/mi_m2294/is_2001_Dec/ai_89239000 which presents an article entitled Body type preferences in Asian and Caucasian college students.

Other issues

Some children and adolescents miss substantial periods at school because of chronic and persistent illnesses such as respiratory problems, asthma and bronchitis, urinary tract infections, migraines, and diabetes (Kearney, 2008; Moonie et al., 2006; Reid, 2005). As a result they may also develop behavioural and learning problems and have restricted opportunities for physical activity. The policy of inclusion means that increasing numbers of individuals with chronic illnesses and impairments will be found in the regular classroom.

Physical safety and legal requirements

As we have discussed in Chapter 3, the early childhood and primary years of schooling coincide with periods of rapid physical growth and motor development during which children are particularly energetic and keen to test out their newly developing physical skills. In adolescence, students, particularly males, engage in more active physical competitive sports. Accidents such as broken arms and legs, concussion, scrapes, and bruises increase sharply at this time (Otters et al., 2005; Sutton et al., 2008) but such injuries can be minimised by appropriate supervision by parents and teachers.

All teachers have a *duty of care* which means that they must be aware of potentially dangerous activities. Increasingly it is being legislated that teachers possess qualifications for sports coaching, and appropriate qualifications for engaging students in various physical activities. Teachers must ensure that for any physical activity there is proper physical conditioning of the students; proper supervision of the sport; well-fitted protective equipment (such as helmets, knee and elbow pads, groin protectors, mouthguards); careful grouping of students according to weight, height and ability; and opportunity for every student who wishes to participate in some sport in accordance with their skills, health and level of physical maturation to do so (Berry, 2007). Teachers are legally responsible to ensure the safety of their students and conducting a risk assessment when planning such activities. In some contexts (e.g. outdoor excursions such as hiking, camping, and other sporting activities) teachers may misjudge the capacity of students to cope with the experiences and ultimately put the students in dangerous situations. Many Departments of Education require teachers supervising excursions to have various first aid certificates. What training and certificates are you receiving as part of your teacher training course? The advice and guidance from the Department of Education can be found at: https://gov.uk/government/uploads/system/uploads/attachment_data/file/335111/DfE_Health_and_Safety_Advice_06_02_14.pdf. This is updated from time to time.

CHAPTER 5

Cognition and cognitive development: infancy to late childhood

Introduction

In the last two chapters we have considered the physical growth of children from early childhood through to early adulthood. We noted that cranial growth during the early childhood years is very significant and by the age of five years has achieved 75% of its adult size. The development of the brain is directly related to the development of motor coordination and a number of other developmental trajectories. Accompanying this cranial growth is also the development of cognition. **Cognitive development** is the development over time of the ability to think and reason and to understand the world in which we live. A knowledge of cognitive development is essential for teachers and educators. Does a child think in the same way as an adult? How does a child process information? When can we expect a child to perform particular mental processes? What is intelligence? What is creativity? Can we measure these? What influences cognitive development? These, and many other questions, are of central importance to educators.

What is cognition? Broadly, cognition refers to the intellectual activity of an individual, i.e. the mental processes; involving all aspects of thought and perception. As with the development of the physical structures of the body, the major cognitive processes that are inherent in being human, mature in an orderly way in children provided the environment contains the normal experiences of childhood such as social interaction, environmental stimulation, and good diet. In other words, a child in any normal environment will develop a full range of cognitive capacities. However, limited environments (that is those restricting the experiences a child has access to, such as poorly run institutional homes, severely abusing and neglectful homes, or severe malnourishment) may impede normal cognitive development.

Continuity and change in cognitive development

As with physical and motor growth, the growth of a child's mind shows continuity as well as change, and as the child grows older there is an increasing differentiation of cognitive capacities. In young children mental abilities are much less separate from one another and from emotions than they are in later childhood. While the emotional content of a situation, such as a parent's denial of the child's desire to play on a dangerous swing, can blind a young child to rational behaviour and explanations, emotions and rationality become increasingly differentiated (in most cases) in older children so that the older child can be very upset or angry but remain (relatively) rational.

In this chapter we consider three important, and contrasting, views on cognitive development, those of Jean Piaget, Lev Vygotsky, and Jerome Bruner. Each believes that learning is an intentional process of constructing meaning from experience, but the means by which this knowledge construction occurs is considered differently. This chapter focuses on elements of these themes that have most implication for pre-adolescent education. In Chapter 6, we look at elements relevant to adolescent education and the educational implications of Piaget and Vygotsky more broadly. We also consider some contemporary views of cognition. Both of these chapters should be read as a unit.

Jean Piaget

Jean Piaget (1896–1980) was a psychologist who has had a profound impact on the way teachers and other professionals think about children (Bibace, 2013). Piaget's background included training as a biologist, and working with Theophile Simon in the Binet Laboratory in Paris. With Alfred Binet, Simon had earlier constructed the first intelligence test. Both of these experiences had an impact on the development of Piaget's theory of cognitive development. His theory has two key dimensions. First, Piaget emphasises that intellectual development occurs through a series of stages characterised by qualitatively discrete cognitive structures. Second, Piaget emphasises the notion that children construct their own understandings through interaction with their environment. Piaget viewed the child as a young scientist, constructing ever more powerful theories of the world, as a result of applying a set of logical structures in increasing generality and power (Inagaki & Hatano, 2006). As such his theory has dual and complementary perspectives that may be termed **structuralism** and **constructivism** (Fosnot, 2013; Morra et al., 2012).

Biological model of cognitive development

Piaget's theory is complex. Our description highlights important elements for your consideration, but in doing so we run the risk of oversimplification. Piaget, as a biologist, was impressed by the way in which all species systematically organise their biological processes into coherent systems and are able to adapt, as necessary, to the environment through processes such as **assimilation** and **accommodation**. He brought his experience as a biologist to the task of explaining the development of cognitive processes in children. Piaget compared the process by which children construct a more intelligent understanding of their world to that used by natural organisms adapting to changes in their environment. He maintained that the growth of intelligence is regulated by the same processes that determine the growth of morphology and changes in the physiology of all living systems (Brown, 2008; Messerly, 2009).

While working with the Binet Laboratory, Piaget was given the task of standardising a French version of a number of English reasoning tests. However, Piaget noted that there was a regularity in the way children miss-answered questions, and decided that it was far more important to discover how each child reasoned out an answer, especially when the answer was wrong, than it was to establish norms for correct answers (Smith, 2009). Furthermore, he became interested in how children learn to correct certain errors in their thinking. Through close examination of his own three children Piaget plotted the course of cognitive development, much of it relating to the children's answers to questions about their environment. He noted how the structure of these answers changed over a period of years.

In order to explain a number of Piagetian constructs we use an analogy how a teacher might use a filing cabinet to store material. Six key concepts developed by Piaget *cognitive structure, organisation, assimilation, adaptation, accommodation,* and *equilibration* can be explored through the analogy of using a filing cabinet. When starting a new job, a teacher might have an empty filing cabinet; material could be filed in different draws or in different folders. Our teacher decides to store teaching materials in the top drawer, student progress data in the middle drawer and practice exam and test materials in the bottom drawer. To begin with, the teacher can store all of their materials for one class in a single file. In Piaget's theory this is called assimilation. However, as the school year progresses and more and more teaching materials build up, one file just isn't enough. Our teacher decides to split one file into several. She or he has to make decisions on how to do this. Is it by term, for instance, or by topic? In Piaget's theory this is called adaptation and our teacher decides to split up the file into three – one for each term. Piaget calls this equilibrium. However, eventually as these three files continue to grow the teacher has to decide whether to split up the files even further or even discard some of their own materials that they might have outgrown. After six years in the job they have a full filing cabinet in their classroom, as well as electronic files stored on their computer and several boxes of materials at home.

 QUESTION POINT

Consider times when you have used the dual processes of assimilation and accommodation. Discuss these with your group. Are there times when one or other process has dominated? Why? And what were the results?

Balance between assimilation and accommodation

Both processes of assimilation and accommodation must act together. If we over assimilate everything is 'housed' in the one file with the potential for retrieval minimised, and flexible action reduced. On the other hand if we set up a new file for each and every new piece of paper (over accommodation) we would be swamped with files.

In a sense this process of developing a filing cabinet to organise one's working world is similar to what Piaget believes happens to children as they become more and more adept at organising and adapting to the world around them. Initially, infants have relatively few functioning cognitive systems (such as reflexes and some rudimentary thought processes) for handling the world of experiences, but great potential to develop increasingly complex means of handling these experiences. Rather like the empty filing cabinet they have the potential to develop ways of effectively interacting with and organising their world. There is, however, a flaw in this analogy. While the filing cabinet is passive, i.e. operated upon to make adaptations and assimilations, the infant actively and internally organises her or his own cognitive structure in interaction with the external world. The infant is an active agent whose mind reconstructs and reinterprets the environment to make it fit in with its own existing mental framework (Smith, 2005). These ways of dealing with experiences Piaget termed **schemas**, and the schemas are organised as cognitive structure.

As novel experiences occur in the child's life the child adapts by relating each new experience to familiar ones through the process of assimilation. At times, however, the experiences require an adjustment on the part of the child to cope with something new through the process of accommodation. So while a child initially develops a schema for food, for example, which is largely related to the stimulus of the mother's breast, at some time the infant could be presented with a plastic bottle and a rubber teat. The infant may cry and not wish to feed on the bottle. From an adult perspective we might say that the child was 'complaining' that it was not what was 'expected'. An adaptation would mean that the infant's schema for feeding underwent accommodation to include the plastic bottle. In adult language we might say that the baby has 'understood' that food may be presented in a different container! Later, rather than milk, the father or mother may present orange juice. While the child might initially baulk, the chances are that if the child is thirsty a quick assimilation will be made to a drink with a novel taste. Many examples can be given and no doubt you can think of ways in which you still learn about the world by these mutual processes of assimilation and accommodation.

When a balance has been struck between the processes of accommodation and assimilation, and the resulting adaptation is satisfying biologically and psychologically, Piaget speaks of the child achieving *equilibrium*. We see this in operation when the child happily sucks on the bottle of juice. The tension between the demands of accommodation and assimilation, when the child adapts to or learns about novel situations, is the power that impels the child to develop new understandings and a new equilibrium (Bloom, 2009; Haroutunian, 2012).

Operative knowledge

For Piaget, cognitive development involves an interaction between assimilating new facts to old knowledge and accommodating old knowledge to new facts and the maintenance of structural equilibration (Atkinson, 2007; Powell & Kalina, 2009). Furthermore, as children mature they develop a series of operations or thought processes that become increasingly able to handle inferential thinking. While the young infant is limited to thinking about problems and experiences in concrete terms, which is termed figurative knowledge, the adolescent is capable of thinking about problems using more sophisticated operational schemas referred to as operative knowledge. We deal with this issue in the next chapter.

Operations, and their groupings, are the main object of Piaget's developmental approach to concept formation. From his many experiments performed by children of all ages Piaget claims that there are five main stages in the development of a concept through which the vast majority of children pass.

Stages of intellectual development

Piaget believed that in each of these stages there is a characteristic way children think about the world and solve problems. We must warn here that these age limits are only guidelines and there are many inconsistencies. At each stage the child develops increasingly sophisticated mental processes, with the ultimate goal being the acquisition of fully logical cognitive operations. We deal with the first three of these in the following sections, and leave formal operations to the discussion of adolescent cognitive development in Chapter 6.

Sensorimotor stage

Piaget believed that during the first two years of life children learn about the world primarily through motor activity. Early Piagetian theory referred to six substages of the sensorimotor period (Case, 2013; Müller, 2009):

1 general assimilating (0–1 month);
2 primary circular reaction (1–2 to 4 months);
3 secondary circular reactions (4–8 months);
4 co-ordination of secondary schemas (8–12 months);
5 tertiary circular reactions (12–18 months);
6 beginnings of thought (18–24 months).

Piaget believed that infants are born with little knowledge about the world and a limited capacity to explore it. In order to develop their rudimentary mental schemas Piaget believed infants used circular reaction. Such reactions occur when infants accidentally

Table 5.1 The four main stages of cognitive development in children, according to Piaget's theory

Stage of intellectual development	Approximate ages
Sensorimotor Stage	Birth to 2 years
Pre-operational	2 to 7 years
Concrete operational	7 to 12 years
Formal operational	12 to 15 years

generate a new experience because of their own motor activity. By a process of trial and error the infant tries to repeat the occurrence and this circular reaction then strengthens the schema (Atkinson, 2007; Case, 2013; Müller, 2009).

The first period of general assimilation is dominated by the basic reflexes of sucking, grasping, crying, and the general movement of parts of the body. This period is characterised by assimilation where the infant assimilates activities to existing schema, such as sucking everything indiscriminately. There is little differentiation. Gradually the infant begins to discriminate, for example, between suckable objects that are satisfying, such as a nipple, and those that are not, such as a blanket. This leads to stage two in which there is the development of differentiation and integration of rudimentary behaviours such as thumb sucking and moving his or her head in the direction of sounds. This process is based on the principles of accommodation and assimilation. **Primary circular reaction** refers to accidental bodily actions that the child repeats because of their satisfying effects, such as watching its waving hand. This repetition establishes a schema for the behaviours, such as hand waving.

The next stage, **secondary circular reactions** refers to actions directed towards objects in the infant's environment as well as to its own body, and involves coordination of activities which are no longer simply reflexive. It is at this time we note infants coordinating movements in order to pull a ribbon on a toy to shake the toy. During this stage there is some progression towards concepts of time and space, causality, and object permanence, which we explain in more detail later.

During the fourth stage, co-ordination of secondary schemas, the concept of **object permanence,** that is, the understanding that objects have a separate, permanent existence becomes more established, and the infant comes to see objects as causes. There is some further development of intentional behaviour and the infant begins to anticipate events. For Piaget, intentional behaviour represents intelligent behaviour and the development of more sophisticated cognitive schemas. During the **tertiary circular reactions** stage the infant actively 'experiments' in order to investigate the properties of objects and events and through these experiments on the environment further develops the central notions of object permanence, causality, space, and time. These new features of thought are incorporated into the infant's mental processes through assimilation and accommodation.

The final stage, beginnings of thought, represents the transition between the sensorimotor stage and the pre-conceptual, or symbolic stage, of preoperational thought. It is marked by the ability of the infant to represent objects mentally and to use this representation in the solution of problems rather than by acting directly on the physical environment. In other words the child is able to internalise action.

In summary, by gradually reorganising their sensorimotor actions infants construct a basic understanding of their environment. Through grasping, sucking, looking, throwing, and generally moving themselves and objects about, children begin to demonstrate an identity separate from their surrounding world; learn about the permanence of objects and certain regularities in the physical world. They develop an elementary understanding of causality, shape, and size constancy. By two, children can solve most sensorimotor problems, e.g. they can get desired objects, can use objects in combination, and can mentally 'invent' means that will permit them to do the things they want. In Piagetian terms children by two have acquired a much larger and more sophisticated set of cognitive schemas as a result of sensorimotor interaction with the environment, and in particular the ongoing processes of assimilation and accommodation that enable children to handle the world more effectively. **Representational thinking**, that is the understanding that a thought can represent an object in a real life setting, which is the basis for anticipating actions mentally, is the outcome of sensorimotor constructions (Case, 2013). By gradually reorganising their sensorimotor actions, infants construct a basic understanding of the permanence of objects in space and a rudimentary ability to represent people and objects not immediately present.

 ACTIVITY POST

Parents play a significant role in stimulating their children in a variety of ways that are important to the children's perceptual and cognitive development. If you work, or have a placement in an early years setting, or perhaps have a friend or family member with a young infant (birth to 3 years), observe the interaction between the parent (or adult carer) and child in one or more play situations. Particularly note visual, auditory, and tactile stimulation. What sorts of interactions would a teacher or early years educator need to know about? Compile a detailed record of the interaction observed and relate your observations to principles of cognitive development discussed in this chapter.

Preoperational stage

With the acquisition of language there is a great leap forward in children's ability to reason about the world around them and to solve problems. During the preoperational period, ages two to seven, children begin to know things not only through their actual actions but symbolically. Symbolic games play an important role in the development of their intellectual abilities. Nevertheless, according to Piaget, preoperational children do not use mature mental operations to solve problems or interpret experiences in the physical world, hence the term preoperational. Pre-operations are internalised actions that have not yet been integrated into complete cognitive systems and so are not yet true operations.

 QUESTION POINT

Why is the acquisition of language so important to the development of cognition? What do you think would be the situation with children who are deaf or mute? Would the cognitive development of such children be delayed? How might this impact on children's learning in the classroom? You should complete an Internet search on this topic to see what the 'experts' say.

Development of perception, language, reasoning, and problem solving skills

Throughout the preoperational period there is a significant development of children's cognitive abilities. This is reflected in their growing powers of perception, increased language usage, more sophisticated reasoning, and problem solving abilities. It is during this period that children's perception becomes increasingly freed from the limits of the physical appearance of objects. Because attention becomes less centred on perceptual clues, and children are able to reorganise and integrate information coming from a range of sources, they become more flexible thinkers. The gradual process of decentring from perceptual stimuli becomes a hallmark of cognitive growth during this period.

Let us look closely at the function of perception as a vital force behind the nurturance of accurate concept development that enables children to selectively detect and interpret relevant environmental information. We consider five essential concepts: size and shape, spatial relationships, class inclusion, quantity concepts, number and time.

 SPOTLIGHT ON PRE-OPERATIONAL THOUGHT

Physiognomic perception

Piaget (Piaget, 1954/2000, 1971/2000, 1973/2015) describes some early features of children's mental characteristics with which parents and teachers are familiar. For example, young children have a tendency to project their anger or fear impulses onto inanimate objects such as chairs and steps, or shadows and cracks in the ground. This attributing of angry feelings onto inanimate objects has been termed **physiognomic perception**.

Phenomenalistic causality

Young children also regard events that happen together as having caused one another. This type of thinking is labelled **phenomenalistic causality**. For example, children often think that raising the blind brings out the sun, or that rain comes to stop children going out to play. At this stage a young child's ready belief in

magic and ritual is tied in with phenomenalistic causality. For young children it is perfectly reasonable that magic things can happen. As children grow older and gain a stronger grasp of causality they begin to try to understand the underlying processes involved in it. As with physiognomic perception this characteristic does not disappear entirely as the child gets older and accounts for the superstition one observes in older children and adults. For example, do you have any preparation rituals for exams? We all know students who get particularly unsettled if they don't have their favourite pen for an exam or are prevented from sitting in a favourite position.

Nominal realism: the power of words

Words are arbitrary constructs to represent objects, actions, feelings, and so on. Young children often invest words and language with a power far beyond the arbitrariness of language implies. This characteristic is termed **nominal realism**. For example, names of things are often sacrosanct and the quality of the object, for example, heat or light, is thought to reside intrinsically in the name of the object, such as sun or moon. Because of this, very young children won't rename objects. Furthermore, words are very powerful. A child hates to be called stupid, because being called stupid may make one stupid. As children become older they begin to realise that not only is the meaning of words arbitrary, but that they can make up their own words for objects and events, and use these as a code to communicate with their peers.

Size and shape constancy

The idea that an object is the same size and shape no-matter from what perspective they are viewed, develops with time. This is referred to as **size and shape constancy**. Many early preschool and kindergarten activities such as stacking objects, labelling positions, looking at things from different angles, and so on are designed to develop perceptual concepts such as 'big' and 'small', 'close' and 'far'. Understanding spatial relationships is especially important for a child's accurate interpretation of the environment. So concepts such as left and right, short and long, near and far, are developed through appropriate experiences.

 SPOTLIGHT ON PERCEPTUAL DEVELOPMENT

A major component of cognitive development is perceptual development (Bjorklund, 2005). Indeed, in the first years of life perceptual development is crucial to children developing schema about the world around them. Knowledge about the nature and time line of perceptual development in children provides information on the quality, limits, and capacities of the senses as children grow older. This is important for at least two reasons. First, knowing about development of the sensory systems allows us to understand the relationship between sensory structures and their function. Second, we are able to discover the relationship between sensory stimulation and brain development. As children mature, changes in perception could be attributable to: a) neural, anatomical, or sensory maturation; b) improvements in attention; c) alterations in motivation or improved task performance; d) experience; or e) combinations and interactions between these.

Most perceptual development occurs in the first year of life, and at the end of this period infants are able to distinguish patterns, depth, orientation, location, movement, and colour (Gerhardstein et al., 2009). As infants grow older their motor skills improve, and further exploration of the environment takes place, guided by perception. This allows the infant to increase its understanding of the world around it.

(continued)

(continued)

With walking comes the capacity of infants to navigate around large spaces, to avoid obstacles, and to adjust their walking to different surfaces such as sloping and spongey surfaces. For example, if a surface is too steep toddlers automatically begin to crawl. As children enter pre-school there is a relationship between perceptual development and school performance. For example, the importance of perception in learning to read is subject of much research. Visual and auditory abilities are implicated in reading performance. Perceptual acuity is also related to children's attention to, and awareness of, environmental dangers, and the influence of educational and entertainment technology on children's perceptual abilities.

While much sensory ability matures by school age, more comprehensive perceptual functioning does not, and children in this age range are believed to undergo rapid growth in integrating perception with their conceptions and verbal descriptions of the world. Research indicates that selective attention, visual integration of shape, and speed of visual information processing vary among children but all generally increase across childhood, reaching maturity about the onset of adolescence. Among the features of perceptual development in children are an increase in efficiency in perceiving perceptual constancies. As we will see in the sections below, perceptual development forms a key element of Piaget's sensori-motor, pre-operational, and concrete operational stages of cognitive development.

Classifying objects into sets

Young children experience difficulties in understanding the relationship that exists between subclasses and classes. For example, if children are presented with four red plastic cars, and two blue plastic cars and are asked to tell whether there are more red or blue plastic cars they answer the question easily. However, if we ask them whether there are more red or plastic cars they will answer that there are more red cars. In other words their thought is dominated by the visual perception of colour, rather than the inclusive set of cars irrespective of colour. As children grow older they classify classes and subclasses effectively.

Perception and judgements of quantity

Preschool children appear to be unable to logically develop accurate quantity discriminations independent of misleading perceptual cues, and frequently appear to make quantity judgements on the basis of perception alone. Concepts such as larger, smaller, less, few, some, and many are frequently bewildering for young children. This is particularly the case when the same volume, such as a drink, is presented in different size glasses. A half full large glass will be considered to have less drink than a full small glass, even if the quantities are exactly the same. In early childhood education there is considerable emphasis on having children master these quantity constructs through a range of activities.

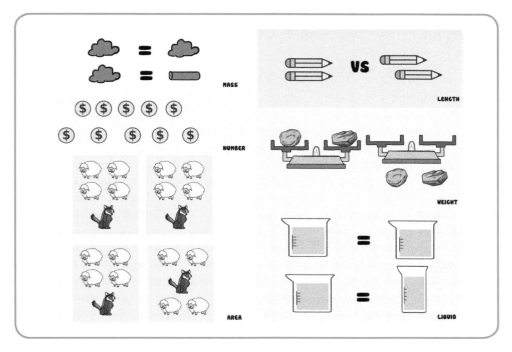

Figure 5.1   **Piagetian Conservation Tasks.**

Number concepts and time concepts

Abstract concepts of measurement, simple addition, and fractional amounts develop with time and there is usually a significant gap between the preschooler's counting abilities and their ability to understand conceptually what is being counted. When mathematical processes are couched in real examples, such as dividing lollies among children, preschoolers show a surprising command of counting principles. Gelman (2006) distinguishes between young children's number abstraction and their numerical-reasoning principles. Prominent among the number abstraction abilities is the preschooler's developing command of five counting principles:

1 Assign one and only one number name to each and every item to be counted (one-one principle).
2 When counting always recite the number in the same order (stable order principle).
3 The final number uttered at the end of a counting sequence denotes the total number of items counted (combinatorial principle).
4 Any sort of entity may be counted (abstraction principle).
5 It does not matter what order you enumerate the objects (order-irrelevance principle).

One of the numerical reasoning principles that children acquire is the number conservation rule that merely spreading the same objects over a larger area does not increase the number of objects in the set.

SPOTLIGHT ON 'TESTS' OF CONSERVATION

A very interesting aspect of Piaget's theory is the method used to distinguish preoperational from more sophisticated cognitive processes. The usual method for distinguishing preoperational thinking from later levels is through 'testing' children on a number of problems which require logical thought and the operations discussed earlier in the chapter (Psaltis & Duveen, 2007; Shayer et al., 2007). A major aspect of preoperational thought is lack of conservation and deductive thinking. Conservation refers to the understanding that objects remain the same volume or quantity despite changes in position or appearance, while deductive thinking involves judgements made on the basis of inferences and logic. There are a number of exercises developed by Piaget and others which demonstrate the level of reasoning children are capable of during the stages of cognitive development. The following activities illustrate characteristic elements in the preoperational child's thinking.

After observing one of two equal lumps of clay being squashed the preoperational child will typically suggest that one lump will have more or less clay than the other in terms of the physical appearance of the two lumps. After witnessing one of two jars of water of equal quantity being poured into a third jar of different size, the child will typically suggest that the amount of water in the new jar (usually a flat, shallow container) contains less than the water in the other full jar. If confronted with two equal pencils lined up on a table with one point protruding past the end of the other pencil, the child will typically argue that one or other of the pencils is longer, and when asked to count two equal rows of coins, one spread out more than the other, the child will typically say that one row has more coins than the other despite having 'accurately'

counted the two rows, and indeed having even seen the two rows of coins lined up equally.

In each of these cases the preoperational child illustrates a preoccupation with visual perception and in particular one feature of the problem. This is called **centration**. Furthermore, the child does not appear to attend to the transformation that occurs from one state to another, for example, that in pouring the water from one container to another one hasn't altered the quantity of water, although the final state may appear different. A simple example of this is to get a child to draw the successive points through which a vertical pencil will move to assume the horizontal position, again the preoperational child cannot answer the problem. And lastly, Piaget believes these experiments demonstrate the child's inability to reverse thinking, that is mentally reverse the operation witnessed to realise that there has been no change in substance, only appearance. Compounding this limited ability of preoperational children to perceive several dimensions of a problem at once is the child's egocentricity whereby the child believes that everyone holds the same perspective.

The characteristics of preoperational thought, described above, function as obstacles to logical thought, and the problems described above are termed problems in conservation. Researchers have been particularly interested in when children acquire the capacity to conserve, and whether this is consistent across a number of domains such as conservation of number, conservation of area, and conservation of volume. There appears to be a sequence with the conservation of number, substance, area, weight, and volume being achieved in that order.

Concepts of time: past, present, and future

During the preoperational stage children ask many time-related questions such as: 'is it morning now?', 'when will it be tomorrow?', 'is it Wednesday or Saturday?', and so on, as they develop their concept of time. By the age of four years, many children measure their week in days at preschool, days with nanna, days with parents or carers, and weekends. Young children also have a limited grasp of the past and the future. However, as they get older they have a growing interest in the concepts of past and future, and a growing control of the elements of time. Concepts of history and the future develop slowly, which has implications for the introduction of historical and other time related studies into the school curricula. An interesting discussion of the development of time, space, and number concepts is also found in Siegler (1991) where some alternative findings and explanations are given.

 QUESTION POINT

Consider each of the points made on size and shape, spatial relationships, class inclusion, quantity concepts, number, and time. Why is an understanding of the acquisition of these concepts by young children so important to teachers? Examine the Key Stage 1 and 2 National Curriculum programme of study for maths (referred to as Foundation Stage in Wales) or the Scottish Curriculum for Excellence first and second levels. How effectively do these reflect children's cognitive capacities at various ages? How are they designed to build upon present stages of cognition while presenting appropriate cognitive dissonance to challenge the children's cognitive growth?

For the English National Curriculum documents see this webpage: https:// gov.uk/government/publications/national-curriculum-in-england-framework-for-key-stages-1-to-4

For the Welsh Foundation stage documents see this webpage: http://learning.gov.wales/resources/improvementareas/curriculum/areas-of-learning/?lang=en

For Northern Irish National Curriculum documents see this webpage:

http://nicurriculum.org.uk/key_stages_1_and_2/areas_of_learning/mathematics_and_numeracy/

For the Scottish numeracy across learning documents see this webpage:

http://educationscotland.gov.uk/learningandteaching/learningacrossthecurriculum/responsibilityofall/numeracy/experiencesandoutcomes/index.asp

ACTIVITY POST

Below are a number of tests of conservation. If you work or have a placement in a primary school give the tests to some children that are at the pre-operational stage of development, and some that are at the concrete-operational stage. Compare the answers given by the children and relate them to characteristics of each stage of development and in particular, criteria for conservation.

1   Place several wooden beads in a dish. All of the beads except two should be the same colour, for example, two yellow, the rest red. You may substitute coloured straws cut into pieces for beads. Ask the children separately and alone 'are there more red beads or wooden beads?' Next ask, 'if I were to string the beads to make a necklace, would the necklace be longer if I used all the wooden beads or all the red beads? Why?'

2   Show the children some fruit, for example, ten raisins and two apples. Ask, 'in what ways are these alike? What do you call them? Are there more raisins than fruit? If we took the fruit and you took the raisins, would we have more, or you? How would you be able to prove who had more?'

3   Show a rubber band to a child. Stretch the rubber band and ask, 'do we have more, less, or the same amount of rubber band as we had before we stretched it? Why?'

Make a report of your findings. Do your results support Piaget's theory?

In summary, preoperational thinking is characterised by **egocentrism**, that is the inability to see things from other's perspective and a belief that everyone else's thoughts, feelings, desires, and perceptions are the same as theirs; confusion between physical and psychological events as represented by animism and physiognomic perception; lack of critical logical thinking represented by inability to conserve; reliance on perception over logic; centration whereby the focus is on a single physical dimension when comparing two or more objects; inability to classify, and transductive reasoning whereby the child combines unrelated facts in a cause and effect relationship such as raising the bedroom blind makes the sun rise (Kesselring & Müller, 2011). During the concrete operational stage each of these characteristic ways of thinking is displaced by logical thought processes.

Concrete operations stage

Following the preoperational stage is the concrete operations stage from approximately seven to 12 years of age. Recent studies indicate however, that some of these ages need to be revised downwards. In contrast to preoperational children, concrete operational children appear to take into account all salient features of the stimulus, and as such thought becomes decentred. The concrete operational child can attend to successive stages in the transformation of an object from one state to another, and mentally reverse the operations that produce an outcome. One good example of the ability to reverse thought is shown through an experiment that has three different coloured balls and a non-transparent tube. The balls are put into the tube in the order red, blue, green, and the child is asked to indicate the order in which they will come out the other side. The child predicts correctly red, blue, green. On the next test the balls are added in the same order, but the tube is rotated through 180 degrees. Again the child is asked to predict the order in which the balls will come out. A preoperational child predicts the order red, blue, green, while a concrete child predicts the right order, green, blue, red. Why?

The clearest indication that children have reached the concrete level of reasoning is the presence of conservation. When asked whether the two lumps of clay mentioned earlier are the same or different, concrete operational children will quickly respond 'the same'. There are three principles of reversibility: *invariant quantity, compensation, reversibility*.

When asked why the two lumps of clay are the same children might answer: 'You didn't add anything or take anything away, you simply changed the shape' (invariant quantity); 'While the pancake is thinner than the ball it is also wider' (compensation); or 'See, I can roll it back up into a ball again' (reversibility).

Seriation and classification

You will recall that preoperational children had difficulty classifying objects. Among other logical operations achieved during the period of concrete operations is the ability to construct classes and subclasses of objects and to organise the elements of a series in either ascending or descending order of size called seriation.

It is obvious, therefore, that concrete operational children are capable of using a variety of logical operations to reason about the world, and to solve problems, however these operations are restricted to concrete experiences, in other words, the content of the operations are real, not hypothetical, objects or situations. When we consider formal operational thought in the next chapter you will see how these limitations are overcome as children mature cognitively as adolescents.

In summary, concrete operational children become less egocentric and differentiate their own perspective from that of others; they increasingly differentiate between physical and psychological events such as imaginations aren't real; they can conserve; they rely on logic rather than perception to solve problems; they are capable of multiple classification; and they can draw an appropriate logical inference from two or more pieces of information (Bibok et al., 2009). However, concrete operational thought is still limited. Logical reasoning is limited to concrete objects that are readily observed; they have an inability to formulate and test multiple hypotheses and an inability to separate, control, and combine variables in a scientific manner, and they lack proportional reasoning such as converting fractions to ratios (Bibok et al., 2009). These cognitive capacities develop during the final stage of cognitive development during adolescence, which we describe in Chapter 6.

Figure 5.2 Piagetian class inclusion test. Question: Are there more teddy bears or fire engines?

SPOTLIGHT ON PIAGET AND PLAY

Piaget described three types of play: practice play, symbolic play, and games with rules, each of which has a relationship to cognitive development. The first of these, *practice play*, relates to the sensorimotor stage of development after about 6 months of age, and describes the intentional repetition of particular actions and use of objects by infants in their exploration of their immediate world of physical objects. For instance, anyone who has had the opportunity to observe an infant over a period of time would notice the rapid transition from initially random movements such as arm waving, which might have caused a toy suspended overhead to swing, to progressively more deliberate efforts to recreate this interesting experience.

Symbolic play begins to emerge as the infant's ability to use mental representations of objects and events develops, especially the ability to imitate, both while the model is present and at a later time. Piaget describes an example of deferred imitation when his daughter of about 16 months exhibited a temper tantrum in her playpen one afternoon, identical in vocalisations and mannerisms to that performed in front of her by a child the same age on the previous day.

At the end of the preoperational stage, children begin to show less interest in games of pretence and engage frequently in *games with prescribed rules* such as hide-and-seek, hand clapping, marbles, or board games. This development follows the shift from pre-operational to concrete-operational thinking or an extension of sensorimotor and constructive activities with the added element of externally defined rules (Dougherty & Ray, 2007; Rakoczy, 2007). Constructive play emerges out of sensorimotor activities when the child has begun to form symbolic representations of experiences and objects: what appears, therefore, as 'playing with blocks' will be represented mentally by the child in constructive play as 'building a house'.

How do children construct knowledge through play? Children's play is full of physical and social activity, conversation and pictures, both real and imaginary. These are the essential elements through which children construct their cognitive, social, and emotional worlds. The role of the carer–educator requires a recognition that it is through play, rather than structured activities in which children receive information about the world and directives on how to behave, that young children learn. Good teachers provide rich opportunities for play with plentiful resources and time without adult interruption unless there is need to refocus because of potentially disruptive behaviour (Gmitrova et al., 2009; Ness & Farenga, 2007).

What is the role of the adult in children's play? During practice play, exploration of the self, others, and the immediate world is what absorbs the young child. For the adult–carer to support this exploration, an environment with a wide range of sensorimotor experiences and modelling of oral language is necessary, along with protection from the physical danger that exploration can bring.

At the stage of symbolic play, the sensitive teacher understands that children come to 'know' by doing; personal experiences and spontaneous actions teach them about the world and about others. The important role for the teacher here is to provide the *tools and symbols* for representing personal reconstructions of experience: models of language (spoken and written) to describe experiences and a range of media for building, making objects, and creating images. Thus, the preoperational child should have available pencils, crayons, and markers with which to 'write' shopping lists and signs; play dough (wet sand or even mud!) for creating objects or just for experimenting with; construction materials such as wood or paper scraps and glue, blocks or toys such as Lego and tools; and costumes for dramatic play with character enactment.

In the concrete-operational stage, where the child is now in formal schooling, the teacher's role is to provide opportunities for the integration of play skills developed in the previous stage into tasks required in the primary school. For example, as children learn to use written symbols to record their stories, they should be encouraged to talk out loud and draw as well (Coates & Coates, 2006). Teacher-designed concrete experiences should provide intellectual challenges for children to discover important concepts while they 'play'. These should be balanced with self-chosen, spontaneous activities in which children can investigate and think critically about their own discoveries. From a Piagetian perspective, such activities allow for the assimilation of new concepts or the experience of cognitive conflict through which accommodation to existing understanding may occur, bringing about a sense of cognitive equilibrium.

As they begin to focus on games with rules during this stage, children of primary school age also need to learn how to use problem-solving skills independently in conflict situations. This should be done through the teacher modelling thinking processes, language, and behaviour.

The role of information technology as a tool for symbolic representation and exploration

(continued)

(continued)

and for the development of higher-order mental processes through play should not be overlooked. With computers today, it is possible to play alone, play cooperatively with others, or play with a virtual community in interactions between children at separate locations and the technology.

What is the role of the social context in cognitive development through play? Not only does there need to be a stimulating environment in which children can investigate and resolve cognitive conflict, but also the encouragement,

guidance, and active involvement of older children and adults in scaffolding children's pretend play has been shown to be very important (Riley & Jones, 2010). For example, Farver and Wimbarti (1995) have shown that older Indonesian children, who often participate in pretend play with their younger siblings more than mothers, act as guides and 'expert partners' (Smolucha, 1992) in stimulating make-believe play by challenging the thinking of their younger siblings and suggesting ideas for making the play more elaborate.

Implications of Piaget for education

Developmentally appropriate education

Piaget's theory has been a great catalyst for the development of educational curricula, methods, and evaluation techniques within our classrooms (Powell & Kalina, 2009). There are a number of important implications of Piaget's theory for the primary and junior high school. Piaget emphasises that children should be *actively engaged* in the content to be learnt and that there should be an optimal match between the developmental stage of the child and the logical properties of the material to be learnt. This approach has been labelled **developmentally appropriate** practice in education (Ojose, 2008; Roskos & Neuman, 2005). You will see this reflected in much curriculum materials in mathematics and science.

Social interaction and cognitive development

From a Piagetian perspective social interaction is crucial for children to progress cognitively because interaction with peers through group work and discussion in the classroom helps liberate children from their egocentrism (Vass & Littleton, 2010). Children's exposure to different points of view forces them to defend, justify, modify, concede, or relinquish their position, all of which obliges them to modify thoughts, that is, to accommodate and assimilate. With peer interaction the mismatch between those operating at slightly higher and lower levels is likely to be optimal, and therefore challenges each individual to progress in their understanding. In order to help children form concepts of living and non-living, of identity and causality they also need experiences in the real world. These experiences help stimulate the growth of logical thinking and the development of language to express thoughts. Later experiences in science and language help them to develop hypothetical and deductive thinking.

Spiral curriculum and curriculum integration

In order to develop increasingly sophisticated ways of thinking, important aspects of the curriculum should be revisited at different stages and the child required to rethink and act at different levels of thought and action. This is referred to as a spiral curriculum. This can be achieved by posing questions at a range of levels to stimulate disequilibrium.

From a Piagetian perspective there is considerable merit in developing themes in which a number of different content areas are combined and integrated. Teachers should thus try to identify structural similarities in different content areas. For example, a thematic approach to 'shapes' could encompass shape in a musical composition, in a poem or story, in mathematical and geometric constructs, in a painting, in social relationships such as 'the shape of my family' and in the natural world.

 QUESTION POINT

Consider your own schooling at both the primary and secondary levels. To what extent to you think it was developmentally appropriate? Compare and contrast your experiences with those of other students.

Lev Vygotsky

Lev Vygotsky (1896–1934) was a contemporary of Piaget. Although he died when he was only 37 years old he has left an impressive legacy of work that is published in the Western world in English and has become increasingly influential. Many of his ideas form a nice counterpoint with those of Piaget, and have had a direct impact on the way teachers teach. A number of these will be described below.

According to Vygotsky's theory, children are born with a wide range of perceptual, attentional, and memory capacities which are substantially transformed through socialisation and education, particularly through the use of cultural inventions such as tools, social structures, and language, to develop human cognition (Daniels et al., 2007; Vygotsky, 1978).

Sociocultural dimensions of learning

In contrast to Piaget, Vygotsky focussed much more on the importance of the sociocultural dimensions and language as important characteristics of formal schooling and learning (Becker & Varelas, 2001; Minick, 2005; Wertsch, 2009). Vygotsky believed that parents, teachers, and peers interact with the child and mediate learning through socially organised instruction. Children are wrapped-around by their culture represented by its tools, inventions, and language and these direct the form and extent cognitive development takes. Tools may consist of pens, paint brushes, notepads, computers, calculators, and various symbol systems. Tools, or cultural artefacts as they are sometimes called (Levykh, 2008; Roth & Lee, 2007), play a double role in learning. First, they provide the means with which individuals and groups act upon the world. In other words the learner does something with the tool that extends the learner's capacity in a particular way. Second, tools act as cognitive scaffolds that facilitate extension of knowledge into related areas (McDonald et al., 2005). Tools not only enrich by developing new capacities in the learner, but also can transform the learner and the learning situation. For example, memory is transformed once an individual acquires reading and writing (language tools). Classroom and learning processes can be radically altered by the common use of computers.

The importance of cultural context

As the tools, inventions, and language of one culture may be significantly different from those of another culture, education must situate learning within the appropriate social and cultural contexts (Sadler, 2009; Sfard & Prusak, 2005). The tools and inventions of a Western society consist of rulers, calculators, computers, mass-transport, supermarkets, and so on. For the child of a family granted refugee status from a developing nation the same assumptions cannot be taken for granted. Language may be spoken and written with an emphasis on the written form as a means for recording and passing on learning within cultures, while in another culture it may be unwritten. In the latter case, oral history and tradition becomes the means by which knowledge is maintained and passed on to succeeding generations. Different cultures also limit who has access to particular information. Our Western society is becoming increasingly an open society with everyone having access to a range of information. In other societies there are severe proscriptions on who can have access to particular information and knowledge. At times this may reflect gender, at other times age, and the taboos associated with these.

 QUESTION POINT

Consider the cultural dimensions of learning as presented above. How would a consideration of these influence teaching in multicultural classrooms? What challenges might the teacher face with a class containing children from immigrant backgrounds or whose family has been granted refugee status? Would the situation be different if a teacher was based in a school that was predominantly Anglo urban?

SPOTLIGHT ON THE ZONE OF PROXIMAL DEVELOPMENT

One of the major elements of Vygotsky's theory is his notion of **zone of proximal development** (Hedegaard, 2005). For Vygotsky teaching is only good when it 'awakens and rouses to life those functions which are in a stage of maturing, which lie in the zone of proximal development' (quoted in Gallimore & Tharp, 1988, p.200). Vygotsky defines the zone of proximal development as the distance between the actual developmental level of a child, as determined by independent problem solving, and the level of potential development, as determined through problem solving under adult guidance, or in collaboration with more capable peers (Vygotsky, 1978). In other words children are constantly on the verge of acquiring new learning, and a zone of proximal development is that area which lies between their existing knowledge or skills and the potential level of development beyond this. A teacher's task is to situate learning within this zone. To do this three characteristics are often listed to guide the teacher:

1 Establish a level of difficulty. This level, assumed to be at the proximal level, must be challenging, but not too difficult.

2 Provide assisted performance. This is referred to as **scaffolded instruction**. The adult provides guided practice to the child with a clear sense of the goal or outcome of the child's performance. As with scaffolding around a building, it is gradually removed so that the child can perform the task independently.

3 Evaluate the independent performance of the child on the task. If the learning experience has been carefully structured and situated within the child's zone of proximal development the child should be able to perform the task independently.

Holistic education

Three key principles underline the effective use of the zone of proximal development to facilitate the cognitive development of children, namely, education must be *holistic*; it must be situated in a social context, and it must allow for change and development in the child.

For Vygotsky, learning must be holistic, i.e. the unit of study should be the most meaningful unit, rather than the smallest or simplest. Division of potentially meaningful material into small skills and sub-skills to facilitate learning is believed to be counterproductive as the essential meaningfulness is lost. The 'whole language' approach to teaching reading, which emphasises that reading comprehension and written expression must be developed through functional, relevant, and meaningful uses of language rather than through the discrete learning of sub-skills (such as phonic decoding) illustrates this idea.

Mediating learning

Vygotsky also emphasised the importance of social interaction between adults and children, and in particular the role played by adults in guiding and mediating learning for children. Central to this is providing instruction that develops in children an increasing mastery of the language of learning and instruction so that they acquire conscious awareness and voluntary control of knowledge (Moseley, 2005). Vygotsky also suggests that formal learning (such as that characterised by learning scientific information) and everyday learning (such as that characterised by learning in the home) are interconnected and interdependent. It is through the use of everyday concepts that children make sense of the definitions and explanations of scientific concepts. However, everyday concepts are also shaped and moulded by exposure to scientific concepts (or schooled concepts), and because of this children become more aware of, and in control of, their everyday worlds (Moseley, 2005). Hence, an effective relationship must exist between the everyday world and the 'schooled world' for learning to be significant, effective, and of practical value.

To facilitate the development of learning that is embedded in the everyday world teachers, students, and peers must interact, share ideas and experiences, solve problems and be interdependent. This interdependence in social contexts is central to a Vygotskian analysis of instruction (Angelova et al., 2006). Because what the child is able to do with assistance and collaboration today, he or she will be able to do independently tomorrow. Learning needs to be structured so that there is an expanding zone challenging children to move forward.

An interesting implication of Vygotsky's approach, which stands in contrast to some of the implications that may be drawn from Piaget's theory, is that children should be challenged to be engaged in activities that appear to be beyond their current level of development. Children can often complete activities with the collaboration of teachers and peers that they could not complete on their own. However, with this assistance and verbal mediation, the needed skills are gradually internalised and the children learn to perform them independently. Hence the zone of proximal development relates to the difference between an individual's current level of development and his or her potential level of development.

 QUESTION POINT

In Vygotskian theory the social context is an essential element of learning and cognitive growth. It would seem that without this social context little cognitive development would, or could, occur. What do you think? How important is the social context to learning for an individual and could a child learn effectively, and hence develop cognitively, without a social context?

Classroom applications of Vygotskian theory

Vygotsky's notions of scaffolding and guided discovery, and his belief in the importance of the continuing interaction between the child and their environment to facilitate the child's understanding of the world about, is essentially a constructivist approach to learning. However, the degree of guidance is more pronounced in Vygotsky's approach than it is in Piagetian views of learning, where the learner is seen more as a solitary explorer. In Piaget's case more emphasis is placed on child-determined exploration and discovery, with little emphasis on direct teaching (Alfieri et al., 2011; Vianna & Stetsenko, 2006).

There are, nevertheless, many similarities in the implications of Vygotsky's and Piaget's theories for the classroom. Both emphasise the importance of active involvement by children in learning, and the process of learning rather than the product. They both emphasise the importance of peer interaction, grounding learning experiences in the real world of experiences for children, and the need for the teacher to take account of individual differences when structuring learning experiences for children.

Piaget suggests the prior need for developmental maturity in order for children to benefit from particular learning experiences, and the importance of unstructured experiences and self-initiated discovery for children's cognitive development, Vygotsky emphasises the need for guidance and assisted-discovery to lead development (Fuson, 2009). Vygotsky (1962, 1978; Vygotsky et al., 2012) also emphasises language as a major means by which cognitive development occurs. Piaget, in contrast, believes that cognitive development occurs independently of language development, and facilitates the acquisition of language.

 ACTIVITY POST

The importance and function of language in cognitive development is debated. Is language a result of cognitive development or does it drive cognitive development? Search the Internet and see if you can shed light on this issue. Write a brief report summarising your findings.

Jerome Bruner

Concept development

An alternative conception of cognitive growth and development was provided by Jerome Bruner. His conceptualisation is still influential today so we provide a brief description for you to consider. For Bruner (1960, 1961, 1966, 1973) the process of intellectual growth and learning consists in children gradually organising their environment into meaningful units by a process called **conceptualisation**. These meaningful units are termed *categories* by Bruner. Depending on the number of effective categories an individual has, they are more or less a functional person in the environment. Through the process of conceptualisation young children begin to develop categories for food, clothing, danger, animals, and so on. The young child passes from the stage of having few functioning concepts and categories to that of an adult who has many.

This process of conceptualisation does not stop as we get older. For example, adults often feel 'at sea' in new environments because we do not have the appropriate categories for interpreting the new environment. The process of forming categories and codes consists of linking ideas together because of common properties. By being exposed to a range of objects and experiences we begin to see these common properties emerge. According to Bruner, categorisation has four major advantages:

1. *Categorisation reduces the complexity of the environment.* For example, a person looking inside a car motor for the first time is struck by the array of different parts and is perhaps overwhelmed by this. Expert mechanics (who have a category for motors) see the motor as an integrated system on which they can operate effectively.
2. *Categorisation permits the recognition of objects.* Car mechanics can work on a lawnmower motor because they can recognise the object in terms of the concept 'motor'.
3. *Categorisation reduces the necessity for constant learning.* We relate to new objects in terms of past experiences and concepts. We are also able to predict qualities of an object without actually testing them by saying that, because it belongs to a certain group, it should have certain properties. For example, general principles learnt in mathematics can lead to solving new problems. We don't need to approach each new problem in a totally fresh way.
4. *Categories provide directions for instrumental activity.* For example, a man lost in a jungle without food will come across a range of unfamiliar growing things. If he categorises an object as food, it will be used to stave off hunger. Indeed, if he is resourceful he could use a log for floating down the river, a banana leaf for shade and shelter, an animal for meat, and a stone for cutting. In a sense, categories define the use to which an object may be put. In learning categories we are learning uses.

Categories are built up through experience and through a procedure Bruner calls *coding*, which refers to the relationship that exists between the general and specific categories. Education is concerned with helping children to encode their experiences, working from the specific to the general – that is, from particular examples to general principles. In brief, this is the foundation of Bruner's theory. Bruner explains the way in which this procedure takes place both theoretically and practically. We are most concerned with describing the practical and less theoretical elements.

The course of cognitive growth

Bruner theorised that children go through three major stages of intellectual development **enactive**, **iconic**, and **symbolic**.

In the **enactive** stage children learn about the world around them by acting on objects. In a sense, an object is what you can do with it. A glass is used to drink from, a bed is to lie in, clothing is to wear, and so on. In the **iconic** stage experiences and objects are represented as concrete images. Children no longer need to manipulate objects in order to learn about them, but can learn through models, demonstrations, and pictures. Children can operate mentally with pictures. In the **symbolic** stage children develop the capacity to think abstractly with symbols and go beyond the present and concrete experiences to create hypotheses. For Bruner, it followed that instruction of children should also be sequenced. In other words, to facilitate learning, children should first experience it, then react to it concretely and finally symbolise it. While progression is believed to be in order through these stages, more mature learners who are already at the symbolic stage often function best when two or more of the modalities are called upon when learning about something new. Bruner's principle is that, at any age, learners learn more effectively if they combine concrete, pictorial, and symbolic presentations of the material.

QUESTION POINT

Think of learning situations where you have learnt most effectively by using two or more modes of thinking and learning. Why do you think multimodalities facilitate learning?

Bruner believes that schools should structure learning experiences so that they are appropriate to each student's level of development.

Ways of thinking

There are two basic types of thinking, analytic thinking and intuitive thinking. **Analytic thinking** characteristically proceeds step-by-step and the learner is, in general, aware of the information and operations involved. This is the type of thinking commonly encouraged in schools, and is most often used in mathematics and science. **Intuitive thinking** is characterised by hunches and solutions not based on formal processes of reasoning. Intuitive thought is based on a feeling one has for a particular subject in its wholeness. As a consequence it does not necessarily advance in carefully defined steps but tends to involve spurts and leaps reflecting the individual's perception of the total problem. Bruner believes that schools should establish an intuitive understanding of materials in children before exposing them to more traditional methods of deduction and proof. Bruner also advocates the use of a **spiral curriculum** for developing concepts at increasingly higher levels of abstraction as children progress from enactive to symbolic thinking. For example, complex mathematical concepts can be related to more elementary concepts developed through the use of concrete materials such as Dienes blocks, and sophisticated notions of comedy and tragedy in literature can be related to more elementary notions of happiness and sadness. In other words the curriculum should build upon integrated material dealt with at varying levels of complexity.

 QUESTION POINT

Think of examples where you have revisited information that you have learnt at earlier times at higher levels of abstraction. What extra insights have you obtained and how is this based on earlier learning? Consider your schooling and tertiary educational experiences. Have you seen evidence of a spiral curriculum in practice?

Discovery learning

Bruner also believed that learning should progress from specific examples to general principles by way of induction. One way to achieve this is through the use of **discovery learning**, which refers to the learning of new information as a result of the learner's own efforts (Olson, 2007; Yilmaz, 2011). The subject matter is not presented to the child in its final form, but rather the child, through their own manipulation of the materials, discovers relationships, solutions, and patterns. Advocates of discovery learning believe that the following advantages characterise this approach:

1 Discovery learning is more meaningful and hence results in better retention. Principles that emerge from discovery are significant because they come from the student's own work.
2 Discovery learning enhances motivation, interest and satisfaction.
3 Discovery learning enhances the development of intellectual capacities, information and problem-solving skills. Students learn how to discover, how to learn and how to organise what they have learnt.
4 Discovery learning encourages transfer of skills to solve problems in new contexts.

Classrooms using discovery learning need to be resource-rich. Teachers need to abandon their role as purveyors of knowledge and become facilitators of children's learning. To perform this function well teachers need to be well prepared and competent in their understanding of the basic underlying principles of their discipline. This is particularly important in handling the range of 'discoveries' and personal proclivities that may characterise any one group of children in the classroom. Teachers must also be willing and able to try a variety of approaches to accommodate the varying needs of the children and their modes of cognitive reasoning (enactive, iconic, and symbolic).

Far from being easy for the teacher, discovery-learning approaches are demanding of organisation and management skills. Novice teachers will need to anticipate thoroughly the sorts of needs the children will have in terms of movement around the learning space, noise and activity levels, resources, and guidance about the purpose of the learning activity. The *quality of learning* needs to be carefully monitored throughout, and interventions made to focus student attention on salient issues emerging from their discovery.

 QUESTION POINT

'Chalk and talk' approaches often appear far easier to manage than discovery learning approaches. Such approaches may also ensure more definitely that concepts the teacher feels are important are learned by the students. What do you think?

Beware – young children do need considerable guidance in their discoveries because they have a developing knowledge base and are inexperienced in drawing 'scientific' conclusions on the basis of random pieces of evidence in the same way as adults do. Maybe discovery learning approaches are better suited to older students. What do you think?

 ACTIVITY POST

Bruner emphasised the importance of discovery learning yet there are many arguments against its use in our classrooms. Do an Internet search on discovery learning and investigate the arguments for and against discovery learning. Consider these arguments and discuss ideas on how the strengths of discovery learning may be enhanced in a classroom while avoiding some of its purported limitations. Design a spreadsheet that outlines 'best practice' in implementing discovery learning.

Language development

A major indicator of development is language acquisition. For young children increasing facility with language opens up rich experiences that help shape the child's cognitive and social worlds. As we have indicated in the sections on Piaget and Vygotsky, both consider language acquisition an essential element of cognitive growth, but from different perspectives. For Piaget language acquisition is an indicator of growing cognitive maturity, as well as facilitating further cognitive growth. For Vygotsky, language acquisition is an essential component of cognitive growth. Language development, and its associated reading acquisition, is an enormous field of study, beyond the scope of this text. In the sections below, we briefly outline some key features of language development but recommend that you consult some further texts that provide more extensive treatment of the topic.

Features of language

Language has certain basic features with which children gradually acquire expertise. These features include the *comprehension* and *production* of language. We are all aware that very young children understand language spoken to them before they are able to speak language to communicate effectively with others. Comprehension of language precedes the production of language. This effect probably persists throughout our lives. Language is a symbol system made up of a *phonology*, the collection of sounds of a language, *semantics*, the meaning given to these sounds (meaning is arbitrary), and a grammatical structure to coordinate these sounds and meanings. *Grammar* consists of three main components: *syntax* which governs word order, *inflections* which alter words for specific meanings (such as 's' for plurals and 'ed' for past tense), and *intonation*, the rising and falling pitch speakers use to denote a question, finality in a statement, surprise, and so on. Finally, language competence depends upon the child knowing how to use language in different contexts; this is referred to as *pragmatics*. Language is modified according to the social situation in which individuals find themselves. For example, a set of language rules apply when one is giving a lecture that are somewhat different to those that apply when one is having a drink with friends at a pub. No doubt, you can think of other examples, such as how one addresses a close friend, a boss, and one's parents in both social and formal situations. Cultural and social conventions, therefore, govern the way in which we use the mechanics of language. Not only do children rapidly master the essential elements of language reception and production, but also a range of registers with which to communicate in particular settings. Schooling is a very important element, therefore, in assisting children to master the complexities of language across a range of settings. These language features, while universal, vary in nature across languages.

Theories of language development

In order to speak, children must have the physiological structures to facilitate sound production as well as the mental structures to select and attend to sounds, and to coordinate these sounds into sequences that ultimately become words and then sentences. There is, therefore, a strong genetic component to language acquisition.

Early behavioural theories held that, while the mechanisms for language production are innate, the formation of sounds and ultimately sentences is the result of conditioning (Skinner, 1957). That is, among the random sounds that infants make some are reinforced by parents, and become established responses, and some are ignored, and therefore fade as responses. Through environmental experience and reinforcement, language is shaped. This is referred to as the environmentalist position on language acquisition. Social cognitive theory of language development holds that language is acquired through a process of modelling and reinforcement (Guo et al., 2010; Hoff, 2006).

Clearly there is evidence that shaping and modelling do effect language acquisition. Children who live in highly verbal homes tend to speak more than those from less verbal homes. Accents and peculiarities of dialect give further evidence that shaping and modelling do occur. However, there are too many problems with this simplistic behavioural approach to language acquisition for it to be plausible as a stand-alone theory. For example, it is unlikely that children are ever exposed to the full range of reinforcing models necessary to explain the complex language they develop.

Second, reinforcement is a rather 'hit and miss' activity. Apart from reinforcing early words, such as 'mama' and 'dada', parents and others typically do not consistently reinforce the early language acquisition of infants, and in particular, they do not appear to reinforce and shape correct syntactic structure, preferring instead to correct semantics. For example, if a child says 'that dog' the mother might correct it to 'no, that is a cat'. If the child then says 'that cat' the mother is likely to say 'yes'. Language is rule driven; however, parents do not typically teach children the rules of language, and reinforce them for their correct usage of the rules.

Third, infants construct 'primitive' language patterns that are rarely modelled or reinforced by parents and which seem to be the result of some type of 'hot wiring' of language development in their brains. Even when corrected children persist with the primitive forms of language for a considerable period of time until more mature speech forms become established. It seems that behavioural reinforcement, while having a role to play in language acquisition is not a sufficient explanation.

In contrast to the environmentalist theory of language acquisition, it has been argued that the acquisition of language is largely innate, and matures according to a timetable that is genetically driven. This theory, often referred to as a **Nativist** approach to language acquisition, is associated with Noam Chomsky (1959, 1995). The basic tenet of this theory is that language is based upon a universal grammar, or set of syntactic rules. Children are born with the capacity to operationalise this grammar whenever they hear language, and this process drives their language development. Chomsky referred to this as an innate language acquisition device (LAD). Hence, from the earliest age, when children hear language their cognitive processes structure their own language competencies in response. For example, children regularise from many examples that 's' is added to a word to produce the plural, and 'ed' to the end of the word to say the thing happened in the past. The over-regularising of the rules such as in 'sheeps', 'tooths', and 'comed', and 'drinked' indicates that a syntactical rule is operating. Children extend their language when rules are confirmed or disconfirmed, which leads to the development of an alternative rule. Language therefore unfolds progressively as the child's mental processing matures in language contexts. This process appears to be universal across language groups.

There are arguments to support this theory. Virtually all children acquire language, and this distinguishes them from apes and other primates, who although make sounds, do not develop language, irrespective of environmental reinforcement. Language spoken in different communities, such as hunter and gatherers, appears no less syntactically complex than that spoken in industrialised countries, although the models presented to children, and the range of purposes of language, might be considerably different. Children acquire language at about the same time and sequence, irrespective of the models to which they are exposed. Finally, children who cannot verbalise, but use sign language, impose on their sign language a set of language rules that seem to be innate, rather than modelled and reinforced (Goldin-Meadow, 2003; Pinker & Jackendoff, 2005).

Criticisms have been levelled at the Nativist approach including its concentration on the development of receptive language rather than on the development of productive language. It has also been criticised for not taking enough account of the impact that speech models have on children's acquisition of speech, and in particular the important role played by parents and caregivers (Ambridge & Lieven, 2011; Spencer et al., 2009). As well as acting as models of language, parents and others, including teachers, help children improve their language usage by three major strategies: expansions, recasts, and clarification questions. Expansions occur when parents and teachers repeat the child's statement in a fuller and more correct form such as 'I want an apple' for the child's imperative 'apple'. Recasts occur when parents and teachers rephrase the child's statement in an alternative form, thus enriching the child's language, for example, 'the bird is being chased by the dog, I hope it flies away safely' for the child's 'the dog is chasing the bird and it will fly away'. Finally, clarification questions are asked by parents and teachers to elicit clearer language from the child as in 'could you please say that again so that I understand what you mean?'. Such clarification questions motivate the child to improve their language. As you can see, these are three very important processes that you will use in your interactions with children mastering the complexities of language.

Interactionist perspective

Because neither environment nor heredity alone seems sufficient to explain language acquisition, it seems that an interactionist theory is probably best able to explain the process. Children appear to have 'hot wiring' that enables their language process to unfold relatively independently of the nature of the environment in which they are located. Nevertheless, their language acquisition is facilitated by the environmental experiences to which they are exposed. In particular, the environment provides the motivational stimulus for children to listen and talk. Teachers, through modelling and reinforcement, play an important role in helping children refine their language skills. Furthermore, social experiences, particularly those at school when children interact with same age and older peers, help develop and refine their language repertoire (see, for example, Mashburn et al., 2008; Tomasello, 2003).

Stages of language acquisition

Considerable research has investigated the stages and nature of language acquisition. There seem to be great regularities in all human societies in the sequence of language development as children progressively master the rules of phonology, semantics, and grammar. Much of this development takes place in the first years of life and by three years of age, children have a vocabulary of approximately 1,000 words and can carry out a reasonable conversation with adults. We will not go into any detail in describing these stages, which include a preverbal period, speech segmentation, child-directed speech, early word recognition and reproduction, the extension of vocabulary and some of its characteristics such as overextensions and under-extensions, and telegraphic speech. We recommend you read some excellent sources on this material such as Clark, 2009; Cohen & Macaro, 2007; Pinker & Jackendoff, 2005; Tomasello, 2003.

By the time children begin school they have mastered much of the complexities of language and have a vocabulary in excess of 10,000 words. They also become involved in much more complex social interactions that further develop their language competencies. These interactions include listening to teacher-controlled sequences, which can be quite complex, such as instructions and information, as well as increasingly complex interactions with their peers. Language interactions with peers occur in both formal and informal settings. Formal settings include classroom activities such as group work during which students need to listen to others' ideas, explain their own thinking, and expand upon and clarify both their own and others language utterances. Informal language interactions occur, for example, in the playground through mastering the rules of games and cooperation, and in the distribution of social knowledge, such as what movies to watch, where to shop, what to eat, and so on. As we have indicated earlier, such social interactions, mediated through language, are believed by both Piaget and Vygotsky, to stimulate cognitive development.

The school connection

Considerable curriculum time in the infants and primary years is dedicated to language arts, which together with reading, is perhaps the major foci of education in the first years of school. A lot of time is spent on pre-reading and pre-writing skills. Children are taught how to listen for comprehension in a variety of genres and how to present verbal ideas so that they are clear to their classmates. This includes conventions such as how to listen, what verbal and non-verbal cues to give to the speaker that one is actively attending, when to interject, when and how to ask questions, and so on. Considerable effort is expended in expanding children's vocabulary, which continues to develop at a great pace, particularly as children begin to read.

6 Cognitive Development: adolescence to adulthood

Introduction

As we discussed in Chapter 5, according to Piaget, intellectual development occurs progressively as the growing child moves through a series of stages, that are characterised by qualitatively different cognitive processes, and is confronted with new experiences that must be adapted to the existing mental schemes of the child. Through the processes of assimilation and accommodation, the child either incorporates new experiences into existing schemes or constructs or alters schemes to make them more useful. As the child develops, these intellectual schemes become more sophisticated, so that at the end of the formal stage the child is capable of the full range of logical operations characteristic of adult thought. In this chapter we examine features of formal operational thought which develop in adolescence and some of the challenges that have been levelled at Piagetian theorising and research. We also consider some further implications of Vygotskian theory in cultural context.

As well as Piaget and Vygotsky there are a number of contemporary cognitive theories that are particularly relevant to adolescent learners, these include metacognition and metacognitive training, situated learning, and distributed cognition. We will examine each of these in some detail and finish the chapter by considering whether there are differences in the ways males and females think and learn.

Piaget and adolescent cognition

Formal-operations stage

Significant cognitive development continues to occur throughout adolescence. During the period Piaget named **formal operational thought** there emerges the ability to think abstractly and in a scientific way. While the preoperational thinker was dominated by perception and an inability to conserve, and the concrete operational thinker was limited to real world activities and problems of limited theoretical complexity, the formal-operational individual possesses a unified logical system with which to explore systematically hypothetical situations and abstract relations independent of content.

Formal thought refers to the ability individuals have to set up and test hypotheses about the world, to think propositionally and to take into account all possible combinations or aspects of a problem without reference to physical reality. Indeed, Piaget described formal operational thought as **hypothetico-deductive** because the formation of hypotheses and the test of deductions from these hypotheses are central to thinking at this stage. In the next sections we describe the elements of formal operational thinking and the 'tests' that have been constructed to illustrate the presence of formal thinking in adolescents and adults.

Combinatorial logic

During the formal stage of cognitive development individuals acquire the capacity to combine discrete elements of problems systematically to test hypotheses about the world. In order to test whether children can set up, test, and confirm or deny hypotheses they are given problems where they must handle several variables at the same time. A common problem is called the colourless liquid problem. In this problem, children are presented with five bottles of colourless liquid and they must decide which combination of three liquids produces a yellow colour. Concrete operational children will simply try various pairs of liquids, or combine all five liquids to no avail, and eventually give up. Formal operational children establish a systematic procedure for testing the liquids in various combinations in order to arrive at the correct solution. They can verbalise the logic they used to solve the problem.

Propositional thinking

Formal thinkers also acquire the capacity for **propositional thinking** that is beyond the capacity of preoperational and concrete thinkers. With propositional thinking formal operational children can work through statements of an argument in the mind. For example, the formal operational child uses deductive logic to answer the syllogism shown in Figure 6.1.

Proportional reasoning

Formal operational children acquire proportional reasoning and are able to apply the concept of ratio and proportion to solve problems. A common problem consists of giving children two cards on which stickmen are drawn, one being two-thirds the height of the other. These stick men are constructed so that they measure four and six jumbo paper clips high respectively. The child is then asked to measure both the stickmen with eight connected jumbo paper clips, and to record the heights in jumbo paper clips. The jumbo paper clips are then replaced with small paper clips and the child is asked to measure only the large stickman with the small paper clips. The child is then asked to decide how high the small stickman is in small paper clips without measuring directly. In other words, the child has to apply proportional reasoning to solve the problem. Another common problem is to have children balance different weights on a scale. Only formal thinkers can explain how a ratio of weight and distance from the fulcrum controls the balance.

Figure 6.1 Propositional thinking.

Figure 6.2 Proportional thinking.

Hypothetical reasoning

Concrete operational children have difficulty mounting a logical argument that follows from a premise that is hypothetical. Formal children can abstract the structure of the argument from its content and argue hypothetically. While debates in the primary school are related to the real world, debates in the secondary school can be related to purely hypothetical issues such as 'if everyone doubled in weight in the world this would be a good thing'.

In summary, hallmark characteristics of formal thinking are combinatorial logic, propositional thinking, proportional thinking, and hypothetical reasoning. It is with these new cognitive capacities that the adolescent thinker and learner can truly engage in more sophisticated learning activities related to mathematics, science, history, and a wide range of academic subjects.

Using formal thinking processes

Studies indicate that simply arriving at the age appropriate to formal thinking does not ensure that formal thought is used (Csikszentmihalyi & Robinson, 2014; Kuhn, 2009). Indeed, adolescents and adults do not show formal-operational thinking under many circumstances. They often think associatively rather than logically. Using formal thinking may be more a product of an individual's domain-specific expertise, based on experience, than of the maturational processes of cognitive development. Consequently, we cannot presume as teachers that all adolescent children think formally. Indeed research demonstrates that the capacity for abstract thinking is limited among adolescents and adults. The theory holds that while they have the capacity, relevant experiences may be necessary to stimulate its use (Endler & Bond, 2008; Powell & Kalina, 2009). It appears that two things are necessary – first, level of cognitive maturity, and second, domain specific opportunities to practice formal thinking. If individuals are not confronted with the necessity to reason formally (in other words if concrete modes of thinking appear more adaptable) then formal thought will not be used. Indeed, most people probably reason at a concrete or preoperational level most of the time. Furthermore, even when individuals are quite adept at formal thinking it is often domain specific. For example, teachers may think formally about issues and problems related to their teaching, but use concrete modes of thought when solving problems related to cooking and carpentry.

 QUESTION POINT

Consider the daily exercises and activities you are involved in. This could be anything from deciding what to eat for breakfast, driving to work or university, to planning a lesson. In what activities do you use formal thought? In which activities do you use concrete and preoperational thought?

SPOTLIGHT ON CRITICISMS OF PIAGETIAN TESTS

In this and the previous chapter we indicated that 'tests' (really reasoning activities) are used to distinguish levels of cognitive functioning and at what stage a child is operating. The following webpages describe how to conduct a range of Piagetian tests: http://ehlt.flinders.edu.au/education/DLiT/2000/Piaget/tests.htm, http://cog.brown.edu/courses/cg63/conservation.html and http://thesocietypages.org/socimages/2009/09/15/piagets-stages-of-cognitive-development-experiments-with-kids/

Many of these are quite straightforward to set up. If you work with children, you should consider administering a range of tests to evaluate for yourself the plausibility of Piaget's theory of stage development in cognitive growth.

These tests have been subjected to considerable critical review with many researchers considering the form of the tests (particularly the language used, relevance of the questions to background experiences and the requirement that children justify their 'correct' answers in the 'correct' way) inadequate (e.g. Twidle, 2006). Many researchers believe that the tests, particularly because of their verbal bias, underestimate what children are cognitively capable of at various ages.

Although it is some years old now, Michael Siegal (1991) wrote a particularly interesting critique of the language framework used in the test of conservation that is now considered to be a 'classic' text. He argues that younger children's apparent inability to conserve and decentre can be explained in terms of a clash between the conversational worlds of adults and children. In particular, Siegal believes that the framework for the Piagetian questions breaks conversational rules that children implicitly hold. While these conventions may be broken for specific purpose in adult speech, young children, in general, abide by them. Specifically, Siegal believes that problems arise because Piagetian experimenters pose questions where the answer is obvious or repeat questions when an answer has already been given. Young children may not recognise that the purpose underlying these departures from conversational rules is to establish their understanding of concepts. Instead, they may assume that, for example, repeated questioning (characteristic of the Piagetian test) implies an invitation to switch the second time around because the first answer was incorrect. For example, in the conservation of liquids test, children who answer that the two jars of water are equal may switch their answers after one jar has been poured into a different container, despite believing the volumes are still the same. They may do this because they want to please the experimenter and give the answer they think is expected. Siegal believes that, when given the appropriate verbal cues that take into account the relative immaturity of their language skills, young children disclose what they know.

What do you think of the arguments put forward by Siegal? In a group, redesign the conservation tests so that they either make use of the language rules of children, or are presented in a non-verbal manner.

Cross-cultural implications

Much of Piaget's theory of cognitive development is based upon the organising principles of perception, and the processes of adaptation, accommodation, and assimilation. There is abundant evidence from cross-cultural and anthropological research that the manner in which individuals perceive, structure, interpret, and relate to their world is a function of what the physical and social environment dictates (Oyserman & Lee, 2008; Robbins, 2005). Consequently, as many of the Piagetian tasks are based upon perception, there is a strong possibility that they may be inappropriate in diverse cultural settings. It is very important therefore for teachers not to jump to conclusions about the cognitive stage of development of children from different cultural groups without taking into account prior experience.

Furthermore, it is very problematic to argue that particular cultural groups lag in cognitive development relative to Western groups. Many studies were conducted in the 1970s that compared children from Western and non-Western backgrounds including Australian native Aboriginal and white children. Findings suggested that in a number of cultural groups, including the Australian Aboriginal, up to 50% of their mature adult population were unable to conserve quantity, weight, or volume, as measured by standard Piagetian tests (Oesterdiekhoff, 2013). This apparent lag is the result of cultural experiences that ill prepare individuals for responding to the Piagetian tests, either through the manner in which they are presented (largely verbal) or the content (perceptually oriented). It is generally accepted today that the nature of culturally different environments, such as that of the Aboriginal or Maori, leads to different types of spatial orientation. Hence, tests devised to assess conservation and formal thinking must take this into account.

 QUESTION POINT

Do an Internet search on cross-cultural studies of Piagetian stages. What is the general consensus of opinion? Do the stages have universal applicability?

Current status of Piaget's theory

Are the stages that Piaget described really universal? Do they cut across domains of knowledge? Do the various cognitive abilities associated with the stages emerge at the ages Piaget predicted? Are the developmental stages he described invariant across individuals and cultures? These and a myriad of other questions have been subjected to research in the last two decades (Feldman, 2004; Tomasello, 2000). There are many opponents of Piagetian stage theory who believe that his theory is an inadequate representation of how children acquire increasingly sophisticated modes of thinking. In particular they object to the supposed relatively inflexible stages through which individuals pass, and the ages at which, various cognitive capacities become evident. In the next section we summarise the current status of Piaget's theory. Alternative views on cognitive development will be presented in Chapter 7.

As the acquisition of conservation provides a hallmark of logical thinking and separates preoperational thinkers from concrete operational thinkers, most research has been conducted in the area of conservation and, in particular, whether the acquisition of conservation is invariant across groups and whether it can be accelerated through various educational programmes (Adey, 2005; Shayer, 2008; Shayer & Adhami, 2007). Research continues to show that the ability to conserve is an important marker of cognitive growth and that it is invariant across groups, although the age at which the ability to conserve occurs has been revised downwards. There is limited evidence that conservation can be accelerated through educational or enrichment programmes. In specific circumstances conservation appears to be responsive to environmental intervention, however, in these circumstances the ability to conserve appears to be limited to the context in which conservation was 'trained', does not appear transferable to other tasks, and is short-lived. Most experts now suggest it is a misuse and misapplication of Piaget's theory to stimulate the early acquisition of conservation through education and schooling (Gordon, 2009; Rowbottom & Aiston, 2011).

In general, there is continuing support for Piaget's theorising, although the ages at which particular types of thinking become accessible to children has been revised downwards. Research using alternative methodologies and new techniques establishes that Piaget underestimated the cognitive capacity of children (Kesselring & Müller, 2011; Moses & Baldwin, 2005; Wellman, 2011). Despite this, there is substantial research support for the basic elements of Piaget's theory. Summarising this research shows that there is evidence that the nature of thinking changes with age and is generally in line with Piaget's stage concept. Elements of thinking characterising different stages, such as centering and conservation, have received considerable support. Piaget's stage theory of cognitive development, therefore, still provides us with a pretty good guide as to when new cognitive abilities are likely to emerge and what they allow the person to do cognitively. The importance of children exploring the environment and having rich social interactions in order to foster cognitive growth has also been demonstrated many times and provides a basis for activity based learning and group work. The processes of accommodation and assimilation are readily demonstrable as key elements of cognitive development.

To this point in time, therefore, the Piagetian perspective still holds a significant place in orienting our understanding of how children's cognition develops. In contrast to the rigid application of Piagetian stage theory to curriculum design, constructivist approaches to learning emphasise two much more flexible implications (Gordon, 2009; Powell & Kalina, 2009).

First, the emphasis shifts from trying to directly foster the characteristics of a future stage of development to maximising the child's opportunities to create and coordinate many relationships of which he or she is currently capable. Second, there is an emphasis on providing children with opportunities to construct meaning out of the experiences presented. Learning is essentially considered a constructive process. Ultimately, elements of Piaget's theory such as the types of experience presented to children, the nature of active learning, and the importance of interest, autonomy, and peer interaction are related to this important notion that children construct their learning from this world of experience.

ACTIVITY POST

The following list provides a number of suggestions for the teacher derived from Piagetian theory. Critique these hints in context of the understanding you have of Piaget's theory.

1 Base learning activities on the stage characteristics of the students' thought processes.

2 Use a wide variety of experiences to maximise cognitive development.

3 Do not assume that children of a particular age are functioning at a particular cognitive level, e.g. reaching adolescence or adulthood does not guarantee the ability to perform formal operations.

4 As each person constructs learning in terms of his or her own schemes no two persons will derive the same meaning or benefit from a given experience.

5 Learning experiences should be individualised so that each student is working at a level that presents an optimal mismatch between what the student knows and the new knowledge to be acquired. Moderate novelty will foster motivation (disequilibrium).

6 Provide concrete experience necessary for the development of concepts prior to the use of these concepts in language.

7 Learning should be considered as an active restructuring of thought rather than an increase in content, and reconstruction (recall) will reflect the particular schema of the learner.

8 Wrong answers should be used to help the student to analyse his or her thinking in order to retain the correct elements and revise misconceptions.

9 Evaluate students in terms of improving his or her own performance. Evaluation should be individualised and should have as its goal the improvement of personal performance.

10 Materials should be used to encourage creative thought. Materials that discourage creative thought should be avoided.

11 Social interaction should be used to promote increases in both interest and comprehension in learning.

(Based on Child, 2007; Fontana, 1995; Webb, 1980)

Further thoughts on Vygotsky

The manner in which children respond to school, and benefit from the experiences presented, reflect the cultural environment in which they are socialised. The cognitive development of children is shaped by personal and cultural histories related to gender, class, race, and family and the self-regulation of valued activities (Molden & Dweck, 2006). These valued activities are set in social, political, and cultural contexts that define what is acceptable and valued. Within these diverse contexts individuals and groups seek to fulfil their self-identities by participating in activities that develop the skills and dispositions needed to excel in their cultural milieu (Adams, 2006; McCaslin, 2009; Oyserman, 2013).

Race, gender, and a range of other labels such as gifted and talented, and special needs, are being increasingly viewed not as inherent or ascribed characteristics of people but as social constructions (Archer, 2010; Lee & Anderson, 2009). In other words, personal identity appears to develop out of the tasks, social relationships, and contexts within which each individual learns. Learning from this perspective is a process through which we become one with the collective through carrying out personal activity in collaboration with other people by using the tools, languages, and social organisations of the group.

This constructivist view of cognitive development, and in particular its sociocultural elements, has significant implications for understanding cultural diversity and our function as educators within culturally diverse educational settings. As we have indicated above, however, as the tools, inventions and language of one culture may be significantly different from those of another culture, effective education must place learning within the appropriate social and cultural contexts. We deal with a number of these social and cultural contexts in the following sections.

Culture and the zone of proximal development

Language and conversational forms and learners' familiarity or lack of familiarity with the use of various conventions (such as questioning) and tools (such as computers) within the school context must be considered by teachers if they are to make education relevant (Grossman & McDonald, 2008). Teachers need to build on the experiences of their students in order to advance their academic and social development. In other words, effective education from a Vygotskian perspective must be situated within the zone of proximal development for individuals. Generally, school practices are consistent with how mainstream students have been socialised in their home culture and with the learning preferences and strengths they have developed. However, effective teaching also requires that teachers make linkages between all students' home culture and classroom practices even when the students are non-members of the mainstream group (Mills, 2008).

Vygotskian perspectives have strongly influenced educators' ideas of effective learning in cultural settings. In particular, the sociocultural milieu of learning affects the following:

- the way individuals go about learning;
- values and goals appropriate to learning;
- definitions of meaningful learning;
- definitions of intelligence and intelligent behaviour;
- the importance of individual versus group activities;
- appropriate measurement and evaluation.

(based on Arievitch & Haenen, 2005)

 ## SPOTLIGHT ON LEARNING THEORIES

As indicated above, Piaget and Vygotsky present views of cognitive development which have implications for structuring learning experiences for students. However, there are a number of other theoretical perspectives on the learning process that guide teachers and educators in their approach to teaching and learning. Three dominant perspectives today are information processing theory, behavioural theory, and social cognitive theory. We deal with information processing theory in some detail in Chapter 8. In the following section, we give a brief overview of behavioural theory and social cognitive theory. Readers are recommended to consult educational psychology texts for a more thorough treatment of these theories (see, for example, McInerney, 2014).

Behavioural learning theory has its roots in the early work of Ivan Pavlov (1849–1936), who found that if you paired a neutral stimulus, referred to as an *unconditioned stimulus*, with a *conditioning stimulus* for a particular response, then the unconditioned stimulus would take on the property of the conditioning stimulus in producing the response, and become a *conditioned stimulus*. The common example of conditioning was pairing a bell with the presentation of meat to a hungry dog. The meat would stimulate the reflex response of salivation by the dog. Eventually, through repeated pairings of bell and meat, the bell alone would produce salivation in the dog. This was then referred to as a learned response. Many examples of what became known as *classical conditioning* exist, such as pairing knee jerk and eye blink reflexes to bells and other noises.

The important feature of classical conditioning for teachers to note is the power of physically associating events to produce new behaviour. Within learning settings, classical conditioning is not usually part of intentional teaching by teachers. However, classical conditioning is the source of much incidental learning, such as the learning of attitudes and emotions towards particular events. For example, if a teacher yells at students when they get a mistake in mathematics, children can learn by association to dislike mathematics. This form of learning operates below the level of conscious awareness.

Pavlov's work was followed up by famous early American psychologists such as John Watson (1878–1958) and Edward Thorndike (1874–1949). Indeed, Watson (1913) coined the term **behaviourism** for this type of learning. Thorndike (1911) investigated the effect of consequences of behaviour on subsequent behaviour and his findings were generalised as the **law of effect**, which proposes that a response is strengthened if it is followed by pleasure, and weakened if followed by pain or distress (physical or psychological).

This principle became the cornerstone of later behavioural theory.

Classical conditioning is used in the treatment of certain psychiatric conditions such as phobias. For example, if a person has a fear of flying, pairing incompatible stimuli such as sitting in a plane with thoughts of being on a beautiful beach sipping cocktails, can help alleviate the fear of flying. This is referred to as counter-conditioning. A more extensive behavioural theory emerged from the work of Burrhus Skinner (1904–1990). His theory, building on the work of Thorndike, became known as **operant conditioning**, or more simply, learning theory. Skinner explored the relationship between reinforcement and the development of learned behaviour. In essence, Skinner found that if a voluntary, but unlearned, response, referred to as an operant, was followed with a pleasant effect, referred to as a reinforcement, the operant became more likely to be repeated (Skinner, 1938). Skinner found that quite complex behaviour could be shaped in animals and humans by chaining a series of behaviours with reinforcement. The common example of operant conditioning was with rats and pigeons, which could learn quite complex behaviour such as pressing levers and doing complex dance routines as a result of being reinforced with food pellets. This process of learning behaviour through the successive reinforcements of approximations to the target final behaviour is known as **shaping**. The quite spectacular routines of dolphins at various oceanariums is the result of shaping through operant conditioning.

In educational settings, operant conditioning is used to shape the behaviour of learners from such simple acts as putting up one's hand to answer a question, through to quite complex behaviours such as solving mathematical problems (Boghossian, 2006; Jordan et al., 2008; Muijs & Reynolds, 2011). The secret to behavioural teaching and learning lies in structuring complex learning episodes into their hierarchical and less complex component parts, and then providing the opportunity for the learner to perform the first elementary response which is then reinforced, and through a cycle of stimulus, response and reinforcement of component behaviours gradually establishing the complex behaviour. This learned behaviour is then sequenced with further behaviour, shaped and established through continuing reinforcement. Reinforcement in the early stages is continuous and then, as the behaviour is established, becomes intermittent. Reinforcement may consist of token reinforcers such as stamps, certificates, or food. It may also consist of praise and reinforcing activities (such as getting an early mark for one's work).

Operant conditioning is the principle behind numerous educational programmes such as **positive teaching**, **programmed instruction**, and **direct instruction** (including many information technology-based learning programmes), and many discipline programmes such as **applied behaviour analysis** (Alberto & Troutman, 2009; Magliaro et al., 2005; Seligman et al., 2009). The primary principle underlying behavioural teaching is the law of effect – that is, that any act that is followed by a pleasant event (such as a reward) is more likely to be repeated in the future. Reinforcement may be **positive** (a pleasant consequence) or **negative** (an unpleasant consequence). In the latter case, something unpleasant happens if the student does not perform an action. On performing the action, the negative reinforcement ceases. An example of this might be having students stand at their seats until they answer questions correctly, and then allowing them to sit down.

(continued)

(continued)

Behavioural theory is used to explain much early learning by children, including learning to talk.

Research typically shows that teaching techniques based on behavioural methods are effective. However, these methods have been subject to much criticism, largely related to the belief that such approaches do not encourage the understanding of material learned, but simply encourage superficial behavioural responses. In fact, cognitive learning theories such as information processing theory are a direct attempt to refocus learning on meaningfulness rather than on overt behaviour. However, you might like to consider when behavioural approaches may be more relevant and when cognitive approaches may be more relevant to particular learning episodes. A learning theory that lies somewhere between the hard-line behavioural approach and the information processing approach is **social cognitive theory**. Social cognitive theory evolved from the early work of Bandura and Walters (1963), but is mostly associated with Bandura (1977). Initially it was referred to as social learning theory and was based on modelling and reinforcement. In brief, social learning theory was based on the belief that individuals learn by modelling the behaviour of others and having this modelled behaviour reinforced. As the theory evolved, it became more explicitly cognitive in orientation (Bandura 1986).

While reinforcement remained a cornerstone of the theory, more emphasis was placed on the learner thinking about, and reflecting upon, modelled behaviour, both the behaviour of others and the effects this behaviour produced in terms of being reinforced or punished, and the potential effects of the learner themself performing the modelled behaviour. This led to the notions of inhibition and disinhibition. In other words, according to social cognitive theory, the fact of observing behaviour means that the behaviour could be modelled. Whether or not modelled behaviour is imitated lies in what are seen as the perceived consequences of performing the behaviour. If the observer or learner believes that the behaviour will be reinforced positively, then the behaviour is *disinhibited* and more likely to be performed. Alternatively, if the observer believes that the behaviour will be punished, it will most likely be *inhibited*. A simple example of this is smoking. Most children observe others smoking. Whether or not they themselves begin to smoke relates to the consequences they perceive may happen as a result. For example, some will see positive consequences, such as being seen as 'cool' and part of the group. Others will see negative consequences, such as being punished by their parents, or poor health. Smoking behaviour will then be either inhibited or disinhibited. Social cognitive theory is used to explain much early learning of children, such as learning to talk, eat, and socialise.

It is also used to explain much social behaviour people learn throughout their lives related to moral judgments, altruistic behaviour, aggression, and violence (see, for example, Bushman & Huesmann, 2006; DeWall et al., 2011). From social cognitive theory has emerged the self-regulated learning model of Zimmerman and others (Cleary & Zimmerman, 2006, 2012; Zimmerman 2008; Zimmerman & Cleary, 2009). More information on behaviourism and social cognitive theory can be found at the following websites: http://psych.athabascau.ca/html/aupr/ba.shtml, http://brembs.net/operant/ and http://psychology.about.com/od/developmentalpsychology/a/sociallearning.htm

Metacognition

There are a number of contemporary views of cognitive development of particular significance to adolescence that relate to the way brain systematically organises information through learning. We consider a number of these views below.

What is metacognition?

In order to learn effectively children need knowledge about how to monitor their cognitive resources, what we call **metacognition**, and how they learn, called *metalearning* (Dinsmore et al., 2008; Schunk, 2008; Veenman et al., 2006).

It is believed that metacognitive knowledge appears early and continues to develop at least throughout adolescence. Adults, because of their greater experience, tend to have more knowledge about their own cognition than younger people, and are also better able to describe it. However, children as young as six can reflect with accuracy on their own thinking, especially when asked to do it with familiar material (Veenman & Spaans, 2005; Whitebread et al., 2009).

Does metacognitive training improve student learning?

Considerable research has been directed towards understanding metacognitive and metalearning processes in the classroom and how these processes may enhance learning (Azevedo, 2005; Berthold et al., 2007). Students develop some metacognitive and self-regulating strategies as a normal part of their own learning and observing others learn, in lieu of explicit instruction (Joseph, 2009; Koriat & Ackerman, 2010). However, while these strategies may be effective they may also be limited and faulty. Consequently, explicit instruction in strategy use with appropriate feedback will, in most cases, enhance student learning and also enable students to develop further their repertoire of strategies. Strategy instruction could begin in later primary school.

Some simple techniques to promote the development of metacognitive skills that should be encouraged in learners are:

- asking questions about processes;
- reflecting on their learning;
- problem-solving by thinking aloud;
- being flexible in their approach to learning;
- developing learning plans;
- learning to summarise.

There are a number of programmes designed to teach students to be self-regulated and metacognitive learners. Three programmes that have been developed and evaluated in the UK are the Reading Edge (Slavin et al., 2009), Thinking Together (Mercer & Sams, 2006) and Lets Think (Adey et al., 2002).

The Reading Edge programme was designed to develop co-operative learning and metacognitive reading strategies in secondary school children aged 11–16. Students worked in four- or five-member teams to help one another build reading skills. Activities included partner reading, story re-telling, story-related writing, word mastery, and story-structure. Three studies have shown that, compared to classes that did not implement this programme, students in Reading Edge classes showed improved scores on vocabulary and reading tests (Chamberlain et al., 2007; Slavin et al., 2007; Slavin et al., 2009). The Reading Edge programme has now been incorporated into a whole school approach to improvement. Details can be found at: http://successforall.org.uk/

The Thinking Together programme is a dialogue-based approach to the development of thinking and learning in primary school children aged 8–11 years. Pupils are explicitly taught about Exploratory Talk – a way of interacting which emphasises reasoning, the sharing of relevant knowledge and a commitment to collaborative endeavour. Pupils work in groups of three, using Exploratory Talk as they work on curriculum-based activities. The role of the teacher is to act partly as a guide for the pupils and partly as a role model to show them how to approach their lesson activities and tasks using Exploratory Talk. A number of studies have shown how pupils in classes that have implemented Thinking Together show more on-task behaviour, more sophisticated language when solving problems, and better scores on IQ tests as well as National Curriculum tests (Mercer, 2013; Mercer & Same, 2006; Mercer et al., 2009). More details about the Thinking Together programme can be found on their website: https://thinkingtogether.educ.cam.ac.uk/projects/

Lets Think is a cognitive acceleration programme than uses principles drawn from Piagetian and Vygotskian theory to enhance the understanding of science concepts for pupils in both primary and secondary schools. A range of approaches are used to enhance the student curriculum that include more cooperative learning, more enquiring and philopsophical approaches to questioning, and for pupils to take more responsibility over their learning. Numerous studies have supported this approach showing how pupils in Lets Think classes show better understanding of maths and science concepts and perform better in maths and science tests than pupils in classes that do not use Lets Think (Adey et al., 2002; Shayer & Adhami, 2007). More details about Lets Think can be found on their website: http://letsthink.org.uk/

 QUESTION POINT

Taking into account what you know about the cognitive development of children consider at what ages students could be introduced to the cognitive skills listed above.

SPOTLIGHT ON TEACHING THINKING SKILLS

How should thinking skills instruction be presented? Two basic approaches are possible. Proponents of the strategy/skill approach argue that it is difficult for most students, and especially for low-achieving students, to learn complex content and skills at the same time. Hence this approach provides explicit instruction of strategies and skills as an adjunct course with some attempt to transfer learning to content areas.

On the other hand, others argue that there should be a dual focus on content and skills. The primary focus should be content objectives, taught by the content teacher, but supported by a repertoire of specific strategies that will help students learn the new content (Abrami et al., 2008). From our perspective the second approach seems more appropriate for use in the regular classroom.

Some authors argue that, as research indicates that most children are able to theorise about their own cognition by the age of four, and are able to use these theories to regulate their performance, it is reasonable to place some degree of emphasis on metacognitive training from the time children enter school, regardless of their basic skills level (Dignath et al., 2008). From this point of view, schools should actively promote the development of metacognitive skills among all students.

Consider one of the metacognition programmes from the three presented above. How would you use it in your classroom?

Cognitive and situated learning

In much of our discussion of Piaget we have been concentrating on a theory of cognitive development which, in a sense, separates the development of cognitive structures from their content and situation, and emphasises the individual construction of learning. As such, this approach provides us with information regarding the ways in which knowledge is structured and the cognitive processes through which new learning can be acquired. Cognitive approaches also provide us with information regarding the kinds of learning experience that will lead best to the acquisition of new knowledge and skills (Kirschner et al., 2006).

An alternative cognitive approach is referred to as **situated learning** (or situated cognition). Proponents of situated learning emphasise that much of what we learn is social in nature, context-bound, and tied to the specific situation in which it is learnt (Korthagen, 2010; Putnam & Borco, 2000; Smith & Semin, 2007).

It is common to find examples of individuals using skills and knowledge to solve specific real life situations, while being unable to use the same operations in classroom-based contexts. For example, research has shown that street vendors can use quite complex maths to work out sums while showing little formal knowledge of mathematics. For this reason, some researchers suggest that learning is most effective when it is in a situated context, and that 'real' learning is a form of apprenticeship in which new members become enculturated into the language, customs, and beliefs of a learning community (Lunce, 2006). An important aspect of situated learning is, therefore, that learning activities in the classroom should be authentic – that is, similar to what real world practitioners do – or at least develop thinking and problem-solving skills that will be useful in out-of-school activities (Braund & Reiss, 2006; Putnam & Borco, 2000).

Distributed cognition

Evolving from the idea of situated cognition is the notion of **distributed cognition**. As we have noted above, the situated learning approach moves away from a belief that learning and thinking is largely an individual process to considering it as a process embedded in social interaction. Hence situative theorists believe that cognition is distributed or 'stretched over' the individual, other persons, and various artifacts such as physical and symbolic tools (Sutton et al., 2010; Zhang & Patel, 2006).

There are many real life situations where it is obvious that cognition (or knowledge) is distributed throughout the group so that the group can function effectively (Hodgkinson & Healey, 2008). In any large organisation such as a complex factory, or a business enterprise, no one individual holds the knowledge and skills necessary for the effective functioning of the organisation. The distribution of cognition across people and tools (e.g. computers and machinery) make it possible for the workers to accomplish tasks beyond the capabilities of any individual staff member.

 QUESTION POINT

How are the notions of situated and distributed cognition similar to Vygotsky's theory of sociocultural learning? How do they differ from Piaget's conception of cognition?

 # SPOTLIGHT ON SEX DIFFERENCES IN COGNITIVE DEVELOPMENT, LEARNING AND ACHIEVEMENT?

There are important school achievement differences between boys and girls, although over the last few years the gap has been closing. Among major concerns are the disproportionate number of males that are placed in special educational settings, and the differential in achievement levels between girls and boys in language, mathematics and science (particularly the physical sciences) (Barro & Lee, 2013; Breen et al., 2010; Hawke et al., 2009; Voyer & Voyer, 2014).

While there are no sex differences in general intelligence, as measured by standard intelligence tests such as the Stanford–Binet or the WAIS-III, there are differences on many subsets of these tests that reflect the differences in achievement levels mentioned above. The most frequently cited difference between males and females is the ability to transform a visual–spatial image in working memory. In general, males perform better on these types of tasks (Kaufman, 2007). These spatial differences between males and females appear early in life and so seem to be more genetically than environmentally influenced. Males also appear to be better in tests of mathematical and scientific ability although females appear to do better in classrooms and grades (Halpern et al., 2007; Spelke, 2005). This is probably related to the visual–spatial strengths of males.

There are a large number of other explanations for gender differences in mathematics and science, including: stereotyping of mathematics and science which encourages different responses from boys, girls, and their teachers (Cvencek et al., 2011; Kiefer & Sekaquaptewa, 2007); lack of interest and salience of mathematics and science for girls (Miller et al., 2006; Shapiro & Williams, 2012). On the other hand, girls appear to have higher levels of ability on a variety of memory tasks such as word recall.

The differences between males and females appear to be strongest in the higher ranges of ability with little differences in the average range (Preckel et al., 2008). Halpern (2013) makes the interesting point that many of the sex differences found in the laboratory are mirrored in the real world. For example, when males and females give directions, males are more likely to use north-south-east-west directions, and are more accurate with these relational strategies. Women, on the other hand, are more likely to use landmarks and left-right directions.

What do your personal experiences suggest?

 ACTIVITY POST

Consider your experiences as a learner, both at school and at university. What examples can you give of learning through behavioural and social cognitive approaches? What application do you think each has in classrooms with which you are familiar? Compare these two perspectives with information processing theory and the theories of Piaget and Vygotsky.

Generate a chart on effective teaching and learning which incorporates perspectives drawn from each of the theories. Compare your chart with that of other students.

ACTIVITY POST

Apart from potential genetic reasons for the difference in performance between males and females on a range of cognitive tasks what other reasons might be possible? You might like to consider issues such as socialisation, teacher expectations, social opportunities and value systems, employment opportunities, peer group influences, learning styles, gender stereotyped curricula, psychobiosocial influences (such as prenatal hormones). The Internet should give you considerable information on each of these potential influences. How would you regulate schooling so that differences between males and females on cognitive functioning was minimised?

CHAPTER 7

Conceptions of intelligence and creativity in childhood and adolescence

Introduction

As we have seen in Chapters 5 and 6 Piagetian theory holds that a child's capacity to reason at various levels is biologically linked, develops in stages, and results from processes of adaptation, assimilation, and accommodation. Piaget was not concerned with individual differences in mental capacity as such, his theory most emphasises the need for each individual to develop their mental capacity through appropriate experiences.

Vygotsky's theory does not consider stages of cognitive development but emphasises the social dimensions of learning and the zone of proximal development as children grow older and become more embedded in their cultural knowledge. Hence, Vygotsky's focus moves beyond what the child currently knows to what is possible, and to the processes most relevant to stimulate this growth. Because of the very strong social and cultural components of Vygotskyian thought, what is considered 'intelligent' behaviour is more broadly viewed than simply being good at school and having a lot of 'knowledge'.

In this chapter we consider the psychometric appoach to intelligence. The psychometric approach is quite different from Piagetian and Vygotskian perspectives as the emphasis is one of measuring the intellectual capacity of individuals relative to others of the same age. It seeks to define and quantify dimensions of intelligence, primarily through the collection of data on individual differences and through the construction of reliable and valid mental tests (Chamorro-Premuzic, 2011; Chamorro-Premuzic & Furnham, 2008; Furnham et al., 2005). There is no attention given to the processes by which children become 'intelligent' which is the focus of both Piaget and Vygotsky.

We also discuss some alternative theories that describe intelligence as multifaceted and finally we consider giftedness and creativity and relate these personal characteristics to conceptions of intellignece and intelligent behaviour. The following website provides further information on key themes covered in this chapter: http://intelltheory.com/index.shtml

Psychometrics and intelligence

While the issues of importance to Piaget related to the nature of, when, and how individuals acquired increasingly sophisticated capacities for thinking, and Vygotsky was most interested in the issue of the social construction of learning and the role it plays in individuals developing as thinkers and knowers, the issues of importance in the psychometric approach relate to designing measurements of intellectual capacity and whether such measurements can be used to predict later intellectual performance. The psychometric approach is also concerned with meaningfully comparing the intelligence of individuals, what factors make up intelligence, and whether these factors change with age? (De Ribaupierre & Lecerf, 2006; Shayer, 2008).

 QUESTION POINT

At this point it is useful to ask yourself to define intelligence. What do you understand by intelligence? How is it demonstrated? How does it develop? What is intelligent behaviour related to?

The mental testing movement, and the concept mental age in particular, stems from the early work of Alfred Binet (1867–1911) and Theophile Simon (1872–1961) in France early last century, when they were given the task of devising a means of distinguishing between children who were retarded and unable to learn and those who could benefit from education and had a capacity to learn (Mackintosh & Mackintosh, 2011). These early psychometricians started with the premise that if children had equal opportunities to learn, those children at a given age who could demonstrate more skills or knew more information, or were better able to solve problems than other children of the same age were showing a greater intellectual ability. From this premise they designed a series of tasks for children to complete which would measure their intellectual capacity relative to others. We deal with elements of the test in further detail below.

The Binet and Simon intelligence test was the forerunner of a whole host of tests that set out to discriminate various levels of intellectual functioning (Sternberg, 2012a). The term intelligence test was an unfortunate one, and still is, as there is no clear definition of what is meant by the concept intelligence. As a result, writers of intelligence tests tend to construct them in line with what they consider the nature of intelligence to be.

One and two factor theories of intelligence

Sometimes intelligence is conceptualised as a unitary construct, in other words if one is bright in one area, then one has the potential to be bright in all areas (see, for example, Sternberg, 2012b). Charles Spearman (1863–1945) was one of the early English pioneers of the psychometric approach to intelligence. He proposed a two-factor theory in which a general factor of intelligence (or *g*) guided performance on mental tests, but that this general capacity was reflected through specific abilities differentially (Spearman, 1927). Hence, although a person might demonstrate different capacities for mental tasks such as maths and English, overall general performance should be consistent. In other words, it should be unlikely to have an individual with a very high level of ability in maths and a very low level of ability in English, or vice versa.

 QUESTION POINT

Do you think that intelligence is an overall capacity which is demonstrated in every activity an individual is involved in or specific to particular areas of behaviour? Give reasons for and examples to substantiate your answer.

Primary mental abilities

It is apparent that individuals do not appear to be equally able or 'intelligent' in all areas of their behaviour hence explaining intelligence as a single or unitary construct, or as a one-factor view, does not seem to explain intelligence very well. In order to explain the obvious differences in performance of individuals across a number of cognitive areas L. L. Thurstone (1887–1955), one of the early American pioneers of the psychometric approach to intelligence, proposed that intelligence consisted of a number of factors, which he called **Primary Mental Abilities** (Thurstone, 1938). These primary mental abilities are verbal meaning, number facility, inductive reasoning, perceptual speed, spatial relations, memory, and verbal fluency. Many tests today are based on these conceptualisations of discrete mental abilities.

Guilford's structure of the intellect

Probably the most extreme case of considering intelligence as multi-faceted is J. P. Guilford's structure of the intellect model (1967). Building on Thurstone's approach, Guilford (1897–1987) proposed that performance on any cognitive task can best be understood by analysing the task into the kind of mental operations to be performed, the type of content or test material on which the mental operation is performed, and the resulting product of performing the particular operation on a particular type of content. Guilford considered five possible kinds of operation, four types of content and six products. These are shown in Table 7.1 and Figure 7.1.

Each of these facets potentially interacts resulting in a particular demonstration of intelligence. In fact, there were exactly 120 factors comprising the structure of intelligence in this original model (5 operations × 4 contents × 6 products). Changes have been made to the model increasing the number of factors to 180 with the figural stimulus content being replaced by auditory and visual stimulus contents, and memory being replaced by memory recording and memory retention (Guildford, 1977; Sternberg, 2012a). The research evidence supporting the model is weak and it has declined in influence over the last few years (Batey & Furnham, 2006; Reeve & Bonaccio, 2011). Nevertheless, the structure of the model suggests some interesting implications for educational use, and we will follow one of these up in our later

Table 7.1 Guildford's structure of the intellect model		
Operations	**Content**	**Product**
Evaluation	Behavioural	Implications
Convergent thinking	Semantic	Transformations
Divergent thinking	Symbolic	Systems
Memory	Figural	Relations
Cognition		Classes
		Units

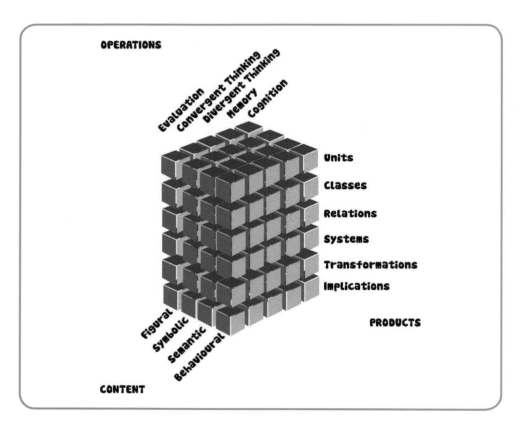

Figure 7.1   Guildford's Model of Intelligence.

discussion of creativity. There are also some links between Guilford's structure of the intellect and the 'Frames of Mind' proposed by Howard Gardner. After reading about Gardner's theory you might like to consider what potential links lie between the two theories.

QUESTION POINT

What do you see as the advantages of such a multifaceted view of intelligence?
What are the disadvantages?

Gardner's 'Frames of Mind'

A contemporary multifaceted view of intelligence is put forward by Howard Gardner in his book Frames of Mind (1983). Gardner argues that there are seven relatively autonomous human intellectual competences, which he calls human intelligences, or frames of the mind. These 'multiple intelligences' are relatively independent of one another, and are fashioned and combined in a multiplicity of adaptive ways by individuals and cultures to produce intelligent behaviour (Gardner, 1983). His theory stems from his beliefs that intelligence should not be reduced to a homogeneous mental construct as in early one- and two-factor theories of intelligence. He also believes that historical and contemporary conceptualisations of intelligence measured by simplistic tests fail to pay sufficient attention to problem solving as it is displayed in the real world characterised by social and cultural diversity.

Gardner believes that intellectual competence entails a set of skills of problem solving that enable individuals to resolve genuine problems or difficulties, and when appropriate, to create an effective product. Gardner also believes that intelligent behaviour must entail the potential for finding or creating problems, thereby laying the groundwork for the acquisition of new knowledge. Intelligent behaviour can be demonstrated in many different ways. The ways in which intelligences are demonstrated reflects a response to the cultural context of the individual and group (Emery et al., 2007; Ng & Earley, 2006). Gardner's theory makes it clear that intelligence in its many facets reflects potentials that must be fostered in the environment. They will not develop fully without stimulation, encouragement, and extensive practice.

Multiple intelligences

Gardner (1983) originally proposed seven intelligences. These are: logical-mathematical, linguistic, musical, spatial, bodily-kinaesthetic, interpersonal, and intrapersonal. These seven were only considered as tentative, and later he proposed an additional three intelligences: naturalist, spiritual, and existential (Gardner, 1999). Each intelligence is characterised by core components such as sensitivity to the sounds, rhythms, meanings of words (linguistic), and capacities to discern and respond appropriately to the moods, temperaments, motivations, and desires of other people (interpersonal). Although few occupations rely entirely on a single intelligence, an individual with a

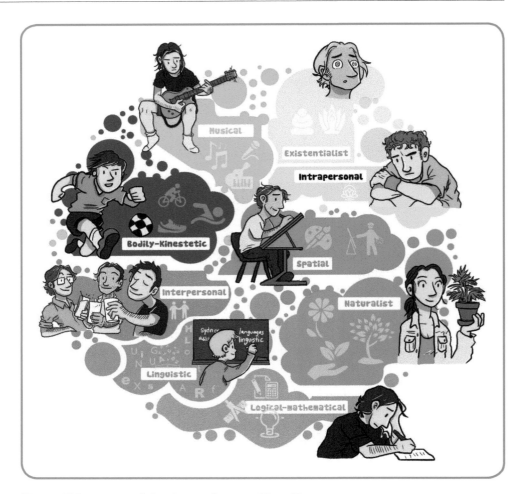

Figure 7.2   Howard Gardner's theory of intelligence.

highly developed intelligence in one of these areas may become a composer (musical), a dancer (bodily-kinaesthetic), or a therapist (interpersonal). Other occupations might require a blend of intelligences (Davis et al., 2011; Shearer & Luzzo, 2009). A surgeon, for example, needs both the acuity of spatial intelligence to guide the scalpel and the dexterity of the bodily-kinaesthetic intelligence to handle it.

Educational implications of multiple intelligences

In most schools there is an emphasis on developing (and measuring) verbal and mathematical behaviour as the core indicators of intelligence. Gardner's theory widens our view of what might comprise intelligent behaviour, and in particular draws attention to the fact that schools should emphasise a broader range of intelligent behaviours. Gardner believes that the assessment of intelligence should no longer be limited

Table 7.2	Gardner's multiple intelligences	
Intelligence	**Core component**	**Career focus**
Logical-mathematical	An ability for numbers, mathematical reasoning, and problem solving	Scientist Mathematician
Linguistic	An ability for language, arts, speaking, writing, reading, and listening	Poet Journalist
Musical	An ability for songs, rhythms, instruments, and musical expression	Composer Musician
Spatial	An ability for learning visually and organising things spatially	Sculptor Architect
Bodily-kinaesthetic	An ability for physical coordination and activity	Dancer Choreographer
Interpersonal	An ability for responding to the emotional states of others and being people-orientated	Counsellor Salesperson
Intrapersonal	An ability for monitoring one's own emotional and physical states	Counsellor Investor
Naturalist	An ability for understanding and relating to the plant and animal world	Farmer Botanist
Spiritual and existentialist	An ability for philosophical and reflective thought	Philosopher Priest

to the simplistic pen and paper (or individual) tests described in the next section of the chapter. Tests of intelligence must be designed which tap into the range of intelligences in culturally relevant ways. The following websites provide further information on multiple intelligences: http://multipleintelligencetheory.co.uk/, http://infed.org/mobi/howard-gardner-multiple-intelligences-and-education/ and http://thesecondprinciple.com/optimal-learning/multiple-intelligence-indicators/

Psychometric approaches to cognitive measurement

Intelligence testing

As we indicated earlier in the chapter, Binet and Simon were the designers of the original intelligence test that has become the basis of intelligence testing generally (see, for example, Fancher & Rutherford, 2012).

One of Binet's basic assumptions was that a person should be thought of as having normal intelligence if he or she can do the things persons of his or her age normally do, below average if performance corresponds to the performance of persons younger than the subject, and accelerated if the performance exceeds that of persons in the subject's own age group. This notion that we can relate an individual's intellectual performance to what is the norm for particular age groups is referred to as the **mental age** of a person. Mental age is judged by comparing the intelligence-test items that a child answers correctly with the average age at which children answer those items correctly. Thus, if a 6-year-old child has a mental age of seven, he is performing as well as the average child whose actual chronological age is seven. Later William Stern (1871–1938), a German psychologist, conceived of the intelligence quotient, which is the ratio of mental age to chronological age multiplied by 100.

$$\text{Intelligence Quotient} = \frac{\text{Mental Age}}{\text{Chronological Age}} \times 100$$

It can be seen, therefore that if a child had an IQ of 100, then performance is average for a child of this age. As the IQ rises above 100 the child is increasingly superior to other children at that age, and as it drops below 100, the child is doing relatively less well than his or her peers. An adjustment was later made to convert the units to standard scores so that IQ's across various age groups were comparable in meaning.

Key principles of the Binet-Simon test

Three general principles underlie this approach to assessing intelligence. First, it is believed that general intelligence is a trait that develops with age; second, that performance in the form of demonstrating skills is, in effect, assessing an underlying capacity to learn; and third, what has been learnt in the past is a measure of what could be learnt in the future. There is no attempt to measure separate mental faculties at work, such as memory, attention, sensory discrimination, and so on. The intention in the Binet-Simon test was to measure general intelligence at work through sampling various types of mental activities such as comprehension, vocabulary, logical reasoning through analogies, opposites, similarities and differences, verbal and pictorial completions, absurdities, drawing designs, and memory for meaningful material and for digits. The test was individually administered and consisted of a series of questions and activities chosen because they were representative of levels of knowledge and abilities at particular ages. The Binet-Simon test later became known as the Stanford-Binet after it was revised a number of times at Stanford University. The latest revision was completed in 2003 (Janzen et al., 2004; Roid, 2003). As well as assessing verbal ability the revised test includes tests of quantitative skill, spatial reasoning, and short-term memory.

Wechsler tests

Individual tests, such as the Wechsler Tests of Intelligence measure independent subscales of intelligence, such as verbal scales and performance scales, as well as obtaining an overall intelligence score. What make these scales different are their measurement of performance as well as verbal and mathematical reasoning. David Wechsler (1896–1981), a psychologist at Bellevue Hospital in New York, worked with children and adults afflicted with various forms of mental illnesses. Considering tests such as the Binet-Simon test inadequate because they were verbally and academically biased, Wechsler set about constructing a test that took more account of intellectual potential in relation to experience, motivation, and personality factors, on the rationale that emotional factors may heighten attention, persistence, and adaptability, or they may impair ability to mobilise intellectual resources. The Wechsler scales were initially intended to assess the intellectual skills of older adolescents and adults and named Wechsler Adult Intelligence Scale (WAIS). The most recent, fourth edition (WAIS-IV) was published in 2008 (Wechsler, 2008). There have been two extensions of the original scale for use with younger children (Kaplan & Saccuzzo, 2013). These are the Wechsler Intelligence Scale for Children (WISC), now in its fourth edition (Wechsler, 2004) designed for use with children aged between 6 and 16 years of age and the Wechsler Preschool and Primary Scale (WPPSI) designed for use with children aged 2 to 7 years of age and now in the third edition (Wechsler, 2002). The Wechsler tests have considerable clinical value. The tests also show up patterns presented by certain psychotic groups and some patterns of brain damage. These tests have been used in the UK and other counties, including Australia and New Zealand, with a number of small changes to a few items.

 QUESTION POINT

Wechsler believed that experience, motivation, and personality factors influenced how intelligently an individual behaves. What evidence do you think there is for this assertion? Obtain a copy of the Stanford-Binet and a Wechsler test (if you are school based, ask your Special Educational Need Coordinator or your school's Educational Psychologist, if you are University based, ask your tutors). What are the similarities? What are the differences?

Sternberg's triarchic theory of intelligence

Wechsler was concerned that the Stanford-Binet test did not measure practical intelligence. Related to this is Robert Sternberg's notion of successful intelligence (Sternberg, 1985, 1997). While Sternberg did not develop an intelligence test as such, his theory of intelligence has spawned a number of instruments to measure successful intelligence and the three components of intelligence.

For Sternberg (1998a, 1998b, 2003), '**successful intelligence**' is defined as that set of mental abilities used to achieve one's goals in life. These skills enable individuals to adapt to, select aspects of, or shape their given environments so that they achieve their goals. Successful intelligence involves three interrelated, but distinct, aspects of thinking: analytical, also called **componential intelligence**; creative, also called **experiential intelligence**; and practical thinking, also known as **contextual intelligence**.

- *Componential intelligence* – ability to acquire knowledge, think and plan, monitor cognitive processes and determine what is to be done;
- *Experiential intelligence* – ability to formulate new ideas to solve problems;
- *Contextual intelligence* – ability to adapt to contexts to optimise opportunities.

As these three intelligences govern intelligent behaviour, the theory has been called a **triarchic theory**. Sternberg believes that, if these modes of thinking are infused in everyday teaching and learning, the achievement of students will be enhanced. He also believes that this will provide a good basis for successful everyday living (Sternberg & Grigorenko, 1997; Sternberg et al., 1998).

 ACTIVITY POST

Design an intelligence test that incorporates measures of componential, experiential, and contextual intelligence. Compare your intelligence test with those of other students. Compile a combined intelligence test which incorporates the best features of individually designed tests. Write a rationale for its use. What do you think are the implications of Sternberg's theory for the classroom?

Group tests of intelligence

There are some major drawbacks in using individual intelligence tests such as the Stanford-Binet and the Wechsler tests. They are time consuming, expensive, and require expert administration and analysis. Because of this they are most used by psychologists or psychiatrists in clinical situations for diagnostic purposes. In order to make intelligence tests cheap and easy to administer *group tests of intelligence* (often called pen and paper tests) were developed. Naturally while making testing speedy and cheap, these tests had to retain accuracy and predictive validity so considerable work goes into their development and validation. Group tests were developed originally during World War I in order to select servicemen for various levels of duty (Rogelberg, 2006). Among common group tests used in the UK are the British Ability Scales (BAS) and the Cognitive Abilities Test (CAT), as well as the UK version of the abovementioned Weschler scales. BIS was originally published in 1979 and is currently in the third edition (Elliot & Smith, 2011) with separate versions for children aged 3 to 8 years of age and 6 to 17 years of age. The fourth version of the CAT was published in 2012 and has seven different versions aimed at specific age ranges anywhere between 6 to 17 years. These tests are typically used by schools to track and monitor the progress of students, group students into ability differentiated classes, and create expected scores for GCSEs and A levels (as well as Scottish lower and higher examinations). Increasingly, psychological tests, such as intelligence and personality tests, are being made available through the Internet with many paper and pencil tests being adapted to completion on computer (Bartram, 2006; Weigold, et al., 2013).

Historically, group tests were used extensively in the UK and other parts of the world to stream students into different levels or types of schooling and for work placement. For instance, the decision whether children with intellectual disability should attend a mainstream or special school was based partly on the results of IQ tests (Farrell, 2010). However, from the 1970s onwards there has been a movement away from this so-called 'deficit model' towards using IQ and ability tests as ways to predict and monitor student progress, and to establish whether particular schools, or teachers, were adding value over and above what would be expected from their IQ or ability scores (Deary et al., 2007).

What do intelligence tests measure?

What the original Binet-Simon intelligence test measured (and other tests following in its footsteps) was actual acquired learning and knowledge. This learning is then used as an index as to what might be expected from the individual in the future. As such these tests have always correlated very highly with each other and academic performance at school, and have been reliable guides as to what an individual might achieve at school, if, and this is important, schools emphasise, as the primary goal of schooling, the acquisition of knowledge in the form of facts and figures, and the development of particular reasoning skills.

 QUESTION POINT

What do you think Howard Gardner would think of convergent intelligence tests? Do you think intelligence tests should be used to stream students into various levels of schooling? If so, why? If not, why?

The notion of what constitutes intelligence in the tests described above is limited to what the test developers define as intelligent cognition and behaviour. It excludes other very valuable forms of expressing intelligent behaviour, such as through creativity, social skills, and physical performance (refer to the earlier section on multiple intelligences). As these tests are based upon having children relate to material they learnt in the past, and are presented in English, they take little account of children who may have had atypical learning experiences such as living in an isolated community or using a non-English first language, therefore, poorly preparing them to achieve in such tests. Personality characteristics are also not well accounted for in group tests, so that a person's score may well reflect his or her concern with diligence or getting the answer right, rather than speed to get as many questions right as possible (many tests have speed of completion as an important criterion of performance).

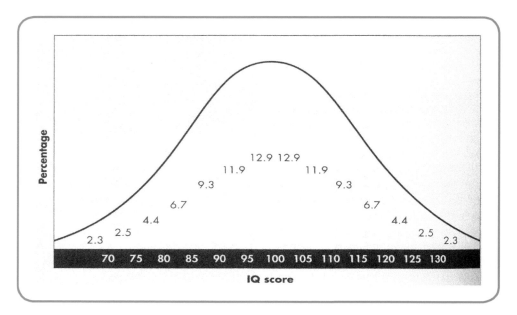

Figure 7.3   **IQ score distributions.**

Non-verbal intelligence tests

To alleviate the language bias inherent in verbal tests a number of non-verbal tests have been designed which measure intelligence through activities such as pattern completion (Raven Progressive Matrices), pictures and diagrams (ACER Junior Non-Verbal Test, Jenkins Intermediate Non-verbal Test, Peabody Picture Vocabulary Test PPVT, Tests of General Ability TOGA), and drawing (Goodenough-Harris Drawing Test). Test writers have also given their attention to developing culture-fair tests and the Raven Progressive Matrices and the Culture Fair Intelligence Test are examples of these. However, whether a truly culture-free and unbiased test can ever be developed is open to further investigation (see, for example, Ardila, 2005; Gipps, 1999; also http://communication.ucsd.edu/MCA/Paper/Cole/iq.html).

Variables that may influence IQ

A fairly large store of confidence is put in intelligence test scores so it is important to consider some of the variables that may influence the accuracy of IQ scores. Among these variables are the following:

1 Different tests measure different attributes, e.g. verbal, motor, perceptual, abstract reasoning, and so on. Intelligence tests seldom tap interpersonal skills, athletic abilities, creativity, and a variety of other desirable human attributes.
2 There may be cultural and social factors operating which influence a person's performance on IQ tests. Harry & Klingner (2006) argue against the use of norm-referenced ability testing with any educational minority group. They argue

that performance estimates based on these tests can be influenced by situational factors, especially schooling, and that there are inherent cultural biases in content and language used which make the tests highly unsuitable.

3   Test norms become quickly dated and unreliable and hence may give a skewed measure of an individual's or groups' intelligence.

4   Individual motivation at the time of sitting for a test may affect the score. Motivation during a test may be influenced by a whole host of issues.

There are also a number of potential factors affecting motivation on intelligence tests. We list a number of these below:

- Parental pressure (you must do well to get into a good high school).
- Positive or negative school experiences (I don't like this school and I'll show them what I think by not bothering about the test).
- Peer affiliations ('too cool for school' – it's not good to be seen doing too well at school).
- Rapport with teachers and testers (I'll try my hardest for my teacher).
- The educational policy of the school (some schools emphasise competition, grading, ability grouping more than others).
- Physical conditions (I don't feel well, or it's a hot stuffy day).
- Personality of the child (test or general anxiety, impulsiveness, persistence, conformity).

An IQ score therefore, may reflect the effect of all the other factors operating on a child at the time of the testing, and the extent to which individuals are consciously acquainted with the rules and procedures of test taking (this is particularly important if the test is being used with groups not used to taking such tests, such as children from immigrant families where IQ tests are not widely used). In the long term any marked changes in an individual's physical or emotional environment, such as moving from the country to the city, losing a parent, or divorce, may result in a change in intellectual performance.

Because of these variables it is dangerous to assume that a child with a high IQ will necessarily perform well, while a child with a low IQ will perform poorly. IQ scores should be used as a guide only. Teachers should primarily consider the individual's ability as demonstrated in class rather than what an IQ score might lead us to expect. IQ scores, to be of much use, should be continually updated, and results from a range of tests should be taken into account.

1   *General information:* These questions relate to a range of information – for example, 'How many hands do you have?' and 'How many pence make up a pound?'

2   *Comprehension:* These questions test practical information and the ability to evaluate past experience – for example, 'What do you do when you cut your foot?' and 'Why do we keep money in the bank?'

3   *Mathematics:* These questions test arithmetical reasoning – for example, eight blocks are placed in a row before the student and they are asked to 'count these blocks with your finger' and 'If 14 apples weigh 4kg, how much do 21 weigh?'

4   *Similarities:* These questions ask in what way certain objects or concepts are similar; measures abstract thinking – for example, 'What is the relation between a piano and a violin?'

5 *Vocabulary:* These questions test word knowledge – for example, 'What is the meaning of knife, table, ... dilatory?'

6 *Digit span:* These questions test attention and memory span by presenting a series of digits auditorily which the individual has to repeat either forwards or backwards.

The following questions are examples of six subtests similar to those in the various Wechsler intelligence scales:

SPOTLIGHT ON EXAMPLES OF GROUP TESTS OF INTELLIGENCE

Group tests of intelligence are often designed to measure individuals' general intelligence as revealed by their performance on verbal and numerical questions. Items are generally arranged in ascending order of difficulty and may include analogies, classifications, synonyms, number and letter series, and questions involving arithmetical and verbal reasoning. These tests are usually timed and typically say:

> This is a test to see how well you can think. It contains questions of different kinds. Some examples and practice questions will be given to show you how to answer the questions.

This is then followed by instructions such as:

> Try each question as you come to it but if you find any question too hard, leave it out and come back later if you have time. Do not spend too much time on any one question. Try to get as many right as possible.

Questions are then asked similar to the following:

1 Foot is to man as claw is to
   1. dog   2. horse   3. lion
   4. cat   5. bird   ( )

2 Book is to library as animal is to?
   1. beach   2. boat   3. house
   4. zoo   ( )

3 What is the next number in this series?
   2, 4, 6, 8, 10 ( )

4 What is the next number in this series?
   1, 5, 2, 5, 3, 5, 4, 5   ( )

5 What group of letters comes next in this series?
   AA, BB, CC, DD   ( )

6 What group of letters come next in this series?
   AC, BD, CE, DF   ( )

7 Four of the following words are alike – what is the other word?
   1. coat   2. shirt   3. singlet
   4. sweater 5. socks   ( )

8 Four of the following words are alike. What is the other word?
   1. laugh   2. giggle   3. chuckle
   4. smirk   5. cry   ( )

9 Large means:
   1. cold   2. big   3. short
   4. funny   5. small

Is Intelligence increasing?

Intelligence levels as measured across the general population appear to be increasing by about 3 IQ points per decade, despite the fact that tests are renormed periodically to adjust for increasing test sophistication (Flynn 2007; Nisbett et al., 2012; Rushton & Jensen, 2010). This is often termed the 'Flynn effect' after James Flynn who has published numerous studies on this apparent increase. What is particularly interesting is that the gains appear greatest on tests that were designed to be free of cultural bias such as the Raven Progressive Matrices. A further interesting aspect of this phenomenon is the lack of relationship between increasing levels of intelligence as measured by intelligence tests and actual school or academic performance, which has not, in general, improved.

 QUESTION POINT

What reasons would you give for the apparent increase in measured intelligence across generations? Do you think people are really becoming more intelligent? In answering this question consider different conceptions of intelligence such as one-factor theories, Guilford's model, and Gardner's Multiple Intelligences.

Three explanations have been given to account for the apparent increase in intelligence across generations. Most people's daily lives have become more complex through exposure to much more information. The many forms of mass media and technology, extended and more sophisticated schooling, and the array of new and ever changing experiences to which people are exposed, may have produced corresponding changes in complexity of mind and in certain psychometric abilities. We have seen in Chapters 3 and 4 that a secular trend in physical development has been attributed to improvements in nutrition. Perhaps improvements in nutrition also contribute to increases in mental functioning. Perhaps brain size is also increasing and affecting intellectual functioning. Lastly, some argue that intelligence as such has not risen but, rather, one aspect of thinking is improving, that of abstract problem solving. This improvement in abstract thinking may be the result of greater exposure of individuals to opportunities to use abstract thought in their everyday lives. As abstract thinking is a major component of IQ testing it is plausible that people will increasingly perform better on this dimension of thinking.

 QUESTION POINT

Consider these three reasons. Do these reflect what you considered as potential factors? What extra reasons did you give?

SPOTLIGHT ON EMOTIONAL INTELLIGENCE

A popular area of interest at the moment is emotional intelligence (Mayer et al., 2008a; Mayer et al., 2008b; Salovey & Grewal, 2005). Emotional intelligence became popularised through a number of articles in the popular press such as *Time* magazine (see Goleman, 1995), and has had an impact on educational policy development in the United States in particular (Ecclestone, 2007; Elias, 2009). Emotional intelligence is defined as the capacity to process emotional information accurately and efficiently, including the capacity to perceive, assimilate, understand, and manage emotion. *Perceiving emotions* involves paying attention to and recognising feelings; *integrating emotion in thought* involves using personal emotions in thought and communication; *understanding emotions* involves reasoning with feelings; and *managing emotions* involves coordinating with the other elements to produce behaviour that is balanced (Mayer et al., 2011). In the last 15 years, there has been a considerable deal of research conducted into emotional intelligence. Some key findings show that children with higher

emotional intelligence have better social skills, friendships, and generally do better at school. However, there are debates over whether emotional intelligence should be considered as a set of specific skills, such as understanding social relationships and managing ones emotions, or whether it consists of a more eclectic mix of traits, such as happiness, self-esteem, and optimism. This diversity in the definition makes it difficult to make clear judgements about the independence of emotional intelligence in contributing to effective or ineffective behaviour over and above personal characteristics and lead some to question whether the concept of emotional intelligence is theoretically sound (Locke, 2005).

Do a search on the Internet and locate the most recent research on emotional intelligence. What does the research say? Based on your findings what is your view of emotional intelligence? Do you think it is a useful concept for teachers and educators? You might find the following website useful: http://helpguide.org/articles/emotional-health/emotional-intelligence-eq.htm

Creativity

In our discussion of intelligence tests above it is obvious that they are very convergent in nature. In other words, they are designed so that there is usually one and only one right answer to a question, if you answer divergently then you will not get a score on that question. But is there a place for different answers and solutions, and what is the relationship between divergent thinking and measures of intelligence that usually require convergent thinking?

The nature of creativity

As with intelligence, there is no agreed upon definition of creativity. As Runco says:

> *Creativity is ... a slippery concept. It takes many forms in different domains, for example, and at different points in the lifespan. It appears that different paths can lead to creative work; none of them is always necessary or always guarantees creative results. Those studying creativity capture these variations by defining creativity as a 'complex' or syndrome. But briefly, creativity is a blend of cognitive, metacognitive, emotional, and motivational components.*

(2005, p. 609)

Some definitions of creativity emphasise personality characteristics, while others focus on the process of thought. Still others emphasise the product of effort as the criterion of creativity (Batey & Furnham, 2006; Beghatto, 2009; Beghetto & Kaufman, 2007; Kaufman et al., 2010; Kaufman & Beghetto, 2009; Runco, 2005; Silvia et al., 2012). Let's look at each of these in turn.

Personality characteristics

Stereotypes abound regarding the personality characteristics of creative people. They are often thought to be bohemian, aloof, amoral, strange, and so on. Indeed, personality characteristics have been one of the most researched areas in the study of creativity. A review of the literature describing creative people came up with the list of descriptions shown in Table 7.3.

As you can see there is quite a variety. One of the early researchers into creativity, Paul Torrance (1962, 1988), found three characteristics that differentiate highly creative children from children who are less creative but equally intelligent. The creative children had a reputation among their peers for having 'wild' or 'silly' ideas, their work was outside the mould of what was anticipated, and it was characterised by humour, playfulness, lack of rigidity, and relaxation.

Since the mid 1980s most research into personality has focused on what are called the 'big-five' personality traits (McAdams & Pals, 2006). These are the five most stable elements of personality that differ between people: Openness, agreeableness, extroversion (or introversion), stability, and conscientiousness. A number of studies have found that various types of creativity (including divergent thinking and creative accomplishments) are more likely in people who are highly open to new experiences (Batey et al., 2010; Furnham & Bachtiar, 2008). People who are open to new experiences tend to be more imaginative, original, and curious in their thinking and these traits allow people to think in more divergent ways and work in ways that involve 'thinking outside of the box'.

The 'big-five' approach is not the only way to look at personality. Feist (2009) believes that social and motivational traits are important components of creativity. Creative

Table 7.3   Personality characteristics of creative people

Independent of spirit	Intuitive	Foolish
Fluent in suggesting solutions to problems	Aesthetic	Productive
Interprets questions flexibly	Unconventional	Inventive
Open to new experiences	Disruptive	Sees things in new ways
Extremely curious	Non-conformist	Highly observant
Non-judgemental	Eccentric	Spontaneous
Restless	Enthusiastic	Reserved
Introspective	Imaginative	Radical
Self-sufficient	Rebellious	Narcissistic
Aggressive	Independent	Accepting of unconventional
Tolerant of ambiguities	Appreciative of complexity	

(Andreasen, 2012; Batey & Furnham, 2006; Feist, 2009; Sung & Choi, 2009)

people are often highly confident in their abilities, and less conforming authoritative and conservative in their opinions and attitudes than others. Highly creative people are more inclined to question, doubt, and reject traditional values. Many creative people also have a strong desire to 'leave their mark on the world' and create a legacy. They can be extremely focused and ambitious. Although the stereotype of a creative person may be as an artist or musician, creative people can include scientists and business people as well as people in most walks in life. Creative people seem to be motivated by an intrinsic enjoyment in the work they are involved in, whether scientists or artists (Prabhu et al., 2008). What is clear from whichever approach to personality is taken, is that highly creative people seem to share and show different traits to others.

Creativity as a way of thinking

Creative thinking, sometimes called the 'small c' approach, involves a process and this process has been studied by a number of researchers (Runco, 2005). According to Abedi (2002) there are four characteristics of creative thinking: originality (discovering new ideas), flexibility (different ideas), elaboration (giving ideas detail), and fluency (the volume of ideas). Highly creative people could be said to have original, flexible, elaborate, and fluent ideas. Various techniques have been used to uncover elements of the creative process including retrospective self-disclosure by creative people, tracking through 'hard data' such as drafts of stories, paintings, and other compositions, psychological monitoring of the process while it is occurring, such as having people report on their thought during or right after a mental activity (Plucker & Makel, 2009). Each of these methods has its drawbacks.

Wallas (1921) described four stages in the creative process. Although these were described in the early part of the twentieth century, this approach is now considered classic and still used today in business and education to teach the creative process (Ames & Runco, 2005; Howard et al., 2008). The four stages are:

1 Preparation – Intense study of the problem at hand.
2 Incubation – A period of rest and reflection and engagement in an activity not related to the work under consideration.
3 Inspiration – The flash of insight that puts the various elements into their proper relationship
4 Verification – A period of intense, systematic work during which the poem is written down, and polished, the theory tested, or the machine built

A number of more contemporary conceptualisations of the creative process have similar stages. Amabile (1996) developed and elaborated on Wallas' four stages, and included a fifth and final stage of creative performance or product. Binnewies, Ohly and Sonnentag (2007) proposed five stages: Problem identification, preparation, idea generation, idea validation, and idea creativity. All five of these stages are influenced by personal initiative and the final four stages facilitated by idea-related communication. Similarly, Basadur and Gelade (2005) describe four creative phases: Idea generation, idea conceptualisation (understanding the problem or the context), idea optimising (a hypothetical solution is developed), and idea implementation (the idea is tested out).

 QUESTION POINT

We are all creative sometimes. Consider when you are at your most creative – what stages do you go through? You need to be somewhat introspective for this exercise as we do not normally think about how we are thinking. Compare your process to those described by other students.

Some authors have found stage descriptions of the creative process unconvincing (Gabora, 2002). Arnheim's analysis of Picasso's creation of Guernica (a famous depiction of the bombing of a Spanish village by the Nazi's prior to World War II) shows it evolving through several versions to its final form with the creative process characterised by an interplay of inferences, modifications, restrictions, and compensations leading gradually to the unity and complexity of the total composition. The work of art did not unfold straightforward as a seed growing, but appeared to grow in what looks like erratic leaps forward and backwards from the whole to the part and vice versa (Arnheim, 2007). While conceptually it is neat to think in terms of stages, in real situations these processes of creation are probably dynamic and interactive, and a combination of new ways of thinking about old ideas (Howard et al., 2008). Nevertheless, such typologies of the creative process discussed above are useful for teachers and parents in providing learning experiences that capitalise on and develop creative thinking processes. A number of techniques such as brainstorming and synectics that are designed to free individuals from inhibitions in thinking and making premature critical judgements, are based on these types of conceptualisations (Dennis et al., 2013; Rietzschel et al., 2006).

Some argue that there isn't any special creative thought process. One has to work hard at being creative. The thought processes used are those used for more conventional thinking, the difference lies in the focus of the question or problem. For instance, creative scientists quite deliberately seek out a problem that is a little off the side of the conventional topics or techniques of their colleagues. They're seeking the challenges, the interesting possibilities. In other words, creative individuals deploy their abilities in distinctive and flexible ways (Dunbar, 1997).

For Sternberg (2006) no single perspective on creativity is satisfying as an explanation and he attempts to integrate across the person and process perspectives by suggesting six ingredients of creativity, namely intellectual skills, knowledge, thinking styles, personality, motivation, and environment. Intellectual skills are required in order to see things in new ways and move beyond conventional ways on thinking, to judge which ideas are worth pursuing and which are not and to know how to persuade others of the value of one's ideas. Knowledge is important because in order to understand a new solution to a particular problem, one needs to understand the problem well. Sternberg, however, does acknowledge that entrenched knowledge can hinder as well as help creativity. A legislative thinking style is useful for creativity. This refers to a combination of deep thinking with the decision to think in new ways. Particular personality traits, such as openness to new experiences, described in the section above, can also assist creative thinking, and has to be accompanied by an intrinsic desire, or enjoyment, in one's endeavours to keep motivated. Finally, one has to be in an environment where creative ideas are valued and supported. Even if all the personal internal resources are in place (intelligent ability, knowledge of the problem, legislative thinking, openness to new experience, and intrinsic motivation) without the right environment person's creative capacity may never have the chance to shine.

 QUESTION POINT

Consider each of these qualities. How important are they to the creative process? How would you support these qualities in children in your classroom?

Creativity as a product

What makes a creative product, or the 'big C approach', is somewhat contentious. For example, as cited by Runco (2005), Picasso's painting was described in 1907 as 'the work of a madman' by Vollard, a highly reputable art dealer of the time. Some products achieve fame because general consensus holds that they are creative. We might list many famous paintings (but by no means all!), famous buildings (we would all list the St Paul's Cathedral, York Minster, the Westminster Abbey, or perhaps the 'Gherkin'), famous household appliances or aids (the Thermos Flask, the paper clip, and stapler). But once we move outside the area of general consensus it is extremely difficult to judge what is truly creative. Some could admire Jackson Pollock's 'Blue Poles' only to hear passers by comment how a class of pre-schoolers could have painted it. Conversely, others are not particularly impressed by Art Gallery collections that include modern art installations made up of crumpled garbage cans, collections of rocks (with a notice nearby saying 'please don't touch and move'), and large canvasses filled with various shades of white (called 'Illumination'). Other viewers may be gushing enthusiastically over the same pieces.

Despite the subjective element involved in making assessments of creative products creative products appear to be characterised by competence, originality, scope, and significance. Some believe that the best indication of whether a person is creative is his or her history of creative activities.

ACTIVITY POST

Select a contentious piece of art or sculpture (conduct an Internet search on Damien Hirst or Tracey Emin if you are not familiar with modern art). Debate with others in your group its artistic and creative merits. Use principles listed above in making your assessments. Was there consensus or disagreement? How would you evaluate the artistic merit of work produced by your students? The work might be verbal, written, drawn, acted, and so on.

The assessment of creativity

Earlier in the chapter we were concerned with the measurement of intelligence. Can creativity be measured? Tests have been designed to measure the creative personality, the creative process, and the creative product (Plucker & Makel, 2009).

Piffer (2012) considered three elements essential to assessing novelty, appropriateness, and impact. In ordinary language this means that creativity involves a fresh or innovative approach to solving a problem and seeing the task through to completion. These criteria underpin the tests of creativity that are used today.

J. P. Guilford (1950, 1987) who was discussed earlier in the context of intelligence, devised a series of tests of creative thinking based upon his model of intelligence, and which attempt to tie together the aspects of the creative process and creative person. The traits Guilford believes related to creativity are the ability to see problems, fluency of thinking (i.e. coming up with a lot of ideas)' originality (no-one else thinks of the idea), redefinition, and elaboration (describing the features of the solution in detail). Guilford believes that these elements may be measured through a series of tests:

1 Word fluency – Write words beginning with 'f' and ending with 't' (the divergent production of symbolic units).
2 Ideational fluency – List the obvious consequences of teachers going on strike for one year (the divergent production of semantic units).
3 Originality – Unusual and clever responses such as the consequences test: What would happen if everyone in the world doubled in size?
4 Spontaneous flexibility – Freedom from inertia in giving a diversity of ideas such as the uses test: How many uses of a newspaper can you think of? (The divergent production of semantic classes.)
5 Adaptive flexibility – The tricky problems test where solutions require ingenuity and unconventional responses. This involves lateral thinking that is seeing a number of possibilities and evaluating them.

Paul Torrance (1962, 1988), who has written extensively on creativity, believes that the creative process is characterised by fluency (that is a fertility of ideas), flexibility (that is the ability to abandon old ways of thinking while initiating new ones), originality (that is the ability to produce uncommon responses and unconventional associations between ideas), and elaboration (that is the capacity to use two or more abilities for the construction of a more complex object). His thoughts have also been reflected in a series of tests that are widely used today (Kim, 2006, 2011). Less formal means of assessing creativity may be through teacher's ratings of children, and pupils' ratings of each other (Hughes et al., 2013).

(?) QUESTION POINT

What do you think is the relationship between intelligence, as measured by intelligence tests, and creativity, as measured by creativity tests? Do you think creative people have to be intelligent?

The validity of creativity tests

Guilford, Torrance and others maintain that tests of creativity measure ability for creative thinking. However some authors believe that to the extent such test have time constraints, involve some level of anxiety (most tests generate some levels of anxiety in most people) and are conducted in an artificial atmosphere they really don't measure creativity as it occurs 'in the real world'. They believe that creativity only occurs in open, stress free situations, and basically the response made must be to a real life situation. Furthermore, to this point in time there is only limited evidence that creativity tests predict to creativity of individuals in later life (Piffer, 2012; Silvia et al., 2012).

Relationship of creativity to intelligence

In view of the fact that creativity and measured intelligence both involve cognitive processes, and in particular problem solving ability, it is reasonable to expect that they would be positively correlated. This relationship is confirmed by a number of studies (Batey & Furnham, 2006; Preckel et al., 2006; Silvia, 2008). However, in the higher ranges of IQ the relationship breaks down somewhat, i.e. you can have very high IQ students who are less creative, and very creative students who are less intelligent. Note however, that we are talking about the higher ranges, in other words they are individuals who are both creative and intelligent, but one or other talent is relatively superior.

8 Cognition and information processing in childhood and adolescence

Introduction

In earlier chapters we have considered how individuals develop cognitively. Part of cognitive development is the increasing capacity for individuals to manipulate and remember information. In this chapter we focus on **information processing theory** as a model for explaining cognition and human learning. We will explore the computer as an analogy for the learning process by examining the way in which information is attended to, encoded, processed, stored, and retrieved.

Results of information processing research apply in three areas of cognitive development and learning. First, information processing suggests that there are limits to the amount of information that learners can attend to and process effectively. This belief stems from the early work of the American psychologist George Miller (1920–2012), one of the founders of the field of cognitive psychology. He proposed that the human mind can only manipulate a limited amount of information at any one time, typically seven units of information, plus or minus two, sometimes referred to as the 'magical number seven' (Miller, 1956). If we overload our processing system, the working memory is unable to cope with the demands and processing becomes inefficient. More recent research suggests that processing capacity is more flexible and depends on a number of factors including the familiarity of the learner with the information, and whether the information is verbal or numerical (Cowan, 2010; Farrington, 2011).

Because of the limited processing capacity of the mind we present many ideas on how long and complex or new and potentially difficult information can be restructured so that mental demand is reduced. Such facilitation can be accomplished by emphasising procedures and activities that are directed towards schema acquisition (i.e. combining elements of information into fewer elements) and automation (i.e. skills for retrieval from long-term memory with less demand on the working memory).

The second finding from information processing research is that the learner needs to be actively engaged in processing the information in order to transfer it from the working memory to the long-term memory. This is referred to as learning for retention. In most theories of learning, active participation of the learner is considered essential.

The third implication from information processing research for learning is that learnt material should be encoded in such a way as to facilitate recall and facilitate transfer to new but related situations. Meaningful material is learnt more easily, retained more effectively, and recalled more efficiently than non-meaningful material. We discuss methods for enhancing meaningful learning later in the chapter.

All the principles of information processing described have application from the earliest years of cognitive development and learning through to old age. However, the neural systems that allow effective information processing to occur mature over time. Young children do not process information with the same facility as older children and adolescents. As children grow older there is an increase in short-term memory capacity and processing and encoding skills, an improvement in retrieval from long-term memory, and increasing development and use of cognitive strategies and self-monitoring meta-cognitive skills to enhance encoding, retention, and retrieval. These developments occur as children are exposed to novel learning experiences, particularly modelling by parents, teachers, and peers. At present it is not possible to say whether these changes reflect structural changes in the child's information processing capacity (akin to Piaget's changes across stages) or whether they are functional capacity changes as the child becomes more expert in cognitive strategy use (Schunk, 2008; Veenman et al., 2006).

To be an effective 'information processer' requires opportunity, experience, motivation, and practice. You will see how these principles apply as the information processing model of cognitive development and learning is described below.

Information processing

Information processing theory is a cognitive theory and, in a sense, attempts to 'look inside' the minds of learners to explore what happens when thinking and learning occurs. Its theoretical perspective focuses on the specific ways in which people mentally think about (process) the information they receive. It is probably the leading conceptual framework for the study of cognitive development and learning today (Kirschner et al., 2009; Steinberg, 2005; Van Merrienboer & Sweller, 2005). In its earliest forms information processing was relatively mechanistic, being based upon a computer analogy, which is described briefly below. The major focus of attention in these early conceptualisations was an examination of inputs, the mental processing of these inputs and the consequent outputs or outcomes, in terms of learned behaviours.

More recent information processing models are concerned with exploring the active involvement of the learner in these processes: how the learner selects, organises, and integrates incoming experience with existing knowledge, and the reconstrucive practices required to retrieve information (Karpicke, 2012; Karpicke & Blunt, 2011).

The information processing approach has challenged some of the fundamental premises of the Piagetian approach, particularly in regard to the mechanics of processing information by younger and older people (Barrouillet, 2011).

(?) QUESTION POINT

How does the information processing approach challenge premises of the Piagetian approach? Does it also challenge premises of the Vygotskian approach?

Cybernetics and information processing

Information processing theories had their origins in **cybernetics**. Cybernetics is the comparative study of the automatic control systems formed by the nervous system and brain and by mechanical–electrical communication systems. Information processing theories conceptualise the mind as a processing system in which knowledge is represented in the form of symbols, and processing is fundamentally symbol manipulation according to a set of mental rules.

Researchers use the information processing model of learning and memory to study how individuals learn, remember, and use the verbal and mathematical symbol systems necessary for communication. Insights gained from information processing theory and research have been enormously useful in understanding how effective learning takes place. Principles derived from this approach are commonly used to design learning experiences and resources for learners. Essential to our understanding of how information is cognitively manipulated are the four processes: *encoding, processing, storing,* and *retrieval*. We deal with these processes later in the chapter.

Information processing theory and computer models

Information processing scientists consider the human mind as a complex cognitive system analogous in some ways to a digital computer (Carandini, 2012; Litta et al., 2006; Sweller & Sweller, 2006). Like a computer, the system manipulates or processes information coming in from the environment or already stored within the system. It processes the information in a variety of ways: encoding, recoding, or decoding it; comparing or combining it with other information; storing it in memory or retrieving it from memory; bringing it into, or out of, focal attention or conscious awareness, and so on.

The ability of a computer to manipulate and process input depends on the quality of the computer software programme and the processing size of the central processing unit (CPU). We will see how these elements work below and then draw an analogy with the human memory processes.

In order to retain a permanent record of our work on the computer we need to save the file. This file may be stored in a variety of forms (e.g. hard drive, USB flash drive (also called thumb drives, pen drives, tokens), CD, or on the Cloud) and the quantity that can be stored depends on the capacity of the storage space. Today storage space is increasing astronomically. The amount of data that can be stored on even small devices like mobile phones far outstrips what even the most sophisticated computers could hold 15 years ago. Finally, having successfully processed the material and stored it, we need to be able to retrieve the file for printing or copying to other files.

These three processes are essential components of a computer's structure. If the information is not input correctly, if there is insufficient memory to process the information, if the information is not saved, or if the information cannot be retrieved then the computer has failed to process the information effectively.

QUESTION POINT

Consider your use of a computer. Can you recall times when any (or all) of these processes have not worked effectively? What were the effects of these malfunctions? How did you solve the problem?

The components of the human information processing system

As you can see, the computer is an integrated system and if any one component is malfunctioning or inefficient the system will be less effective. The computer analogy is actually quite a good model of one view of what happens conceptually when a person thinks and learns. Each of the components of the human information system are also integrated, and must function effectively for the system as a whole to be effective.

Sensory receptors, working memory, and long-term memory

Figure 8.1 presents the components of the human information processing system. The **sensory receptors** (such as our eyes, ears, touch, smell, and taste) are the senses through which we perceive external stimuli and record the memory for a very short period of time, perhaps less than half a second for vision, and about three seconds for hearing in sensory memory. Depending on an individual's orientation and attention, particular stimuli are selected for further processing in the working memory. The **working memory,** also referred to as the short-term memory, is that part of the person's mind that processes information, first in the short-term memory (which has limited capacity for registering the sensory input for processing by the working memory), and then through conscious and active rehearsal which manipulates the information. Only limited chunks of information can be worked on, and the information can only be stored for a brief period. In a sense, the working memory is the 'workpad' or 'jotter' of the mind (Baddeley, 2012; St Clair-Thompson & Gathercole, 2006), the place where the construction process occurs – that is, the place where incoming information makes contact with prior knowledge and the interaction between the two produces an interpretation of the incoming information (Morrison, 2005). As such, the working memory functions very much like the Random Access Memory (RAM) in a computer system (rather than the long-term storage of information in the hard drive or on a USB flash drive).

Long-term memory is the repository of stored information (Brown et al., 2007) and is very much like the hard drive or USB flash drive. The long-term memory is a permanent store of information and appears to be unlimited in capacity (unlike computer storage systems). Most of us, however, use only a limited amount of our capacity, and a lot of what is stored is irretrievable. At the end of processing, a response is performed

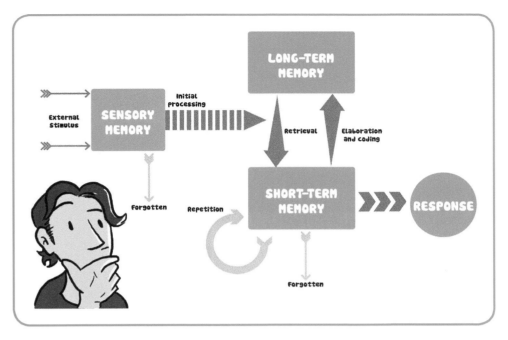

Figure 8.1   The human information processing system.

by the person's muscle systems on instruction from the working memory which calls up information from the long-term memory for enacting behaviour (akin to making a computer printout).

The information processing model is, therefore, very useful in helping us understand how cognitive tasks should be structured so that they are most easily perceived with attention, actively memorised, effectively stored, and retrieved, for future action by the learner.

For sensory input to be effective the senses must be fully operational. Just as a faulty keyboard will prevent the effective input of information to the computer, so the learner who cannot see or hear properly or who is poorly oriented to attend to appropriate stimuli will not be in a position to input information effectively into the working memory.

Sensory problems often become obvious during the early years of life and should be remediated as soon as possible in order that learning not be impeded (see Chapters 2 and 4). Simple examples of this are hearing and visual impairment. Remedial action may be as simple as moving students who cannot see or hear properly to the front of the room, or more intensive interventions such as the use of hearing aids and eyeglasses may be needed. With the mainstreaming of special needs students into regular classrooms, it is even more critical for teachers to pay attention to how well individual students can perceive and receive the sensory stimulation of the classroom. Very often, however, poor attention (or poorly focused attention) is the root cause of faulty input, and so teachers must always be aware of the need to orient students to attend to appropriate stimuli.

? QUESTION POINT

Consider the following websites: http://education.com/reference/article/information-processing-theory/ and http://edpsycinteractive.org/topics/cognition/infoproc.html. List the extra insights you had into information processing as a theory of learning. What elements can you apply to your teaching?

SPOTLIGHT ON PERCEPTION AND EFFECTIVE LEARNING

In order for the learner to attend to the correct cues or stimuli, salient features of the stimuli need to be prominent. Features that are attended to are referred to as *figure*, and background features are referred to as *ground*. Learners are continually distinguishing main figures from the background in order to perceive patterns accurately.

When Figure and Ground are ambiguous or not easily distinguishable, problems in interpretation occur. Examine Figure 8.2. What do you see? Some people instantly see an old woman, others instantly see a young woman. If you focus on the white, the white is the figure and the black the ground. If you focus on the black it is the figure. You cannot focus on both figure and ground at once, although you can fluctuate between making the white the figure and then the ground. Some people are so fixated on black as ground that they find it inordinately difficult to see the old woman. Conversely some people can only see the young woman. Visual illusions such as these are informative about

Figure 8.2   Figure and Ground.

fundamental perceptual processes involved in cognition and learning (Burge et al., 2010; Wagemans et al., 2012). Figure and ground can also be thought of as auditory concepts in which background noise is distinguished from salient auditory cues that are `structured for meaning. For example, coughing in a concert can become the focus of attention and distract the audience from the musical piece being played.

Figure 8.3   Figure and Ground in reading.

What do you see here? Do you see the word 'HELLO'? Or, a bunch of black splotches? Women are able to spot the word 'HELLO' easily. Men find it difficult to see the word 'HELLO'.

Distinguishing Figure from Ground has important implications for learning to read, doing mathematics, and other subjects. In reading, for example, if students focus on the white page as the figure and the black marks as background they will have great difficulty reading. Look at Figure 8.3. If you concentrate on the white what do you see? If you concentrate on the black what do you see. Drawing a line across both top and bottom of the figure will assist you in seeing a meaningful pattern.

For most students their teacher's lessons and questions are the main focus of their attention, and background noise stays in the background. If a student perceives the buzz of fluorescent lights, the hum of the heater or air conditioner or the shuffling of feet and papers as the figure, and the teacher's voice as background, learning will suffer. This often happens when the teacher is boring or dealing with overly difficult material. It also occurs when students are bored and tired. Small distractions can become the centre of attention.

Does everyone perceive things in the same way or is their perception grounded in the same experiences? It is clear that this is not the case. One person may focus on the 'bigger picture' and see an organising structure with many interrelationships between the various parts (or other stimuli). Others, however may focus on the fine detail and the individual parts. Just because one person perceives the world in a particular way does not mean that others have the same perception (Nicolaou & Xistouri, 2011). When explaining or introducing new objects, ideas, or concepts to children it is important to understand that not all children will perceive or understand them in the same way. It is important for the teacher to provide the right level of context to guide children's understanding and, where appropriate superimpose structure to allow children's understanding to develop.

In classrooms students' perceptions of the nature of a task may not include those critical features that teachers assume they are aware of. Furthermore, the knowledge structures that teachers assume students use while investigating scientific concepts, for example, may not be the ones actually used by students, usually because students lack the assumed prerequisite knowledge or are unable to grasp the mental set required. As if this were not enough, at the output level the students' perceptions relating to the significance of the task outcomes achieved may not be those the teacher assumes are perceived! For example, a student might perceive the major task outcome of a verbal presentation to be fluency with which the presentation is made, for the teacher the student showing a thorough understanding of the topic may be the most important outcome to be measured.

Consider figure and ground in classroom learning exercises. Give examples of when children might not be focussing on the figure the teacher is teaching about but on a different figure. Remember, figure and ground are mobile, what a teacher believes is the figure may not be what the student perceives as the figure.

Remembering and forgetting

A major concern of teaching is getting students to remember things, or conversely, stopping them from forgetting. Effective remembering involves efficient encoding: the means by which we gather and represent information mentally. It also involves efficient retention: the means by which material is retained in the memory for later retrieval; and it involves efficient retrieval: the means by which we get information from long-term memory when it is needed. There are strategies by which each of these processes may be facilitated to enhance remembering and alleviate forgetting.

Just as the CPU of a computer processes a large amount of information with a combination of relatively few basic instructions, so information processing psychologists assume that the number of fundamental processes underlying human cognition is relatively small and attempt to identify these. They also seek to discover how higher-order intellectual functions are formed from more elementary cognitive processes. In the following sections we outline some of the elements considered important for effective encoding of new information (see Bjork et al., 2007; Driscoll & Driscoll, 2005).

Meaningfulness and encoding

Probably the most important aspect of the material being presented in order for it to be easily encoded and remembered is its *meaningfulness*. Meaningful material is encoded and stored more efficiently than non-meaningful material. But what do we mean by meaningful material? Remember the computer analogy? All computers require a software programme of some kind in order to recognise material being fed into the computer. With many computers, when you plug in a USB flash drive, you get a message or menu to let you know whether the computer system can read the files or not. In other words, the computer has an existing framework for recognising and incorporating commands. In information processing terms, your short-term memory operates as a system that processes new information more readily when it is related to information already held in the long-term memory. So, in effect, **meaningful material** really means material that can be related to already existing schemes of knowledge in the long-term memory. The new material is recognised in terms of prior knowledge and concepts already understood. When adults are given a mental task to perform in an area in which they have little knowledge, they often process the information less efficiently than children who have knowledge in that area (Gathercole & Packiam-Alloway, 2007). The conceptualisation of meaningfulness relates to the processes of assimilation and accommodation discussed in Chapter 5. Consider the following websites which provide further information on mind tools to enhance learning and memory: http://mindtools.com/memory.html and https://understood.org/en/school-learning/learning-at-home/homework-study-skills/8-working-memory-boosters

Strategies to help learning

Can we help learners structure their learning so that encoding, storing, and retrieval are made easier? There are a number of learning strategies that can assist learners to encode, store, and retrieve difficult information. These include **chunking**, **story grammar training**, self questioning, and summarisation.

As its name suggests, chunking involves reducing complex material to smaller patterns (fewer units to learn) that can be remembered more easily. Some techniques of chunking involve acrostics and rhymes which are described below.

Story grammar training consists of teaching students to ask themselves five questions which structure their attention as they read stories:

1 Who is the main character?
2 When and where did the story take place?
3 What did the main characters do?
4 How did the story end?
5 How did the main character feel?

Children are more actively involved in mentally processing the elements of the story when they ask and answer these questions so that encoding, retention, and recall are facilitated (Glaser & Brunstein, 2007).

With **question generation** students are taught how to generate integrative questions concerning text that capture large units of meaning. This facilitates encoding because readers become more active and, in particular, monitor their own reading, so that problems in their comprehension become more apparent. One way of using questions is to turn text headings into questions and then to read the text material with answering the question in mind.

Reading to answer a question is a prominent feature in the SQ3R (Survey, Question, Read, Recite, Review) approach (Jariam et al., 2014; McDaniel et al., 2009) and the PQ4R (Preview, Question, Read, Reflect, Recite, Review) variation (Donndelinger, 2005). With the PQ4R, the reader *previews* the material to be read, generates *questions* from the headings, *reads* the material for the main ideas and supporting details, *reflects* on connections between the new information and what was previously known, *recites* the answers to the questions, and *reviews* what is known and still left unanswered. Try it for yourself while you are reading this chapter.

The active generation of summaries has also been found to facilitate the comprehension and retention of textual material (Bugg & McDaniel, 2012; Leopold et al., 2013). There are many techniques suggested for using summaries (Engstrom, 2005; Kobayashi, 2007) that are too extensive to develop in this text. No doubt you are familiar with some of them (e.g. marginal notes, underlining topic sentences, highlighting key ideas). Many of these techniques are quite structured and methodical. For students to use them successfully they need to be actively taught the strategies. However, the usefulness of summarisation training for children younger than about 10 years of age is not conclusive.

SPOTLIGHT ON PRIOR KNOWLEDGE AND EFFECTIVE LEARNING

The activation of prior knowledge about a topic before presenting new material is very important as it can act as a springboard for further learning (Nesbit & Adesope, 2006). The assessment of the learner's prior knowledge by the educator (or indeed the learner) can offer valuable information regarding the direction instruction should take by identifying existing knowledge to which the new material can be linked, or by identifying inaccuracies and misconceptions that can be detrimental to learning. Prior knowledge, 'helps learners to relate new information to existing knowledge. This will lead to rich knowledge structures, because it increases the number of relations between concepts and facilitates activation of knowledge.' (Dolmans et al., 2005, p. 733).

The assessment of prior knowledge is, however, difficult as any one measure might not give a full indication of knowledge conceptions and misconceptions. For example, in class, a teacher might use a multiple choice test or an essay to evaluate the level of prior knowledge of students before beginning a new topic. The technique used may only give a limited slice of information. Hence, it is always advisable to use multiple forms of assessment in order to be confident about students' prior knowledge.

As we have indicated earlier in this chapter, the structure and accessibility of knowledge stored in the long-term memory influences how effectively it can be used for learning new material. This is referred to as *top down processing*. Prior knowledge also interacts with a number of other key components of the learning episode, such as the structure and

content of the information to be learnt, the learning materials used, the learning strategies used, the activities involved, level of motivation and interest, and so on. Research is currently being conducted in these areas to examine the relationship of prior learning to these factors in order to derive further principles that might guide educators in establishing effective learning environments.

Informal knowledge

The informal knowledge that students bring to the learning situation can hinder effective learning and can be quite resistant to change. For example, all of us have intuitive understandings about scientific and natural processes. At times we need to learn new material that conflicts with our pre-established intuitive understandings. Because the new material is non-meaningful in terms of the learners' pre-existing schema it is difficult to learn and teachers need to ensure that this informal knowledge does not interfere by correcting misconceptions. Doing this is not easy, and involves helping learners see the limitations in their understandings and convincing them of the merits of the alternative (McNeil & Alibali, 2005; Wagner et al., 2000). The problems of incompatible prior knowledge become particularly important during adolescence as students are introduced to many scientific, historical, and social concepts.

McNeil (2008) describes a study in which children in the second and third year of school in which children were being taught simple arithmetic (e.g. 6 + 4 = 10). The question was whether simple arithmetic interferes with a slighty more complex form of arithmetic, equivalence problems. This refers to when the left and right-hand sides of an equation represent the same value (e.g. 7 + 3 = 2 + 8). In one condition, children were given simple arithmetic problems to solve before, being given unlimited time to solve equivalence problems (e.g. 5 + 4 + 8 = 5 + _); (4 + 8 + 9 = 4 + _). In another condition children were asked to solve the equivalence problems without starting with simple problems. The children given the simple arithmetic problems first were less likely to correctly solve the equivalence problems. The simple arithmetic problems trigger what NcNeil calls a 'mindless understanding' that the left-hand side of the equations represents the mathematical operation and right-hand side of the equations represents the answer. So for instance, a child might think the correct answer to the problem 5 + 4 + 8 = 5 + _ was 17

by adding up 5 + 4 + 8 rather than 12 to balance the equation. Such 'mindless understanding' triggered by prior knowledge can lead to learning failures.

Can you think of any examples of where your preexisting knowledge base interfered with new learning? How did you overcome this? What implications does this hold for your teaching? Think here, for example, about the phases of the moon and whether these are caused by the shadow of the earth falling on the moon, or because of the view of the moon we have from any particular vantage point on the earth. Which do you think it is? (You might need to consider an encyclopedia or online search to find out the answer, does it conflict with your preconceived notions?)

How would you handle the kind of situation presented in the reading example above? Discuss your strategies with those of other students and compile a list of 'helpful hints to teachers'.

 QUESTION POINT

Consider each of the strategies described above. Have you used any of these? Which is your favourite method for memorising complex and long material?

Learning non-meaningful material

We have all faced the situation of having to memorise material that is non-meaningful to us such as lists of dates, telephone numbers, the names of a class, algebraic formulae, spelling words, periodic tables (perhaps even multiplication tables which for many appear non-meaningful). Non-meaningful material puts an extra burden on the processing unit to encode the material and hence it is essential that we reduce the number of elements we have to learn to what we can mentally manipulate and to impose, where possible, some element of meaning on the material. There are a number of strategies to improve the encoding, storage, and retrieval of such material. As we have suggested these strategies revolve around simplifying the material, and superimposing patterns on it so that it becomes, to some extent, meaningful (Karpicke & Grimaldi, 2012).

Number of units of information that can be processed

As indicated above, part of the problem of learning complex and long material, as well as non-meaningful material, is that our short-term memory is limited in the number of units of information we can process at one time. This is usually estimated to be between three and seven, depending on age, although some people appear to be able to process more. The units are *chunks* rather than number of physical units. A letter, a number, a word, or a familiar phrase can function as a single chunk because each is a single unit of meaning. Thus it is as easy to remember a set of three unrelated words with nine letters (e.g. hit, red, toe) as it is to remember three unrelated letters (e.g. q, f, r) (Gobet, 2005; Miller, 1956). *Chunking* is a mental strategy by which we break long and complex series into smaller chunks to facilitate learning and recall. For example, if we have to learn to spell the word antidisestsablishmentarianism it is probably easier if we learn anti-disestablish-mentarianism.

Mental imagery

Another way of encoding material is through using *mental imagery* to impose some kind of meaning and structure on the material. There are two different types of image that can be constructed to assist with retention and recall of verbal material. The first, called **representational images**, exactly represent the content of the prose to be learnt. For example, 'the car crashed into the tree' can be directly represented, as we can form an image of each element in the prose that will facilitate recall. There is consistent research evidence that active construction of representational images, that is, creating visual images of what one is reading or hearing, facilitates children's learning of text (at least from the age when children begin to process concrete stories).

Mnemonic images

Sometimes it is more difficult to imagine elements of prose and in these cases aids may be used to stand for elements to be remembered to aid our memory. These aids are called **mnemonic images** (Evans, 2007). Mnemonic imagery is useful when we are trying to learn information about totally unfamiliar concepts such as scientific, geographical, or financial concepts. It seems especially useful when there are many previously unknown concepts that must be acquired in a relatively short time. There are simple mnemonic devices, such as rhymes, acrostics and acronyms, and more complicated forms, such as the keyword method, in which we link ideas to key words that are easier to remember. With the **keyword method** a word is keyed to the prose so that it triggers off a rich set of associations that recall the prose (Fitz et al., 2007; Wyra et al., 2007). For example, individuals commonly use HOMES to remember the Great Lakes Huron, Ontario, Michigan, Erie, and Superior. We use mnemonics when we deliberately impose some sort of order on the material we want to learn. Again the principle is to reduce the amount that has to be encoded into a form that is easily retrievable later.

Other strategies that are useful are *peg-type mnemonics*, where particular concepts to be remembered are located in some space (such as a living room) and identified with common objects (e.g. in the living room). This is called a method of *loci* peg-type mnemonic and has been used for centuries. Greek and Roman orators advised their students to remember the points in a speech they were to make by forming images of the points and locating them at successive places along a familiar path. When they were to give the speech, they could retrieve the points they wished to make by mentally walking down the path and 'looking' to see images of the different points (Putnam, 2015).

A *pegword mnemonic* associates an item with a rhyme such as in one-bun, two-shoe, three-tree, and so on. Another device, the *link method*, simply constructs an overall image in which the items to be remembered form component and interacting parts. You could, for example, visualise items on a shopping list interacting in some way, such as a milk carton balancing on an egg surrounded by flour, and so on. Some great feats of memory are the result of well-applied mnemonics (Buzan, 2006; Hagwood, 2006).

 ACTIVITY POST

Consider a range of material you have to learn, such as information in this textbook. Develop a number of memory devices to help you remember specific material. Distinguish between meaningful material (which we hope comprises the majority of the book!) and non-meaningful material. Illustrate the use of each memory device with an example. Share your memory devices with other students in your group. Do you think such devices are helpful? When are they most helpful to you? When are they least helpful to you?

What mnemonics (memory aids) do you use? Discuss this with fellow students and compile a list of commonly used memory aids. Further information on mnemonics and other cognitive skills may be obtained at: http://mindtools.com/memory.html

Why do mnemonics work?

Mnemonics assist with encoding because they provide meaning through associations with more familiar, meaningful information. Forming images of the material to be learnt greatly aids later recall. Mnemonics also assist learners to organise unrelated and often abstract material. Importantly, mnemonics associate the material to be learnt with retrieval cues – for example, with the peg method we have only to remember one-bun and the incongruous image will be triggered.

In order to be effective mnemonics should be easy to learn, interesting, and fun. Indeed, some of the strongest evidence favouring the teaching of mnemonic imagery skills is that students appear to be impressed by how effective these strategies are when they use them and tend to incorporate them into their learning styles (Putnam, 2015).

There are a couple of dangers in using mnemonics. We may become quite inflexible in our recall, or if an element of the mnemonic is missing we may not be able to retrieve the rest. Most of us have to recite the little poem on the months of the year to remember the number of days in each. When flexibility of recall is important the encoding should not be tied too tightly to a rigid mnemonic, and of course the most useful devices of encoding are those that are inherently meaningful in themselves.

Classifying to help learning

We have already emphasised that remembering becomes easier when the learner is able to link new information to old information through mental schemas. Indeed, we also discussed this with regard to Piaget's theory and early learning in Chapter 5. For many cognitive psychologists it is these linkages and relationships between pieces of information that are the hallmark of understanding and effective learning (Powell & Kalina, 2009; Tse et al., 2011). The adequacy of the organisational structure connecting elements of the knowledge to be retained determines the accessibility or availability of the information at a later time. It seems reasonable therefore that if we can help learners to categorise information into structural relationships we will facilitate coding, storage, and retrieval.

Coding is particularly useful for structuring both meaningful and non-meaningful material so that it is more easily learnt and recalled later. Some quite elaborate coding systems have been devised to assist students see the connectedness of information and to facilitate the encoding and retention of quite difficult material. Often all one has to do is to remember one element of the structure and all the other elements will also be remembered. Coding frames and classification systems assist memory such as in Figure 8.4.

The organisation of this material into a form of hierarchical tree makes it more meaningful, and therefore encoding, retention, and retrieval should be enhanced (Davies, 2011; Karpicke, 2012).

Concept mapping

Concept mapping (Adesope & Nesbit, 2009; Nesbit & Adesope, 2006), a more elaborate form of coding, is a useful strategy for teaching students about concepts. A **concept map** is a two-dimensional diagram representing the conceptual structure of subject matter. To construct a concept map we first identify the concepts and principles to be taught. Then, the content elements are arranged in a hierarchical order from general to detailed, top to bottom. Finally, a line is drawn between each two related elements to show the linkage (Yin et al., 2005). Figure 8.5 represents a concept map. Concept mapping, once learnt, becomes a very valuable evaluation tool. Concept mapping allows the learner to combine elements into meaningful statements or propositions. This linking helps students to see the relationships between concepts and build on their conceptual framework.

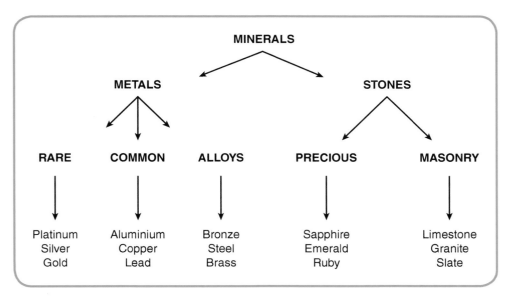

Figure 8.4 Mineral classification system.

Networking

Another form of concept mapping is **networking**. Networking requires students to identify the important concepts or ideas in the text and to describe the inter-relationships between these ideas in the form of a network diagram using nodes and links. Students' application of this networking technique should result in their improved comprehension and retention of material since the network diagram provides a visual, spatial organisation of the information and helps the student see an overall picture of the material (McCrudden et al., 2007). A teacher-made network can be used as an advance organiser (Cañas et al., 2005; Eppler, 2006) and incomplete or inaccurate networks completed by students can be used by the teacher to assess their level of comprehension and any misconceptions they might have.

In order to make good use of networking and concept maps students have to be trained before they can use the techniques proficiently (Novak & Cañas, 2007). It is also important to clearly represent the many types of relationships (conceptual, propositional, procedural, cause–effect, factual) that are present simultaneously and linked by intertwined lines and words, so that students are not confused. Because of the complexity of much learning, concept maps and networking may oversimplify relationships so that much important information is left out. Nevertheless, this approach is beneficial in facilitating learning and recall, and also helps learners to make clear to themselves what similarities there are between concepts, thereby improving generalisations of learning (Adesope & Nesbit, 2009).

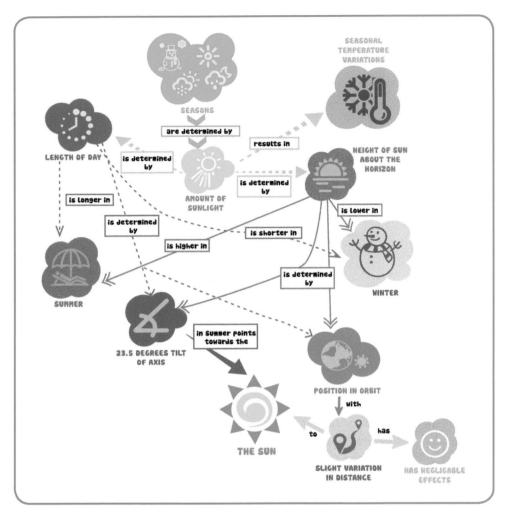

Figure 8.5   A concept map to explain why we have different seasons (based on Novak & Cañas, 2008).

 SPOTLIGHT ON STRATEGIC LEARNERS

Cognitive strategies such as those described above enhance learning (see, for example, Nesbit & Adesope, 2006; Novak, 2010). The appropriate use of strategies depends on how familiar the learner is with the material to be learnt, and is also domain specific (Marewski & Schooler, 2011). The aim of strategy use is to minimise the demands on the working memory, and to make learning and responses as automatic as possible (Raghubar et al., 2010). When students already know a great deal about a topic they really don't need to use strategic routines for acquiring new concepts. Effective learners know when they need to be strategic and when they do not.

Strategies that are appropriate in one domain may be inappropriate in another. For example, it may be important to give extra attention to numerals in mathematics and history, but it would be unimportant in most language studies. Rehearsing information with attention to temporal or serial order may be useful in some domains (such as history) but inappropriate in others. Attention to the subjective content of some material may be essential (such as in literature) but in other areas it could interfere with processing information (such as physics). Weak strategies in particular domains may be strong strategies in others (Veenman & Spaans, 2005).

Many students are not strategic learners and they should be taught to monitor their use of strategies and their effectiveness. In line with this, students should be taught when and where to use particular strategies and to be flexible – that is, if a particular approach is unsuited to a specific learning task they should adopt another strategy (Dignath et al., 2008; Perels et al., 2005). It is also important to teach strategies within the context of real learning events such as mathematics, language, and social science.

How should learning strategies be taught? Teachers should describe the strategy to students and model its use (Bell & Kozlowski, 2008; Dignath & Büttner, 2008). This modelling should include think-aloud statements about how to perform the procedure. These 'think-alouds' should also include important information on *why* and *when* the strategy could be used. Teacher-guided practice with the strategy should be given to students, followed by detailed feedback by the teacher on how individuals might improve strategy use. The practice–feedback loop continues until students can use the strategy efficiently.

To facilitate acquisition, practice may begin with easier material and progress to harder tasks. To train for transfer of the strategy, the practice examples should be drawn from different content areas, and the strategy can be employed at various times during a day's instruction and as part of homework exercises. As you can see from this description, teaching effective strategy use to students should be explicit, intensive, and extensive. The goal is for students to use the learned strategies autonomously, skilfully, and appropriately.

It is probably best to teach only a few strategies at a time and teach them well. Ultimately, the type of strategies employed by learners should be related to the amount of prior knowledge they possess, the nature of the material to be learnt, and the kind of outcome the learner is trying to achieve (Amadieu et al., 2009; Conley, 2008). At times simple mnemonics will be appropriate; at other times concept maps will be more suitable.

Remembering and forgetting

We have considered important elements of coding information so that it is easier to remember. In this section we will consider procedures that facilitate or inhibit the effective retention of information. Much of the material presented to our senses each day is not remembered because we do not attend specifically to the stimuli.

Factors affecting remembering

The long-term retention of learning is quite complex and influenced by many factors (Cepeda et al., 2006; Custers, 2010). As we have already indicated the degree of organisation and structure of the material being learnt is a very important factor and, in particular, if this structure relates to **prior knowledge**, retention should be enhanced.

Practice, relearning, advanced training, and continued exposure to the content being learnt also facilitate retention because they increase the degree of original learning. Instructional techniques also have an effect. In particular, research indicates that **mastery learning** approaches, which are highly structured around achievement goals and provide opportunities for practice, recall, feedback and review, produce superior academic performance.

Instructional techniques that require the active involvement of the learner also facilitate remembering and recall. Finally, remembering is also affected by the nature of the assessment tasks. Tasks that call on recognition appear to stimulate remembering better than tasks that rely on recall. This is probably because the prompts for recognition are more explicit. Individual differences in ability also play a role in retention (Brandt et al., 2005).

A period of time is necessary for learning to become established and consolidated in long-term memory. The actual physiological processes involved in this have attracted considerable attention from psychologists and physiologists but are beyond the scope of this text (Alberini, 2005). We will concentrate on the mechanics of learning for retention.

There are a number of techniques that may be used to enhance retention: whole and part learning, repetition and drill, overlearning and automaticity, and distributed practice.

Whole and part learning

Most complex learning consists of a number of elements or units. *Whole and part learning* refers to the nature of the unit chosen for learning and memorising (Driscoll & Driscoll, 2005; Martens, 2012; Van Merriënboer et al., 2006). With the whole learning approach, the integrity of the block of material to be remembered is maintained and encoded as a unit. For example, when learning a speech most people would choose the whole method and read through the speech as a unit until they had mastered it, perhaps using one of the mnemonic techniques described above, such as the link method.

With the part method a large block is broken into smaller subsections and then put together again at the end. For example, in a long piece of music most musicians would practice particular phrases until they were mastered and then combine them again into one piece.

The most effective method is determined by the nature of the material to be learnt and the age and ability of the learner. Whole and part learning approaches have implications for a range of learning activities such as learning the piano (should we learn one hand and then the other or both together?), poetry (stanza by stanza?), music (the whole piece or phrase by phrase?).

There are no hard and fast rules for using whole or part methods, but there are some important principles when adopting one or the other approach. The whole method binds material together at the outset into a meaningful whole, however, learning may seem slower. Part learning supplies immediate goals, shows more rapid learning, and is therefore more satisfying. But part learning does not necessarily transfer to the whole, and to complete a learning of individual parts may inhibit later learning of the whole.

Repetition and drill

All of us as learners have used repetition and drill to remember material. No doubt you can remember 'swotting' for a test. Repetition, in itself, does not lead to greater retention; the important criterion for the usefulness of this as a technique is that it must be an active process, based on attention and understanding. The belief that if a learner does it often enough they will catch on is quite erroneous. Learners can write out a list of spelling words many times without learning them if they are not attending to what they are doing; a learner can practise writing skills without improving in penmanship; and a learner may do a series of exercises by following the steps indicated in the example without mastering the principles involved. Basically, repetition is a very effective technique if it is active and has the interest, attention, and purpose of the learner and is associated with meaningful learning; it is most useful in refining and improving the retention and recall of material already learnt.

Overlearning and automaticity

Continuing repetition of the material past the point of first mastery, called **overlearning**, is also beneficial in facilitating retention and recall. This repetition is also necessary for the development of *automaticity*. Automaticity refers to a skill or behaviour that has been repeated to the point of being 'automatic'. That is to say the skill or behaviour can function with little mental effort while other thinking occurs. Another characteristic of automaticity is that skills requiring several steps of behaviour are 'chunked' into a single unit. Consider people learning to drive a manual car for the first time. They have to discern where the various pedals, indicators, and mirrors are, when to press what, when to look where, what position the hands and feet must be in to drive and change gears, and then drive. Early on, this process can fill the limited space in the working memory. Driving can be very rough! Repeated practice can lead to automaticity which connects all the steps necessary to produce proficient driving, thereby taking up less space in the working memory.

(?) QUESTION POINT

Consider the mind aids presented in the following websites: http://mindtools.com/pages/main/newMN_TIM.htm and http://memory-improvement-tips.com/best-study-skills.html. How effective do you think they are? How might they be taught to children?

Distributed practice

Practice may be concentrated into relatively long, unbroken periods, or spread over several short sessions. When practice is concentrated in long periods it is called **massed**. When it is spread over time it is called **distributed**.

Almost without exception, studies concerned with the relative effectiveness of distributed and massed practice, whether it is with motor skills (such as writing) or verbal learning (such as reading), show that practice should be spaced for the best results (Cepeda et al., 2006; Seabrook et al., 2005). A few words in spelling each day for a week will be mastered better than a large number to be learned over one night.

When the amount of work involved in a task is complex and involved, or perhaps not so meaningful, there should be regular practice periods separated by rest periods to allow for the consolidation of the material. This particularly applies to situations where a high level of attention or energy is required (such as learning to use complex machinery) and where the possibility of errors increases as individuals become fatigued. The length of the rest period is not so crucial as the fact of having a rest. A five-minute break may be all that is necessary to allow the consolidation of information to take place, and to alleviate potential fatigue effects.

Massed practice periods are nevertheless very useful for tasks that are meaningful or already partially learnt. They are also useful for revising material or bringing the individual or group to a peak level of mastery on the material (Cepeda et al., 2009; Toppino et al., 2009).

Serial position effect

When faced with learning a long list of things such as the alphabet, mathematical tables, spelling lists, historical dates, a poem, or a song, the material presented early is most easily remembered; material near the end is remembered relatively easily; but there is often great difficulty remembering the middle sections of the material. Students tend to make spelling errors in the middle of words and in the middle of spelling lists; they get up to 4 × 6 easily in their tables but forget the next in the sequence until they sigh with relief at 4 × 10, 11, and 12. Students forget the middle of songs or poems, and pronunciation errors are made in the middle of words (e.g. chimbley).

This fall-off in retention in the middle of the sequence is known as the **serial position effect**. It doesn't apply only to lists of things. Students' attention and task focus may waver over the course of a lesson, or activity, as a result of many things including their interest, instructional approach, and home/background factors, such as having a good night's sleep.

This phenomenon of retaining and recalling the first part of a list more easily is referred to as the **primacy effect**, and the phenomenon of retaining and recalling the last elements of a list more easily than the middle section is referred to as the **recency effect**. It appears that the serial position effect may be explained by a fall-off in attention in the middle, so encoding is therefore less effective and retention and recall are lessened.

Another problem with learning material in serial order for retention and recall is that the order in which we learn the material determines the order of easiest recall.

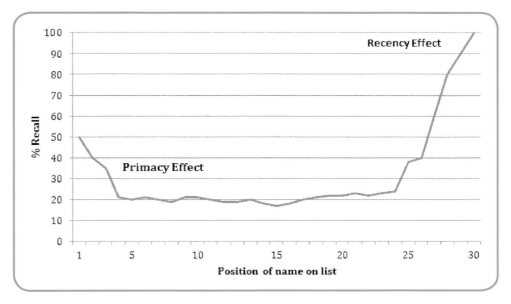

Figure 8.6   The serial-position effect for recall of list of 30 names.

In general, if we have slavishly learnt material in a serial form it is very hard to recall items without resorting to the whole list. For example, how many people have to go through a large part of the alphabet in order to recall a letter's position or right through a multiplication table to locate a particular sequence? If we require flexibility of recall, items should not be learnt in a serial fashion.

(?) QUESTION POINT

How would you make use of the information on the primacy and recency effects to structure learning episodes to facilitate retention and recall? In particular consider situations such as teaching a long song or piece of music, teaching mathematics tables, teaching material that is a mix of easy and difficult concepts, or presenting a long explanation of a complex phenomenon?

Why do we forget?

There are a number of reasons given why we forget. Ineffective processing of the information initially through lack of attention, lack of rehearsal, ineffective encoding of the prompts needed for recall, and interference effects.

In our description of the encoding and retention processes above we emphasised the importance of encoding material in such a way that particular cues can be used to recall the information. Indeed, successful mnemonics depend upon cues that are easy to remember, acting as the trigger for remembering more difficult material. The effectiveness of retrieval cues depends on their relation to the nature of the stored material. For example, if you are given the word *bank* to remember, and it follows the words *river*, *creek*, and *stream* in a list, you are likely to encode it as a geographical term. Later, you are more likely to recall *bank* if you are given the retrieval cue *geographical term* than if you were simply left on your own to remember the word. If you were given the word *bank* among a list of accounting terms such as *money*, *statements*, and *balances*, and you were given the retrieval cue *accounting term*, you would probably also remember the word *bank* as belonging to the list. On the other hand, if the word was included in a list of geographical terms and you were given the retrieval cue *accounting* you may very well have difficulty retrieving the word (Sederberg et al., 2008).

Interference effects

Some argue that the basic reason we forget is not that we have lost the available information from memory but that the memory is blocked from retrieval because of competing responses. In other words, events occurring before or after events that are to be remembered interfere with recall of the to-be-remembered events. This effect on retention is known as the **interference effect** and, depending on the direction of the interference, we have either proactive interference or retroactive interference.

Proactive interference occurs when earlier learning interferes with new learning; for example, a person learning new word processing software may have difficulty because he confuses the processes with those of an earlier word processing package. In general, when we find it difficult to respond to new situations because of our established ways of responding, we have proactive interference. There are many examples of this effect – driving on the right-hand side of the road in Europe, learning to touch type, correcting a well-established spelling error, driving a manual car after an automatic car, and so on.

When new learning impedes the retention of the old learning we have an example of **retroactive interference**. We have all experienced the difficulty of learning new computer software, as we have indicated above. Once the new programme is learned, however, it becomes equally difficult to remember how to use the old software.

In order to avoid this effect learning experiences should be sequenced so that present learning does not inhibit the retention and recall of earlier or subsequent learning. For example, if we were to give students a spelling list that contained 'ie' words such as *achieve* and *piece*, any subsequent list should not contain 'ei' words, such as *conceive* and *receive*, until the earlier material is consolidated. We all use the rhyme 'i before e except after c' to try to sort this out. The problem most of us still have with ie/ei words indicates the power of the interference effects.

QUESTION POINT

Think of occasions when proactive and retroactive interference effects interfered with your learning. How strong were the effects and which of the two types seemed more distracting? Discuss these examples with other students in your group.

In contrast to inhibition, sometimes learning one thing can help a person learn similar material (Chan, 2009; Panzer et al., 2006). For example, learning Spanish first may help a student learn Italian, a similar language. This is known as proactive facilitation. If we are teaching children how to spell 'ie' words and we follow up the initial learning with further lists containing 'ie' words, the earlier learning should be consolidated. This is known as retroactive facilitation. Facilitation and inhibition effects are related to **transfer of learning**, which we discuss below.

 QUESTION POINT

Think of occasions when proactive and retroactive facilitation effects facilitated your learning. How strong were the effects and which of the two types seemed more facilitating? Discuss these examples with other students in your group.

How do experts differ from novices in information processing?

In general, adults are more cognitively mature and capable of more sophisticated information processing than children. However, as illustrated earlier, when adults are given a mental task to perform in an area in which they have little knowledge, they often process the information less efficiently than children who have more knowledge in that area. This raises the question of the relationship between the amount of knowledge possessed and its impact on cognitive processing.

Not surprisingly, the evidence shows that the expert knows more domain-specific concepts than the novice does, and that these concepts are more differentiated and interrelated, with each of the expert's concepts closely connected in long-term memory with many other concepts (Bradley et al., 2006; Chi, 2006). Hence encoding, storage, and retrieval are facilitated. Experts also appear to be more likely to use cognitive strategies such as planning and analysis before processing information. In many cases this simplifies the processing procedure as the experts call to mind appropriate templates for cognitive action from their rich 'bank' of stored experiences and memories. In other words, the expert's response can be more automatic, unconscious, and effortless (Brand-Gruwel et al., 2005; Erricson, 2006; Meade et al., 2009). Generally adults are expected to perform better on unfamiliar material than children because they can draw on their larger experiences, and greater store of cognitive strategies. If a child has more experience in an area he or she could perform better than an adult.

 ## SPOTLIGHT ON TRANSFER OF LEARNING

A key concern of education is to provide students with skills and knowledge that they can transfer broadly to other situations (see, for example, Burke & Hutchins, 2007; Hager & Hodkinson, 2009). In other words, mathematics that we learn in the classroom should help us with our shopping, English should help us with writing business letters, keyboard and computing skills should transfer to a range of other electronic equipment, learning one language should assist in learning another, and so on (Gainsburg, 2008).

This elementary and simple notion of transfer of learning is, however, not so simple and has spawned an enormous amount of research examining the issue over the last 100 years (see, for example, De Corte, 2003; Haskell, 2000). The reason for this is that the rules we think should apply to transfer don't seem to work that well. It is a common occurrence that individuals do not transfer skills and knowledge across contexts, and the further one context is from another the less likely transfer is to occur. So, for example, students who are taught mathematical solutions for particular problems may transfer these to similar problems (what we might call specific or direct transfer), but are less likely to transfer them to different but related problems, for example, in physics (what we might call general transfer).

Even if the principles behind the solutions are relevant, as the context becomes less similar students become less likely to transfer them to the new context. This is of course a great problem, and is the reason why so much research and theorising has gone into studying transfer of learning. We would like to be more certain as educators that what we teach in one context will broadly transfer to similar and related contexts.

Most research on transfer has been concerned with examining the transfer of elements of learning to other particular situations, what might be termed the direct application of principles, skills, and knowledge to new situations. There is another way of looking at transfer, and this is to consider it as preparation for future learning (Schwartz et al., 2005). In this case transfer is not demonstrated by the direct application of specific skills and knowledge to new situations so much as by the broad application of skills and knowledge in new situations.

Bransford and Schwartz believe that this view of transfer is more in keeping with how the world of learning actually operates. Our aim as educators is, of course, to facilitate transfer and there are some broad principles (based on Bransford & Schwartz, 1999; Schwartz et al., 2005) that should be applied.

- Effective transfer requires a sufficient degree of original learning.
- Practising through to automaticity of cognitive and metacognitive skills in a range of related areas facilitates transfer.
- The degree to which learning has made the retrieval of relevant knowledge 'effortful' or relatively 'effortless' affects transfer.
- Developing abstractions and principles to apply in future situations facilitates transfer.
- Embedding learning in a community of shared knowledge and demonstrating the links between components of knowledge rather than emphasising discrete components facilitates transfer.
- Emphasising meaningfulness and understanding facilitates transfer.
- Using appropriate prompts and guides to show the links between existing knowledge and skills and new applications of these facilitates transfer.
- Emphasising understanding and active involvement of the learner facilitates transfer.
- Using concrete examples facilitates transfer.
- Learning in multiple contexts facilitates transfer.

 ACTIVITY POST

Utilising a range of the features of teaching for transfer outlined above, design a series of lessons in which you teach for transfer of knowledge to a new, but related area of knowledge. Clearly outline the elements you have implemented to enhance transfer.

Using the information processing approach in the classroom

There are a number of applications of information processing in the classroom. These are presented in Table 8.1.

Table 8.1   Using the information processing approach in the classroom

Principle	Example
1 Gain the students' attention. 2 Bring to mind relevant prior learning. 3 Point out important information. 4 Present information in an organised manner.	• Use cues to signal when you are ready to begin. • Move around the room and use voice inflections. • Review previous day's lesson.

(continued)

Table 8.1 *(continued)*

Principle	Example
5 Show students how to categorise (chunk) related information. 6 Provide opportunities for students to elaborate on new information. 7 Show students how to use coding when memorising lists. 8 Provide for repetition of learning. 9 Provide opportunities for overlearning of fundamental concepts and skills.	• Have a discussion about previously covered content. • Provide handouts. • Write on the board or use transparencies. • Show a logical sequence to concepts and skills. • Go from simple to complex when presenting new material. • Present information in categories. • Teach inductive reasoning. • Connect new information to something already known. • Look for similarities and differences among concepts. • Make up silly sentence with first letter of each word in the list. • Use mental imagery techniques such as the keyword method. • State important principles several times in different ways during presentation of information (STM). • Have items on each day's lesson from previous lesson (LTM). • Schedule periodic reviews of previously learned concepts and skills (LTM). • Use daily drills for arithmetic facts. • Play form of trivial pursuit with content related to class.

From http://teach.valdosta.edu/whuitt/col/cogsys/infoproc.html.

9 Personal and social development in childhood

Introduction

In this and the following chapter we examine personal and social development from childhood through to adolescence. What is **personality**? Personality refers to characteristics of people that are obvious in a variety of situations. Personality is stable; that is, we do not change into fundamentally different people from day-to-day. Personality is also organised, that is, its attributes are interrelated. It is certain that personality is formed through the interaction between innate biological mechanisms for particular behaviours and the environment. Personality is also distinctive, each personality being unique (Chamorro-Premuzic, 2011). It is important for educators and other professionals dealing with children to understand some aspects of personality, and personality development, in order to facilitate the development of children.

The foundations for personal and social development are set within the family. The family is very important during childhood as it is the major setting for learning about social interactions, appropriate sex roles, and achieving personal interdependence and independence. School is also very significant as it is the first wide social environment of the child that facilitates the development of attitudes towards social groups and institutions, learning to get along with age-mates and, more broadly, life skills.

As children become more mobile, and expert at language, they become resentful of being babied. They want to test out their independent skills. However, they also want to remain connected to safe and loving caregivers. This 'tension' between the need to remain secure in a loving and supportive social environment while developing independence marks the beginning of personal and social development.

By middle-age childhood children tend to display very distinctive individual characteristics, argue over fairness and may become, at times, aggressive and quarrelsome, all hallmarks of growing independence.

In the following sections we examine a number of theories of personality which look at the personal and social dimensions of personal development. We start with Freud.

Sigmund Freud

Freud (1856–1939) likened the mind to an iceberg in which the smaller visible part represents the region of the consciousness, while the much larger mass below the water represents the region of the unconscious (1913, 1960). The *conscious mind* is what you are aware of at any particular moment, your present perceptions, memories, thoughts, fantasies, and feelings. Working closely with the conscious mind is what Freud called the *preconscious* mind dealing with anything that can easily be made conscious. The larger part of the mind is the *unconscious mind*. In this vast domain of the unconscious is a great underworld of vital, unseen forces that exercise a strong control over the conscious thoughts and deeds of individuals. The unconscious mind is the source of motivation for our desires and activities, although, as we will see below, our motives, according to Freud, may be kept hidden from us or available to us only in a disguised form.

The life energy of personal action is called **Libido** (the creative energy in all individuals) and **Thanatos** (the destructive energy in all individuals). The interaction between these two energies mobilises personality growth. In Freudian theory healthy personality growth depends on individuals passing through a series of **psychosexual stages**. These psychosexual stages are developmental phases proposed by Freud that reflect changes in the focus of sexual energy on different bodily organs. The stages describe the psychological consequences of transformations in sexuality (Jarvis, 2004). Through these experiences mature adults achieve a balance between three components of personality: the **id**, the **ego**, and the **superego**. The id is the source of basic biological needs and desires and is driven by the *pleasure principle* to satisfy needs immediately; the ego is the conscious, rational part of personality and is driven by the reality principle which represents reason which puts limits on dangerous and impulsive acts that the id wants to indulge; and the superego is the seat of conscience, which distinguishes right from wrong irrespective of whether the contemplated action or desire is 'safe'. The superego represents cultural norms and standards internalised by the individual. The id predominates in infancy, the ego develops out of interactions with the world of experience as the child becomes increasingly independent, and the superego emerges as the child begins to conflict with familial and societal realities and demands.

While these three systems can be identified as separate hypothetical structures, behaviour for the mature person is nearly always the product of an interaction between the three. Rarely does one system operate to the exclusion of the other two, except in cases where the balance is broken.

 ACTIVITY POST

According to Freud, personality growth occurs through the resolution of conflict between the id, ego, and superego. Consider the definitions of id, ego, and superego presented above. Develop a series of scenarios in which there is conflict between id desires, ego rationality, and superego conscience. Develop scenarios in which one or other component of personality dominates. Develop scenarios in which a harmony is developed out of the conflict. Discuss your scenarios with other students.

Stages of psychosexual development

As these three mental systems evolve, individuals experience five clearly distinguishable developmental stages. Each of these can be defined in terms of individuals satisfying needs through three erogenous zones – the mouth, the anus, and the genital organs. Actions by children involving these zones bring children into conflict with their parents, who for Freud are the major influencing factor on the development of personality. The resulting frustrations and anxieties, as well as satisfying experiences, stimulate the development of a large number of adaptations, defences, compromises, and sublimations which are ultimately incorporated into the mature personality (Berzoff, 2011; Carducci, 2009; Jarvis, 2004).

Infants' lives are dominated through their mouth with breast feeding the primary focus of attention. Indeed throughout this period much of their learning occurs through the mouth with most objects being explored orally. This period has been called the *oral* stage, and Freud believed that the quality of nurturing that children receive during this time affects their feelings of dependence and trust in the world.

When infants are very young little attention is paid to toilet training, however, toilet training becomes a major focus from about 2 years of age. This period has been termed the *anal* stage of development. During this period parents begin to establish controls on the child in toileting behaviour. Toilet training generalises to parents trying to control much instinctual behaviour of the child. This leads to a developing sense of control or lack of control in the child, as parents begin to increasingly control the actions of the child. Freud believed that if the training and discipline emphasises positive independence and control, feelings of confidence in self are developed. Alternatively, if experiences during this time are overly restrictive or punitive, negative personal characteristics develop such as destructiveness, messiness, and so on.

From about four, young children develop an interest in their genitalia, noticing differences between boys and girls, and sexual feelings associated with the functioning of the genital organs are the focus of activity. This has been termed by Freud the *phallic* stage. This is the time when the individual identifies with the same-sex parent and sexual identity is developed. Important in the process of identity formation is the **Oedipal crisis** and **Electra crisis**. According to Freud, during this stage boys are sexually attracted to their mothers and are hostile to their fathers. They wish to supplant the father in the mother's affection. However, the reality is that the father is stronger and may castrate the boy (called castration complex in Freudian theory). As a result (and unconsciously) the boy sublimates his sexual feelings and enjoys the mother vicariously through identifying with the father. A similar, although less well described process, referred to as the Electra crisis, occurs for the female. Freud believed that girls of this age are sexually attracted to their father and hostile to their mothers. However, as the father is unattainable girls identify with the mother. Sexual identity is therefore established during the phallic period. At this time the superego begins to form which is the basic conscience that guides moral behaviour.

Finally, after a period of *latency*, children enter the *genital* stage when there is the transformation of the individual into a reality-oriented, socialised adult. During adolescence, sexual attraction, socialisation, group activities, vocational planning, and preparations for marrying and raising a family begin to come to the fore in well-stabilised behaviours. Each of these stages are presented in Table 9.1.

Anxiety and personal development

As we have suggested, throughout Freud's personality development stages there is a dynamic interaction between the three elements of personality: Id, ego, and super-ego. Depending on the nature of the conflicts experienced and on the modes of resolving them, individuals will develop positive or negative personality characteristics. Freud considered it vital that these three systems remain in balance, with a smooth transfer of energy from id to ego to superego. When the balance is upset the personality may break down into excessive anxiety. As any one of the three systems

Table 9.1	Freud's stages of psychosexual development	
Stage	**Ages**	**Description**
Oral	Lasts about one year	The mouth is the principal focus of dynamic activity. Sucking and biting are favourite activities. The world is explored through the mouth. The residual satisfaction of learning about, and controlling the world through the mouth leaves an imprint on personality.
Anal	2 to 4 years	The anus is the principal focus of dynamic activity. Control over toilet functions such as holding in and letting go are a source of pleasure and power. Power can be demonstrated through either the parent controlling the child's toileting, or the child controlling the parent through resistance or compliance. These features of toilet training leave an imprint on personality.
Phallic	4 to 5 years	The sex organs are the principal focus of dynamic activity and masturbation is a common activity. Preoccupation with sexual activities and the satisfaction derived from this leaves an imprint on personality.
Latency	Approximately 6 years to pubescence	Period during which sexual impulses are held in a state of repression. It is not clear that all children have a period of latency, for many children an interest in sexual activity continues throughout childhood, however, it might be more covert and disguised.
Genital	Puberty through to adulthood	The genitals are the principal focus of dynamic activity. Sexual activity becomes a primary concern and a way of establishing relationships.

can dominate, this means that we can have three distinct forms of anxiety: neurotic, realistic, or moral (Berzoff, 2011; Harari, 2001).

Neurotic anxiety occurs when the individual fears that the instinctive forces of the id will control their behaviour. **Realistic anxiety** exists when the individual is dominated by the ego to such an extent that id-driven behaviour (such as eating or sexual behaviour) becomes impossible to enjoy, and the individual is unable to devote energy to any superego demands such as the welfare of others. **Moral anxiety** occurs when the superego dominates and the individual becomes trapped in an over-rigid value system taken over from their parents. The individual is excessively scrupulous and compulsively on guard against anything that might arouse feelings of guilt. They reject both the pleasure principle of the id and the reality principle of the ego and inhabit, instead, an unreal world of taboos and forbidden things (Berzoff, 2011; Harari, 2001).

 ACTIVITY POST

Revisit the exercise in the previous Activity Post and categorise each scenario according to the three types of anxiety: neurotic, realistic, and moral.

 SPOTLIGHT ON DEFENCE MECHANISMS

One of the goals of ego behaviour is to protect and enhance one's sense of self. As children grow and are developing a sense of self, defence mechanisms play an important role in protecting an individual's sense of self (Cramer, 2006). All defence mechanisms have two characteristics in common:

1 They deny, falsify and/or distort reality.
2 They operate unconsciously so that the person is not aware of what is taking place.

While the use of defence mechanisms is normal (and all of us resort to them unconsciously from time to time), overuse of them impedes the development of a mature personality. The major defences are:

1 repression;
2 reaction formation;
3 rationalisation;
4 regression;
5 fixation;
6 projection;
7 fantasy;
8 denial.

Repression refers to the defence mechanism of removing from consciousness painful or shameful experiences and thoughts, or the process of preventing unacceptable impulses or desires from reaching consciousness. The purpose is essentially to protect the ego

(continued)

(continued)

from processes that are incompatible with the individual's high evaluations of self. For example, a hit and run driver may flee the accident in a moment of fear and be found later, with absolutely no recollection of what has occurred.

Reaction formation occurs when a repressed feeling or emotion is replaced by its opposite; for example, a feeling such as hatred may be hidden from awareness by the substitution of its opposite. A woman with an abusive husband may unconsciously wish to be rid of him, but this negative wish may be expressed as unusual concern for his welfare and tolerance of his behaviour.

Rationalisation is a commonly used defence mechanism. It occurs when we unconsciously give socially acceptable reasons for our conduct in place of real reasons. We may tell ourselves that we should go to the movies with our friend instead of studying because the other person is lonely and needs our company. A child might say that he couldn't do his homework because he had to help his mother with the shopping.

Regression occurs in order to reduce tension and anxiety and consists of children and adults engaging in behaviour more characteristic of an earlier stage of development. A child might begin to wet its pants when going to school for the first time, or a child might begin to suck its thumb when a new baby arrives home. The child fears being displaced and seeks attention, but can't express it consciously because the need arises out of jealousy and is therefore unacceptable, and hence engages in thumbsucking. While some forms of regression are indicative of severe problems, such as the adult psychotic who plays with dolls when under stress, most forms of regression are relatively mild. Many adults chew pens during an exam, eat excessively when worried, or masturbate when stressed. In each case the individual retreats to an earlier level of coping with anxiety.

Fixation occurs when an immature form of defence mechanism is consistently used rather than a more mature defence mechanism, such as sublimation. In extreme cases, this may lead to the emergence of a personality disorder in which the further growth of character is blocked by an obsessive personality pattern (Peterson et al., 1992).

Projection occurs when we ascribe our own unconscious motivation to other people, such as when we accuse others of being angry, hateful, or deceitful as a defence against our own anger, hatred, or deceit. Students at school might accuse the teacher of being lazy because they themselves are too lazy to do their school work.

Fantasy is a defence mechanism that protects the ego by seeking imaginary satisfactions in place of real ones. Today, there is much debate over video pornography in which violence is portrayed and its supposed effect on reducing or increasing sexual crimes. One argument goes that individuals who may otherwise engage in such activities use these videos to fantasise and sublimate their sexual drives in a relatively harmless way. What do you think?

Denial functions as a defence when an individual denies the existence of painful experiences and thoughts (such as a refusal to accept that a loved one has died). Some grossly overweight or underweight people deny that they have a problem and distort their body image accordingly.

QUESTION POINT

Consider each of the defence mechanisms listed above. Which ones do you think you or others may have used? Give examples. Consider school and classroom situations. Which of these defence mechanisms may be more commonly used by students? Discuss your thoughts with others in a group.

Current status of Freud's theory

While few psychologists today accept all Freud's major theoretical concepts, the theory is still considered very important. It provides a broad insight into the development of personality, especially the importance of our unconscious in motivating behaviour, as well as the influence of early socialisation within families on subsequent personality development. In this sense, Freud's theoretical framework helps us understand the emotional development issues of children.

On a broader level, Freud's theory has been influential in the development of many other theoretical perspectives on personality development. Educational and psychological literature on personality development very often presumes that the reader has some basic understanding of Freudian psychology (Havighurst, 2013; Jarvis, 2004; Larsen & Buss, 2013; Leary et al., 2009). Nevertheless, Freud's theory has been criticised for two basic reasons. First, many consider that his theory overemphasises the sexual nature of personality development. In his emphasis on critical events related to the oral, anal, and phallic stages, and the successful resolution of problems at these times, he appears to have neglected other important dimensions affecting the development of personality. Furthermore, Freud's emphasis that the early years of development, and in particular the effects of parenting, leave an indelible mark on the personality seems to be contradicted by evidence that the personality is in a state of continual development, and that later life experiences can and do make up for inadequate experiences in early life (Rudnytsky, 2008). Other criticisms relate to the lack of clear definitions of some of the components of his system, and the difficulty inherent in empirically testing and measuring these components (Dufresne, 2005; Greenwood & Loewenthal, 2005). More information on Freud and other personality psychologists may be found on the following website http://simplypsychology.org/personality-theories.html

 QUESTION POINT

What other important dimensions affecting the development of personality might Freud have neglected? What other limitations do you see in Freud's theory of personality development?

Classroom implications of Freud's theory

There are many elements of Freud's theory that are useful for teachers in understanding behaviour in the classroom. **Identification, anxiety, displacement,** and **defence mechanisms** are very useful concepts for teachers.

Much personality development results from children incorporating values held by significant others through the process of **identification,** and teachers as well as parents are powerful models in this process.

Earlier we discussed three forms of anxiety: neurotic anxiety, realistic anxiety, and moral anxiety. Children can develop neurotic anxiety if they are not helped by teachers and parents to recognise and come to terms with their instinctual behaviour. They need to recognise that instinctual drives are normal but that they need to strive to strike a balance between what is an acceptable/unacceptable satisfaction of these drives. A preoccupation with these instinctual drives can develop into neuroticism. Neurotic anxiety sometimes displays itself in *acting-out behaviour,* for example, when an apparently placid and well-controlled child has a violent outburst of rage.

Realistic anxiety may be caused by brutal shocks or frightening experiences such as violence and sexual abuse, but it may also be caused in children by such things as excessive demands for academic success or standards of behaviour, by a background of domestic strife, or the uncertainties of having to start a new school with a new teacher.

Moral anxiety may be produced by repressive moral training and may provoke self-punishment in children through feelings of unworthiness or inadequacy. Sometimes ritualistic gestures such as excessive handwashing (called obsessional–compulsive behaviour) develop in an attempt to remove such feelings symbolically (Berzoff, 2011; Harari, 2001).

Sometimes children engage in *displacement* in the classroom. For example, children may be 'out of sorts' at times, owing to a range of causes, and will displace their annoyance, aggression, and anger on their peers and teachers. Children who are abused at home may act in very antisocial ways at school. It is well to remember that children's behaviour (as well as our own) is the result of a complex interplay of unconscious forces and we, as teachers and parents, must take the time to work through the possible reasons for specific behaviour, particularly when the behaviour is different from the typical or is apparently inexplicable.

When under stress, children may unconsciously resort to defence mechanisms to protect their ego, that component of the personality that suffers the anxiety feelings. The most common defence mechanisms used by children are regression, projection, rationalisation, and fantasy. For example, while under stress some children may regress and resort to thumb sucking or wetting themselves. Stress related to school work, or tests, may lead to children procrastinating, working slowly, not making an effort, or disturbing the work of others. These types of behaviours can be used to avoid the source of anxiety while creating an 'excuse' for underperformance or slow progress. More serious stressors, resulting from bullying or an unstable home life (e.g. parental substance abuse), can result in an inability to cope with the situation and subsequent withdrawal or bizarre behaviour. For example, graffiti, school vandalism, and school refusal (where the child refuses to attend school) may be examples of both regression and 'acting-out' behaviour. Again, when such behaviour is severe, it is important to investigate the reasons for the behaviour and attempt to alleviate the conditions causing it.

Many accusations and counter accusations between children at school are the result of projection; for example, Mary says she doesn't want to play with Bill because Bill doesn't like her, when the truth is that Mary is afraid that Bill doesn't want to play with her. Some children may project that their teacher is lazy and a poor teacher when the student is in fact the lazy one.

Children often use rationalisation to excuse sloppy work, cheating, and a range of inappropriate behaviour within the school context. For example, many children say that they don't work hard at school because it is boring, or that they didn't do their homework because they had to help their mother with the shopping. Fantasy or daydreaming is used to relieve boredom and inability to cope. You can find more detail on Freud's psychosexual theory at the following website as well as on the other personality theories described below: http://ship.edu/~cgboeree/perscontents.html. You might also find the following website on Great Ideas in Personality useful: http://personalityresearch.org/

Erik Erikson

Erikson's stages of personal development

Erik Erikson (1902–1994) has made a major contribution to the way in which we think of personality development from childhood through to old age. Although derived from Freud, Erikson's theory takes a life span approach, and is, in general, more appealing to teachers and many other professionals as it promotes the idea of positive personal growth more specifically than Freud's theory. Side-by-side with the stages of *psychosexual development* described by Freud are Erikson's **psychosocial stages** of ego development, in which the individual establishes new basic orientations to the social world (Erikson, 1963, 1968; Kroger, 2004, 2007). There are eight stages of development encompassing youth to old age. A healthy personality is, by and large, one that has successfully accomplished the tasks appropriate to each stage. While at each stage there is the potential for positive and negative experiences Erikson allows for the fact that earlier, poorly resolved conflicts may be compensated for, in part, by later fulfilling experiences. Freud's theory seems to hold that significant earlier negative experiences will have a continuing dominant effect throughout life.

Table 9.2 lists these eight stages and compares them with Freud's psychosexual stages. In this chapter we will consider the stages relevant to early and late childhood. In Chapter 10 we will discuss adolescent and adult personal development. In each stage there is a dichotomy between two elements of personality which are resolved as the personality grows.

Table 9.2 Erikson's eight stages of personality development

Period of development	Freud's psychosexual stages	Erikson's psychosocial stages
Birth to 1 year	Oral stage	Basic trust versus mistrust
1 to 3 years	Anal stage	Autonomy versus shame and doubt
3 to 6 years	Phallic stage	Initiative versus guilt
6 years to puberty	Latency stage	Industry versus inferiority
Adolescence	Genital stage	Identity versus role confusion
Young adulthood		Intimacy versus isolation
Middle adulthood		Generativity versus self-absorption
Old age		Ego integrity versus despair

Trust and mistrust

Infancy and early childhood is a period of *trust* and *mistrust* where consistent loving caregiving leads to feelings of well-being and a sense of the world as a safe place in which to be. Inconsistent or rejecting care fosters within children a basic mistrust, fear, and apprehension of the caregivers, which may be generalised to other people and to the world at large. The dichotomy between trust and mistrust arises at each successive stage of development. While it is important that children generally develop a trusting nature, a healthy amount of mistrust is also part of a balanced personality.

Autonomy and shame

As children become more mobile and gain a greater command of language they test out their *autonomy*. Depending on the amount of autonomy allowed and support given, children develop a sense that they are able to control themselves. On the other hand, if the caregivers are overly restrictive, harshly critical or impatient, and consistently do for children what they could do for themselves, children may develop a sense of *shame* and *doubt* about their capacities to do things. It is essential that parents and teachers provide safe and realistic opportunities to develop a sense of autonomy. As with each of the dichotomies presented in the theory some level of the opposite quality, in this case doubt, is necessary so that individuals do not have an unrealistic sense of their autonomy and power.

Initiative and guilt

In order for children to develop confidence and be assured of their own motor and intellectual abilities it is important to give them opportunities to initiate many activities. This is particularly the case during early to middle childhood. Children who are

Table 9.3 Characteristics of Erikson's stages

Stage	Ages	Psychosocial crisis	Significant relations	Psychosocial modalities	Psychosocial virtues	Maladaptations and malignancies
I Infant	0–1	Trust versus mistrust	Mother	Safety and security	Trust, reliance	Sensory distortion – withdrawal
II Toddler	2–3	Autonomy versus shame and doubt	Parents	Personal control	Willpower, choice	Impulsivity – compulsion
III Preschooler	3–6	Initiative versus guilt	Family	To play	Reason, courage	Ruthlessness – inhibition
IV School-age child	7–12 or so	Industry versus inferiority	Neighbourhood and school	To accomplish	Ability	Narrow virtuosity – inertia
V Adolescence	12–18 or so	Ego-identity versus role-confusion	Peer groups, role models	Independence	Trust, loyalty	Fanaticism –repudiation
VI Young adult	the 20's	Intimacy versus isolation	Partners, friends	Secure relationships	Love	Promiscuity – exclusivity
VII Middle adult	late 20's to 50's	Generativity versus self-absorption	Household, workmates	Career and family	Care	Overextension – rejectivity
VIII Old adult	50's and beyond	Integrity versus despair	Mankind or 'my kind'	Reflection	Wisdom, understanding	Presumption – despair

Table based on http://ship.edu/%7Ecgboeree/erikson.html

given freedom and opportunity to initiate and test their newly acquired powers of communication and physical agility develop *initiative* and self-assurance. In contrast, if children are overly restricted or made to feel that they are engaging in a 'silly' or 'wrong' activity, making a mess or taking up too much time, they may develop a sense of *guilt* over self-initiated activities that will persist through later life stages.

Often, different expectations are held for girls than for boys, such that differential restrictions are applied by parents (and at times by teachers) (Fontana, 1986). This can lead to problems when children wish to initiate activity in supposed gender-inappropriate areas. For example, boys who want to dance and girls who want to play football sometimes come in for a hard time and are made to feel uncomfortable and guilty over their choices. Schools are implementing anti-sexism programmes to address this problem, although many homes still strongly support children's initiatives in sex-stereotyped areas.

 QUESTION POINT

Have you seen any examples of differential treatment of boys and girls in opportunities provided for them to develop a sense of autonomy and initiative? What might the consequences of this be?

Industry and inferiority

As children grow older they become more industous and inquisitive about the world. This is a period of *industry* versus *inferiority*. Children at this time are capable of increasingly sophisticated thought and argument and it is a time to encourage them in their productivity and creativity as they make and build things. Children who are restricted, criticised, told not to make a nuisance of themselves, or a mess may develop feelings of inferiority.

The child's peer group becomes an increasingly important influence as the peer group gives feedback to children about their abilities which helps to reinforce feelings of industry or inferiority. Following the period of industry and inferiority is the period labeled identity formation versus role confusion which characterises the adolescent period which we describe in Chapter 10.

 # SPOTLIGHT ON ERIKSON'S STAGES IN RELATION TO PLAY

In the context of Erikson's stages of psychosocial development there are three stages that are particularly relevant to children's play. Between the ages of about one and three children enter a *period of exploration* that has grown out of the trust consolidated in the earlier stage of infancy. In terms of exploratory play, a sense of independence grows as the caring adult demonstrates respect for the child's growing capabilities in their beginning language and physical actions on the world, and shows warmth in the relationship with the child. Where doubt is expressed about the child's abilities by significant others, self-doubt may develop.

During the second stage referred to as the *period of play*, between three and six, before children begin formal schooling, the exercise of initiative becomes paramount. (Frost et al., 2008), In the course of play, this may be demonstrated in rough-and-tumble games, investigations into unknown places and things, and acts of physical and verbal daring. The danger of dampening a child's sense of initiative and turning it to guilt is very real in countless experiences of such play. According to Erikson, the ability to choose, plan and accomplish actions without anxiety during this stage is the key to healthy psychosocial development.

When children are in middle childhood and at school, they enter the third stage known as the *period of investigation* in which they develop a sense of personal control rather than a sense of incompetence and inferiority. Play activities through which this development can be fostered include both physical and social games such as sports or hand clapping, marbles and card or board games, as well as the investigative classroom experiences designed by teachers. Structured cooperative learning activities during this time allow children to learn and practise social skills such as turn-taking, encouraging others, and negotiating, as well as language and communication skills such as asking questions, active listening, clarifying, and explaining. Once again, support from the child's social environment helps to resolve the developmental conflict at this stage and leads into the period of identity formation during adolescence.

We discuss different types of play later in this chapter. However if you want to explore the different types of play that children engage in at different ages, the following webpages are a good source of information: http://childdevelopmentinfo.com/child-development/play-work-of-children/pl2/ and http://child-development-guide.com/stages-of-play-during-child-development.html

Parental and grandparental involvement in school

Increasingly research shows that good quality parent and grandparent involvement in school leads to increased school motivation and achievement (Anderson & Minke, 2007; Gonzalez-DeHass et al., 2005; Hill & Tyson, 2009; Jeynes, 2007). Erikson's theory gives a sound rationale for parent and grandparent involvement in schools. This involvement can be as simple as paying attention to children's play and responding to their questions, listening to children read, acting as a sounding board for ideas (when parents and teachers are too busy), modelling different attitudes and values for children to incorporate into their growing sense of self, reinforcing children for their efforts and, finally, even direct involvement in the instruction of children (see, for example, Knollmann & Wild, 2007). Childcare settings and schools should actively encourage parental and grandparental involvement in their programmes, and develop appropriate structures to facilitate this. Of course, there are tremendous benefits for the older people as well. In being involved in the education of young children, older people are extending their period of generativity and maximising the positive forces that will lead them to feel a sense of integrity for a life well spent.

 ACTIVITY POST

Design a questionnaire or interview to examine the issue: 'why do some parents become involved in school activities and others don't?' Question respondents about what they consider 'good quality' involvement to be? Also ask them how they think schools and other educational settings might encourage good quality involvement? Compare your answers with those of other students.

 ## SPOTLIGHT ON WHY PARENTS BECOME INVOLVED IN THEIR CHILDREN'S EDUCATION

Among the reasons for parents becoming involved in their children's education are: (1) the parents' beliefs about their role in the child's life; (2) the parents' belief that they can help their child succeed at school; and (3) the general invitations, demands, and opportunities for parental involvement provided by both the child and the child's school (Deslandes & Bertrand, 2005; Hoover-Dempsey et al., 2005; Pomerantz et al., 2007).

The parents' construction of their role as parents refers to their beliefs about the appropriate actions they should undertake for, and with, their children in order for them to be successful at school. Many of these roles are 'defined' through social rules and expectations of what makes a good parent and by the social supports provided to parents. This varies according to the social and community groups the family belongs to, the nature of the family structure (e.g. single-parent or two-parent family) as well as to the life events such as divorce or job redundancy impacting on parents at any given time (Johnston & Swanson, 2006; Vincent & Ball, 2007).

In communities that value education and believe that parents should be involved, more parents are likely to be involved. This may vary by socioeconomic or cultural grouping (Anderson & Minke, 2007; Lee & Bowen, 2006). For example, some groups believe that schooling and teaching is the prerogative of teachers and parents should not be involved. For some other groups, a strong feeling of alienation from schooling might induce parents not to participate in their children's schooling. This could, for example, characterise parents from ethnic or social groups that are stigmatised (e.g. children of traveller parents) or immigrant families who may not understand the schooling system in the United Kingdom.

In some instances parents might value education and perceive that it is appropriate to be involved but nevertheless do not participate in the schooling of their children. This might be because they lack a feeling of efficacy for helping their children at school. **Parental self-efficacy** concerns parents' beliefs about their general ability to influence their child's developmental and educational outcomes, about their specific effectiveness in influencing the child's school learning, and about their own influence relative to that of peers and the child's teacher (Hornby & Lafaele, 2011; Jeynes, 2007). Many parents believe they cannot help, or cannot provide the materials, such as books and computers, needed to assist their children effectively. Lack of efficacy may characterise many parents who are poorly educated themselves, not well off financially or from a cultural and language background different from the school. Conversely, parents who feel they can help their children are more likely to be involved in their children's schooling. Feelings of efficacy are related to a parent's belief that with effort children can improve and so it is worthwhile helping children put in the extra effort.

It is likely that parents' feelings of efficacy change as their children move through schooling. Parents who feel competent to help their children at primary levels might feel less competent as children progress through high school. Indeed, there is commonly a drop-off in parental involvement at the high school level. This might be because the subject matter becomes more difficult or because schools become less inviting places for parents.

Finally, in order for parents to become involved they need to feel that both the children and the school want them to become involved (Anderson & Minke, 2007; Hoover-Dempsey et al., 2005). In other words parents may value education and believe they can help, but feel excluded from the process. It is important, therefore, that schools encourage parents to feel that their involvement is welcome. When parental involvement is required by schools, achievement outcomes of students are enhanced (Hill & Tyson, 2009). It is also likely that as children become older, and begin to focus on independence and autonomy, they become less welcoming of their parents' involvement in their schooling. Indeed, a whole host of personality variables characterising individual children will impact on a decision of particular parents to become involved or not.

Humanism and personal development

Another group of psychologists, referred to as humanists, also developed ideas on how individuals develop personally. While Freud and Erikson considered the interaction between the individual and the environment (in particular parents as a major part of the environment) important for the development of personality, **humanistic psychologists** throw more emphasis on the innate potential of humans to develop. They perceive people as free and unique, self-directed, capable of setting goals, making choices, and initiating action. Humanist psychologists further believe that, in order to function most effectively and to maximise their potential, individuals must first become aware of their internal thoughts and feelings regarding themselves and the world. By consciously describing such thoughts and feelings, individuals become more aware of how these influence their behaviour and may therefore be better able to control them.

The thoughts and feelings that individuals have about themselves focus around three broad areas (Moss, 2015):

1 *Identity:* Who am I? Where am I going?
2 *Connectedness:* How do I fit or relate with other people? Do people like me?
3 *Power:* What are my limits? What control do I have over my life?

For humanist psychologists, personal development is a process of answering these questions. Humanism further holds that a critical aspect of this learning process is the ability to judge whether or not our thoughts and feelings are personally productive, and then make whatever modifications are necessary. The ultimate goals of this search for self-knowledge are greater self-control and more positive living. This process of self-knowledge depends on people's interactions with one another as it is through these interactions that we become aware of our own identity.

Carl Rogers

A major figure in the development of the humanistic view of personal development is Carl Rogers (1902–1987). Rogers' personality theory is based on two major assumptions (Kirschenbaum, 2007):

1 Human behaviour is guided by each person's unique self-actualising tendency.
2 All humans need positive regard.

Rogers believes that individuals strive to fulfil themselves and that all of us, given a supportive interpersonal environment, have the necessary resources within ourselves to achieve this. In other words, an individual's personal growth towards healthy, competent, and creative functioning is largely inner controlled and driven rather than outer controlled and directed (Rogers, 1951, 1961). When this principle is translated into helping individuals develop it is referred to as *client-centred counselling* (as opposed to directive approaches to counselling). It has become one of the most common and widely used approaches in counselling practice (Mearns et al., 2013).

Rogers also believes that an individual's 'real' world is what the individual *perceives*, rather than what may actually be. In other words, reality is personal and subjective. Perceived reality is known as our *phenomenological field*. Simply speaking, if we perceive that we are boring, untalented and unlikeable, objective evidence to the contrary may make little difference to our sense of self. Instead, our phenomenological field has to be altered so that 'reality' may be perceived in a different light. Hence, facilitators of children's development must become part of the child's phenomenological world, and therefore be 'real' to the child.

QUESTION POINT

What do you think being 'real' to a child means? How would 'realness' operate in the classroom and school setting?

We saw that with Freud and Erikson parents and other significant others have a significant impact on the development of an individual's personality. For humanists, such as Rogers, the role of parents and teachers in childrearing and education is to facilitate children's growth in a caring but non-controlling environment. Parents and teachers best become facilitators of children's development by supplying appropriate opportunities, resources, support, and non-evaluative feedback to promote their growth, development, maturity, and ability to cope with life. In order to be facilitators parents and teachers must be caring, trustworthy, dependable, and consistent. Independence, creativity, self-reliance, and self-evaluation should all be supported, and children should be encouraged to take responsibility for their own learning and development.

As you can see, there is a strong emphasis in this approach on interpersonal relationships and feelings, and allowing children the freedom to grow. Parents and teachers are perceived as joint voyagers with children on the way to self-discovery. Indeed, the approach suggests that, as teachers and parents, we too grow through this process and that unless we also develop as 'real' people we cannot hope to be facilitators of others' growth to realness.

Further information on Roger's personality theory may be found at http://wynja. com/personality/rogersff.html.

 QUESTION POINT

Consider the different emphases of the humanist and Freudian theories. Which do you think offers more for the teacher in the classroom?

Abraham Maslow

Maslow's hierarchy of needs

Abraham Maslow (1908–1970), a humanist psychologist, considered that personal growth occurred through a series of stages which present alternatives for growth. Very young children are dominated by physiological needs, while older children are interested in testing themselves out in the environment, especially in relation to their physical abilities and their capacity to avoid danger. In middle childhood, as well as satisfying these needs, children increasingly test themselves out in the social world, where the need for affection and belonging becomes relatively more important. Last, as children grow older they develop clearer ideas about themselves as individuals with varying capacities which they wish to test. Thus, the need to feel competent, and to receive approval and recognition from others, becomes increasingly important. Each of these growth characteristics is reflected in Maslow's hierarchical system which we describe below.

According to Abraham Maslow (1968, 1970, 1976) physiological needs come first. These are often referred to as *deficiency needs*. If children are hungry, thirsty, or sleepy they will be preoccupied with satisfying these needs and will have little interest in other activities. These needs are cyclical, once they are filled they remain dormant until hunger or thirst arises once more. Many schools in low socioeconomic areas are instigating breakfast programmes for children who come from homes where they may not have been adequately fed in the morning. The purpose is, of course, to feed children so that they can concentrate more effectively on learning, a need higher up in

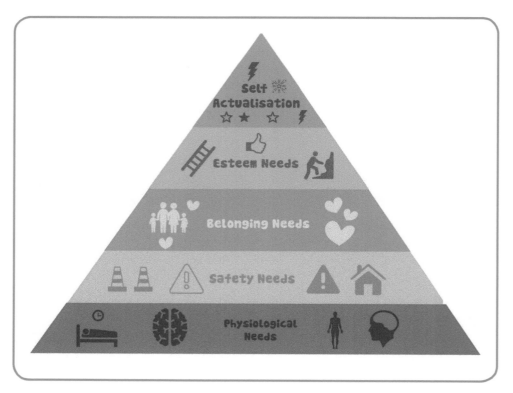

Figure 9.1   **Maslow's hierarchy of needs.**

the hierarchy, often referred to as a *growth need or metaneed*. The physiological needs do not have to be as graphic as illustrated by chronically hungry children. Just being too cold, or too hot, or too hungry for 'little lunch' is enough to distract children (and teachers) from the task of learning.

Children also have a need to feel safe and secure which is referred to as *safety needs*. Students learn best in environments in which they feel safe. If children are preoccupied with their physical welfare they will not learn well. Such conditions will predispose them to be fearful children. There is growing concern today about the level of bullying, especially cyberbullying, in our schools (Due et al., 2005; Rigby & Smith, 2011) which is incompatible with a safe learning environment. Bullying devalues, isolates, and frightens people so that they no longer believe in their ability to achieve. It has long term effects for those doing the bullying, their targets, and the onlookers. Every student has the right to expect that he or she will spend the day – both in and out of the classroom – free from bullying and intimidation. In the UK it is a legal responsibility for all state-funded schools to have a behaviour policy that includes measures to prevent all forms of bullying among students. All teachers, students, and parents must be informed of this policy (DfE, 2014).

Another example of this need for safety is children who come from homes where physical abuse is prevalent. These children often withdraw from involvement in classroom activities as they are preoccupied with the events that dominate their lives at that time at home (Cook, 2005; Pirrie et al., 2011). Continued insecurity makes it very difficult for them to reacquire confidence in themselves and, of course, confidence is a prerequisite of effective learning.

Most schools have well-established pastoral care programmes to alleviate problems related to abuse and insecurity of various types, those endemic to the school, and those related to the wider society from which the students come. Schools need to be safe and secure environments in which children can work. According to Maslow, teachers need to work within this basic needs framework to make learning environments satisfying to students and to maximise their motivation. As basic needs are satisfied, the metaneeds, or the needs related to self-actualisation, become important.

The third level of Maslow's hierarchy is the *need to belong*. Belongingness is initially satisfied through the family, but as children widen their social network this need must also be fulfilled through contact with others outside the family. A feeling of being one of the group and having a cohort with whom to identify within the school is important to children (Baker, 2006; Baskin et al., 2010). Isolates and outcasts, or children scorned by others, can be distracted from their schoolwork. Children can be cruel to each other and great unhappiness often results when an individual feels isolated from the group. Teachers must be aware of this and facilitate good interpersonal relationships and a sense of belonging within the classroom which fosters good classroom relationships (Jennings & Greenberg, 2009; Rigby, 2005). Even at the adult level the need for belongingness is very strong. Many companies and sports teams have group bonding sessions and team building exercises to encourage their members to feel part of the group. Companies and teams believe this enhances the happiness of their members and therefore leads to better motivation and productivity, and an identification with, and loyalty to, the company or team.

QUESTION POINT

Have you ever experienced a team building exercise? What was the nature of the exercise? What activities were conducted to help the group feel cohesive? What was the balance between formal and informal activities? Discuss your experiences with other members of your group. What application would such activities have for schools and classrooms? Is there any scope for team building among the staff of a school and what might the nature of such team building be?

The fourth, need for **self-esteem**, relates to an individual's need to feel worthwhile and important in the eyes of others. Again, the initial way in which this is fulfilled is through the family. However, we are all aware that there are times when children are denigrated within the family and come to school with negative thoughts and feelings about themselves. In these cases the school programmes and procedures, as well as classroom practices, must be designed to maximise students' feelings of self-worth.

 ACTIVITY POST

Complete an Internet search for self-worth programmes. What are the characteristics of these programmes. What is the research evidence that they are useful in enhancing students' feelings of self-worth?

Finally, according to Maslow, is the need for **self-actualisation**. At this level, individuals strive to satisfy their need to grow intellectually and spiritually.

 ACTIVITY POST

Maslow notes that human needs appear to arrange themselves in a hierarchical order, and that success at one level of need usually requires prior satisfaction of another more prepotent need. However, human motivation is affected by biological, cultural, and situational forces, all interacting and at times it appears that human behaviour does not seem to follow this hierarchical sequence. For example, many people will persist at a task long after they become hungry or thirsty because they are intensely interested in their work. At times, people are motivated to behave in ways that appear to contradict their basic needs for safety and belongingness because of the functioning of a higher need such as self-esteem or self-actualisation. Do a literature search on famous people in which you find exceptions to Maslow's hierarchy. Report your findings to a group. Why do you think these exceptions occur?

Classroom implications of humanistic perspectives

Realness, acceptance, and empathy

There are many applications of humanist psychology in the classroom stemming from the belief that effective teaching and classroom management is largely a function of positive teacher student and student–student relationships. The teacher's role is central in building positive interpersonal relationships and promoting a positive socioemotional climate (Farmer et al., 2011; Humphrey, 2013). In order to be effective humanists believe that teachers must understand themselves and be prepared to disclose their feelings to others, and they must also value learners as worthy partners in learning, entitled to have their own beliefs and values. Teachers should also be empathetic to the student being sensitively aware of the way learning and other experiences appear to students. Rogers (1961) referred to these three characteristics as realness, acceptance, and empathetic understanding.

 QUESTION POINT

How important do you think these three characteristics are to effective teaching? Have you seen evidence of these three characteristics in teachers you have known? If so, how did they exhibit these qualities? How are you sensitised to these humanistic qualities of teachers in your teacher education programme?

Open education

According to humanist educators the healthy socioemotional climate of classrooms is fundamental to effective teaching. Many teachers in the 1970s attempted to develop a range of teaching approaches that more clearly reflect humanistic philosophy. These have included **open education**, **open classrooms**, open scheduling and many forms of curricula that emphasise affective learning such as values clarification (Fraser, 2012; Hill, 2010).

Open education is a form of education, the goal of which is to respond to students on the basis of their individual behaviours, needs, and characteristics (Cahn, 2011). Open classrooms are based on the educational philosophy that children are active agents in their own development and learn at different rates. Teachers share decision making with students and students are evaluated in relation to their own previous performance rather than with the performance of other students. More information on open education may be obtained on the following website: http://edpsycinteractive. org/topics/affect/humed.html

Proponents of this approach see free access to resources as a more democratic approach to education which means that it is not limited to those persons or countries with access to wealth (Carson, 2009; Lane, 2008). This has been made partly possible by the advances in data storage and mobile technology. It is now possible to access and download resources from all over the world in a way that was not possible a decade ago.

Many other practices encouraged by the humanist approach are now part of mainstream educational practice: child-centred teaching, individualising instruction, encouraging independent work, pupil choice and responsibility, de-emphasising competition, and emphasising cooperation. Alternative forms of assessment such as observation and portfolios, negotiated curricula, and negotiated assessment, together with an emphasis on criterion-referenced evaluation rather than norm-referenced evaluation, also fit within a humanist philosophy of child-centred education.

 ACTIVITY POST

Using the Internet, look-up information on mainstreaming, open classrooms, individualising instruction, cooperative learning, alternative assessment modes, portfolios, negotiated curriculum, and criterion referenced evaluation. Examine the philosophy underpinning such educational practices and demonstrate how they reflect a humanistic approach to teaching and learning. How strong is the research support base for the effectiveness of these approaches compared with more traditional classroom practices such as norm references testing, direct instruction, and teacher dominated classroom instructional modes?

Humanist psychology has also had a strong influence on discipline and management programmes in schools. Noteworthy among these are Ginott, Glasser, Gordon, and Dreikurs who have developed humanistic ideas for the classroom, particularly with regard to forms of communication and discipline. As we have indicated earlier, teachers are an integral part of the interactive process in their classroom. By modelling interpersonal communication skills, teachers may help to initiate and facilitate teacher–student and student–student interaction which in turn will guide students in learning to use these skills.

ACTIVITY POST

Complete an Internet search on the management and discipline approaches of Ginott, Glasser, Gordon, and Dreikurs. Outline the key elements of each approach. Determine when each approach might be most appropriate. What is the research support base for the effectiveness of each approach? Which is the most popular approach in schools with which you are familiar?

 ACTIVITY POST

We have covered some important theories of personality in brief. Further details can be found on the following website: http://ship.edu/~cgboeree/perscontents. html. Using this website construct a table which illustrates the relative strengths of each theory for teachers and related professionals. List the criticisms that have been levelled at each theory. Which theory or combination is most satisfying to you?

 SPOTLIGHT ON BULLYING

Bullying and victimisation in the school have been recognised universally as damaging the psychological, social, and even physical development of children (Berger, 2007; Monks & Smith, 2006; Pepler et al., 2008; Smith, 2011). Those students who engage in bullying behaviour are predisposed to later antisocial, criminal, delinquent, and violent behaviour (Bender & Lösel, 2011; Farrington & Ttofi, 2011). Bullying incorporates a wide range of behaviours: name calling, extortion, physical violence, slander, exclusion from the group, damage to others' property, and verbal intimidation (Wang et al., 2009). When these behaviours occur through the medium of mobile phones, the internet, emails, or social media sites it is referred to as cyberbullying. Bullying is differentiated from other forms of aggressive behaviour in that it involves a more powerful group/individual dominating through violence, aggression, or intimidation of a less powerful group/individual over an extended period of time (Olweus, 2010, 2011). The extent of bullying is apparently extensive. Rigby and Smith (2011) reported that 14% of 8–16 year olds were bullied in English schools at least once in the previous four weeks. Similar situations were found in schools in Canada, Scandinavia,

(continued)

(continued)

and Ireland (see, for example, Due & Holstein, 2008; Modecki et al., 2014).

The causes of bullying are not clear. A controversial view is that bullies are trying to protect or boost low self-esteem, although research has resulted in mixed findings; some supporting this view, others not (Gendron et al., 2011). An important distinction to make, when considering the likely causes of bullies and victims is that rarely are children exclusively one or the other. Many bullies are also victims (Pollastri et al., 2009). One of the paradoxical aspects of bullying in schools is that it is sometimes tolerated as part of a child's 'growing up'. Indeed, bullies are often socially reinforced for bullying because of the sense of power they have satisfied in the view of onlookers. Evidence suggests, however, that bullying has detrimental effects on children and should not be a normal part of growing up. In fact, it should not be a part of any caring educational environment.

Anti-bullying programmes

In order to alleviate bullying in schools (and other educational settings such as training camps and apprenticeship programmes) many schools and institutions are introducing anti-bullying intervention programmes to indicate clearly that bullying is an unacceptable form of behaviour no longer condoned by teachers, parents or other students. These programmes have some common features. They usually adopt a whole-school-community approach which attempts to shape the ethos of the school so it is clearly anti-bullying. They seek to help both bullies and victims come to understand the negative effects of bullying, use strategies at the individual level, provide information and support to students, teachers, and families and integrate the programme into the school curriculum. One of the most commonly researched anti-bullying programmes implemented in schools all over Europe and North America, that incorportates these features, is the Olweus Bullying Prevention Programme, developed by Dan Olweus (Olweus & Limber, 2010). The website can be found here: http://violencepreventionworks.org/public/index.page

 QUESTION POINT

Consider a number of school anti-bullying policies. They can often be found on a school's website. What are their key features? What are their similarities and differences? Do they reflect any of the values discussed earlier in this chapter? How effective do you think these policies would be? Do you have any reservations about the policies and any suggestions for their improvement?

Social and emotional development in childhood

The social worlds of children play a very important role in their cognitive, personal, and social development. Children observe and model social and academic skills and standards for performance displayed by others, and they are rewarded for behaving in ways that are valued by teachers and peers. Children must also be socially as well as intellectually adept if they are to be successful students (Cohen, 2006; Durlak et al., 2011; Humphrey, 2013). The development of a social identity becomes increasingly important to children as they grow older. What is the importance of family relationships to social and emotional development? Sociability has its roots in the interactions of the baby and its parents or other caregivers, and these early experiences will either encourage or deter the baby's tendency to approach other human beings, and to feel secure about exploring the world.

Attachment

It is essential that a strong, affectionate bond be established between the child and caregivers (Brumariu & Kerns, 2011; Ebbeck & Yim, 2009). This is referred to as **attachment**. Attachment continues to be important throughout adolescence, and, in a wider sense, we all need a continuing feeling of attachment to caring others throughout our lives. Effective attachment depends upon mutual, warm, and loving engagement between the caregivers and the child. The infant may initiate these interactions through crying, clinging, smiles, and cooing. Caregivers may instigate them through nurturing and attending to the child's needs physically and emotionally. These interactions are mutually reinforcing and provide the basis for the development of interpersonal relationships and a sense for each individual of being part of a social network (Nickerson & Nagle, 2005). Ainsworth has classified four different levels of attachment which has implications for how adults should respond to children in particular situations that are now widely accepted (Ainsworth et al., 1978). These levels are secure attachment, insecure-avoidant attachment, insecure-resistant attachment, and disorganised and disoriented attachment. You might like to do an Internet search on attachment theory to see what these implications might be.

The nature of attachment changes as children grow older. In the early years in the home, parents and siblings are the most important elements in the development of a child's social self. As children grow older, mothers typically spend less time with them while fathers become more important influences in their development, involving themselves more in children's activities, such as hobbies, sports, and clubs. Siblings also act as important socialising influences on each other. The most persuasive characteristics of this relationship are competition and concern about being treated equally by parents.

While competitive interaction is a fact of sibling life, there are many positive and neutral interactions that benefit the child's social and emotional development. Someone close in age to the child may be able to communicate more effectively than parents can. In areas such as dealing with peers, coping with difficult teachers, and discussing taboo subjects, siblings are often of more assistance and support than parents. Older siblings may model appropriate behaviour and attitudes to a range of events dealing with identity, physical appearance, and sexual behaviour – areas in which the parents may be unwilling or incapable of helping the child. Of course, sometimes the reverse can occur with older siblings modelling inappropriate behaviour and attitudes.

SPOTLIGHT ON PARENTING STYLES

In our Western society parents begin to give their children increasing independence as they grow older (although this is not a universally practised custom). Many parents encourage their children to take on part-time paid work and to achieve independent goals, thereby fostering a sense of industry. Indeed, parenting styles reflecting involvement, autonomy, and support may promote the development of a healthy sense of autonomy (see, for example, Joussemet et al., 2008; Soenens & Vansteenkiste, 2010). Parenting styles are often classified in three basic ways: **authoritative, authoritarian, permissive**. Authoritative parenting is characterised by parents who provide a loving and supportive home, hold appropriate and high expectations for their children, have clear rules on acceptable behaviour and enforce rules consistently, and include children in decision making. This type of parenting is most associated with well-adjusted children. In contrast, authoritarian parenting is characterised by restrictive rules and lack of warmth, while permissive parenting is characterised by lack of concern and control. Children from authoritarian homes tend to be unhappy, anxious, and lacking social skills, while those from permissive homes tend to be selfish, unmotivated, impulsive, and disobedient (Chan & Koo, 2011; Hoeve et al., 2009).

While it might be tempting to say that parenting styles cause these behaviours in children the findings are based on correlational research which means that the interactions between parents and children are reciprocal. In other words, parents will be responding to their children's behaviours as well as children responding to their parent's behaviours. Although parents might begin by being authoritative, children's behaviour might lead the parents to become more authoritarian, or perhaps even laissez-faire. How would this happen? (See for example the article in *Current directions in psychological science* by Serbin and Karp (2003).)

Social and emotional development

Often personal, social, and emotional problems begin to surface as children enter school, with rates of referral for primary children being considerably higher than for preschool children. Common problems are oppositional and acting-out behaviour, poor discipline, and personal characteristics such as shyness, unhappiness, and withdrawal. Many of these emotional and behavioural problems are related to the home backgrounds of the children. Indeed, the changing nature of society and family structure has put new pressures on young children and brought new responsibilities to the school and teachers.

In many households both parents work, so increasing numbers of children leave for school and arrive home after school without adult supervision. Many children in our classrooms come from single-parent homes, the result of separation, divorce, or parental death. In the 2014 General Household Survey there were two million single parent families with dependent children living in the UK and 91% of these were women (Office for National Statistics, 2015a). Many children suffer trauma as a result of such effects of divorce as custodial arrangements, the nature of the custodial parent–child relationship, and the availability and reliance on support systems (Fabricius & Luecken, 2007; Lansford, 2009; Lansford et al., 2006). In this, and in other circumstances where children lose parents, the classroom teacher becomes an important element in the child's support structure. During middle and late childhood, peers, teachers, and other adults become more important (Bokhorst et al., 2010; Nickerson & Nagle, 2005).

 QUESTION POINT

How should teachers and other school personnel support a child going through emotional difficulties resulting from a trauma such as divorce of his or her parents, or death of a parent or sibling? What other professional agencies outside the school could be used to assist and provide advice?

The peer group

As children progress through school the peer group becomes more important. Many children organise themselves into more or less exclusively girl or boy **cliques**. Indeed, in late childhood groups of children are more often than not single sex. Rituals and rules may be established to keep other individuals out of the group, but cliques become less rigid as children approach puberty and groups become more heterosexual. Most schools now implement non-sexist practices that cut across sex-based cliques, although in out-of-school activities most children prefer to get together in single-sex groups.

QUESTION POINT

Can you remember being part of a single sex group at school? When was this? Were there any rules for being part of the group? When did your friendship groups become less exclusively single sex? Are adolescence and adulthood groups still predominantly single sex for many activities? If they are, why do these single sex groupings persist?

Small friendship groups are very important to the identity of the child as they give a secure base from which the child can test out their growing ideas of the world across a wide range of areas, including areas in which they would be reluctant to seek information and advice from their parents and other adults. The characteristics of students' friends, and the features of their friendships, may influence students' self-perceptions, attitudes, and behaviours (Aikins et al., 2005; Bissell-Havran & Loken, 2009; Nelson & DeBacker, 2008). Through *peer modelling* and reinforcement, children can acquire and test out their growing personal, social, and physical skills in a group that is supportive (Vitaro et al., 2007).

Peer interactions are reciprocal, that is, they have a mutual impact on each other. An important aspect of these friendships is in the area of *emotional development*. In coping with emotional conflict, young friends express considerable emotion, sympathy, and support for each other (Findlay et al., 2006; Nickerson et al., 2008). Family and cultural backgrounds play critical roles in the development of both informal and formal peer groups. Children's perception of security in the mother–child relationship, for example, has been shown to be related to the formation of positive peer relationships in middle childhood (Kerns et al., 2006). Therefore, even though children and adolescents often spend greater amounts of time with their peers than with their parents, isolation from parental values does not necessarily ensue (Bokhorst et al., 2010; Smetana et al., 2006).

Sociometry

As we have indicated above, having friends is related to school adjustment (Waldrip et al., 2008). At times it is useful to find out the friendship networks of groups of children in order to understand some of the dynamics that characterise their academic and social behaviour at school. A measurement technique commonly used to measure the social structure of groups is called a **sociometric test** (Cillessen, 2009). A sociometric test consists of asking each member of a group to name the people with whom he or she would like to associate in various situations. When each child has given its answer they are tabulated on a summary sheet from which a number of features of social interaction can be evaluated. These features include clusters (groups of children who are friends), stars (children who are chosen by many members of the group), and isolates (children who choose one or more children within a group but no one chooses them). By counting the number of times a child is chosen you can discover the degree to which he or she is accepted by other members of the group. This is called **sociometric status**. A sociometric test reveals the structure of the group as a whole. Is it made up of cliques or is it well integrated? Is there a cleavage between the boys and girls? Is there a cleavage between ethnic groups? Are there any children who cross barriers and act as integrating members of the group as a whole? Who are the leaders and who are the followers? Figure 9.2 illustrates a sociometric analysis of a pre-school classroom.

The most practical use of sociometric tests is to help organise and arrange actual classroom groups. The children's sociometric choices are a valuable guide in working out desk arrangements or setting up groups. Sociometric tests may be given at different times of the year in order to discover how the group structure and individuals' sociometric status and personal relationships have changed over the year. This is particularly useful if a teacher has implemented some type of intervention to improve social dynamics within the classroom.

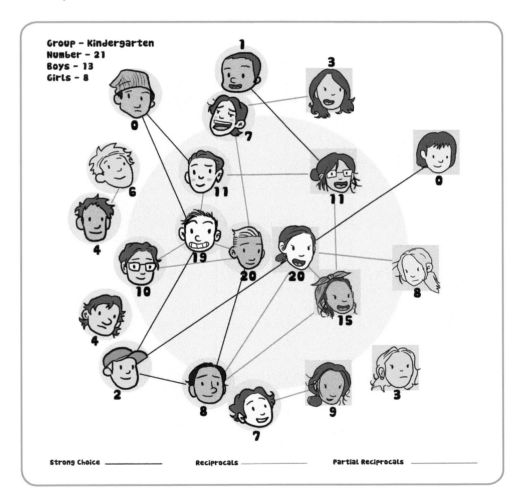

Figure 9.2   Sociometric analysis of a pre-school classroom.

There are limitations in sociometric tests. They only give information about children and their relationships within the group tested, results can't be extrapolated to other social situations. The test shows who a person's friends are, but does not give information about the depth or nature of the relationship. In and of themselves sociometrics do not reveal anything about the children's actual social behaviour, nor indicate what kinds of social skills they have. In order to evaluate this, sociometric results need to be supported by observations.

Having said this, sociometric techniques allow us to routinely identify children as popular, sociable, withdrawn, isolated, neglected, unpopular, rejected, aggressive, controversial, average, normal (Cillessen & Rose, 2005; Košir & Pečjak, 2005). Popular status and social acceptance are related to successful academic performance, and rejected status and low levels of acceptance to academic difficulties. Therefore two groups that are important to identify are sociometrically rejected children, those who are infrequently nominated as someone's best friend and are actively disliked by their peers, and sociometrically popular children, those who are frequently nominated as a best friend and rarely disliked by their peers (Sandstrom & Cillessen, 2006). In general, when compared to average-status peers, popular students are more cooperative, helpful, sociable, demonstrate better leadership skills, and are more self-assertive. In contrast, rejected students tend to be less compliant, less self-assured, less sociable, and more aggressive, disruptive, and withdrawn than their average-status peers.

 ACTIVITY POST

Conduct a sociometric test among a group of students by conducting a friendship survey. This might be a classroom group, a club, or a sporting team. It is usual to ask individuals who they like to be with for particular activities such as play, seatwork in class, or organised group activity. The number of questions can be variable and should suit the age of the students. It is important to ask questions that elicit from the student who they like rather than choosing on the basis of particular skills and technical abilities that another student might have. A good example of a question is: Suppose your class was going on a field trip and you were travelling by car. Each car would take four students. Who would you like to have ride in the same car that you were going in?

The situation for the 'test' should be informal as possible and your instructions clear. Do not force individuals to give a response. Tabulate the results in such a way that you can ascertain visually where the relationships lie. This should indicate the individual's sociometric status, number of individuals who chose each person, the number of choices made by each individual, the number of different individuals each person chooses, reciprocal choices, sub-groups, and cliques. A way of coding responses such as coloured arrows between individuals, and double headed arrows for reciprocal choices, etc. can be useful.

You should never give the results of the test out to the students, although they can be usefully used to discuss elements of class dynamics in general.

SPOTLIGHT ON PLAY AND PERSONALITY DEVELOPMENT

Play is very important to the social and emotional development of children (Ginsberg, 2007; Newton & Jenvey, 2011). The interpersonal interactions between peers during play, particularly those involving prosocial or aggressive interactions, influence social development. Exposure during play to the opinions, ideas, feelings, and feedback of peers enables children to move beyond egocentric thought to consider the point of view of others (Lillard et al., 2013). It is also believed that positive play experiences at school enhance an individual's learning behaviours, for example, motivation, feelings of competence, persistence, and positive attitudes, while reducing classroom behaviour problems. Children who engage in less positive play experiences are more likely to lack motivation and to engage in disruptive behaviour (Uren & Stagnitti, 2009). Indeed, so important is play to the cognitive, social, and physical development of children that many educational settings beyond the early school years include both free and structured play opportunities within the formal school programme as an instructional strategy, over and above what happens spontaneously in play at break times (Annetta et al., 2009; Honeyford & Boyd, 2015).

Conversely, at many other schools the opportunity for play becomes significantly reduced as students move from kindergarten to first grade and beyond. In effect, the reduction in free and structured play limits the opportunities for students to learn through social interaction with peers.

Play researchers believe that play develops through a series of stages and should be intrinsically motivating, spontaneous, self-initiated, and free from too many rules. The idea that play develops through a series of stages was first identified by Parten as long ago as 1932. She identified five stages:

1 *Solitary:* the child plays alone, unaware of others.
2 *Onlooker:* the child looks on at the play of others but is not directly involved in it.
3 *Parallel:* children play alongside others doing similar things, but with little or no interaction.
4 *Associative:* children play as a group, using the same materials, but do not appear to share a plan of action or common purpose.
5 *Cooperative:* children play with each other, making up and taking turns in games that have a shared goal.

As children develop, so do the complexity and social nature of their play. While *solitary* and *onlooker* play is characteristic of young children, and *associative* and *cooperative* play is more typical of the older child, it is inaccurate to use the categorisation of social play as a marker of social maturity. Just as young children may take part in the interactive games or associative play when they play pretend games and chatter to each other (Lillard et al., 2011; Lillard et al., 2013), so older children may also engage in solitary play in which they play quietly for a period by themselves, showing that they are now able to concentrate on a task (Smith, 2005). As for onlooker play, even adolescents may remain on the side until they have worked up the confidence to participate in a group 'game' to which they are newcomers.

(continued)

(continued)

As some children are less socially competent in interactive play situations teachers should also foster interactions between children at various levels of interactive play competence. This may help alleviate inappropriate classroom behaviour and help develop social competence in children (Michnick-Golinkoff et al., 2006).

In addition to social skills, many language and interpersonal skills are learnt through cooperative and associative play as children have to interact with one another in the business of problem solving, negotiating, resolving disputes, turn-taking, and sharing resources. The teacher has an important role to play in providing the language needed to describe the conflicts that erupt in children's play and in assisting children in understanding the perspective of others who may often inadvertently thwart them.

10 Personal and social development in adolescence

Introduction

In Chapter 9 we introduced a number of personality theories which help us understand the process of personality development during childhood. We now turn our attention to personal development during the period of adolescence. In order to make sense of the continuity in development you should read Chapter 9 before this chapter.

Of critical importance during adolescence is the formation of healthy emotions and personal and social identity. Social development and identity formation during the adolescent years acquire more significance than they had at any previous time. Essential to this is the relationship adolescents continue to have with their parents and siblings, as well as the developing relationships they have with their social networks through their expanding interpersonal contacts at school and elsewhere. We cover important aspects of these interconnections in this chapter specifically by looking at the development of healthy relationships in which elements of autonomy, independence, interdependence, and connectedness are developed. We also consider conflict situations with parents, peers, and others that might lead to adolescent alienation.

One of the most important personal developments that occurs during adolescence is the development of a sense of **identity** which refers to people's self-constructed definition of who they are, what they find important, and what goals they want to accomplish in life. There are a number of explanations and interpretations of how identity is formed. Influential in our understanding of identity formation during adolescence has been the work of Erikson and Marcia. We dealt with elements of Erikson's psychosocial theory of personal development in Chapter 9. In this chapter we specifically consider Erikson's and Marcia's views of identity formation during adolescence. Important elements of a healthy identity are a positive self-concept, self-regulation, and positive self-efficacy. We deal with each of these in some detail.

Social and emotional development, social identity, and adolescence

Few developmental periods are characterised by so many changes at so many different levels as adolescence (Laursen & Collins, 2009; Wigfield et al., 2006). We have considered a number of these changes, such as physical and cognitive, in earlier chapters. While it is not uncommon for adolescents to experience some problems during this time, most pass through puberty and adolescence without significant psychological or emotional difficulties. Most adolescents develop a positive sense of personal identity and manage to form adaptive peer relationships at the same time as maintaining close relationships with their families.

Some adolescents experience difficulties that cause deep emotional stress and anxiety that leads them into a downward spiral that ends in academic failure and difficulty in attending school. Indeed, research shows that poor socioemotional adjustment and conduct problems are associated with past, present, and future academic achievement problems (Fantuzzo et al., 2005; Masten et al., 2005). Parents and educators should be sensitive to the needs of all adolescents at this time in order to provide the emotional supports needed for healthy personal, social, and emotional development (Aviles et al., 2006; Jennings & Greenberg, 2009).

When considering overall social development during adolescence, attention should be focused on four important aspects. The first of these is the continuing process by which a sense of personal identity is established. We consider this in some detail later in the chapter. The second aspect is the nature of the family relationships and its effect on the adolescent's self-reliance, independence, and interconnectedness. The third, peer group interaction, focuses specifically on the development of interpersonal relationships and group acceptance. The fourth aspect deals with the opportunities provided by social environments, including the school, for healthy personal and social development of the individual.

Family relationships, social development, and relationship to academic adjustment

Parenting styles

Research has shown that parenting styles have a considerable impact on social development and academic adjustment (Smetana et al., 2006; Spera, 2005). The original work of Baumrind (1967) highlighted three possible patterns of parenting styles – **authoritative parenting**, **permissive parenting**, and **authoritarian parenting**. We examined elements of these parenting styles and their potential effects in Chapter 9. Later theorists (Maccoby & Martin, 1983) expanded this to four prototypic patterns of parenting which included warmth and demandingness dimensions: authoritative style (high warmth and high behavioural demandingness); authoritarian style (low warmth and high demandingness); indulgent-permissive (high warmth and low demandingness), and rejecting-neglectful (low warmth and low demandingness). Research clearly shows that the most effective parenting style for personal and school adjustment is the authoritative style (Silva et al., 2007; Turner et al., 2009). Further information on parenting styles and their relationship to personal development may be found at the following website: http://psychology.about.com/od/developmentalpsychology/a/parenting-style.htm

We also saw in Chapter 9 that effective attachment to caregivers is very important for healthy personal development. The importance of attachment continues through adolescence. Indeed, probably the most critical factor in the development of identity is the nature of the relationship adolescents continue to have with their parents. Research findings suggest that attachment to parents may facilitate adolescents' social competence and well-being, reflected through self-esteem, emotional adjustment, and physical health (Laible, 2007; Nickerson & Nagle, 2005). Adolescents who have secure relationships with their parents have higher self-esteem and better emotional well-being. Attachment to parents during adolescence serves the adaptive function of providing a secure base from which adolescents can explore and master new environments and a widening social world in a psychologically healthy way (Brumariu & Kerns, 2010).

Connectedness to parents

In the last decade, developmentalists have begun to explore the role of *connectedness to parents* in adolescent development. Adolescents continue to seek help from their parents for both major and minor developmental problems, including interpersonal, health, and educational problems (Ackard et al., 2006). This connectedness to parents also promotes competent peer relations and positive close relationships outside the family (Barber & Schluterman, 2008).

 QUESTION POINT

Consider your own personal development. What role did your parents play? Using the typology presented by Maccoby and Martin what style of parenting characterised your childhood? How does this differ to the experience of other students in your class?

Autonomy and independence

As we saw in Chapter 9, establishing autonomy and independence are important elements in the development of personality. As children enter adolescence autonomy and independence become quite crucial issues discussed by parents and their children. Younger children are easier to 'control' and boundaries on behaviour are more easily established. Because adolescents want greater autonomy than that granted to them as children, there is typically a temporary increase in family conflict over autonomy and control while the elements of these are renegotiated (Baumrind, 2005). The degree of difficulty that the adolescent encounters in establishing independence depends on a number of factors: the consistency, rate, extent, and complexity of independence training that is sanctioned by society as a whole, and reflected in organisations such as schools, together with the child-rearing practices and models of behaviour provided by the parents (Pomerantz et al., 2005).

QUESTION POINT

Consider the cultural group to which you belong. What are the major elements of independence training? At what time do major developmental milestones in independence training occur? Compare your answers to those of students in your class from other cultural groups.

In optimal situations parents reinforce and stimulate this process of growing autonomy, self-determination, and independence (Goldstein et al., 2005; Pomerantz et al., 2005; Ryan & Deci, 2006; Soenens et al., 2007). Important in this is the opportunity given to adolescents to have an input into family decision making. It appears that those who feel they have such an input have higher self-esteem and greater school motivation. It appears that such children also make an easier transition into high school (Hill & Tyson, 2009). In contrast, excessive parental control is linked to lower intrinsic school motivation, to more negative changes in self-esteem following high school transition, to more school misconduct associated with this transition, and to greater investment in peer social attachments and even delinquency (Fan & Williams, 2010; Guay et al., 2008). It is not possible to determine whether the parental control is the cause or result of these aspects of adolescent behaviour. They probably interact. It is also necessary to add that too little parental control also leads to significant negative consequences.

Erikson: identity formation

In Chapter 9 we considered Erikson's first four stages of personal development which coincided with childhood. The fifth stage, **identity** versus **role confusion**, coincides with adolescence and according to Erikson, is a particularly important stage for the development of self-identity. This period occurs during a time of increasing social contacts. Adolescents integrate what they have learnt about themselves and begin to test their identity out in the wider world. In particular, adolescents compare their experiences with their peers, and become interested in relationships, religions, politics, and society in general. Becoming members of sporting associations, religious groups, and social networks outside the family grows increasingly important and helps to define for individuals where they belong.

Role confusion results when an adolescent feels lost, unattached, or confused in social identity. This might be the result of inadequate opportunities to form social networks outside the family or residual from poorly resolved conflicts in earlier stages. For example, individuals who already feel inferior and guilty may choose not to test themselves in the wider community of peers and relationships and, therefore, deny themselves further opportunities for personal growth. Conversely, individuals with a poorly developed identity may either go to extremes to become part of a group or engage in antisocial or antipersonal behaviour, such as delinquency and substance abuse, to reduce their sense of confusion.

ACTIVITY POST

The media is full of stories these days of youths and youth groups that engage in antisocial behaviour. Over a period of two weeks collect a portfolio related to youth culture and antisocial behaviour. What are the defining features of the youth culture and antisocial behaviour? What reasons are given in the articles and other media for antisocial behaviour? Categorise the behaviours according to principles of personal development covered in this Chapter 9 and this chapter.

Erikson: young adulthood and beyond

As adolescents become young adults they develop greater intimacy with others, and they begin to share with others and care about other people selflessly in ways that were not characteristic of earlier stages of personal development. This period is considered to be one of developing *intimacy* versus *isolation*. It is through selfless caring that individuals develop a sense of intimacy with others. If a sense of intimacy is not established with friends or a marriage partner, the result, according to Erikson, is a sense of isolation, of being alone without anyone to share with or care for.

In the earlier stages of personality development people are somewhat self-absorbed in the sense that experiences are interpreted in terms of what they mean to the individual. As psychologically healthy individuals progress through the stages they become more oriented to other people. In the seventh stage, which occurs during middle adulthood and is referred to as *generativity* versus *self-absorption*, individuals become aware of, and more involved with, things and people outside their immediate families. They become concerned for the future of the world and the younger generation. Those who fail to establish a sense of generativity stagnate in a state of self-absorption in which their personal concerns and comforts become of primary concern.

In the final period, *integrity* versus *despair*, there is still the potential for personal growth. Integrity characterises the older individual who looks upon life's journey as an adventure of self-discovery, in which positive and negative experiences have been melded into a personality with which the individual is content. On the other hand, old age may bring to the individual despair and regret for lost opportunities and direction. The task of sharing wisdom and encouraging others is accepted with enthusiasm by those who develop integrity.

As with the earlier stages, society has an important role to play here in fostering within individuals a sense of integrity. Communities and families that respect the elderly and give them opportunities to be productive facilitate the development of a sense of integrity. On the other hand, elderly people who are substantially isolated from events of importance, such as sharing in the rearing and teaching of children, may feel undervalued and despair. Further useful information may be obtained at the following website that provides details on the eight stages of development and provides information on Erikson's notion of identity crisis: http://simplypsychology.org/Erik-Erikson.html

Classroom applications of Erikson's theory

Importance of teachers and peers

There are several features of Erikson's theory that make it attractive to people in the helping professions such as teaching. We noted earlier that Freud's theory suggests that the early years of life and, in particular, parenting practices related to feeding, toilet training, and the inculcation of sexual identity and values have the major role to play in personality development, with other events and interpersonal contacts being of relatively minor importance. On the other hand, Erikson, while agreeing that there is an initial onus on parents to support positive personal growth in children, argues strongly that other people, such as teachers and peers, become increasingly important as children grow older, and that personality development is a continuous process, with growth, development, and change occurring whenever children are given positive or negative experiences.

Furthermore, earlier negative experiences such as parental neglect, which leads to a sense of mistrust in children, can be alleviated by later positive experiences such as a caring school and teacher, thereby fostering a sense of trust within the children. Children who have their sense of industry derogated at home can have it revitalised at school through the actions of caring and stimulating teachers. We must add here, however, that action can occur both ways. A child who comes to school with a well-developed sense of trust may have it undermined by an uncaring teacher or bullying peers, and a child who is always building and inventing at home may lose interest in a classroom dominated by regulation and a National Curriculum that does not foster creativity.

A key to understanding Erikson's theory is the knowledge that, at each period of development, experiences can be positive or negative and the total personality at any particular time reflects the balance struck between them. If children experience basically negative or confusing experiences, they may be unable to establish a sense of self-identity, a process that Erikson called *role confusion*. This may be reflected in delinquent behaviour, losing one's identity in the group or extreme identification with atypical groups (such as religious extremism) or substance abuse. Children and adolescents may emotionally and cognitively disengage from their education and in extreme cases become 'school refusers'.

Identity crisis

Some psychologists suggest that, unless adolescents go through some type of **identity crisis**, where they clarify and become aware of personal values that they commit themselves to, little psychological growth can occur. Research suggests that many adolescents do not go through such a crisis and therefore fall short of mature identity achievement. Instead, **identity foreclosure** results, in which adolescents prematurely

Figure 10.1   Identity Crisis.

identify with the values and goals of their parents without questioning whether they are right for them (Marcia, 1980; see also 1966, 1967).

James Marcia

Basing his work on that of Erikson, James Marcia proposed four identity statuses that resolve the identity crisis. Each status relates to an individual's commitment to a career, personal value system, sexual attitudes, and religious beliefs. Some resolutions are more positive for the personality than others.

1 **Identity diffusion**: where there is no crisis and no commitment. This is exemplified in the adolescent or young adult who flits from job to job, commitment to commitment and relationship to relationship with little personal investment. Identity diffusion may be the product of earlier unresolved conflicts, or may result from perceived blocks in the environment, such as parental disapproval or cultural barriers. It is often characterised by self-doubt, anxiety, depression, and apathy.

Figure 10.2   Identity Diffusion.

2 **Identity foreclosure**: where there is no crisis and commitment is based on the will of the parents or other significant people, such as ministers of religion or romantic partners. This is exemplified by the young adult who becomes a lawyer or chemist because 'Dad and Mum expect it' or goes into Dad's business, without any personal valuing of the career. It might also occur as a result of an adolescent falling into a career in which they already have a perceived interest or talent (e.g. sporting or artistic skills), without leaving scope to develop other areas of interest. Identity foreclosure can lead to discontent in later life.

3 **Identity moratorium**: where the individual is experiencing crisis and working out roles and commitments. This is exemplified by the young adult who tries out a variety of personal and social options before making a commitment. The delay in making a commitment may be the product of family events, socioeconomic position, educational deprivation, and other social barriers. An individual may drop out of university for a period of time to 'sort out' whether this is really the right career path. Choosing to return, or to go in a different direction, facilitates the achievement of identity. Some students delay making a choice until they have temporarily broken the ties of their families and schooling. Again, this process can facilitate the ultimate choice in which there is a personal commitment.

4 **Identity achieved**: having already explored alternatives, identity-achieved individuals are committed to a clearly formulated set of self-chosen values and goals. They feel a sense of psychological well-being, of knowing who they are and where they are going. When asked about career or life changes they might respond that they are pretty sure that what they are doing is right for them.

Identity achievement and moratorium are considered healthy alternatives, whereas adolescents who can't proceed past the identity diffusion or identity foreclosure stage have difficulties in adjustment. They need extra assistance and counselling to answer the important question 'Who am I?'

QUESTION POINT

Consider your choice of university course or career. How did you decide to do the training you are now doing? Can you classify your decision-making according to Marcia's typology. Do the reasons for your career decision differ with those of other students?

SPOTLIGHT ON IDENTITY FORMATION IN CROSS-CULTURAL CONTEXTS

Identity formation is influenced by salient and societally important cultural factors. Does Marcia's typology of identity formation therefore have general application in countries such as the United Kingdom, the United States, and Australia that are characterised by ethnic and cultural diversity? Cross-cultural research seems to indicate that the same patterns do occur across cultures (Hughes et al., 2006). However, Marcia's interpretation certainly highlights the individualistic component of identity formation in which the individual is reacting to social situations shaping identity rather than being embedded within and part of the social milieu. As we have discussed earlier in our treatment of Vygotsky, a social contructivist view of identity formation would emphasise the idea that a person's identity may be inseparable from the group identity in which it is situated (see, for example, Postmes et al., 2005).

Erikson emphasised that one of the important elements of identity formation is for it to be validated by others in the community. Hence an individual's cultural identity, nurtured by members of their own cultural community, is essential to personal identity formation. In many societies the idea of individual identity, as we understand it in Western societies, may be contradictory to identity as it is understood

(continued)

(continued)

in those societies in which social identity takes precedence over individual identity.

The notion of identity formation and identity crisis is certainly thrown into strong relief when we consider individuals who come from ethnic minority groups in multi-ethnic societies such as the United Kingdom, the United States, Australia, New Zealand, and Canada. In their case, there may be an even stronger clash of forces orienting the development of their sense of identity. For example, while children from a traditional Western background are socialised within a world in which society at large, family and peer groups share many common values and traditions, children whose families may originate from Asian or African counties (e.g. Syria, Sudan, China, or Iran), may well find that they are influenced by conflicting forces. For example, while traditional Western children are encouraged by society, and family and peer groups to develop individuality and autonomy, many children from other cultures may be encouraged by their families and cultural groups to remain interdependent. Therefore these children receive conflicting messages from the wider society, school, peers, and their cultural community. On multiple levels

such as moral values, dress, use of spare time, political views, dating, education, career choice, and religion there is potential for conflicting messages and identity conflict (Shih & Sanchez, 2005). This may be further exacerbated for females who traditionally are given even less freedom to make personal decisions (on such matters as dating, education, and career choice) than males in particular ethnic communities.

State schools in England have statutory responsibility to teach 'Fundamental British Values' (Department for Education, 2014). These are: Democracy, the rule of law, individual liberty, and mutual respect and tolerance of those with different faiths and beliefs. How might children from non-Western cultural backgrounds respond to these values? Are these values exclusively British and who decides what these values should be? What might the implications of this be for parents, teachers, and other professionals involved with adolescents? What special issues are related to individuals forming an ethnic identity?

The Department for Education guidance document can be found at: https://gov.uk/government/uploads/system/uploads/attachment_data/file/380595/SMSC_Guidance_Maintained_Schools.pdf

Parental involvement and identity formation

Probably the most critical factor in the development of a sense of identity is the nature of the relationship that children and adolescents maintain with their parents (Luyckx et al., 2006; McLean, 2005; Smetana et al., 2006). Establishing a strong identity is facilitated if a sufficiently rewarding, interactive relationship exists between the child or adolescent and both parents. It is important that the same-sex parent serves as an adequate model for personally and socially effective and appropriate behaviour. It is also important that the opposite-sex parent is an effective individual, and approves of the model provided by the same-sex parent and the child's own identification with this model.

Because adolescents challenge cherished values, such as religious beliefs, moral values, political allegiances, and parental authority this period can be quite trying for parents (Smetana, 2005; Smetana et al., 2005). This time can also be a period of change and personal stress for parents which may exacerbate difficulties experienced with adolescent children. Many parents of adolescent children are entering their middle years; as well as having ambivalent attitudes towards the growing independence of their children and often lacking expertise in handling the developmental problems of this age, parents may also be experiencing their own emotional problems and conflicts that impact on parent–child interactions – problems such as marital dissatisfaction, economic burdens, career re-evaluation, and health and body concerns such as menopause (Davis-Kean, 2005; Morrison et al., 2005). If this parental perspective is taken into account the lack of communication between parents and adolescents and the conflicts that often result can be better understood, and better advice given. Such problems may be further exacerbated for migrant parents who see, as well, cherished cultural values dissipating as their adolescent children become increasingly assimilated into the cultural norms of their new country.

At the time that adolescents are moving away from parent dependency, they often substitute peer dependency (Wigfield & Wagner, 2005). As I indicated above, adolescents seek out and listen to the advice of peers on many issues, especially those involving immediate consequences, such as clothes, entertainment, fads, and so on. Peers exert a great deal of pressure on each other to conform. They also give each other the opportunity to express the frustrations and problems they have at home. However, adults often exaggerate the power of the peer group, particularly as it relates to sexual behaviour, substance abuse, and delinquency. It is important to note that, as well as parents and peers, other forces within society strongly influence the adolescent, including the popular media and other adults such as teachers, coaches, and part-time employers.

 QUESTION POINT

What do you think are the other major influences on adolescent identity formation; what are the positive aspects of their influence; what are the potential negative aspects?

Conflict with parents

During adolescence children move in wider social circles and are increasingly exposed to the values and models of behaviour of their peer group and to belief systems of different families. Often this leads to conflict as adolescents compare what their peers are able to do with what their parents allow them to do (Steinberg et al., 2006). It is important that there is effective communication between the adolescent and the parents, and that parents and adolescents use problem-solving procedures to reduce conflict. Under the best circumstances the adolescent (and parents and teachers) learn to compromise rather than being hostile and confronting (Smetana, 2005). Adolescents should be encouraged and helped to be empathetic, take the perspective of others, and be less confrontational.

Parental aspirations and expectations for their children, parenting styles (such as authoritarian and authoritative), level of parental support and involvement in monitoring school work, level of contact with the school, as well as their involvement in stimulating children's development, are very important to student achievement at school (Hill & Tyson, 2009; Jeynes, 2007; Lee & Bowen, 2006; Spera, 2005).

 ACTIVITY POST

In multi-racial countries such as the United Kingdom and Australia, the norms for autonomy and independence training vary widely from one cultural group to another and from one set of parents to another. This variation can cause considerable difficulty for some children from groups that do not encourage independence in the same way as some Western groups. There can be a cultural clash when children are expected to behave in contradictory ways depending on social circumstances. Interview some adolescent students from varying cultural backgrounds and examine the issue of cultural similarities and differences in the development of autonomy and independence. Write a brief report on your findings and compare them with those of other students in your group.

 SPOTLIGHT ON PARENTING STYLES AND CULTURAL DIFFERENCES

It is important that concepts such as *authoritarian* and *authoritative* be interpreted through cultural lenses. People from an Asian heritage may have a different set of labels appropriate to describing beneficial and less beneficial parenting styles from the point of view of achievement than those appropriate to Western groups. For example, international comparisons show that authoritarian parenting is negatively related to academic achievement in most countries (e.g. the United States, Australia, mainland China), but positively related to academic achievement in Hong Kong (Spera, 2005).

Research with American children in Years 3 through 5 (Lee & Bowen, 2006) has shown that parental beliefs and attitudes differed across sociodemographic groups. Parental expectations did not differ across ethnic groups, but parents from economically disadvantaged backgrounds, and who may not have formal school qualifications themselves, were less optimistic about their children's education. Similar levels of help with homework were reported across groups, however children from Hispanic or Latino backgrounds (an ethnic minority group in the United States) were more likely to limit children's leisure activities during the school week to allow for extra time to be devoted to homework. Involvement in school was greatest among parents whose lifestyle and culture was similar to the culture of the school. Parents of children from minority groups were less likely to become involved with school due to a lack of confidence in their own interactions with the schooling system.

A study in the United Kingdom by Crozier and Davies (2005) examined school involvement from the parents of Pakistani and Bangladeshi heritage families. Interviews with parents showed that they generally had very little involvement with their children's schools, knew very little about the education system and in some cases what their children were learning in school. Although characterised by the schools as being 'hard to reach' these parents were not uninterested in their children's education. Rather, they trusted the schools in their role as providers of education. Furthermore, schools may be unintentionally making it difficult for these parents to become more involved by assuming that parents would already understand the ways in which they could become involved, not considering the ethnic makeup of the student body (being 'colour blind' to race) and not indicating to parents, who may have poor English, that bilingual assistants were available to support meetings.

Both of these studies highlight the 'psychological barriers' that may exist to school involvement in certain groups. Why is it important for teachers to be sensitive to cultural differences in parenting styles and expectations? Have you experiences and instances where there has been a difference between your beliefs and values and those of parents of children with whom you are engaged?

The importance of the peer group to adolescents

Peers play a vital role in the psychological development of adolescents. At the time when adolescents are moving away from parent dependency, they substitute peer dependency. The quality of their peer interactions will have a bearing on a range of behaviours including academic performance and school behaviour (Roseth et al., 2008; Stewart, 2008). Peers exert a great deal of pressure on each other to conform. Adolescents seek out and listen to the advice of peers on many issues, especially regarding clothing, entertainment, and fads.

Changes in the structure of Western society such as a decline in the extended family, increased divorce rates, growing numbers of two-career families, and the increasing institutionalisation of age segregation, for example, through care homes, cheaper insurance for over-50s, and fewer employment opportunities for those over 50 have had an impact on adolescent development. These factors, as well as expanded communication networks among the young especially through the use of the Internet,

Figure 10.3   **Peer Interaction.**

social media, mobile phones, and delayed entrance into adult society through extended education for most, have increased the importance of the peer group as a developmental influence.

(?)   **QUESTION POINT**

Through the use of the mobile phone, social media, and Internet communication between adolescents these days is constant and immediate. What are the potential positive aspects of this constant and immediate communication? What are the potential negative effects?

Reeve (2012) proposes three processes by which peers interactions are thought to influence learning:

1 *Relatedness*: perceiving oneself as being related to others in the school context.
2 *Competence*: perceiving oneself as capable in school activities.
3 *Autonomy*: experiencing choice and control in one's school activities.

While feelings of autonomy are most likely to be influenced by teachers and parents, relatedness, and competence, while influenced by parents and teachers, are also likely to be strongly influenced by the quality of one's interaction with the peer group (Pianta et al., 2012; Wentzel, 2005). Negative peer relationships may foster feelings of loneliness and lack of relatedness that then affect one's feeling of competence. Competence has been shown to predict academic achievement (Marsh & Martin, 2011). There is evidence in support of the negative impact of loneliness and peer rejection on students' academic performance (Buhs, 2005; Buhs et al., 2006; Schwartz et al., 2005). However, research also indicates that parents can influence their children to a much greater extent than peers and that, even in cases where students do not have friends, the negative effects of peer rejection can be offset by being liked by the teacher (Hughes & Kwock, 2006; Roorda et al., 2011).

Positive and negative peer effects

Adults often exaggerate the negative power of the peer group, particularly as it relates to sexual behaviour, drug use, and delinquency (Arnett, 2007; Haynie & Osgood, 2005). The influence of the peer group and, in particular, special friends is just as likely to be positive as negative, depending on the friends' characteristics. For example, students whose friends have high grades are likely to improve in their own grades, while students whose friends are disruptive in school are likely to become more disruptive themselves (Mrug & Windle, 2008; Nelson & DeBacker, 2008; Stewart, 2008). Wentzel (2005) says the bulk of evidence on the influence of the peer group supports a model in which clear expectations and opportunities for academic goal pursuit, instrumental help, safety and responsivity, and emotional support represent provisions of positive peer relationships that support students' pursuit of academic goals and subsequent actual achievements. Other groups, such as adults, teachers, coaches, and part-time employers, also strongly influence adolescents' attitudes and behaviour (Wentzel 2005; Wigfield & Wagner, 2005).

Friendships

Research on friendships during adolescence has identified these important characteristics of strong, positive relationships (Way & Greene, 2006):

- loyalty and faithfulness;
- avoidance of intense competition, while aiming for equality through sharing;
- the perception of relationships as emotionally supportive.

Friendships are very important to adolescent development and the quality of the friendship determines whether particular friendships will be influential on a range of behaviours. It appears that if students have a high-quality friendship they are more likely to be influenced than if the friendship is of low quality. High quality friendships are ones in which friends validate and care about each others' emotional well-being, support intimacy and self-disclosure, resolve conflicts effectively, and provide instrumental help and companionship (Stanton-Salazar & Spina, 2005; Waldrip et al., 2008; Wentzel, 2005). It is important, therefore, for teachers not to group poorly adjusted students together in groups as they may form high-quality friendships that will mutually reinforce the alienation. Research suggests that individuals with positive friendships are higher in classroom involvement, perceive their conduct as better, feel they are more accepted by their peers, and have higher general self-esteem than students with less positive friendships (Woods et al., 2009). It is more beneficial to help poorly adjusted students form friendships with better adjusted students.

Adolescent grouping

Group membership is also very important to adolescents. The nature and structure of groups vary considerably. At the most inclusive level is the **crowd**. While this seems a vague term it describes those large congregations of adolescents that hang out together in shopping malls, beaches, and sporting events. The members of a crowd meet because of their mutual interest in particular activities, such as sporting activities, rather than because they are mutually attracted to each other. Individual members of crowds may or may not interact with one another. There are often names for crowds such as the 'toon' army for supporters of Newcastle United Football Club (apparently after the the way that the word 'town' is pronounced in Newcastle). In school, groups might include 'goths', 'chavs', and 'nerds'. Crowds give adolescents an identity embedded within a larger social structure and have a considerable impact on relationships and dating patterns that might limit the opportunity for adolescents to explore new identities and crowd memberships (McFarland & Pals, 2005). The influence of the crowd begins to wane in late adolescence as more adolescents create their own personal values and morals and no longer see it necessary to belong to a particular group and are content to be separate from particular crowds (Smetana et al., 2006).

The next grouping of importance is the clique which is smaller and includes a degree of intimacy between members and has more group cohesion than crowds. Cliques typically are small groups who maintain similar ethnic, age, gender, and social class parameters. During middle adolescence cliques move from being almost exclusively single sex to integrated, and might be characterised by overt characteristics such as modes of dress, behaviours, and speech (Killeya-Jones et al., 2007).

Finally, as indicated above, adolescents develop a number of personal friendships vital to their emotional and social development (Dishion & Tipsord, 2011; Rose & Rudoplph, 2006; Wentzel, 2005). Simply having a friend at school appears to be related to a range of positive outcomes. Children with friends tend to be more sociable, cooperative, and self-confident compared to their friends without peers. Children with friendships that are reciprocated also tend to be more independent, emotionally supportive, altruistic, and less aggressive than those who do not have such friendships. As with other peer relationships, having friends has been related positively to grades and test scores and students with friends appear to be more engaged in school-related activities (Wentzel, 2005).

While popularity and peer acceptance may be stable from childhood to adolescence, sexual maturation and heterosexual behaviour provide new influences that affect an adolescent's behaviour within a group. Among some of these new factors and influences affecting peer group acceptance are dress, entertainment, sport, dating, drugs, dropping-out, and politics. The group or clique one belongs to makes a statement about the values held by the individual in a social context. Group identity at this time often overrides individual identity (Kroger et al., 2010). The following website contains further information and useful links related to crowds and cliques: https://psychologytoday.com/blog/the-modern-teen/201011/jocks-brains-populars-crowds-effects-you

 QUESTION POINT

Reflect back on when you were an adolescent. Were you a member of a crowd and a clique? What were the characteristics of these groups; were there any distinquishing features which made them more or less exclusive? How many personal friendships did you have and what were the features of these friendships? Have any of these personal friendships continued until today? If so, what are the primary reasons for the continuance of these friendships? Are friendships equally important in adulthood? Why or why not?

Adolescent sexuality

Sexuality is a special development during adolescence. Puberty equips the adolescent for mature sexual relationships and for reproduction. Adolescent sexuality is related to and impacts on almost every level of development, physical, social, emotional, intellectual, and moral. It also relates to parental influences and peer group associations. Sexual maturity on one level leads to a growing sense of independence and maturity in the adolescent, while on another it may lead to rebellion against the mores of both parents and society (Ream & Savin-Williams, 2005). The values and mores of parents may be in sharp contrast to those espoused by youth culture, fueled by the mass media, access to information and experiences, and the ease with which adolescents communicate with each other through social media, the smart phone, and Internet. Many adolescents find sexual adjustment difficult (Moore & Rosenthal, 2006; Steinberg, 2005). Integrating sexuality meaningfully with other aspects of the adolescent's developing sense of self and of relations to others, with as little conflict and disruption as possible, is a major developmental task for both girls and boys (Collins & Steinberg, 2008; Montgomery, 2005).

QUESTION POINT

What issues are likely to be contentious between adolescents and their parents? What influence is media and ease of communication between adolescents likely to have on these issues? What were the issues you had with your parents as an adolescent? Do these differ from issues experienced by adolescents today? Ask some older and younger students you are studying with about their issues. Does the salience of issues differ according to how old a person is?

Social development and alienation

In our rapidly changing world many children and adolescents become alienated. The roots of youth alienation are very complex and may include family background, personality characteristics (such as self-esteem), and school influences. Alienation may involve four dimensions:

- powerlessness;
- social estrangement;
- meaninglessness; and
- normlessness.

Some adolescents feel a lack of control and power in their lives. Others may feel physically and mentally isolated from their situation, socially estranged. Others may feel a sense of the meaninglessness and irrelevance of what is happening to them. Others may wish to reject the norms and rules of society (Eccles & Roeser, 2011; Stanton-Salazar & Spina, 2005). While each of these features of alienation are conceptually distinct they may act in concert or alone. In other words an adolescent might feel powerless and the meaninglessness of what they are doing, yet not be socially estranged.

Alienation may lead some students to completely disengage with their education, truant, engage in delinquent behaviour, and engage in substance use and abuse (Hascher & Hagenauer, 2010). At its most severe, alienation can also manifest itself in psychophysiological and psychological disturbances such as obesity, anorexia nervosa, migraine, gastrointestinal upsets, anxiety, phobias, and depression – and, in its most extreme form, suicide (Lilenfeld et al., 2006; Rayce et al., 2009; Smith et al., 2009).

Students at risk of alienation need to be identified early in order to receive intervention and treatment. Each of the components of alienation described above indicates different strategies for intervention. Among potential intervention strategies are alternative teaching approaches, counselling and curricula adaptations, alternative and vocational education programmes, flexible school structures – such as high schools and authority, and power sharing through student participation in decision making, counselling, work experience programmes, and parental and community involvement in schooling.

Programmes that appear most successful in reducing alienation are those that improve students' sense of belonging while alleviating social estrangement, allow students to actively engage in the curriculum and empower students to make decisions, thus alleviating meaninglessness. These programmes may include practical options, such as work experience and prevocational and life skills training, which are perceived by students as increasing the meaningfulness of learning (D'Angelo & Zemanick, 2009).

Social skills, antisocial behaviour, and academic achievement

Social skill involves 'the ability to interact with others in a given context in specific ways that are socially acceptable or valued and at the same time personally beneficial, mutually beneficial, or beneficial primarily to others' (Combs & Slaby, 1977, p. 162). Poor social skills in childhood and adolescence have been linked to poor academic achievement, low self-esteem, antisocial and aggressive behaviour, a higher incidence of contact with the police and the juvenile system, and antisocial or delinquent behaviour in adulthood including loneliness, alcoholism, substance abuse, criminal behaviour, marital difficulties, employment problems, and mental health problems (Cook et al., 2008; Durlak et al., 2010).

The roots of antisocial and delinquent behaviour are quite complex and may include family variables such as socioeconomic status and employment history, family size and parenting characteristics (such as poor supervision), lack of parental involvement, parents' rejection of the child, and parental aggressiveness (Alltucker et al., 2006; Hoeve et al., 2009). Appropriate social skills intervention programmes are an important element to include in school social development programmes.

 ACTIVITY POST

Complete an Internet search for social skills development programmes. Describe the nature of these programmes and critique their potential effectiveness. The following website gives you a good point from which to start your Internet search: http://naspcenter.org/factsheets/socialskills_fs.html

Adolescent suicide

In the past two decades suicide rates in the UK fell slightly. In 1995 there were approximately 9.8 suicide deaths per 100,000 individuals and in 2013 approximately 8.8 deaths per 100,000 individuals (Office for National Statistics, 2015b). Rates for males are higher than for females. Rates for adolescent suicide are lower, and have fallen in the UK since 2001 (Hagell et al., 2013). The most recent data, from 2013, show that there were an average of 0.26 male suicides and 0.07 female suicides deaths per 100,000 individuals in the age group 10–14 years; rising to 6.05 male suicides and 1.39 female suicides deaths per 100,000 individuals in the age group 15–19 years (Office for National Statistics, 2015b). For the those aged 15–19 years, suicide is the most common cause of death after motor accident (Hagell et al., 2013). Although figures are low and falling, they remain, along with self-harm, a significant cause of concern (Department of Health, 2014).

The difference in completed suicide rates between males and females may be explained by the different methods used, with males more likely to impulsively use violent methods, such as shooting and hanging. In contrast, females more often use less violent methods, such as overdoses of substances, which allow time for treatment if the person is found alive. Furthermore, as females in general have a greater reliance on interpersonal relationships for support and more positive help-seeking attitudes and behaviours than males this might protect them from suicide (Eschenbeck et al., 2007). Suicide has also been linked to antisocial, aggressive behaviour and as the incidence of this is greater among males this could also partly explain their greater levels of completed suicide.

Ethnic differences

There are ethnic differences in suicide rates with males from Western backgrounds more likely to commit suicide than males from other ethnic groups, such as persons from an Asian heritage. This difference appears to reflect religious and cultural values that establish *protective taboos* within particular groups, and perhaps the *extended social network* in which adolescents from particular ethnic groups receive more immediate support (Evans et al., 2005). For young people living in the UK, those from Irish, Black Carribean, Pakistani, Bangladeshi, and Indian backgrounds were all less likely to contemplate a suicide attempt than persons from a white-British background (Crawford et al., 2005). These rates, however, changed as people got older where Irish and Black Carribean men and women in the 35–54 years age bracket were as, or more, likely to attempt suicide than white-British men and women.

Risk factors in adolescent suicide

While the rate of adolescent suicide is cause for great concern it is still a relatively infrequent occurrence. Psychologists and psychiatrists try to identify risk factors that might be implicated in an adolescent's contemplation of suicide so that these individuals might be identified in order for targeted intervention to be provided. Because of the relatively small number of suicides it is difficult to discover clearly the primary factors that cause adolescents to attempt suicide. Table 10.1 presents a list of risk factors that might be implicated in suicide.

However, suicide more often than not seems inexplicable. In many cases of attempted suicide and suicide none of the factors in Table 10.1 appears to play an obvious part, while in many other cases adolescents who have exposure to some or all of these factors do not attempt suicide. In short, it is very difficult to predict suicidal behaviour.

Table 10.1 Suicide rick factors	
Primary risk factors	**Other suggested risk factors**
• drug and alcohol abuse • previous suicide attempt • affective illness such as depression • anti-social or aggressive behaviour • family history of suicidal behaviour • the availability of an illegal firearm	• stressful life events, such as family turmoil • increased pressure on children to achieve and to be responsible at an early age • severe parent–child conflict • overly demanding or protective parenting • abusive or neglectful parenting, and mass media giving publicity to suicide which encourages social imitation

(Based on Bridge et al., 2006; Nock & Kessler, 2006; Silenzio et al., 2007)

It appears that in cases of completed suicide there has been a preceding shameful or humiliating experience, such as an arrest, a perceived failure at work or school, a rejection by a loved one such as a parent, or difficulties resulting from sexual orientation such as homosexuality. There are many websites related to teen suicide which you should consult for further information on this topic. A good starting point is: http://focusas.com/Suicide.html

Preventing mental health problems

The 2004 British Child and Adolescent Mental Health Survey showed that 9.6% of children and young people (aged 5–16 years) had a mental disorder (Office for National Statistics, 2004). This figure was higher for boys (11.4%) than girls (7.8%) and higher in the 11–16 years age bracket (11.5%) than the 5–10 years age bracket (7.7%). However, few of these receive formal help from specialist mental health services (Sayal, 2006; Wilson, 2007). These social, emotional, and behavioural difficulties may impact on student motivation and the ability of individuals to benefit from schooling and, because students then fall behind scholastically, the emotional, social, and behavioural problems may become further exacerbated. In other words there is a reciprocal relationship between mental health and school achievement (Bond et al., 2007).

It is very important that teachers, counsellors, and school personnel are well informed about student mental health problems, know how to recognise students at risk and have in place appropriate support procedures to assist individuals and their families (see, for example, Han & Weiss, 2005; Levitt et al., 2007; Reinke et al., 2011). Table 10.2 presents some warning signs of suicide. When an individual's behaviour becomes atypical and includes a number of these features it might be an indication that the adolescent is thinking about suicide. At these times, effective counselling, pastoral support, and referral to Child and Adolescent Mental Health Services are necessary.

Table 10.2   Signs of suicide

- Putting personal affairs in order, such as giving away treasured possessions and/or making amends.
- Talking about suicide directly or indirectly ('you won't have to worry about me much longer') and/or saying goodbye to family and friends.
- Protracted periods of sadness, despondency and/or 'not caring' any more.
- Extreme fatigue, lack of energy, boredom.
- Emotional instability – spells of crying, laughing.
- Inability to concentrate, becoming easily frustrated and/or distractible.
- Deviating from usual patterns of behaviour (e.g. decline in grades, absence from school, and/or discipline problems).
- Neglect of personal appearance.
- Change in body routines (e.g. loss of sleep or excessive sleep, eating more or less than usual, and/or complaints of headache, stomach ache, backache).

(Based on Rudd et al., 2006)

There are a number of programmes developed to help prevent adolescent suicide. Two common approaches are *telephone crisis counselling* and *curriculum-based programmes* part of personal, social, and health education to educate children and young people about the signs and causes of suicide as well as the different types of support that are available. Although curriculum programmes are not common in the UK, reviews suggest that they can be effective in reducing thoughts about contemplating suide, actual suicide attempts and depression (Horowitz & Garber, 2006; Miller et al., 2009). These programmes can be used at the universal level, for all individuals in a class or a school, at the selected level to target children at risk. Not surprisingly, selected programmes are more effective.

Many of the primary factors associated with youth suicide are common to other alienated behaviours, such as delinquency and substance abuse. As a result, some primary prevention programmes have been designed to address negative behaviours such as depression, lack of social support, poor problem-solving skills, and hopelessness in students before problems arise. In addressing these it is thought that the root source of much adolescent suicidal behaviour is also addressed. Many schools, therefore, have personal development, health and physical education programmes which aim to increase the adolescent's self-esteem, social confidence, regulation of emotion, and ability to anticipate and solve problems (Baily, 2006; Fergus & Zimmerman, 2005; Karcher, 2005). In particular, it is felt that problem-solving skills training and self-efficacy enhancement for adolescents may be the most effective suicide prevention programmes (Miller et al., 2009).

Family support programmes have also been instigated for families undergoing crises and these appear to alleviate a range of problems, including substance abuse and delinquency. As these factors are also associated with adolescent suicide, it is thought that family support programmes provide a primary preventative against suicide as well. This is particularly important as there is considerable evidence that strong parental attachments and expressions of warmth and caring have been found to protect adolescents from depression and anxiety. Hence, it is important to support families in developing the strategies to provide a cohesive family that provides for close supportive relationships rather than ones characterised by conflict (Pinkerton & Dolan, 2007; Piquero et al., 2009).

Self-concept, self-esteem, and effective learning

We have discussed above the importance of identity formation to adolescents. Aspects of identity that appear to be important and related to school achievement are an individual's **self-concept** and **self-esteem**. Self-concept refers to a person's beliefs about themselves in specific areas such as physical ability, physical appearance, peer relationships, parent relationships, academic ability, and self-worth. For example, an individual might describe himself or herself as good at mathematics, but not good at music. These descriptions are part of the person's self-concept. If the person evaluates these beliefs as positive or negative the person is giving an indication of his feelings of self-esteem (Marsh & O'Mara, 2008; Schunk & Pajares, 2005).

What people believe they are good at probably influences their motivation to engage in the task, as well as the achievement levels sought and attained. For example, if individuals believe they are good at mathematics they will make a greater effort in mathematics lessons. The relationship between self-concept and behaviour (particularly in terms of success and failure) is presumed to be reciprocal (see, for example, Marsh et al., 2005). This means that if we feel good about ourselves in a particular area we are more likely to try hard, trying hard leads to success, success makes us feel good about ourselves and the cycle continues.

Most researchers consider that self-concept has many dimensions, and that individuals do not have an overall generalised self-concept that characterises their beliefs about themselves across all areas (Marsh & Craven, 2006). More likely, individuals believe they are good at some things and not so good at other things; these may cluster into broader categories of self-concept such as academic and non-academic self-concepts. Research shows that self-concepts in specific school subjects are significantly related to subsequent choices of what subjects students want to continue to study and the choices of what they actually do pursue (Marsh & Martin, 2011).

How is self-concept formed?

Self-concept seems to be formed largely through social interaction and social comparison. Social *frames of reference* indicate to us what our capacities and qualities are under particular circumstances. When we compare ourselves with others who appear to be superior we are likely to develop a relatively negative self-concept, whereas if we believe we are superior to others then we are likely to develop a relatively positive self-concept, and this is irrespective of our actual ability. Hence, someone objectively good at science may consider him or herself superior or inferior to others in their group and hence believe they are relatively good at science or relatively bad at science. This *external frame of reference* is very important in the formation of our self-concepts. Feedback from significant others such as parents, siblings, peers, and teachers is influential in the growth of one's self-concept.

 QUESTION POINT

Consider your own self-concepts. In what do you have a positive self-concept? Are there any areas in which you have a negative self-concept? How influential was your comparison with others in the formation of your self-concepts?

We are not generally equally positive or negative about our ability across a wide range of areas even though we might be equally strong in a range of activities and behaviours. An *internal frame of reference* also comes into play in the formation of our self-concepts. We tend to compare our self-perceived skills in one area (such as mathematics) with our self-perceived skills in another (such as English) and use this internal, relativistic impression as a second basis for arriving at our self-concept in particular areas (Möller et al., 2011). Hence, someone who is relatively good at both mathematics and English may believe they are better at English, and hence have a positive self-concept for English and a relatively negative self-concept for maths. Research shows that while academic achievement scores across a range of unrelated academic areas (such as mathematics and English) are strongly positively correlated, self-concept ratings for these unrelated academic areas are largely non-correlated.

Developmental changes in self-concept

There appear to be some changes in self-concept foci as children grow older. Young children seem to focus on behavioural and physical characteristics, whereas older children focus on more abstract psychological characteristics (Robins & Trzesniewski, 2005; Sebastian et al, 2008). As children's notions of what constitutes effort, ability, achievement, success, and failure develop over time, so do their beliefs about their competencies (and hence self-concept).

It appears that in the infants and early grades children's self-concepts across a range of areas are uniformly high and less differentiated than older children's. As children have more academic and non-academic experiences, their self-concepts become more differentiated and begin to be less positive. Throughout high school, individuals revise aspects of their self-concept, and some aspects become more positive relative to others. After adolescence (beginning in Year 9 or 10), self-concept becomes more positive once more in a variety of areas and becomes relatively stable (Marsh et al., 2005; Marsh & Craven, 2006; Marsh & Martin, 2011).

QUESTION POINT

Much research seems to show that there is a decline in academic and non-academic self-concepts during the early years of secondary school (Years 7 to 9). Can you speculate on reasons why this might occur? List primary factors that might be implicated in this decline and compare your list to that of other students. What interventions could be instigated to alleviate such declines?

Big-fish–little-pond effect

Herb Marsh (e.g. Marsh et al., 2007, 2008) believes that as self-concept is formed in interaction with others, educational settings are very important in the formation of an individual's self-concept. For this reason Marsh believes it is often better for a bright individual to be a big fish in a little pond. That is, doing well among a mixed-ability group, than to be a little fish and performing at an average level in a high-ability group. In the former case it is easier for students to establish and maintain positive feelings about their academic accomplishments, which serve to reinforce further academic pursuits. In selective educational environments (such as Grammar schools where children must take an entrance exam, often referred to as the '11+'), where the average ability of students is high, it is more difficult to establish and maintain these positive feelings. Selective secondary schools, and gifted and talented classes may, therefore, be disadvantageous to some students because of this 'big-fish–little-pond' effect (see Marsh et al., 2007, 2008). In these selective settings, high-ability students may choose less demanding coursework and have lower academic self-concepts, lower achievement scores, lower educational aspirations, and lower occupational aspirations than similar students in non-selective educational environments. It appears from this evidence that high-ability students may be better off in non-streamed schools.

QUESTION POINT

The big-fish–little-pond effect is controversial and seems to undermine the value of selective schools and selective classrooms and streaming; what do you think? Compare your views to those of other students. Discuss this issue with students who have attended both selective and non-selective schools.

Self-regulation and adolescence

Other elements of importance to adolescent formation of identity are **self-regulation** and **self-efficacy**. Both of these processes are derived from the work of Albert Bandura and the social cognitive theory of human development. Self-regulation refers to the regulation of one's own cognitive processes in order to learn successfully. Self-regulation involves such things as goal setting, planning and time management, attention control, self-motivation, flexible use of learning strategies, self-monitoring, asking for help when needed, and self evaluation (Cleary & Zimmermnan, 2012; Zimmerman, 2008; Zimmerman & Cleary, 2009). Given the span of cognitive qualities associated with self-regulation you can see why it develops to its fullest during adolescence and is important during those years.

The way in which learners self-regulate is a function of a number of important cognitive processes regarding their knowledge and beliefs (Cleary et al., 2008). These processes include their interpretation of the tasks and goals they set themselves, which may be influenced by: their understanding of typical task demands; their beliefs about factors responsible for successful and unsuccessful performance (which are called attributional beliefs); and task-specific perceptions of their self-efficacy. Learners' understanding and mastery of learning strategies may also influence the degree and manner in which they self-regulate. These self-regulatory processes are not innate. There is an important role to be played by teachers in helping students analyse tasks, set appropriate short and long term goals, and establish appropriate criteria for success and appropriate attributions for success and failure.

Self-regulated learning is related to academic motivation and academic achievement. Research indicates that students who are academic high achievers practise a greater range of self-regulatory strategies, and more often, than low achievers (Helle et al., 2013). In particular, high-achieving students report greater use of organising and transforming information, reviewing notes, and seeking assistance from adults (Fishman, 2014; Villavicencio & Baernardo, 2013). They may also make greater use of the full range of strategies such as self-evaluating, goal setting and planning, keeping records, and monitoring and reviewing texts (Berger & Karabenick, 2011). There is some evidence for gender differences in the use of self-regulating strategies, with high-achieving females using more record keeping and monitoring, structuring the environment to assist learning, and goal setting and planning than high-achieving males. The reasons and implications for this are not yet clear and this issue is currently under research.

As we mentioned above, the skills of self-regulation detailed above don't occur naturally or spontaneously in learners. Indeed, the development of such skills is complex and long term. Teaching episodes need to be developed to encourage learners to develop these skills across a range of subjects so that, in the long term, self-regulating becomes a generalised capacity (see Cleary & Zimmerman, 2012; Zimmerman & Kitsantas, 2005).

Self-efficacy and adolescence

A feeling of positive *self-efficacy* is essential for an adolescent's feeling of well-being because efficacy beliefs influence how they feel, think, motivate themselves, and behave. Albert Bandura believes that students' beliefs in their efficacy to regulate their own learning and to master academic activities determine their aspirations, level of motivation, and academic achievements. Bandura believes that the higher individuals' perceived self-efficacy the higher the goal challenges they set for themselves and the firmer their commitment to them (Bandura, 1986, 1997; see also Schunk & Mullen, 2012; Schunk & Pajares, 2005).

Self-efficacy has to do with self-perception of competence rather than actual level of competence. Some individuals may display a lot of skill in an area and yet evaluate themselves negatively because of the high personal standards they have set themselves (Pajares, 2008; Usher & Pajares, 2008). It is believed that students base their appraisals of ability on a wide range of sources including their actual performance, feedback from others and vicarious (observational) experiences such as seeing others performing in a like manner being praised, ignored, or ridiculed.

High self-efficacy (or perceived ability) for a particular activity does not in itself necessarily lead to motivated behaviour. The perceived value of the activity and outcome expectations also influence level of motivation. However, without a sense of self-efficacy it is unlikely that individuals will engage in activities, irrespective of whether they are perceived as important or not.

Research suggests that students who are low in self-efficacy for learning avoid seeking help because it implies that they are less able than other students. On the other hand, students who are high in self-efficacy seek help more often (Bong, 2008; Kitsantas & Chow, 2007; Skaalvik & Skaalvik, 2005). This contrast is exacerbated depending on the nature of the motivational goals established in the classroom. For example, if classrooms emphasise relative performance on tasks through competition and ranking then students low in self-efficacy are even more likely to avoid seeking help. This means that students low in self-efficacy put themselves at a greater disadvantage for learning and achievement. This danger is reduced in classrooms that emphasise personal improvement, understanding, mastery, and the intrinsic value of learning. The difference in help-seeking behaviours between high- and low-efficacy students is also reduced in classrooms that emphasise good interpersonal relationships and provide a warm and supportive environment (Meece et al., 2006).

Bandura (1997) proposes four sources of efficacy beliefs:

- *Mastery experiences*: being able to successfully complete a lesson activity.
- *Physiological and emotional states*: feeling interested rather than bored in a lesson.
- *Vicarious experiences*: watching others succeed and thinking 'I can do that too'.
- *Social persuasion* (others have a belief in you).

When an individual masters a situation or activity, self-efficacy is enhanced and expectations for future success are also enhanced. The reverse also applies. One's emotional states when engaged in activities also impact on self-efficacy beliefs. Engagement is indicated by excitement and level of energy expended. High engagement in a successful or unsuccessful activity will have more impact than low engagement. Watching the effects on others of success and failure in particular activities also influences the development of personal self-efficacy. In other words, the effects of seeing someone perform an activity well and get praised for it, and seeing their efficacy is enhanced, will flow to us as enhanced personal self-efficacy if we think we have equal capacity as the model. Finally, social persuasion can also influence one's feelings of efficacy. Valued friends, family, and teachers can heighten our feelings of self-efficacy by telling us 'You can do it!', provided the individual trusts the persuader.

 QUESTION POINT

Review each of these elements: mastery, engagement, vicarious involvement, and social persuasion. Consider areas in which you have high and low self-efficacy. Analyse each area using these four elements. Using this analysis is it possible to develop high self-efficacy in an area in which you currently have low self-efficacy? Discuss your analysis with other students. How could you apply this information to enhance the self-efficacy of students at school?

There are a number of ways of helping to develop and maintain self-efficacy among students, including teaching goal setting and information processing strategies, using models, and providing attributional feedback and rewards (Hattie & Timperley, 2007; Usher & Pajares, 2008). The setting of challenging but attainable goals and the achievement of these goals enhances self-efficacy and motivation (Liem et al., 2012; Locke & Latham, 2006; Martin, 2015). Teachers need to assist students to set both **short-term goals** and **long-term goals**. Andrew Martin suggest that students be encouraged to set personal best goals. Personal best goals are goals that are set by students themselves in conjunction with a teacher or learning mentor. Martin further suggests that in order to be effective they should be specific (e.g. a specific subject such as English, or aspect of that subject, such as grammar), challenging (as least as high or higher than that of a previous best), and personal rather than in comparison to other students.

 QUESTION POINT

What other techniques might be useful in teaching students how to set goals? Are there any developmental differences in the manner in which goals should be set to encourage students to be self-regulated?

If students are taught information processing strategies (i.e. their **metacognitive** and **metalearning** skills are developed) they are more likely to feel competent in a range of learning situations and therefore more motivated to continue in these activities. Classroom models (both teachers and peers) may also be used to demonstrate that particular tasks lie within the range of ability of particular students. Observing others succeed can convey to observers that they too are capable, and can motivate them to attempt the task.

To enhance self-efficacy, feedback on student performance should emphasise goals achieved or gains made rather than shortfalls in performance. For example, we can tell students that they have achieved 75%, emphasising progress, or we can highlight the 25% shortfall in their performance. Accenting the gains enhances perceived self-efficacy, while highlighting deficiencies undermines self-regulative influences with resulting deterioration in student performance (Bandura, 1997).

High school environments and the development of adolescents

It is an interesting phenomenon that during adolescence, along with all the other physical, cognitive, and social changes taking place, profound changes also occur in the individual's educational environment. From the security and predictability of the primary school with its organised schedule of activities, single teacher classrooms and stable peer cohorts, adolescents find themselves in an educational world with multiple changes. Multiple teachers, multiple peer cohort groups, multiple classrooms, multiple subjects and activities, and new and complex demands. It is at this stage that many children who were doing well at and enjoying school begin to lose interest and develop patterns of behaviour that hinder achievement (see for example, Yeung & McInerney, 2005). Many educationalists suggest that this occurs because there is a mismatch between what the school offers in terms of a supportive social and intellectual environment for adolescents, and what they actually need (Eccles & Roeser, 2009; Urdan & Schoenfelder, 2006). Research has suggested that the following school social environment dimensions facilitate or inhibit student adjustment to high school (Lam et al., 2012; Wang & Halcombe, 2010; Wentzel, 2012):

- *Students' belief that their teacher cares about and supports them.* Perceiving their teacher as supportive is especially important for students' confidence relating to the teacher, self-regulated learning, and disruptive behaviour.
- *Students' belief that they are encouraged to interact with their classmates.* Regarding academic work which is highly correlated with motivation and engagement in learning.
- *Students' belief that the teacher encourages mutual respect and social harmony among classmates.* Students' perception of being in a classroom where the teacher encourages classmates to respect their ideas and not to laugh or make fun of them

is the most important dimension of the social environment in predicting changes in academic self-efficacy and self-regulation of school work.

- *Students' belief that they are encouraged to be competitors in the classroom.* Students who perceive that their actions will be compared directly to others in the class, express less confidence in their ability to relate well to their teacher and also report engaging in more disruptive behaviour.

Mismatch between school and adolescent needs

Eccles and Roeser (2009) argue that a decline in motivation for learning as adolescents enter high school is not an inevitable result of the students' adolescent development, but rather reflects non-adaptive school and classroom practices which lead to these declines. With appropriate school and classroom strategies in place, adolescents can proceed through high school with enhanced motivation for learning.

 ACTIVITY POST

Consider the differences between primary and secondary school. Did you have any trouble adjusting to the changing environment? What issues caused you most difficulty? How did you adjust? What strategies could secondary schools use to alleviate the stress that might be caused by the new demands put upon adolescents entering high school? Discuss your answers with other students. Compile a list of suggestions for schools to facilitate adolescent adjustment in high school. Share your list with other students.

CHAPTER 11

Moral development in childhood and adolescence

Introduction

In all organised societies a framework of rules exist to govern and control human behaviour. These rules relate to behaviour as diverse as being faithful in marriage, to paying taxes, to speeding in a car, to public nudity. Sometimes these rules are directly related to religious precepts and these can vary from group to group and society to society. For example, multiple wives might be acceptable in a fundamentalist Muslim culture, while unacceptable in a Western Christian or secular society. At other times rules emanate from, and are controlled by, the political and judicial systems operating in any society. So, for example, driving with a proscribed alcohol level is illegal in many societies, however, the actual proscribed level of blood alcohol can vary widely from the common 0.05% to 0.1% to 0.01%, and the levels are set by the political and legal system of the country, state, or even town. There is no inherent religious reason why a person should not drink and drive.

Some rules, whether emanating from religious or political systems seem to be universal. So, for example, murder and theft are illegal universally. However, the interpretation of what constitutes murder and theft in a given society may vary. For example, in some societies the killing of an unfaithful wife is not considered murder but a 'just' retribution. In other cases rules seem culturally specific. For example, whether a church marriage is necessary to ratify the union. The mix of rules and obligations in any society are quite complex. The mix becomes even more complex when many rules are defined as legal obligations but not necessarily moral obligations (such as drinking and driving), while some moral mores may not be legally mandated (such as being faithful in marriage). The lines between what is morality and legality are often quite blurred, and we expect that quite a number of readers, coming from their own religious or secular perspectives, would think that drink driving is not only illegal but also immoral. In this particular instance the issue is complicated when one considers whether drink driving goes from being illegal to illegal *and* immoral at some particular alcohol blood level reading.

Last, the issue is even further complicated when one considers that there are many norms of moral behaviour that are relatively idiosyncratic. An example of this would perhaps be strict veganism where individuals will eat no product from a living creature considering such an act immoral. Given this complexity of rules, mores, and morality how do growing children cope?

From even an early age children have a rudimentary understanding of rules. As children and adolescents develop a greater social and personal identity and become more independent they develop a more refined understanding of legal rules and moral rules and begin to distinguish the two. In this chapter we consider moral development in detail and examine closely the work of Piaget, Kohlberg, neo-Kohlbergian approaches, Gilligan, and Turiel. Piaget's stages of moral reasoning are discussed, together with the notions of a morality of constraint and a morality of cooperation. In line with recent thinking about Piagetian stage theory, we provide a critique of his approach to moral development. Kohlberg's stages of moral development (preconventional, conventional, and postconventional) are described and the current status of the theory is explored. In particular, we examine sex differences in moral development, the relationship between moral reasoning and moral behaviour, and cross-cultural implications. Neo-Kohlbergian developments which address some of the criticisms of the original theory are examined. Turiel's views on the acquisition of moral values in social contexts are also considered. Useful information on a number of these theories and their implications for moral education may be found at the following website: http://psychology. jrank.org/pages/431/Moral-Development.html

Moral development

From a cognitive psychological perspective, the process of development of moral concepts arises from children's personal cognitive growth and experiences in the social world. The appreciation of the moral component of social experiences depends upon the cognitive level at which the child is functioning. It is in making sense of these social experiences that children perceive their salient moral aspects, for example pain or injustice, and generate ideas on how people should act towards each other. These moral rules are not based on given rules or adult influence but, rather, children construct their own judgments through abstractions from their experiences. As children grow older they re-evaluate existing concepts and construct new ones that are qualitatively different. Moral development, therefore, presents an interplay between individual cognitive development and cognitive development within the social context.

As caregivers, parents, and educators, we are intimately involved in the process of communicating values to children and adolescents. It is helpful to understand, therefore, the ways in which the development of the moral self is believed to occur. Widely differing conceptions exist of how we develop a sense of morality and whether morals are universal or culturally based and acquired through socialisation. In the following sections we look at the theories put forward by Piaget, Kohlberg, neo-Kohlbergians, Gilligan, and Turiel.

 QUESTION POINT

Before we begin examining theories of moral development consider how you yourself developed a 'moral self'. What are the components of your moral self? What were the primary influential factors in the development of your moral values? Are your moral values different from the moral values of other people. If so, what are the differences, and how did these develop? Is there a relationship between religious values and moral values? If so, how and why? If not, why?

Jean Piaget's stage theory of moral development

The developmental theory of Piaget presents the view that increasingly sophisticated moral reasoning develops through an invariant sequence of stages. Piaget contends that all morality consists of a system of rules that is handed from adults to children. Through training, practice, and developing intellect, children learn to nurture respect for these standards of conduct (Carpendale, 2009; Piaget, 1965).

Piaget questioned scores of Swiss children aged between 5 and 13 years about their understanding of rules, and their interpretations of right and wrong. For example Piaget asked children about stealing and lying. When asked what lying is young children consistently answered that it is using 'naughty words'. When asked why they should not lie the younger children usually could not verbalise beyond reiterating because it is a naughty word. In contrast, older children were able to explain that one shouldn't lie because it is wrong and not true. In particular, Piaget examined the relationship between *intention* and notions of *right* and *wrong*. Children were given two stories (shown in Table 11.1) and asked to judge which of the two boys in the story was naughtier: the boy who was well intentioned but caused more damage, or the boy who was not well intentioned and caused less damage. Children were asked to give reasons for their answers.

Piaget found two different *moral orientations*, one typical of preoperational children (pre 7 years) and one typical of children in the late concrete substage (10–12 years). He found that younger children tend to focus on observed consequences of actions and believe in absolute, unchanging rules handed down by outside authorities. Piaget named this stage one of **heteronomous morality** or **moral realism**, in which children adopt the morality of constraint ('heteronomous' means under the authority of another). Children in this stage tend to view behaviours as totally right or wrong, and think everyone views them in the same way. Children judge whether an act is right or wrong on the basis of the magnitude of the consequences, the extent to which it conforms to established rules, and whether the act is punished.

This heteronomy results, in part, from the egocentric thinking characteristic of young children in which they are not able to consider the perspective of other people

---

Table 11.1   Stories used by Piaget to study moral reasoning

Story A: A little boy called John is in his room. He is called to dinner. He goes into the dining room. But behind the door there was a chair, and on the chair there was a tray with 15 cups on it. John couldn't have known that there was all this behind the door. He goes in, the door knocks against the tray, bang go the 15 cups, and they all get broken.

Story B: Once there was a little boy whose name was Henry. One day when his mother was out he tried to get some jam out of the cupboard. He climbed up on a chair and stretched out his arm. But the jam was too high up and he couldn't reach it and have any. But while he was trying to get it he knocked over a cup. The cup fell down and broke.

simultaneously with their own, and hence they project their own thoughts and wishes on to others. It is also associated with moral realism, that is that young children are more concerned about the consequences of actions rather than the intentions behind the act. In other words, the letter of the law is valued above the purpose of the law. Moral realism is associated with the young child's belief in **immanent justice** which refers to their belief that punishment automatically follows from wrongdoing. Heteronomous moral thinking is also reflective of the social power relationships between adults and children. Children are relatively powerless and rules are handed down from above. Right and wrong is what is determined by others, and reinforced through reinforcment and punishment. Younger children have a rigid view of discipline and punishment, while older children distinguish between punishment and guilt.

Older children, however, differentiate punishment from wrongdoing; in other words, they will maintain their innocence in the face of punishment. Older children also recognise that others may hold different points of view, and in their judgments of right and wrong stress intentions as well as consequences. Punishment should fit the 'crime' rather than being capriciously applied by someone who is more powerful than the child. As older children mix in wider social circles, and in particular with their peers, inferred intentions behind the act becomes the focus and a belief that rules can be constructed and changed by social agreement. Greater flexibility of thought therefore characterises the moral reasoning of older children. Piaget named this **autonomous morality** where children adopt the **morality of cooperation** (Fox & Riconscente, 2008; Haidt, 2008; Narvaez, 2010; Turiel, 2014). The ability to act from a sense of reciprocity and mutual respect is associated with a shift in the child's cognitive structure from egocentrism to perspective taking. Thus, Piaget viewed moral development as the result of interpersonal interactions through which individuals work out mutually fair resolutions.

In the context of Piaget's stories, therefore, younger children believe that John is the naughtier because he broke more cups, despite the fact that he didn't break them on purpose. Older children judge that Henry is the naughtier child because they take into account the intention behind the act leading to the damage.

While children in the heteronomous stage show a great concern for rules and believe they can't be changed, children at the autonomous stage no longer view rules as fixed, but rather as flexible, socially agreed upon principles of cooperation that can be changed with the agreement of others affected by the rules. A greater sense of *reciprocity* characterises the moral reasoning of older children; that is, the welfare of others and a concern for fairness is important, because it is only then that one can expect fairness in return. At this stage, the belief in a morality of reciprocity means that duty and obligation are no longer defined in terms of obedience to authority, but as a social contract reflecting the mutual needs of oneself and others, called a **morality of reciprocity**.

The development from stage one to stage two reflects the growing ability of children to decentre, that is, to take the perspective of others. This development is facilitated by peer interaction through which one's individual perspective is challenged by the perspectives, needs, and demands of other individuals.

ACTIVITY POST

Select a group of younger and older students. Tell them the two stories recounted above. Ask them which child in the two stories is naughtier. Record their answers and the reasons for their answers. Categorise the answers according to Piaget's approach. Are there developmental differences in the answers and reasons given? Are there any features of their answers that are not easily categorised according to Piaget's approach? Are there potential problems with the scenarios presented to the students that might limit their responses?

Critique of Piaget's theory

Research generally supports Piaget's view that children pass from a morality of constraint to a morality of cooperation, and that this is facilitated by intellectual growth, peer interaction, and a diminution in adult authority (Carpendale, 2009). However, as with Piaget's theory of cognitive development, this theory has also been subjected to considerable criticism. In particular, it appears that even quite young children can distinguish between social-conventional and moral rules, with the former far more rigid. We discuss this further in the next section on Kohlberg. Furthermore, it is believed that the stories told by Piaget underestimated children's moral understanding. If you refer back to stories A and B you will see that the good intention was coupled with more damage, while the poor intention was coupled with less damage. It is possible that this confused children in their understanding of intention versus consequences, and they focused their answers on the consequences.

Preschool and primary children appear quite able to judge the difference between well-intentioned and ill-intentioned behaviour in terms of naughtiness when changes are made to the stories' structure (Nobes et al., 2009; Smetana et al., 2014). When stories focus on intentions rather than the consequences by holding the consequences constant while varying the intentions, children distinquish between well-intentioned and ill-intentioned acts. Children also distinguish between well-intentioned and ill-intentioned acts when the character's intentions are given last in the story, or by making story events very meaningful to children by role playing the behaviour.

 QUESTION POINT

Do you think Piaget's two-stage developmental sequence in moral development is sufficiently complex to explain moral development as it occurs across the lifespan?

The next section deals with the work of Lawrence Kohlberg, who brings a lifespan view to moral development that he relates to the complex life events of developing individuals.

Lawrence Kohlberg's stage theory of moral development

Piaget's initial ideas were built on by Lawrence Kohlberg (1927–1987), who developed the most extensive theory of moral development to date. Kohlberg's developmental stage theory (Kohlberg 1976, 1977, 1978, 1981; see also Gibbs, 2013) is based on four core assumptions:

- The theory is cognitive, that is, it emphasises thought processes involved in moral decision making rather than alternative possibilities, such as socialisation processes.
- The theory emphasises the personal construction of knowledge about morality. In other words the meanings of 'rights', 'duties', 'justice', 'social order', and 'reciprocity' are personally constructed through experience, albeit formed within the context of wider ideologies and practices within a particular cultural or social group.
- The theory is developmental. Kohlberg believed that moral development occurs as an invariant sequence no matter what the national or subcultural group happens to be. Each level of moral judgment must be attained before the individual can perform at the next higher level, and the attainment of a higher level of moral judgment appears to involve the reworking of earlier thought patterns rather than an additive process of development.
- The theory emphasises moral development as a growth from conventional to postconventional moral thinking.

Kohlberg's methodology

Kohlberg also used the clinical method to assess the level of cognitive reasoning of children and adolescents. Children were presented with three moral dilemmas on which they had to make a moral judgment. Depending on the justification given for their judgment, children were categorised as belonging to a particular stage of moral development (rather like children being categorised as preoperational, concrete, or formal thinkers on the basis of their answers to Piagetian problems; see Chapter 5).

 **ACTIVITY POST**

Kohlberg Dilemmas

Select a group of students of varying age and read them the following moral dilemmas.

Dilemma I

Joe is a 14-year-old boy who wanted to go to a football training academy very much in his summer holiday. His father promised him he could go if he saved up the money for it himself. So Joe worked hard with his weekend job and saved up the £40 it cost to go, and a little more besides. But just before the training was going to start, his father changed his mind. Some of his friends decided to go on a special fishing trip, and Joe's father was short of the money it would cost. So he asked Joe to lend him the money he had saved from the job. Joe didn't want to give up going to football training, so he thinks of refusing to give his father the money.

1   Should Joe refuse to give his father the money?

1a   Why or why not?

2   Does the father have the right to tell Joe to give him the money?

2a   Why or why not?

3   Does giving the money have anything to do with being a good son?

3a   Why or why not?

4   Is the fact that Joe earned the money himself important in this situation?

4a   Why or why not?

5   The father promised Joe he could go to camp if he earned the money. Is the fact that the father promised the most important thing in the situation?

5a   Why or why not?

6   In general, why should a promise be kept?

7   Is it important to keep a promise to someone you don't know well and probably won't see again?

7a   Why or why not?

8   What do you think is the most important thing a father should be concerned about in his relationship to his son?

(continued)

(continued)

8a   Why is that the most important thing?

9   In general, what should be the authority of a father over his son?

9a   Why?

10   What do you think is the most important thing a son should be concerned about in his relationship to his father?

10a Why is that the most important thing?

11   In thinking back over the dilemma, what would you say is the most responsible thing for Joe to do in this situation?

11a Why?

Dilemma II

Judy is a 12-year-old girl. Her mother promised her that she could go to a special music concert coming to their town if she saved up from babysitting and lunch money to buy a ticket to the concert. She managed to save up the £20 the ticket cost plus another £5. But then her mother changed her mind and told Judy that she had to spend the money on new clothes for school. Judy was disappointed and decided to go to the concert anyway. She bought a ticket and told her mother that she had only been able to save £5. That Saturday she went to the concert and told her mother that she was spending the evening at her friend's house. A week passed without her mother finding out. Judy then told her older sister, Louise, that she had gone to the concert and had lied to her mother about it. Louise wonders whether to tell their mother what Judy did.

1   Should Louise, the older sister, tell their mother that Judy lied about the money or should she keep quiet?

1a   Why?

2   In wondering whether to tell, Louise thinks of the fact that Judy is her sister. Should that make a difference in Louise's decision?

2a   Why or why not?

3   Does telling have anything to do with being a good daughter?

3a   Why or why not?

4   Is the fact that Judy earned the money herself important in this situation?

4a   Why or why not?

5   The mother promised Judy she could go to the concert if she earned the money. Is the fact that the mother promised the most important thing in the situation?

5a   Why or why not?

6   Why in general should a promise be kept?

7   Is it important to keep a promise to someone you don't know well and probably won't see again?

7a   Why or why not?

8   What do you think is the most important thing a mother should be concerned about in her relationship to her daughter?

8a   Why is that the most important thing?

9   In general, what should be the authority of a mother over her daughter?

9a   Why?

10   What do you think is the most important thing a daughter should be concerned about in her relationship to her mother?

10a   Why is that the most important thing?

11   In thinking back over the dilemma, what would you say is the most responsible thing for Louise to do in this situation?

11a   Why?

Dilemma III

Two young men, brothers, had got into serious trouble. They were secretly leaving town in a hurry and needed money. Karl, the older one, broke into a shop and stole £1,000. Bob, the younger one, went to a retired old man who was known to help people. He told the man that he was very sick and that he needed £1,000 to pay for an operation. Bob asked the old man to lend him the money and promised that he would pay him back when he recovered. Really Bob wasn't sick at all, and he had no intention of paying the man back. Although the old man didn't know Bob very well, he lent him the money. So Bob and Karl left town, each with £1,000.

1   Which is worse, stealing like Karl or cheating like Bob?

1a   Why is that worse?

2   What do you think is the worst thing about cheating the old man?

2a   Why is that the worst thing?

3   In general, why should a promise be kept?

4   Is it important to keep a promise to someone you don't know well or will never see again?

4a   Why or why not?

5   Why shouldn't someone steal from a store?

6   What is the value or importance of property rights?

(continued)

(continued)

7 Should people do everything they can to obey the law?

7a Why or why not?

8 Was the old man being irresponsible by lending Bob the money?

8a Why or why not?

> (Dilemmas adapted from http://3.haverford.edu/psychology/ddavis/p109g/
> kohlberg.dilemmas.html)

Typically, answers to the dilemmas will range across a range beliefs (see Cushman et al., 2006; Kutnick, 2011).

Categorise the answers according to the stages in Table 11.2. What do you notice about the answers; were there differences according to age and sex; did you have difficulty in categorising the answers? If so, what issues made it difficult to categorise them? If you included some individuals from ethnically or religiously diverse backgrounds were there any differences according to ethnic and religious background?

Kohlberg's stages of moral development

Kohlberg categorised responses to these dilemmas under three major levels of moral development: **preconventional morality**, which reflects a concern for avoiding punishment and moral judgments are characterised by a concrete, individual perspective; **conventional morality**, which reflects a concern with rules and regulations. Individuals at the conventional level of reasoning have a basic understanding of conventional morality, and reason with an understanding that norms and conventions are necessary to uphold society. They tend to be self-identified with these rules, and uphold them consistently, viewing morality as acting in accordance with what society defines as right; and **postconventional morality,** which reflects higher-level ethical principles (Kohlberg, 1981). Post conventional individuals reason based on the principles which underlie rules and norms, but reject a uniform application of a rule or norm. While two stages have been presented within the theory, only one, Stage 5, has received substantial empirical support. These levels are described more fully in Table 11.2.

For classifying level of moral reasoning the reason given for the decision is more important than the actual decision. In other words the same decision could be justified by quite different moral perspectives.

More often than not it is relatively easy to group answers to moral dilemma stories into one of three basic categories: a morality that seems to reflect a concern for *avoiding punishment* and *egocentric concerns*; a morality that seems to reflect an understanding of *rules and regulations* and their function in a society; and a morality that seems to be concerned with *ethical principles* which may take precedence over laws which broadly reflect Kohlberg's three major levels of moral development – preconventional, conventional, and postconventional (Kohlberg, 1981). Did you find it easier to categorise the responses into these three major divisions or was it possible for you to classify

Table 11.2 Aspects of moral reasoning

Level and stage	Individual's moral persepctive
Level 1 Preconventional	At this level, the child is responsive to cultural rules and labels of good and bad, right or wrong, but interprets the labels in terms of either the physical or hedonistic consequences of action (punishment, reward, exchange of favors) or the physical power of those who enunciate the rules and labels.
Stage 1: Punishment and obedience	A person at this stage doesn't consider the interests of others or recognise that they may differ from one's own. Actions are considered in terms of physical consequences such as to avoid punishment and obtain rewards. Those in authority have superior power and should be obeyed. Punishment should be avoided by staying out of trouble.
Stage 2: Individualism, instrumentality, and exchange	Right action consists of what instrumentally satisfies one's own needs and occasionally the needs of others. A person at this stage is aware that everybody has interests to pursue and that these can conflict, so integrates conflicting demands through instrumental exchange of services, letting others meet their own interests and being fair. However, the needs of the individual are paramount, and it's all right to do things (such as cheating, bribing, and stealing) if you get away with it and no one else is hurt in the process. Elements of fairness, reciprocity, and equal sharing are present, but they are always interpreted in a physical, pragmatic way. Reciprocity is a matter of 'you scratch my back and I'll scratch yours', not loyalty, gratitude, or justice.
Level 2 Conventional	At this level, the individual perceives the maintenance of the expectations of family, group, or nation as valuable in its own right, regardless of immediate and obvious consequences. The attitude is not only one of *conformity* to personal expectations and social order, but of loyalty to it, of actively maintaining, supporting, and justifying the order and identifying with the persons or group involved in it. The level consists of the following two stages.
Stage 3: Mutual interpersonal expectations, relationships, and conformity	Good behaviour is what pleases or helps others and is approved by them. There is much conformity to stereotypical images of what is majority or 'natural' behaviour. Behaviour is frequently judged by intention – 'he means well' becomes important for the first time.

(continued)

Table 11.2 *(continued)*

Level and stage	Individual's moral persepctive
	One earns approval by being 'nice'. A person at this stage is aware of shared feelings, agreements, and expectations that take primacy over individual interests. Believes in the Golden Rule, putting oneself in the other person's shoes. Does not yet consider generalised system perspective, and likes to be seen as doing the right thing by other people. Behaviour conforms strictly to the fixed conventions of society in which one lives.
Stage 4: Social system and conscience	The individual is oriented toward authority, fixed rules, and the maintenance of the social order. Right behaviour consists in doing one's duty, showing respect for authority, and maintaining the given social order for its own sake. A person at this stage takes the viewpoint of the system, which defines roles and rules. The individual 'does one's duty', shows respect for authority and believes in maintaining social order for its own sake. An individual considers individual relations in terms of place in the system. In other words, the individual is willing to go against social convention and the desire to be one of the crowd and please others in order to uphold laws that are seen as important for the stability of the community.
Level 3 Postconventional or principled	The individual makes a clear effort to define moral values and principles that have validity and application apart from the authority of the groups of persons holding them and apart from the individual's own identification with the group. The level has the two following stages:
Stage 5: Prior rights and social contract	The person at this stage is aware of values and rights prior to social attachments and contracts. Norms of right and wrong are defined in terms of laws or institutionalised rules, which are seen to have a rational base such as expressing the will of the majority and maximising social utility or welfare, and are necessary for institutional or social cohesion and functioning. Duty and obligation are defined in terms of contract, not the needs of individuals. At this stage, laws can be challenged as being 'good' or 'bad', and indeed the interpretation of the law itself can be challenged. Lawyers, Supreme and High Court judges spend much of their time arguing at this level. Fundamentally, laws are viewed as human inventions and, as such, are modifiable and not sacrosanct.

Table 11.2 *(continued)*	
Level and stage	**Individual's moral persepctive**
Stage 6: Universal ethical principles	Right is defined by the decision of conscience in accord with self-chosen ethical principles that appeal to logical comprehensiveness, universality, and consistency. These principles are abstract and ethical (the Golden Rule, the categorical imperative); they are not concrete moral rules like the Ten Commandments. At heart, these are universal principles of justice, of the reciprocity and equality of the human rights, and of respect for the dignity of human beings as individual persons. In stage 6, individuals consider circumstances and the situation, as well as the general principles and the reasons behind the rules. Orientation is not only to existing rules and standards, but to principles of moral choice involving appeal to logical universality and consistency. Although law is important, moral conflict is resolved in terms of broader moral principles. Indeed, at times it may be moral to disobey laws.

(Snarey & Samuelson, 2014)

them into five or six sub-stages? A lot of very useful information on Kohlberg's theory can be found on the following websites: http://simplypsychology.org/kohlberg.html and http://pegasus.cc.ucf.edu/~ncoverst/Kohlberg's%20Stages%20of%20Moral%20Development.htm

Current status of Kohlberg's theory

Although the basic ideas behind Kohlberg's theory appear to have stood the test of time, the theory has experienced a number of challenges over the years and changes have been made to the theory. Evidence has accumulated that individuals do move from very unsophisticated and egocentric forms of moral reasoning to increasingly sophisticated forms, and the stages outlined by Kohlberg, by and large, have received empirical support. The progression appears to be invariant, that is, an individual doesn't regress from a typically higher form of reasoning to a typically lower form, and stages are not skipped (Haidt, 2008; Millen, 2007).

Nevertheless, in the light of subsequent research there have been a number of modifications and elaborations to the theory (Gibbs et al., 2007; Krebs & Denton, 2005). It is now clear that principled reasoning does not emerge in any substantial way during the secondary school years, and that most children up to about Year 10 are functioning at stage 2 and stage 3, with stage 2 rapidly declining. In the latter years of high school and early adulthood, stage 1 thinking has virtually disappeared, stage 2 thinking is considerably reduced, and stage 3 begins to decline with the rise of stage 4 thinking. Basically, the ages at which various levels of moral reasoning decline and rise have been revised upwards in the light of new evidence and a re-evaluation of old data (Hart & Carlo, 2005). Furthermore, because postconventional thinking was so rare among the subjects interviewed, stage 6 has been dropped from the reformulation of the theory, while stage 5 has been modified to include some of the features of stage 6 (Garz, 2009; Gibbs, 2013; Snarey & Samuelson, 2014).

It has also become apparent that individuals do not reason at one stage exclusively but, rather, while typically reasoning at one stage, called the *modal stage*, they also understand and value reasoning at the next level up on the scale. Part of their reasoning is also at one stage lower (Haidt, 2007; Krebs & Denton, 2006). It is important to note here that the dynamism for moving from one stage to the next higher stage appears to be the cognitive conflict engendered when one is confronted with a level of reasoning higher than one's current level. For educators and parents this gives a rationale for holding moral dilemma discussions among individuals functioning at varying (but close) stages of moral reasoning. However, research tends to indicate that the challenge should not be too great, for example, when there is a mismatch between a stage 2 and a stage 4 or 5 thinker (see Ellis & Shute, 2007; Nucci & Turiel, 2009; Smetana, 2006).

 ## SPOTLIGHT ON INTERVIEWS AND MORAL REASONING

Kohlberg believed that the responses of children to moral dilemmas presented in interview situations represent underlying forms or structures of moral thought which are universal – that is, not dependent on particular socialisation practices within particular cultural communities. He also felt that moral development is an active process with children generating moral structures through interaction with other persons and through role taking in social situations. In particular, children are stimulated to move on to a higher stage of moral development when confronted with some genuine moral conflict that calls into question their typical beliefs.

In order to investigate and demonstrate this Kohlberg put a lot of faith in the interview method, which 'has been assumed to provide a clear window into the moral mind. The interview method presumes that a person both is aware of his/her own inner processes and can verbally explain them' (Rest et al., 1999, p. 295). However, others have questioned the value of interviews in uncovering the depth of moral reasoning that might characterise individuals.

For example, in questioning the belief that young children are incapable of advanced moral reasoning, Shweder, Mahapatra, and Miller (1990; see also Rest et al., 1999; Thoma, 2006) make the intriguing point that language (which is used to elicit moral judgments) is very often a quite inadequate means of explaining how individuals reason and think. Shweder et al. (1990, p. 143) states:

Kohlberg's theory of moral development is about the development of moral understandings, yet his moral dilemma interview methodology is a verbal production task that places a high premium on the ability to generate arguments, verbally represent complex concepts, and talk like a moral philosopher. It is hazardous to rely on such a procedure when studying moral understandings because one of the most important findings of recent developmental research is that knowledge of concepts often precedes their self-reflective representation in speech. Young children know a great deal more about the concept of number, causation, or grammaticality than they can state.

Children and adults may be able to reason at a higher moral level than their feeble attempts at explanation indicate. It might help to explain why so few individuals are classified as operating at the principled level. It appears that those who have been classified as such (e.g. Mahatma Ghandi, Martin Luther King, and Mother Teresa) were also skilled communicators of their thoughts!

 QUESTION POINT

Consider the argument put forward by Shweder et al. Do you think using verbal activities to evaluate moral reasoning is flawed? If you consider it flawed what alternative techniques would you use?

Elliot Turiel's domain theory of moral development

Within **domain theory** a distinction is drawn between the child's developing concepts of morality, and other domains of social knowledge, such as social convention. According to domain theory, the child's concepts of morality and social convention emerge out of the child's attempts to account for qualitatively differing forms of social experience associated with these two classes of social events. The unprovoked hitting of someone, for example, causes harm irrespective of whether there are or are not social rules controlling such actions. For this reason a contrast is drawn between *conventional rules* and *moral imperatives*. Conventional rules deal with issues that have no intrinsic interpersonal consequences, such as saying please and thank you, but facilitate the smooth running of society. Conventions provide a way for members of the group to coordinate their social exchanges through a set of agreed upon and predictable modes of conduct. Concepts of convention then, are structured by the child's understandings of social organisation. In contrast, morality is structured by concepts of harm, welfare, and fairness.

At times, however, breaking conventional rules is considered the same as breaking moral rules. Writers such as Turiel and Nucci (Nucci & Powers, 2014; Nucci & Turiel, 2009; Turiel, 2008) argue that an understanding of social conventions such as rules of dress, greetings, and appropriate behaviour in social settings progresses through developmental levels reflecting underlying concepts of social organisation, and that this development is different from the stages of moral development relating to issues that are universal and unchangeable such as proscriptions against stealing, injury, and slander. Moral transgressions are viewed as wrong, irrespective of the presence of governing rules, while conventional acts are viewed as wrong only if they violate an existing rule or standard. Children's and adults' responses to events in the moral domain focus on features intrinsic to the acts (such as harm or justice), while responses in the context of conventions focus on aspects of the social order (rules, regulations, normative expectations). Moral transgressions are viewed as more serious than violations of convention, and acts performed for a moral reason are considered more positive than ones performed because of convention (Helwig & Turiel, 2011; Smetana & Turiel, 2008; Turiel, 2014).

Of course, some rules have both an implied moral and conventional dimension, and conformity to the rule may reflect either moral or conventional reasoning, or a combination of both forms. In this way moral reasoning can be seen as more variable and flexible than is allowed for in Kohlberg's theory. For example, many drivers don't exceed the proscribed alcohol level while driving because they generally feel that it is immoral to endanger the lives of other drivers on the road. Other drivers obey the law because they are afraid of random breath testing and the consequences if they are over the limit. Most people are probably influenced by both motives.

Three important influences on our moral behaviour are:

- the moral values we have internalised through our socialisation;
- our exposure to models of moral behaviour; and
- the informational assumptions that provide the basis for our decision making.
(Turiel, 2014)

An individual's informational beliefs and assumptions about relevant aspects of reality have a bearing on the individual's interpretation of an event. For example, the belief that a foetus is a person makes abortion comparable with murder. On the other hand, if a foetus is not considered human life then abortion is seen as a personal choice that does not involve a moral transgression. It is for these reasons that people can have so many different moral perspectives on the same act (Smetana & Turiel, 2008; Turiel, 2014).

Moral actions and conventional actions

A major difference between the domain perspective and those of Kohlberg and Piaget is the belief that even very young children can differentiate between actions that are moral and those that are conventional. For example, children believe that they shouldn't break the classroom rule against talking (conventional rule), but that talking would be okay if the rule were removed. On the other hand, children believe it is wrong to hurt another child irrespective of the existence of a rule forbidding it. Because of this differentiation, moral and values education should reflect this distinction.

Young children are also able to distinguish just and unjust authority, and take into account the age and status of authority figures, their formal position in the social hierarchy, their ability to sanction and punish, and the extent of their expertise and knowledge. For example, children accept parental commands regulating activities such as house chores, but reject parental commands to steal or cause harm (Turiel, 2008, 2014).

For Turiel and others, it seems that children's moral judgments do not simply and directly reflect adults' values, teaching and commands, or the attitudes and opinions of significant groups such as religious ones. Rather, it appears that moral and social understandings and decisions result from a developmental process that stems from the child's social interactions and observations, which are then interpreted and modified according to the child's understandings and assumptions.

Moral reasoning and moral action

Research examining the relationship between moral reasoning and moral action has found only a weak relationship. Nevertheless, the relationship is in the expected direction. In other words, people who have been classified as functioning at a higher level of moral reasoning will avoid behaviour, such as cheating, more often than those who have been classified as functioning at a lower level (Hardy, 2006; Hardy & Carlo, 2011).

Various reasons are given for the weak link between moral reasoning and moral behaviour. We are all aware that circumstances can facilitate or inhibit what we believe to be moral behaviour irrespective of our moral beliefs. For example, for a woman with a large family of young children, the possibility of another pregnancy may persuade her to practise contraception, even though this may be against the rules of her church. All of us have had tussles of conscience when competing demands make a simple direct relationship between moral beliefs and behaviour problematic.

 QUESTION POINT

What reasons do you give for the relatively weak association between moral reasoning and moral actions. Have you engaged in actions that you could not justify through moral reasoning? Compare your responses to those of other students.

Carol Gilligan and gender differences in moral development

Carol Gilligan (1977, 1993) also challenged Kohlbergs's view of moral development, and in particular his methodologies. Gilligan believes that Kohlberg's stage theory and methodology is gender biased leading to men being classified as functioning at higher levels of moral reasoning than females. She argues that, because all Kohlberg's original subjects were male, the 'model' reasons derived for moral decisions used to structure the stage theory reflect a male perspective rather than a universal one. For example, she believes that men speak of rights, while women speak of responsibilities; men highlight rationality, while women highlight caring and concern; men are seen as searching for general principles that can be applied to any moral dilemma and women as concentrating on particular situations, relationships, and people. Gilligan maintains that Kohlberg's system of scoring the interviews, therefore, based upon male reasoning, penalises women so that more women are represented at lower levels of moral reasoning relative to men. Furthermore, she believes that, as the stages are based on a male perspective, they present a very limited view of moral reasoning.

QUESTION POINT

Gilligan lists a range of differences between men and women in their moral reasoning such as men highlighting rights and rationality and women responsibility and caring. What evidence have you seen for these purported differences between men and women in their moral reasoning?

While Gilligan and her colleagues argue that traditional Kohlbergian measures are biased against females, most research shows that Kohlberg's measurement methods and scoring schemes do not yield reliable gender differences in moral judgment scores (Jorgensen, 2006; Walker, 2006).

Morality of care

Despite the apparent controversy, Gilligan has nevertheless highlighted some important dimensions of moral reasoning not emphasised in Kohlberg's theory. While Kohlberg emphasises the **justice perspective** – a perspective that focuses on the rights of the individual: individuals stand alone and independently make moral decisions – Gilligan (1993) focuses on a **care perspective** that views people in terms of their connectedness with others and concern for others.

In studies with girls aged from 6 to 18 years of age Gilligan (1993) shows that girls consistently reveal a detailed knowledge about, and interest in, human relationships. Gilligan believes that this causes a dilemma for many girls who perceive that their intense interest in intimacy and relationships is not highly regarded in a male-dominated culture. Although society values women as caring and altruistic, such characteristics may limit females' opportunities in society at large. Females who choose to adopt achievement-driven values characteristic of the male may be considered selfish. If they don't, they may not be regarded as the equal of males! Gilligan believes that the conflict experienced can have a serious impact on the development of the female's self-concept and lead to depression and eating disorders among adolescent girls (Perry & Pauletti, 2011; Shaw & Dallos, 2005).

There has been considerable research support for Gilligan's claim that the moral reasoning of females and males is concerned with different issues. Some schools have taken seriously Gilligan's ideas that girls should have greater value placed on their **morality of care**, rather than being encouraged to be independent and self-sufficient. They have done so by emphasising cooperation rather than competition across the curriculum. It is also believed that boys benefit from such teaching approaches.

It is important to note that there is not an absolute gender difference and the two perspectives are not incompatible (Perry & Pauletti, 2011; Walker, 2006). Males can express deep concern for the welfare of others and develop intimacy and altruistic characteristics, while females can be justice oriented. In many cases neither perspective dominates.

SPOTLIGHT ON MORALITY AND CROSS-CULTURAL CONSIDERATIONS

In the theories described earlier there is an implicit asssumption that children acquire moral values relatively independently of their social environment, as if some of the development was 'hot wired' and naturally unfolds as children grow older. Given this belief it would appear that moral values would be universal. Shweder, Mahapatra, and Miller (1990) argue that young children acquire their social knowledge through a process of cultural transmission. From this perspective the cultural milieu of the child takes on a greater role in shaping moral responses, leading to a relative rather than a universal stance on questions of right and wrong (see also Vaisey, 2009).

Naturally, Kohlberg's comprehensive theory of moral development, with its claims to universalism, has been tested in a wide range of cultural contexts. Two issues are worth noting here. First, the original stories constructed by Kohlberg reflect a Western, middle-class orientation and, as such, may not be suited for use in other cultural contexts. Attempts have been made to rewrite the stories for particular cross-cultural use (Gibbs et al., 2007; Haste & Abrahams, 2008).

Second, and a greater problem than culturally suitable stories really hits at the heart of the theory, and this is the conception that there are universal moral values that characterise postconventional moral thinking, values such as liberty, equality, safety, the elimination of suffering, and the preservation of human life. Other writers (Schwartz, 2006) suggest that, far from being universal, demographic, economic and political factors influence specific moral values within different cultures. For example, the value of free speech and human individual dignity may very well reflect a democratic perspective rather than a universal value. Even on contentious issues within the United Kingdom, we see a diversity of opinion on laws related to abortion, euthanasia and same sex marriage, so that when we move to other cultures the complexity becomes even greater. For example, birth control is considered immoral in many cultures, while polygamy is considered moral. Those holding to the universalistic notion argue that, irrespective of the recognition of wrongness (in behaviour such as polygamy or abortion), certain behaviours are wrong regardless of social mores and man-made laws. In his latest formulation of the theory, Kohlberg paid greater attention to this issue (Kohlberg et al., 1983; Shweder et al., 1990). As you can see, this is a very complicated issue, and one that is far from resolution.

ACTIVITY POST

How universal are moral values? In order to consider this question have a discussion with a group representing different cultural and religious backgrounds. What are common moral beliefs? Where are there divergent views about morality? Given the possibility that people will hold different moral perspectives reflecting their cultural and religious backgrounds how should moral issues be handled within school contexts characerised by diversity? Write a brief report outlining your findings and compare these with other students in your group.

Neo-Kohlbergian approaches to moral development

Defining Issues Test (DIT)

Because of the perceived limitations in Kolberg's theory a number of theorists are developing a new approach that has been termed neo-Kohlbergian (Haidt, 2007, 2008; Thoma, 2006). Essential differences between the neo-Kohlbergian approach and that of Kohlberg are the way in which theorists assess moral development and the direct links drawn between moral thinking and information processing. Instead of interviews neo-Kohlbergians use multiple-choice recognition tasks which ask participants to rate and rank a set of items that are designed to activate moral schemas. This 'test' is called the Defining Issues Test (DIT).

Instead of referring to stages of moral development neo-Kohlbergians refer to moral schemas. Moral schemas are more concrete conceptions of the moral basis of behaviour than Kohlberg's stages, which are relatively abstract, particularly at the higher levels. In other words, the content of an act (indicated through a schema) can be used as a measure of moral thinking as well as the structure of the reasoning (cognitive operations represented in stages in Kohlberg's theory, and assessed content free through interviews on moral dilemmas). Rather than thinking of moral development as a step-like procedure as in Kohlberg's theory, neo-Kohlbergians emphasise the more fluid overlapping of ways of thinking about moral issues that characterise individuals as they move from more primitive ways of thinking to more advanced. Finally, neo-Kohlbergians believe that morality is a social construction that reflects the community's experiences, particular institutional arrangements, deliberations, and aspirations that are supported by the community (Gibbs, 2013). In contrast, as we have noted earlier in this chapter, Kohlberg argued for the universality of moral reasoning and values.

Moral schemas in the DIT

There are three moral schemas represented in the DIT: the Personal Interests schema, the Maintaining Norms schema, and the Postconventional schema. The *Personal Interests* schema develops in childhood, while the other two are typically developed in adolescence and adulthood (Myyrya et al., 2010). The Personal Interests schema includes elements of Kohlberg's stages 2 and 3 and justifies a decision by appealing to the personal stake that a person has in the consequences of an action as well as concerns for those with whom the person has a personal affectionate relationship. Society-wide norms are not apparent or relevant to decision making.

The *Maintaining Norms* schema, drawn from Kohlberg's stage 4, implicates society-wide norms. Indicative of this level of reasoning is reference to the necessity of having and maintaining societal norms that facilitate the harmonious working of society and that are applied even with strangers. Formal law, that is publicly set and known by everyone, is used for ensuring social norms are applied uniformly across society. Individuals, in adhering to the law, anticipate that others will also do their duty by the law. There is a partial reciprocity implied as obeying the law might not benefit all the participants in the same way. In the Maintaining Norms schema there is a duty orientation, which emphasises the need to obey authorities out of respect for the social system. There is a strong link between law and order in this schema. In essence, maintaining the social order through adherence to laws defines morality in this schema.

The *Postconventional schema* reflects moral obligations that are based on shared ideals that are reciprocal and open to debate, tests of logical consistency, and the experience of the community (Myyrya et al., 2010). Four elements are proposed as comprising Postconventional schema. First, the person believes that laws and regulations are social conventions that can be renegotiated to address a new moral purpose rather than being immutable. Second, laws and regulations should reflect higher ideals regarding human interaction or organisation. Many laws today have overturned earlier laws in order to address ideals such as equal opportunity, minimal rights and protection for everyone, privacy and intimacy, and so on. Third, these ideals that shape codes of behaviour should be sharable, that is, embraced by others and justifiable through rational critique. Fourth, the Postconventional schema holds that laws should be fully reciprocal, that is, they should not only apply to everyone equally but be equally just to everyone. That is, there should not be laws that favour particular groups over others. Both the Maintaining Norms and Postconventional schemas seek to establish consensus. In the first schema this is through appeals to existing practice and existing authority, while in the latter it is through appealing to ideals and logical coherence.

As with Kohlberg's theory there is considerable debate over the merits of the neo-Kohlbergian approach and the methodology used and considerable research effort has been directed at examining these issues, which is beyond the scope of this book (see Gibbs, 2013; Myyrya et al., 2010; Thoma, 2006). If you are interested you should follow up this material by reading some of the research and associated literature and, in particular, examine the DIT.

 ACTIVITY POST

Complete an Internet search to critique the neo-Kohlbergian approach. In particular consider the strengths and weaknesses of the DIT. If possible, utilise the DIT and one or more of Kohlberg's moral dilemma stories with a group of late childhood and adolescent students. Examine similarities and differences in the classification of each student's level of moral reasoning.

Classroom applications of moral development theory

Our consideration of theories of moral development has highlighted a number of important issues for educators and parents. First among these is the notion that moral reasoning increases in sophistication as children get older, and that there is a relationship between moral reasoning and cognitive development. We cannot therefore expect children to hold the same moral perspective as ourselves and, indeed, children may consider it all right to cheat and lie if, for example, it's for a good reason or can be concealed. Sermonising to children about their 'immoral' behaviour may well be a fruitless exercise if we are using arguments based on stages more than one in advance of the child's modal level.

Second, our discussion has drawn attention to the importance for moral growth of the child's own direct social experience and their active efforts to draw meaning from its contradictions. Clearly, the school and classroom supplies the first large environment in which children test out their moral rules. Cooperative grouping will provide a good environment for peer interaction that will promote cognitive and moral growth.

Approaches to teaching moral values

There are two basic approaches to teaching moral values. The first approach reflects a behavioural/social cognitive approach. In this approach children learn to be good by being exposed to virtuous deeds and actions through models (such as texts and films) and being reinforced for appropriate behaviour. The values to be learnt are predetermined and programmed into the curriculum (see, for example, Narvaez et al., 2006; Nucci & Powers, 2014; Smetana, 2006). The second approach, cognitive developmental, reflects the theories of Piaget, Kohlberg, and others, and emphasises the personal or social construction of moral beliefs and values (Jensen, 2008; Snarey & Samuelson, 2014).

 ACTIVITY POST

The discussion above calls into question many of the more traditional didactic methods of 'teaching' moral values. It has been common practice for social studies and other texts to present moral stories based on the lives of famous people such as Abraham Lincoln, Lewis Carroll, Helen Keller, Florence Nightingale, Mahatma Ghandi, and Albert Schweitzer. It was anticipated that the child would learn to be moral by reading about moral behaviour. What is the research evidence that such didactic approaches are effective (or not effective)? Are these didactic practices still in common use? If so, discuss examples of these with your fellow students. What extra complications arise if these materials are used in educational settings characterised by diversity? (See, for example, Gibbs et al., 2007; Schwartz, 2006.)

Four-component framework of moral education

Understanding moral development is a complex thing. Effective moral education should, therefore, account for the complexities of social and moral reasoning (Nucci & Turiel, 2009). It should be geared towards stimulating the development of moral concepts, fostering an understanding of the distinctions, relations and conflicts between moral and social concepts, as well as guiding children's comprehension of the ways access to information modifies social and moral decisions. One such approach to guide the development of moral education programmes, was originally proposed by James Rest and subsequently elaborated by Darcia Narvaez and Muriel Bebeau in a four-component framework (Bebeau & Monson, 2014; Narvaez, 2014). Each of these components highlights an issue to be addressed in order to encourage and develop moral behaviour.

1 *Moral sensitivity* (interpreting the situation as moral). This emphasises that moral behaviour can only occur if an individual assesses the situation as moral and is aware of how one's actions affect other people.
2 *Moral judgment* (judging which of the available actions are most moral). This emphasises the selection process, choosing one action over another.
3 *Moral motivation* (prioritising the moral over other significant concerns and personal values such as careers, affectional relationships, institutional loyalities, and so on). This emphasises the choice made to be moral over other possible behaviours that are valid and significant.
4 *Moral character* (being able to construct and implement actions that service the moral choice). This emphasises the processes by which one constructs an appropriate course of action, avoids distractions and maintains the courage to continue.

Nel Noddings and caring schools

In order to encourage the development of moral values and behaviour in students, educational environments should be moral places. Today there is considerable emphasis on schools having a culture of caring in which interpersonal relationships are considered very important to the social, moral, and cognitive development of students (Battistich, 2014; Thapa et al., 2013; Watson & Battistich, 2006). This is in line with humanist perspectives on education considered earlier and links have also been drawn with Vygotsky's social constructivism and, in particular, the notion of the Zone of Proximal Development (see, for example, Daniels et al., 2007, and Chapter 5). Caring refers to teachers' abilities to empathise with and invest in the protection and development of young people (Maxwell & DesRoches, 2010).

According to Noddings caring has three components:

- receptivity;
- engrossment; and
- motivational displacement.

QUESTION POINT

Some argue that schools are established to teach children the three 'r's' (reading, writing, and arithmetic) and that widening the curriculum in many other ways to include issues such as caring behaviour and moral education is moving beyond what schools are established to do. What is your opinion on this issue?

Reflecting a curriculum of caring, changes have been made to many school organisations, curriculum content and emphases, and there has been a development of community service education and extensions of contact with parents and communities. What is your experience with caring school environments? In what ways has your teacher training provided you with the skills to encourage caring values among the students you teach?

Consider the implications of each of the theories covered in this chapter for children whose families might be recent migrants or seeking asylum. These children might not have been brought up in Western settings and with Western values. What different factors are likely to affect moral development in each case?

Receptivity refers to full openness to the other person and a compelling obligation to respond. *Engrossment* refers to fully receiving and experiencing what the other person is saying or presenting as if one were that person. *Motivational displacement* refers to the willingness the carer has to give primacy to the goals and needs of the cared for. The caring relationship has to be reciprocal with the cared for receiving the caring that is offered. This is indicated when the cared for responds in word or deed in a way that recognises that care has been given. It is through this recognition and response that the carer receives validation for the caring act, thus completing the cycle (Owens & Ennis, 2005). The cared for's response is the carer's reward and is the impetus for continued caring (Noddings, 2010).

The roles of carer and cared for are not fixed but are characterised by reciprocity and mutuality. In other words the carer and cared for can reverse roles as opportunities arise. In the school context students can learn to be both carers and cared for.

Noddings (2005, 2006) suggests four central components of a moral education that reflects a caring perspective. First, teachers and other adults must model caring behaviour. Second, students should be engaged in open-ended dialogue with each other in order to gain understanding, insight, appreciation, and empathy. In this way both the caring and cared for share the experience and grow through it. Third, students should be encouraged to practice caring behaviour, hence schools and homes should provide the opportunity for such practice. Finally, students should be encouraged to affirm caring behaviour in others.

Glossary

Accommodation: A cognitive process defined by Piaget as the modification of existing cognitive structures by new elements.

Adolescence: The period of development between childhood and adulthood.

Amniocentesis: A medical technique that involves inserting a hollow needle into a woman's abdomen during pregnancy to test amniotic fluid to provide information on the chromosomal constitution of the foetus and for diagnosing problems with metabolism.

Analytic thinking: (Bruner) Characteristically proceeds step-by-step and the learner is, in general, aware of the information and operations involved.

Anorexia nervosa: Severe eating disorder in which individuals restrict their eating to such an extent that they become painfully thin. The malnutrition that accompanies the illness leads to additional side effects such as brittle, discoloured nails, pale skin, fine dark hairs appearing all over the body, and extreme sensitivity to cold. Menstrual periods also cease.

Applied behaviour analysis: The application of behavioural learning principles to understand and change behaviour.

Applied research: Deals with the application of knowledge to solve specific practical problems.

Assimilation: A cognitive process defined by Piaget as the integration of new elements into existing cognitive structures, the child adapts by relating each new experience to familiar ones.

Asynchrony: Differential rate at which different body parts grow. Asynchrony can be interpersonal, where development varies from individual to individual, or intrapersonal, where there is an uneven progression of development within an individual.

Attachment: A strong, affectionate bond established between the child and caregivers.

Attention deficit hyperactivity disorder (ADHD): Children characterised by low attention to task and high physical activity levels.

Authoritarian parenting: A form of parenting characterised by restrictive rules and lack of warmth.

Authoritative parenting: A form of parenting characterised by a loving and supportive home, appropriate and high expectations for children, clear rules on acceptable behaviour, consistent enforcement of rules and inclusion of children in decision making.

Autism: An individual's extreme inability to relate to other people and a tendency to withdraw from real life, indulge in day-dreaming and bizarre fantasies and behaviour.

Automaticity: A process that occurs when information or operations are overlearned and can be retrieved and used with little mental effort.

Autonomous morality: In Piaget's theory when children view moral rules as flexible, socially agreed-on principles that can be changed (also referred to as a morality of reciprocity).

Basic research: Deals with the generation of new knowledge or the extension of existing knowledge.

Behavioural genetics: The study of the relative contribution of environmental and heredity factors to differences in human thought and behaviour.

Behaviourism: A theory of learning that focuses on external events as the cause of changes in observable behaviours.

Bulimia nervosa: Uncontrollable binge eating followed by a combination of purging of the stomach contents through laxatives, diuretics or self-induced vomiting, strict fasting, and strenuous exercise.

Canalisation: The tendency for heredity to restrict the development of some human characteristics to just one or a few outcomes.

Care perspective: In moral reasoning a focus on nurturance and concern for others.

Catch-growth: Physical growth returns to its genetically determined path after being delayed by environmental factors.

Centration: A preoperational child's preoccupation with visual perception and in particular one feature of a problem.

Cephalocaudal development/growth: Development of physical and motor systems from the head down.

Cerebral palsy: A form of paralysis resulting from brain injury.

Chorion biopsy: Often referred to as chorionic villus sampling, involves inserting a thin tube into the uterus either through the vagina or through a thin needle into the abdomen, and taking a small sample of tissue from the end of one or more chorionic villi. Cells are examined for genetic defects.

Chromosomes: Strands of DNA (deoxyribonucleic acid) molecules that carry genetic information.

Chunking: A strategy to enhance learning through reducing complex material to smaller patterns (fewer units to learn) that can be remembered more easily.

Clinical method: A procedure whereby a psychologist probes for information by asking a respondent questions in an interview setting, and supplements the information obtained in this manner with observations, projective techniques and perhaps some activities (such as completing a relevant task).

Cliques: Small groups who maintain similar ethnic, age, gender, and social class parameters.

Cognitive development: The development over time of the ability to think and reason and understand the world in which we live.

Componential intelligence: The ability to acquire knowledge, think and plan, monitor cognitive processes, and determine what is to be done.

Concept map: A two-dimensional diagram representing the conceptual structure of subject matter.

Conceptualisation: (Bruner) The process of intellectual growth through which children gradually organise their environment into meaningful units.

Concurrent validity evidence: When data from measurements are compared at the same time and lead to the same conclusions.

Construct validity evidence: When procedures such as factor analysis are used to support the underlying dimensions being measured by a test.

Constructivism: Piaget's view that children construct their own understanding through interaction with their environment.

Content validity evidence: Evidence that the measure, such as a questionnaire, intelligence test, or biological measure, reflects the appropriate domain of investigation.

Contextual intelligence: The ability to adapt to contexts to optimise opportunities.

Conventional morality: A form of morality that reflects a concern with rules and regulations.

Correlational research: Research designed to examine the relationship between variables, in particular the co-variation between variables of interest to the researcher.

Criterion validity evidence: Evidence that the results of a specific measurement, such as a new intelligence or personality test, converge with the results of other established measurements.

Cross-sectional design: A research design that studies a large number of participants at a given point in time for comparison.

Crowd: A term used to describe large congregations of adolescents that hang out together in shopping malls, beaches and sporting events.

Cybernetics: The comparative study of the automatic control systems formed by the nervous system and brain and by mechanical-electrical communication systems.

Denial: A defence mechanism through which an individual denies the existence of painful experiences and thoughts (such as a refusal to accept that a loved one has died).

Developmentally appropriate education: An educational environment that provides an optimal match between the developmental stage of the child and the logical properties of the material to be learnt.

Differentiation of motor movements: The gradual separation of children's motor movements from gross movement patterns into more refined and functional movements as they mature.

Direct instruction: A highly structured, goal-oriented approach to teaching, characterised by teacher presentation, teacher modelling, and student practice with feedback.

Discovery learning: Subject matter is not presented to students in its final form, but rather students, through their own manipulation of the materials, discover relationships, solutions, and patterns.

Distributed cognition: Knowledge is distributed through a group so that the group can function effectively.

Distributed practice: Practice of an activity is spread over time.

Dizygotic twins: So-called fraternal twins developed from two fertilised ova.

Dominant gene: In a heterozygous situation the gene that has most power in expression.

Domain theory: A theory of moral development that draws a distinction between a child's developing concepts of morality, and other domains of social knowledge such as social conventions.

Down syndrome: A chromosomal abnormality resulting from the presence of three rather than the normal two on chromosome 21 that leads to unusual physical features, increased health problems, and increased potential for mental retardation.

Ectomorphs: Skinny, angular people, likely to be non-sociable, intense, shy, and intellectual (cerebrotonia).

Ego: In Freud's theory the conscious, rational part of personality driven by the reality principle which represents reason and which puts limits on dangerous and impulsive acts of the id.

Egocentrism: (Piaget) The preoperational child's inability to see things from other's perspective and a belief that everyone else's thoughts, feelings, desires, and perceptions are the same as theirs.

Electra crisis: In Freud's theory, a stage between 3 and 6 years of age when girls are sexually attracted to their fathers and hostile to their mothers.

Enactive stage: (Bruner) Children learn about the world around them by acting on objects.

Endomorphs: Large, round people, likely to be sociable, jolly, happy, placid, and slow-moving (viscerotonia).

Environmentalist position: A belief that individual potential is very malleable and, provided the environment is healthy and stimulating, individuals may develop many different physical and psychological skills and talents, irrespective of supposed limitations from their genetic inheritance.

Experiential intelligence: The ability to formulate new ideas to solve problems.

Experimental research: Research in which the researcher manipulates one or more independent variables (those factors perceived as important by the researcher) in order to observe their effects on one or more dependent variables (outcomes seen to be important by the researcher).

Face validity evidence: Indicates that the task or measure in the research, at least on the surface, measures what it purports to measure.

Factor analysis: A statistical technique for reducing a large set of data to smaller parcels of data usually called 'factors' or 'components'. Patterns in the overall data are therefore more easily observable.

Fantasy: In Freud's theory a defence mechanism that protects the ego by seeking imaginary satisfactions in place of real ones.

Fetoscopy: The insertion of a small light and camera into the uterus to inspect the fetus for defects of the limbs and face. It can also allow a sample of fetal blood to be taken which can be analysed for hemophilia and sickle cell anemia as well as neural defects.

Fine motor skills: Small precise movements of the body, especially the hands and fingers, such as in using scissors, or writing.

Fixation: In Freud's theory an immature form of defence mechanism is consistently used rather than a more mature defence mechanism, such as sublimation.

Formal operational thought: (Piaget) The ability to think abstractly and in a scientific way.

Genes: About 20,000 DNA segments carried on any one chromosome that serve as the key functional units in hereditary transmission.

Genetic counselling: A process of informing people who have a family history of particular genetic problems of the probability of a genetic defect, its likely seriousness and treatment, in order to inform their decision to have a child or not.

Genotype: The 23 pairs of chromosomes (22 matched and the twenty-third sex chromosomes) that provide the basic blueprint for an individual's development.

Gross motor skills: Large movements of the body that allow movement around the environment, such as walking.

Grounded theory: A systematic research method in which questions, themes, and issues arise from the analysis of the data themselves.

Growth charts: Graphs representing chronological norms of development for height, weight, skeletal structure, muscles, internal organs, the brain, and the sexual system.

Haemophilia: A congenital tendency to uncontrolled bleeding, usually affects males and is transmitted from mother to son.

Hereditarian position: The belief that individual development reflects genetic potential and that no amount of environmental engineering can alter the course of development of the individual.

Heredity: Genetic blueprint passed on to each child by its parents.

Heteronomous morality: In Piaget's theory of moral development younger children tend to focus on observed consequences of actions and believe in absolute, unchanging rules handed down by outside authorities (also referred to as moral realism).

Heterozygous: If the alleles from both parents for a particular genetic characteristic are different.

Humanistic psychologists: Psychologists that emphasise the innate potential of humans to develop. They perceive people as free and unique, self-directed, capable of setting goals, making choices, and initiating action.

Hypothetico-deductive reasoning: A term used by Piaget for formal operational thought related to adolescents forming hypotheses, testing these hypotheses and making deductions based on these tests.

Iconic stage: (Bruner) Experiences and objects are represented as concrete images.

Id: In Freud's theory the source of basic biological needs and desires, driven by the *pleasure principle* to satisfy needs immediately.

Identification: In Freud's theory, the process that motivates children to try to become like their same-sex parent in all-important respects. More broadly applied, children incorporating values held by significant others.

Identity: People's self-constructed definition of who they are, what they find important, and what goals they want to accomplish in life.

Identity achieved: In Marcia's theory identity-achieved individuals are committed to a clearly formulated set of self-chosen values and goals.

Identity crisis: In Marcia's theory a period in which individuals clarify and become aware of personal values.

Identity diffusion: In Marcia's theory a stage of identity development that occurs when individuals fail to make clear choices for their future.

Identity foreclosure: In Marcia's theory a stage of identity development that occurs when individuals prematurely adopt the ready-made positions of others, such as parents.

Identity moratorium: In Marcia's theory a stage of identity development that occurs when individuals pause and reflect on what their future might hold as individuals.

Immanent justice: A categorical morality which means that if punishment has been given, wrong must have been done.

Infant marasmus: A marked breakdown in the normal development of a child, illustrated by poor physical growth and intellectual impairment.

Information processing theory: Theoretical perspective that focuses on the specific ways in which people mentally think about (process) the information they receive.

Integration of motor movements: Various opposing muscle and sensory systems being brought into coordinated interaction with one another.

Integrative review: A review that primarily synthesises and interprets findings on a topic across a range of relevant research articles.

Interference effect: The intrusion of similar memories on one another which inhibits learning.

Internal consistency reliability: Scores on comparable halves of the test are similar.

Inter-rater reliability: Scores obtained from different raters are consistent.

Intuitive thinking: A form of thought characterised by hunches and solutions not based on formal processes of reasoning.

Justice perspective: In moral reasoning a focus individual rights.

Keyword method: Memory device associating new words or concepts with similar-sounding cue words and images.

Klinefelter syndrome: A chromosomal abnormality that usually results from the presence of two X chromosomes and one Y chromosome. Children with this syndrome are phenotypically male but never produce sperm.

Law of effect: Any action producing a pleasant effect will be repeated in similar circumstances to produce a similar effect.

Libido: In Freud's theory the creative energy in all individuals.

Literature review: A form of research that involves a secondary analysis across related studies to evaluate overall findings.

Longitudinal design: A research design that usually studies a number of participants continuously over a longer period of time.

Long-term memory: The repository of stored information for relatively long periods of time.

Massed practice: Practice of an activity is concentrated in long periods.

Mastery learning: A teaching approach where students must learn one unit and pass a test at a specified level before moving to the next unit.

Meaningful material: Material that can be related to already existing schemes of knowledge in the long-term memory.

Meiosis: A type of cell division that results in daughter cells each with half the number of chromosomes of the parent cell.

Mental age: An index of a child's intellectual ability relative to that of other children the same age. Mental age is judged by comparing the intelligence-test items that a child answers correctly with the average age at which children answer those items correctly.

Mesomorphs: Muscular, solid people, likely to be forceful, aggressive, unsympathetic, loud, direct, and action oriented (somatonia).

Meta-analysis: A form of literature review that takes the primary statistical findings from related studies and derives a measure of overall significance of the findings.

Metacognition: People's ability to think about their thoughts and control their cognitive processes.

Metalearning: A process by which the learner plans, sets goals, organises, monitors, and evaluates their learning.

Mnemonic images: Memory devices that aid retrieval including method of loci, keyword systems, and eidetic imagery.

Monozygotic twins: So-called identical twins developed from the one fertilised ovum.

Moral anxiety: The superego dominates an individual's behaviour and the individual becomes trapped in an over-rigid value system.

Morality of care: A morality based upon connectedness and concern for others.

Morality of cooperation: Children perceive rules as simple social constructs that society believes are correct and necessary for the cohesion of the society.

Morality of reciprocity: Duty and obligation are not defined in terms of obedience to an authority but as a social contract reflecting the mutual needs of oneself and others.

Moral realism: The belief that there are objective moral facts and values that are independent or beliefs, feelings, or attitudes.

Motor development: Age-related changes in motor skills including crawling, walking, and running.

Myelinisation: The sheathing of the nerve fibres in the brain and nervous system with fatty tissue which improves the efficiency of message transfer.

Nativist approach: A view that human development is largely determined by genetics.

Negative reinforcement: Reinforcement that strengthens a response because the response removes some painful or unpleasant stimulus or enables the individual to avoid it.

Networking: A form of concept map that requires students to identify the important concepts or ideas in the text and to describe the interrelationships between these ideas in the form of a network diagram using nodes and links.

Neurotic anxiety: An individual fears that the instinctive forces of the id will control their behaviour.

Niche-picking: The tendency for an individual to actively choose environments that complement their heredity.

Nominal realism: (Piaget) The power of words in creating 'reality'.

Object permanence: The understanding that objects have a separate, permanent existence.

Oedipal crisis: In Freud's theory a stage between 3 and 6 years of age when boys are sexually attracted to their mothers, and are hostile to their fathers but are not fully conscious of their feelings.

Ontogenetic development: Development influenced by environmental factors.

Open classrooms: A form of education in which the goal is to respond to students on the basis of their individual behaviours, needs, and characteristics.

Open education: A form of education in which the goal is to respond to students on the basis of their individual behaviours, needs, and characteristics.

Operant conditioning: Learning in which voluntary behaviour is strengthened or weakened by consequences or antecedents.

Overlearning: A technique to enhance remembering material through continuing repetition of the material past the point of first mastery.

Parental self-efficacy: Parental beliefs about their ability to influence their child's developmental and educational outcomes, about their specific effectiveness in influencing the child's school learning, and about their own influence relative to that of peers and the child's teacher.

Permissive parenting: A form of parenting characterised by few demands being placed on children. It is non-directive and lenient.

Personality: The characteristics of people that are fairly stable over time and obvious in a variety of situations.

Phenomenalistic causality: (Piaget) Young children regard events that happen together as having caused one another.

Phenotype: The expressed genes that form an individual's observable characteristics.

Phenylketonuria (PKU): A digestive disorder that makes it impossible for a child to metabolise the amino acid (phenylalanine) that is commonly in milk products leading to a build up of a toxic substance, phenylpyruvic acid that can lead to mental retardation.

Phylogenetic development: Genetic unfoldment best understood in processes such as seeing, walking, and talking.

Physical development: Physical and neurological growth over time.

Physiognomic perception: (Piaget) Young children attributing life-like qualities onto inanimate objects.

Positive reinforcement: A stimulus that increases the probability of an operant (behaviour) recurring as a result of its being added to a situation after the performance of the behaviour. It usually takes the form of something pleasant.

Positive teaching: Identifying records relevant to students and making these records contingent on appropriate social and academic behaviour.

Positivistic research: Research based on a priori theorising seeking for answers to research questions.

Postconventional morality: A morality that reflects mutual obligations based on shared ideas that are reciprocal, open to debate, tests of logical consistency, and the experience of the community.

Preconventional morality: A form of morality that reflects a concern for avoiding punishment and moral judgment characterised by a concrete, individual perspective.

Predictive validity evidence: When data are able to predict a criterion such as school performance or job promotion.

Primacy and recency effects: The ability to retain and recall the first and last elements of a list more easily than the middle section.

Primary circular reaction: Accidental bodily actions which the infant repeats because of their satisfying effects.

Primary mental abilities: Core components of intelligence proposed by Thurstone including verbal meaning, number facility, inductive reasoning, perceptual speed, spatial relations, memory, and verbal fluency.

Prior knowledge: The knowledge, skills, or ability that students bring to the learning process.

Proactive interference: Earlier learning interferes with new learning.

Programmed instruction: Instruction which emphasises reinforcement by providing the student with immediate feedback for every response. Information is provided sequentially in small units, and the learner does not proceed to a new unit until mastery of the present one is demonstrated.

Projection: In Freud's theory a defence mechanism through which individuals ascribe their own unconscious motivation to other people.

Propositional thinking: A characteristic of formal thinking through which individuals work through statements of an argument in the mind.

Proximodistal development/growth: Growth from the central axis of the body outward.

Psychosexual stages: In Freud's theory, the stages of personality development related to the sexual and aggressive drives of children.

Psychosocial stages: Erikson's description of the distinct phases of development that are consequences of the social experiences and major events of the human life cycle.

Pubescence: Derived from the Latin 'to grow hairy' – refers to changes that occur to individuals that result in sexual maturity.

Qualitative research: An alternative approach to quantitative research that uses relatively little standardised instrumentation and does not depend on extensive statistical analysis.

Quasi-experimental research: Research similar to experimental research in which independent variables cannot be controlled to the same degree as in a true experiment.

Question generation: A strategy to enhance learning through which students are taught how to generate integrative questions concerning text that capture large units of meaning.

Randomisation: A strategy for determining the assignment of subjects to experimental conditions in such a way that the probability of being assigned to a particular condition is the same for all participants.

Rationalisation: In Freud's theory a defence mechanism through which individuals unconsciously give socially acceptable reasons for their conduct in place of real reasons.

Reaction formation: In Freud's theory a defence mechanism through which a repressed feeling or emotion is replaced by its opposite.

Realistic anxiety: An individual is dominated by the ego to such an extent that id-driven behaviour (such as eating or sexual behaviour) becomes impossible to enjoy, and the individual is unable to devote energy to any superego demands such as the welfare of others.

Recency effect: *See* primacy and recency effect.

Recessive gene: In a heterozygous situation the gene that has least power over the other is called the recessive gene. In general, recessive genes are expressed if the allele for this characteristic is the same from both parents.

Regression: In Freud's theory a defence mechanism through which tension and anxiety are reduced by children and adults engaging in behaviour more characteristic of an earlier stage of development.

Reliability (in testing): Measures used are stable and consistent over time.

Representational images: A form of mental imagery through which the imagery exactly represents the content of the prose or material to be learnt.

Representational thinking: The understanding that a thought can represent an object in a real life setting.

Repression: In Freud's theory a defence mechanism through which painful or shameful experiences and thoughts are prevented from reaching consciousness.

Research design: Comprises the research question(s), an identification of the appropriate data, the sample of participants needed to obtain these data, the method for gathering them, and the analytical tools and approaches to be used for analysing the data.

Retroactive interference: New learning impedes the retention and retrieval of earlier learning.

Role confusion: In Erikson's theory an individual's inability to establish a sense of self-identity.

Scaffolded instruction: (Vygotsky) Support and assistance provided by parents and teachers to support children's learning. Support and assistance are reduced as children become more capable of completing cognitive tasks independently.

Schemas: Cognitive structures for organising perception and experience.

Scientific method: Based on controlled experiments in which cause and effect may be examined.

Secondary circular reactions: Actions directed towards objects in the infant's environment as well as to its own body, and involve coordination of activities that are no longer simply reflexive.

Secular trend: A trend towards accelerated maturation in height and weight among males and females over the last century.

Self-actualisation: Individuals strive to satisfy their need to grow intellectually and spiritually.

Self-concept: A person's beliefs about themselves in specific areas such as physical ability, physical appearance, peer relationships, parent relationships, academic ability, and self-worth.

Self-efficacy: One's perceptions of one's own ability to succeed on valued tasks.

Self-esteem: Judgments about one's worth and the feelings associated with these.

Self-regulation: The regulation of one's own cognitive processes in order to learn successfully. Self-regulation involves such things as goal setting, planning and time management, attention control, self-motivation, flexible use of learning strategies, self-monitoring, asking for help, and self-evaluation.

Sensory receptors: The senses (eyes, ears, touch, smell, and taste) through which we perceive external stimuli and record the memory for a very short period of time.

Serial position effect: Remembering the beginnings and ends of lists while forgetting the middle of the list.

Shaping: In Behavioural theory reinforcing progressive steps towards a desired goal or behaviour.

Situated learning: A view that learning is most effective when it is in a situated context, and that 'real' learning is a form of apprenticeship in which new members become enculturated into the language, customs, and beliefs of a learning community.

Size and shape constancy: The knowledge that objects are the same size and shapes no-matter from what perspective they are viewed.

Social cognitive theory: A theory of learning that emphasises learning through observation of others.

Social skills: The ability to interact with others in a given context in specific ways that are socially acceptable or valued, and at the same time personally beneficial, mutually beneficial or beneficial primarily to others.

Sociometric status: A term used to indicate the social status of an individual in the social structure of a group.

Sociometric testing: Methods used for assessing the social status of specific persons in the social structure of a group.

Spiral curriculum: A form of curriculum in which concepts are presented at higher levels of abstraction as learning develops.

Story grammar training: A strategy to enhance learning through which students are taught to ask themselves questions that structure their attention as they read stories.

Structuralism: Piaget's belief that intellectual development occurs through a series of stages characterised by qualitatively discrete structures.

Successful intelligence: (Sternberg) That set of mental abilities used to achieve one's goals in life including adapting to, selecting aspects of, or shaping their given environments.

Superego: In Freud's theory the seat of conscience, which distinguishes right from wrong irrespective of whether the contemplated action or desire is 'safe' and represents cultural norms and standards as internalised by the individual.

Symbolic stage: (Bruner) A stage of cognitive development in which children develop the capacity to think abstractly with symbols and go beyond the present and concrete experiences to create hypotheses.

Teratogens: Chemicals and drugs introduced to the prenatal environment that can stunt physical and mental growth so that the child is born with birth defects.

Tertiary circular reactions: Infants actively 'experiment' in order to investigate the properties of objects and events and through these experiments on the environment further develops the central notions of object permanence, causality, space, and time.

Test-retest reliability: A test that produces similar results on two separate occasions.

Thanatos: In Freud's theory the destructive urge in all individuals.

Transfer of learning: The application of knowledge learnt in one context to another related context.

Triarchic theory of intelligence: (Sternberg) Based on three interrelated but distinct aspects of thinking: analytical, also called componential intelligence; creative, also called experiential intelligence; and practical thinking, also know as contextual intelligence.

Turner syndrome: A chromosomal abnormality that results from the presence of only one sex chromosome, X. Children with this syndrome are phenotypically female but sterile.

Ultrasound: In pregnancy – the use of high frequency sound waves that are bounced off the fetus and then translated into pictures on a video screen that shows the size, shape, and position of the fetus. This is a useful technique for determining fetal age, multiple pregnancies, and the identification of gross abnormalities.

Validity in measurement: Refers to whether what is being measured is what is intended to be measured. More importantly, validity refers to the appropriateness of a measure for the specific inferences or decisions that result from the scores generated by the measure.

Working memory: (Also referred to as the short-term memory) That part of the person's mind that actively processes small amounts of information.

Zone of proximal development: (Vygotsky) The distance between children's apparent level of cognitive development when working independently and their level when solving problems under adult guidance or working with more capable peers.

References

Abedi, J. (2002). A latent-variable modeling approach to assessing reliability and validity of a creativity instrument. *Creativity Research Journal, 14*(2), 267–276.

Abrami, P. C., Bernard, R. M., Borokhovski, E., Wade, A., Surkes, M. A., Tamim, R., & Zhang, D. (2008). Instructional interventions affecting critical thinking skills and dispositions: A stage 1 meta-analysis. *Review of Educational Research, 78*(4), 1102–1134.

Ackard, D. M., Neumark-Sztainer, D., Story, M. & Perry, C. (2006). Parent–child connectedness and behavioral and emotional health among adolescents. *American Journal of Preventive Medicine, 30*(1), 59–66.

Adams, M. (2006). Hybridizing habitus and reflexivity: Towards an understanding of contemporary identity? *Sociology, 40*(3), 511–528.

Adesope, O. O. & Nesbit, J. C. (2009). A systematic review of research on collaborative learning with concept maps. In P. Lupion Torres and R. de Cássia Veiga Marriott (Eds.) *Handbook of research on collaborative learning using concept mapping* (pp. 238–251). Hershey, PA: Information Science.

Adey, P. (2005). Issues arising from the long-term evaluation of cognitive acceleration programs. *Research in Science Education, 35*(1), 3–22.

Adey, P., Robertson, A. & Venville, G. (2002). Effects of a cognitive acceleration programme on Year 1 pupils. *British Journal of Educational Psychology, 72*(1), 1–25.

Aikins, J. W., Bierman, K. L. & Parker, J. G. (2005). Navigating the transition to junior high school: The influence of pre-transition friendship and self-system characteristics. *Social Development, 14*(1), 42–60.

Ainsworth, M. D. S., Blehar, M. C., Waters, E. & Wall, S. (1978). *Patterns of attachment: A psychological study of the strange situation*. Hillsdale, NJ: Erlbaum.

Alberini, C. M. (2005). Mechanisms of memory stabilization: Are consolidation and reconsolidation similar or distinct processes? *Trends in Neurosciences, 28*(1), 51–56.

Alberto, P. A. & Troutman, A. C. (2009). *Applied behavior analysis for teachers*. Upper Saddle River, NJ: Pearson.

Alfieri, L., Brooks, P. J., Aldrich, N. J. & Tenenbaum, H. R. (2011). Does discovery-based instruction enhance learning? *Journal of Educational Psychology, 103*, 1–18.

Alltucker, K. W., Bullis, M., Close, D. & Yovanoff, P. (2006). Different pathways to juvenile delinquency: Characteristics of early and late starters in a sample of previously incarcerated youth. *Journal of Child and Family Studies, 15*(4), 475–488.

Amabile, T. M. (1996). *Creativity in context*. Boulder, CO: Westview.

Amadieu, F., Van Gog, T., Paas, F., Tricot, A. & Mariné, C. (2009). Effects of prior knowledge and concept-map structure on disorientation, cognitive load, and learning. *Learning and Instruction, 19*(5), 376–386.

Ambridge, B. & Lieven, E. V. (2011). *Child language acquisition: Contrasting theoretical approaches*. Cambridge: Cambridge University Press.

American Psychiatric Association (2013). *Diagnostic and statistical manual of mental disorders* (5th edn), pp. 5–25. Arlington, VA: American Psychiatric Publishing.

Ames, M. & Runco, M. A. (2005). Predicting entrepreneurship from ideation and divergent thinking. *Creativity and Innovation Management, 14*(3), 311–315.

Anderson, K. J. & Minke, K. M. (2007). Parent involvement in education: Toward an understanding of parents' decision making. *The Journal of Educational Research, 100*(5), 311–323.

Andreasen, N. C. (2012). Creativity in art and science: Are there two cultures? *Dialogues in Clinical Neuroscience, 14*(1), 49.

Angelova, M., Gunawardena, D. & Volk, D. (2006). Peer teaching and learning: Co-constructing language in a dual language first grade. *Language and Education, 20*(3), 173–190.

Änggård, E. (2011). Children's gendered and non-gendered play in natural spaces. *Children Youth and Environments*, *21*(2), 5–33.

Annetta, L., Mangrum, J., Holmes, S., Collazo, K. & Cheng, M. T. (2009). Bridging realty to virtual reality: Investigating gender effect and student engagement on learning through video game play in an elementary school classroom. *International Journal of Science Education*, *31*(8), 1091–1113.

Anton, M. (2003). Files reveal state-supported sterilisation. *Sydney Morning Herald*, 19–20 July.

Antrop, I., Buysse, A., Roeyers, H. & Van Oost, P. V. (2005). Activity in children with ADHD during writing situations in the classroom: A pilot study. *British Journal of Educational Psychology*, *75*, 51–69.

Arcelus, J., Mitchell, A. J., Wales, J. & Nielsen, S. (2011). Mortality rates in patients with anorexia nervosa and other eating disorders: A meta-analysis of 36 studies. *Archives of General Psychiatry*, *68*(7), 724–731.

Archer, L. (2010). *Urban youth and schooling*. Maidenhead: McGraw-Hill Education.

Ardila, A. (2005). Cultural values underlying psychometric cognitive testing. *Neuropsychology Review*, *15*(4), 185–195.

Arievitch, I. M. & Haenen, J. P. (2005). Connecting sociocultural theory and educational practice: Galperin's approach. *Educational Psychologist*, *40*(3), 155–165.

Arnett, J. J. (2007). The myth of peer influence in adolescent smoking initiation. *Health Education & Behavior*, *34*(4), 594–607.

Arnheim, R. (2007). *The genesis of a painting: Picasso's Guernica*. Berkeley, CA: University of California Press.

Arselan, R. C. & Penke, L. (2015). Zeroing in on the genetic of intelligence. *Journal of Intelligence*, *3*, 41–45.

Asbury, K. & Plomin, R. (2013). *G is for genes: The impact of genetics on education and achievement*. Chichester: Wiley.

Atkinson, C. (2007). *Making sense of Piaget*. Oxon: Routledge.

Aviles, A. M., Anderson, T. R. & Davila, E. R. (2006). Child and adolescent social-emotional development within the context of school. *Child and Adolescent Mental Health*, *11*(1), 32–39.

Azevedo, R. (2005). Computer environments as metacognitive tools for enhancing learning. *Educational Psychologist*, *40*(4), 193–197.

Baddeley, A. (2012). Working memory: Theories, models, and controversies. *Annual Review of Psychology*, *63*, 1–29.

Bailey, R. (2006). Physical education and sport in schools: A review of benefits and outcomes. *Journal of School Health*, *76*(8), 397–401.

Bailey, S. M. (1993). The current status of gender equity research in American schools. *Educational Psychologist*, *28*, 321–339.

Baker, J. A. (2006). Contributions of teacher–child relationships to positive school adjustment during elementary school. *Journal of School Psychology*, *44*(3), 211–229.

Balla, D. & Zigler, E. (1975). Preinstitutional social deprivation, responsiveness to social reinforcement and IQ change in institutionalized retarded individuals. *American Journal of Mental Deficiency*, *80*, 228–230.

Bandura, A. (1977). *Social learning theory*. Englewood Cliffs, NJ: Prentice-Hall.

Bandura, A. (1986). *Social foundations of thought and action: A social cognitive theory*. Englewood Cliffs, NJ: Prentice-Hall.

Bandura, A. (1997). *Self-efficacy: The exercise of control*. New York: Freeman.

Bandura, A. & Walters, R. H. (1963). *Social learning and personality development*. New York: Holt, Rinehart & Winston.

Banister, P., Dunn, G., Burman, E., Daniels, J., Duckett, P., Goodley, D., ... & Whelan, P. (2011). Qualitative methods in psychology: A research guide (2nd edn). Maidenhead: Open University Press/McGraw Hill.

Barber, B. K. & Schluterman, J. M. (2008). Connectedness in the lives of children and adolescents: A call for greater conceptual clarity. *Journal of Adolescent Health*, *43*(3), 209–216.

Barkley, A. R. (1998). *Attention-deficit hyperactivity disorder* (2nd edn). New York: The Guildford Press.

Barro, R. J. & Lee, J. W. (2013). A new data set of educational attainment in the world, 1950–2010. *Journal of Development Economics*, *104*, 184–198.

Barrouillet, P. (2011). Dual-process theories and cognitive development: Advances and challenges. *Developmental Review*, *31*(2), 79–85.

Bartram, D. (2006). The internationalization of testing and new models of test delivery on the Internet. *International Journal of Testing*, *6*(2), 121–131.

Basadur, M. & Gelade, G. A. (2005). Modelling applied creativity as a cognitive process: Theoretical foundations. *Korean Journal of Thinking and Problem Solving, 15*(2), 13.

Baskin, T. W., Wampold, B. E., Quintana, S. M. & Enright, R. D. (2010). Belongingness as a protective factor against loneliness and potential depression in a multicultural middle school. *The Counseling Psychologist, 38*(5), 626–651.

Batey, M. & Furnham, A. (2006). Creativity, intelligence, and personality: A critical review of the scattered literature. *Genetic, Social, and General Psychology Monographs, 132*(4), 355–429.

Batey, M., Furnham, A. & Safiullina, X. (2010). Intelligence, general knowledge and personality as predictors of creativity. *Learning and Individual Differences, 20*(5), 532–535.

Battistich, V. A. (2014). The child development project: Creating caring school communities. In L. Nucci, T. Krettenauer and D. Narvaez (Eds.) *Handbook of moral and character education* (pp. 328–351). New York: Routledge.

Baumrind, D. (1967). Child care practices anteceding 3 patterns of preschool behavior. *Genetic Psychology Monographs, 75*(1), 43–88.

Baumrind, D. (2005). Patterns of parental authority and adolescent autonomy. *New Directions for Child and Adolescent Development*, (108), 61–69.

Bearman, S. K., Presnell, K., Martinez, E. & Stice, E. (2006). The skinny on body dissatisfaction: A longitudinal study of adolescent girls and boys. *Journal of Youth and Adolescence, 35*(2), 217–229.

Bebeau, M. J. & Monson, V. E. (2014). A theoretical and evidence-based approach for designing professional ethics education. In L. Nucci, T. Krettenauer and Narvaez (Eds.) *Handbook of moral and character education* (pp. 507–534). New York: Routledge.

Becker, J. & Varelas, M. (2001). Piaget's early theory of the role of language in intellectual development: A comment on DeVries account of Piaget's social theory. *Educational Researcher, 30*, 22–23.

Beghatto, R. A. (2009). Creativity in the classroom. In J. C. Kauffman and R. J. Sternberg (Eds.) *The Cambridge handbook of creativity* (pp. 447–463). Cambridge: Cambridge University Press.

Beghetto, R. A. & Kaufman, J. C. (2007). Toward a broader conception of creativity: A case for 'mini-c' creativity. *Psychology of Aesthetics, Creativity, and the Arts, 1*(2), 73.

Bell, B. S. & Kozlowski, S. W. (2008). Active learning: Effects of core training design elements on self-regulatory processes, learning, and adaptability. *Journal of Applied Psychology, 93*(2), 296.

Belsky, J. & Pluess, M. (2009). Beyond diathesis stress: Differential susceptibility to environmental influences. *Psychological Bulletin, 135*, 885.

Belsky, J., Bakermans-Kranenburg, M. J. & Van Ijzendoorn, M. H. (2007). For better and for worse differential susceptibility to environmental influences. *Current Directions in Psychological Science, 16*, 300–304.

Bender, D. & Lösel, F. (2011). Bullying at school as a predictor of delinquency, violence and other anti-social behaviour in adulthood. *Criminal Behaviour and Mental Health, 21*(2), 99–106.

Berger, B. J. & Karabenick, S. A. (2011). Motivation and students' use of learning strategies: Evidence of unidirectional effects in mathematics classrooms. *Learning and Instruction, 21*(3), 416–428. doi: 10.1016/j.learninstruc.2010.06.002

Berger, K. S. (2007). Update on bullying at school: Science forgotten? *Developmental Review, 27*(1), 90–126.

Berry, J. (2007). *Teachers' legal rights and responsibilities: A guide for trainee teachers and those new to the profession*. Hatfield: University of Hertfordshire Press.

Berthold, K., Nückles, M. & Renkl, A. (2007). Do learning protocols support learning strategies and outcomes? The role of cognitive and metacognitive prompts. *Learning and Instruction, 17*(5), 564–577.

Berzoff, J. (2011). Freud's psychoanalytic concepts. In J. Berzoff, L. Melano-Flanagan and P. Hertz (Eds.) *Inside out and outside in: Psychodynamic clinical theory and psychopathology in contemporary multicultural contexts* (pp. 17–47). Lanham, ML: Rowman and Littlefield.

Bhutta, Z. A., Das, J. K., Rizvi, A., Gaffey, M. F., Walker, N., Horton, S., ... & Maternal and child nutrition study group. (2013). Evidence-based interventions for improvement of maternal and child nutrition: What can be done and at what cost? *The Lancet, 382*, 452–477.

Bibace, R. (2013). Challenges in Piaget's legacy. *Integrative Psychological and Behavioral Science, 47*(1), 167–175.

Bibok, M. B., Müller, U. & Carpendale, J. I. M. (2009). Childhood. In U. Müller, J. I. M. Carpendale and L. Smith (Eds.) *The Cambridge companion to Piaget* (pp. 229–254). Cambridge: Cambridge University Press.

Biesta, G. (2009). Good education in an age of measurement: On the need to reconnect with the question of purpose in education. *Educational Assessment, Evaluation and Accountability, 21*(1), 33–46.

Binnewies, C., Ohly, S. & Sonnentag, S. (2007). Taking personal initiative and communicating about ideas: What is important for the creative process and for idea creativity? *European Journal of Work and Organizational Psychology, 16*(4), 432–455.

Bissell-Havran, J. M. & Loken, E. (2009). The role of friends in early adolescents' academic self-competence and intrinsic value for math and English. *Journal of Youth and Adolescence, 38*(1), 41–50.

Bjork, E. L., de Winstanley, P. A. & Storm, B. C. (2007). Learning how to learn: Can experiencing the outcome of different encoding strategies enhance subsequent encoding? *Psychonomic Bulletin & Review, 14*(2), 207–211.

Bjorklund, D. F. (2005). *Children's thinking: Cognitive development and individual differences*. Belmont, CA: Wadsworth Publishing Company.

Blachman, B. A. (2011). *Foundations of reading acquisition and dyslexia: Implications for early intervention*. Oxon: Routledge.

Black, R. E., Allen, L. H., Bhutta, Z. A., Caulfield, L. E., De Onis, M., Ezzati, M., ... & Maternal and child undernutrition study group. (2008). Maternal and child undernutrition: Global and regional exposures and health consequences. *The Lancet, 371*, 243–260.

Blair, C. & Raver, C. C. (2012). Child development in the context of adversity: Experiential canalization of brain and behavior. *American Psychologist, 67*(4), 309.

Blanco, J., Gabau, E., Gomez, D., Baena, N., Guitart, M., Egozcue, J. & Vidal, F. (1998). Chromosome 21 disomy in spermatozoa of the fathers of children with trisomy 21, in a population with high prevalence of Down syndrome: Increased incidence in cases of paternal origin. *American Journal of Human Genetics, 63*, 1067–1072.

Bleidorn, W., Kandler, C., Riemann, R., Angleitner, A. & Spinath, F. M. (2012). Genetic and environmental influences on personality profile stability: Unraveling the normativeness problem. *Journal of Personality, 80*, 1029–1060.

Bloom, J. (2009). Piaget on equilibration. In U. Müller, J. I. M. Carpendale and L. Smith (Eds.) *The Cambridge companion to Piaget* (pp. 132–149). Cambridge: Cambridge University Press.

Boghossian, P. (2006). Behaviorism, constructivism, and socratic pedagogy. *Educational Philosophy and Theory, 38*(6), 713–722.

Bogin, B. (2010). Evolution of human growth. In M. Muehlenbein (Ed.) *Human evolutionary biology* (pp. 379–395). Cambridge: Cambridge University Press.

Bokhorst, C. L., Sumter, S. R. & Westenberg, P. M. (2010). Social support from parents, friends, classmates, and teachers in children and adolescents aged 9 to 18 years: Who is perceived as most supportive? *Social Development, 19*(2), 417–426.

Bond, L., Butler, H., Thomas, L., Carlin, J., Glover, S., Bowes, G. & Patton, G. (2007). Social and school connectedness in early secondary school as predictors of late teenage substance use, mental health, and academic outcomes. *Journal of Adolescent Health, 40*(4), 357e9–e18.

Bong, M. (2008). Effects of parent-child relationships and classroom goal structures on motivation, help-seeking avoidance, and cheating. *The Journal of Experimental Education, 76*(2), 191–217.

Borghi, E., De Onis, M., Garza, C., Van den Broeck, J., Frongillo, E. A., Grummer-Strawn, L., ... & Onyango, A. W. (2006). Construction of the World Health Organization child growth standards: Selection of methods for attained growth curves. *Statistics in Medicine, 25*(2), 247–265.

Bradley, J. H., Paul, R. & Seeman, E. (2006). Analyzing the structure of expert knowledge. *Information & Management, 43*(1), 77–91.

Brand-Gruwel, S., Wopereis, I. & Vermetten, Y. (2005). Information problem solving by experts and novices: Analysis of a complex cognitive skill. *Computers in Human Behavior, 21*(3), 487–508.

Brandt, K. R., Cooper, L. M. & Dewhurst, S. A. (2005). Expertise and recollective experience: Recognition memory for familiar and unfamiliar academic subjects. *Applied Cognitive Psychology, 19*(9), 1113–1125.

Branje, S. J., Van Lieshout, C. F. & Gerris, J. R. (2007). Big five personality development in adolescence and adulthood. *European Journal of Personality, 21*(1), 45–62.

Bransford, J. D. & Schwartz, D. L. (1999). Rethinking transfer: A simple proposal with multiple implications. *Review of Research in Education, 24*, 61–100.

Brantlinger, E. (1997). Using ideology: Cases of nonrecognition of the politics of research and practice in special education. *Review in Education, 24,* 61–100.

Braund, M. & Reiss, M. (2006). Towards a more authentic science curriculum: The contribution of out-of-school learning. *International Journal of Science Education, 28*(12), 1373–1388.

Braungart, J. M., Plomin, R., DeFries, J. C. & Fulker, D. W. (1992). Genetic influence on tester-rated infant temperament as assessed by Bayley's Infant Behavior Record. Nonadoptive and adoptive siblings and twins. *Developmental Psychology, 28,* 40–47.

Breen, R., Luijkx, R., Müller, W. & Pollak, R. (2010). Long-term trends in educational inequality in Europe: Class inequalities and gender differences. *European Sociological Review, 26*(1), 31–48.

Bridge, J. A., Goldstein, T. R. & Brent, D. A. (2006). Adolescent suicide and suicidal behavior. *Journal of Child Psychology and Psychiatry, 47*(3–4), 372–394.

Bronfenbrenner, U. (1979). *The ecology of human development: Experiments by nature and design.* Cambridge, MA: Harvard University Press.

Bronfenbrenner, U. & Morris, P. A. (2006). The bioecological model of human development. In W. Damon and R. Lerner (Eds.) *Handbook of child psychology* (pp. 793–828). Hoboken, NJ: Wiley.

Brooks-Gunn, J. & Peterson, A. C. (2013). *Girls at puberty: Biological and psychosocial perspectives.* New York: Springer Science & Business Media.

Brown, G. D., Neath, I. & Chater, N. (2007). A temporal ratio model of memory. *Psychological Review, 114*(3), 539.

Brown, M. (2008). Comfort zone: Model or metaphor. *Australian Journal of Outdoor Education, 12*(1), 3–12.

Brumariu, L. E. & Kerns, K. A. (2010). Parent–child attachment and internalizing symptoms in childhood and adolescence: A review of empirical findings and future directions. *Development and Psychopathology, 22*(01), 177–203.

Brumariu, L. E. & Kerns, K. A. (2011). Parent–Child Attachment in Early and Middle Childhood. In P. K. Smith and C. H. Hart (Eds.) *The Wiley-Blackwell handbook of childhood social development* (2nd edn) (pp. 319–336). Chichester: Wiley.

Bruner, J. S. (1960). *The Process of education.* Cambridge, MA: Harvard University Press.

Bruner, J. S. (1961). The act of discovery. *Harvard Educational Review, 31,* 21–32.

Bruner, J. S. (1966). *Toward a theory of instruction.* Cambridge, MA: Belknap Press.

Bruner, J. S. (1973). *The relevance of education.* New York: Norton.

Bryman, A. (2012). *Social research methods.* New York: Oxford University Press.

Bugg, J. M. & McDaniel, M. A. (2012). Selective benefits of question self-generation and answering for remembering expository text. *Journal of Educational Psychology, 104*(4), 922.

Buhs, E. S. (2005). Peer rejection, negative peer treatment, and school adjustment: Self-concept and classroom engagement as mediating processes. *Journal of School Psychology, 43*(5), 407–424.

Buhs, E. S., Ladd, G. W. & Herald, S. L. (2006). Peer exclusion and victimization: Processes that mediate the relation between peer group rejection and children's classroom engagement and achievement? *Journal of Educational Psychology, 98*(1), 1–13.

Burge, J., Fowlkes, C. C. & Banks, M. S. (2010). Natural-scene statistics predict how the figure–ground cue of convexity affects human depth perception. *The Journal of Neuroscience, 30*(21), 7269–7280.

Burke, L. A. & Hutchins, H. M. (2007). Training transfer: An integrative literature review. *Human Resource Development Review, 6*(3), 263–296.

Burn, S. M. (2005). *Women across cultures: A global perspective.* New York: McGraw-Hill.

Burrowes, N. (2013). *Body image–a rapid evidence assessment of the literature: A project on behalf of the Government Equalities Office.* London: HMSO.

Bushman, B. J. & Huesmann, L. R. (2006). Short-term and long-term effects of violent media on aggression in children and adults. *Archives of Pediatrics & Adolescent Medicine, 160*(4), 348–352.

Buss, D. M. (2009). How can evolutionary psychology successfully explain personality and individual differences? *Perspectives on Psychological Science, 4*(4), 359–366.

Buzan, T. (2006). *Use your memory.* Harlow: Pearson Education.

Cahn, S. M. (2011). *Classic and contemporary readings in the philosophy of education.* New York: Oxford University Press.

Cairns, R. B. & Cairns, B. D. (2007). *The making of developmental psychology.* In W. Damon and R. Lerner (Eds.) *Handbook of child psychology* (pp. 89–165). Hoboken, NJ: Wiley.

Cameron, N. & Bogin, B. (2012). *Human growth and development.* London: Academic Press.

Cañas, A. J., Carff, R., Hill, G., Carvalho, M., Arguedas, M., Eskridge, T. C., ... & Carvajal, R. (2005). Concept maps: Integrating knowledge and information visualization. In S.-O. Tergen and T. Keller (Eds.) *Knowledge and information visualization* (pp. 205–219). *Tübingen:* Springer Berlin Heidelberg.

Carandini, M. (2012). From circuits to behavior: A bridge too far? *Nature Neuroscience, 15*(4), 507–509.

Carducci, B. J. (2009). *The psychology of personality.* Chichester: Wiley.

Carpendale, J. I. (2009). Piaget's theory of moral development. In U. Müller, J. I. Carpendale and L. Smith (Eds.) *The Cambridge companion to Piaget* (pp. 270–286). Cambridge: Cambridge University Press.

Carson, S. (2009). The unwalled garden: Growth of the OpenCourseWare Consortium, 2001–2008. *Open Learning, 24*(1), 23–29.

Case, R. (2013). *The mind's staircase: Exploring the conceptual underpinnings of children's thought and knowledge.* Hove: Psychology Press.

Castilho, L. V. & Lahr, M. M. (2001). Secular trends in growth among urban Brazilian children of European descent. *Annals of Human Biology, 28,* 564–574.

Castle, L., Aubert, R. E., Verbrugge, R. R., Khalid, M. & Epstein, R. S. (2008). Trends in medidation for ADGD. *Journal of Attention Disorders, 10,* 335–342.

Cepeda, N. J., Coburn, N., Rohrer, D., Wixted, J. T., Mozer, M. C. & Pashler, H. (2009). Optimizing distributed practice: Theoretical analysis and practical implications. *Experimental Psychology, 56*(4), 236–246.

Cepeda, N. J., Pashler, H., Vul, E., Wixted, J. T. & Rohrer, D. (2006). Distributed practice in verbal recall tasks: A review and quantitative synthesis. *Psychological Bulletin, 132*(3), 354.

Chamberlain, A., Daniels, C., Madden, N. A. & Slavin, R. E. (2007). A randomized evaluation of the Success for All Middle School reading program. *Middle Grades Reading Journal, 2*(1), 1–22.

Chamorro-Premuzic, T. (2011). *Personality and individual differences.* Chichester: Blackwell.

Chamorro-Premuzic, T. & Furnham, A. (2008). Personality, intelligence and approaches to learning as predictors of academic performance. *Personality and Individual Differences, 44*(7), 1596–1603.

Chan, J. C. (2009). When does retrieval induce forgetting and when does it induce facilitation? Implications for retrieval inhibition, testing effect, and text processing. *Journal of Memory and Language, 61*(2), 153–170.

Chan, T. W. & Koo, A. (2011). Parenting style and youth outcomes in the UK. *European Sociological Review, 27*(3), 385–399.

Chavkin, W. (1995). Substance abuse in pregnancy. In B. P. Sachs, R. Beard, E. Papiernik and C. Russell (Eds.) *Reproductive health care for women and babies.* New York: Oxford University Press.

Chelly, J., Khelfaoui, M., Francis, F., Chérif, B. & Bienvenu, T. (2006). Genetics and pathology of mental retardation. *European Journal of Human Genetics, 14,* 701–713.

Cherney, I. D. & London, K. (2006). Gender-linked differences in the toys, television shows, computer games, and outdoor activities of 5- to 13-year-old children. *Sex Roles, 54*(9–10), 717–726.

Cherney, I. D., Seiwert, C. S., Dickey, T. M. & Flichtbeil, J. D. (2006). Children's drawings: A mirror to their minds. *Educational Psychology, 26*(1), 127–142.

Chi, M. T. H. (2006). Two approaches to the study of experts' characteristics. In K. A. Ericsson, N. Charness, P. J. Feltovich and R. R. Hoffman (Eds.) *The Cambridge handbook of expertise and expert performance* (pp. 21–30). New York: Cambridge University Press.

Child, D. (2007). *Psychology and the teacher.* London: Bloomsbury.

Chomski, N. A. (1959). A review of B. F. Skinner's verbal behavior. *Language, 35,* 25–58.

Chomski, N. A. (1995). *The minimalist program.* Cambridge, MA: MIT Press.

Christie, D. & Viner, R. (2005). Adolescent development. *British Medical Journal, 330,* 301–304.

Cillessen A. H. (2009). Sociometric methods. In K. H. Rubin, W. M. Bukowski and B. Laursen (Eds.) *Handbook of peer interactions, relationships, and groups* (pp. 82–99). New York: Guilford Press.

Cillessen, A. H. & Rose, A. J. (2005). Understanding popularity in the peer system. *Current Directions in Psychological Science, 14*(2), 102–105.

Clark, E. V. (2009). *First language acquisition.* Cambridge: Cambridge University Press.

Clark, J. E. (2007). On the problem of motor skill development. *Journal of Physical Education, Recreation and Dance, 78*(5), 39–44.

Clark, L. & Tiggemann, M. (2006). Appearance culture in nine-to 12-year-old girls: Media and peer influences on body dissatisfaction. *Social Development, 15*(4), 628–643.

Clay, D., Vignoles, V. L. & Dittmar, H. (2005). Body image and self-esteem among adolescent girls: Testing the influence of sociocultural factors. *Journal of Research on Adolescence, 15*(4), 451–477.

Cleary, T. J., Patten, P. & Nelson, A. C. (2008). Effectiveness of self-regulation empowerment program with urban high-school students. *Journal of Advanced Academics, 20*(1), 70–107. doi: 10.4219/jaa-2008–866

Cleary, T. J. & Zimmerman, B. J. (2006). Teachers' perceived usefulness of strategy microanalytic assessment information. *Psychology in the Schools, 43*(2), 149–155. doi: 10.1002/pits.20141

Cleary, T. J. & Zimmermnan, B. J. (2012). A cyclical self-regulatory account of student engagement: Theoretical foundations and applications. In S. L. Christenson, A. L. Reschly and C. Wylie (Eds.) *Handbook of research on student engagement* (pp. 237–257). London: Springer. doi: 10.1007/978-1-4614-2018-7_11

Cleary-Goldman, J., Malone, F. D., Vidaver, J., Ball, R. H., Nyberg, D. A., Comstock, C. H., ... & Timor-Tritsch, I. E. (2005). Impact of maternal age on obstetric outcome. *Obstetrics & Gynecology, 105*, 983–990.

Coates, E. & Coates, A. (2006). Young children talking and drawing. *International Journal of Early Years Education, 14*(3), 221–241.

Cohane, G. H. & Pope, H. G. (2001). Body image in boys: A review of the literature. *International Journal of Eating Disorders, 29*(4), 373–379.

Cohen, A. D. & Macaro, E. (Eds.) (2007). *Language learner strategies: Thirty years of research and practice.* Oxford: Oxford University Press.

Cohen, J. (2006). Social, emotional, ethical, and academic education: Creating a climate for learning, participation in democracy, and well-being. *Harvard Educational Review, 76*(2), 201–237.

Cole, T. J. (2003). The secular trend in human physical growth: A biological view. *Economics & Human Biology, 1*(2), 161–168.

Collins, W. A. & Steinberg, L. (2008). Adolescent development in interpersonal context. In W. Damon and R. M. Lerner (Eds.) *Handbook of child psychology* (pp. 3–15). New York: Wiley.

Combs, M. L. & Slaby, D. A. (1977). Social skills training with children. In B. B. Lahay and A. E. Kazdin (Eds.) *Advances in clinical child psychology* (pp. 161–201). New York: Plenum Press.

Conley, M. (2008). Cognitive strategy instruction for adolescents: What we know about the promise, what we don't know about the potential. *Harvard Educational Review, 78*(1), 84–106.

Cook, L. (2005). Schools without walls: Reconnecting the disconnected. *Support for Learning, 20*(2), 90–95. doi: 10.1111/j.0268-2141.2005.00367.x

Cook, C. R., Gresham, F. M., Kern, L., Barreras, R. B., Thornton, S. & Crews, S. D. (2008). Social skills training for secondary students with emotional and/or behavioral disorders: A review and analysis of the meta-analytic literature. *Journal of Emotional and Behavioral Disorders, 16*(3), 131–144.

Cowan, N. (2010). The magical mystery four how is working memory capacity limited, and why? *Current Directions in Psychological Science, 19*(1), 51–57.

Cramer, P. (2006). *Protecting the self: Defense mechanisms in action.* New York: Guilford Press.

Crawford, M. J., Nur, U., McKenzie, K. & Tyrer, P. (2005). Suicidal ideation and suicide attempts among ethnic minority groups in England: Results of a national household survey. *Psychological Medicine, 35*(9), 1369–1377.

Creswell, J. W. & Clark, V. L. P. (2007). *Designing and conducting mixed methods research.* Thousand Oaks, CA: Sage.

Crothers, L. M., Kehle, T. J., Bray, M. A. & Theodore, L. A. (2009). Correlates and suspected causes of obesity in children. *Psychology in the Schools, 46*(8), 787–796.

Crow, S. J., Mitchell, J. E., Roerig, J. D. & Steffen, K. (2009). What potential role is there for medication treatment in anorexia nervosa? *International Journal of Eating Disorders, 42*(1), 1–8.

Crozier, G. & Davies, J. (2005). Hard to reach parents or hard to reach schools? A discussion of home–school relations, with particular reference to Bangladeshi and Pakistani parents. *British Educational Research Journal, 33*(3), 295–313.

Csikszentmihalyi, M. & Robinson, R. E. (2014). Culture, time, and the development of talent. In M. Csikszentmihalyi (Ed.)

The systems model of creativity (pp. 27–46). Dordrecht, The Netherlands: Springer.

Cushman, F., Young, L. & Hauser, M. (2006). The role of conscious reasoning and intuition in moral judgment testing three principles of harm. *Psychological Science, 17*(12), 1082–1089.

Custers, E. J. (2010). Long-term retention of basic science knowledge: A review study. *Advances in Health Sciences Education, 15*(1), 109–128.

Cvencek, D., Meltzoff, A. N. & Greenwald, A. G. (2011). Math–gender stereotypes in elementary school children. *Child Development, 82*(3), 766–779.

D'Angelo, F. & Zemanick, R. (2009). The twilight academy: An alternative education program that works. *Preventing School Failure, 53*(4), 211–218.

Dalvand, H., Dehghan, L., Hadian, M. R., Feizy, A. & Hosseini, S. A. (2012). Relationship between gross motor and intellectual function in children with cerebral palsy: A cross-sectional study. *Archives of Physical Medicine and Rehabilitation, 93*, 480–484.

Daniels, H., Cole, M. & Wertsch, J. V. (2007). *The Cambridge companion to Vygotsky.* Cambridge: Cambridge University Press.

Davies, M. (2011). Concept mapping, mind mapping and argument mapping: What are the differences and do they matter? *Higher Education, 62*(3), 279–301.

Davis, E. E., Pitchford, N. J. & Limback, E. (2011). The interrelation between cognitive and motor development in typically developing children aged 4–11 years is underpinned by visual processing and fine manual control. *British Journal of Psychology, 102*(3), 569–584.

Davis, K., Christodoulou, J., Seider, S. & Gardner, H. (2011). The theory of multiple intelligences. In R. J. Sternberg and S. B. Kaufman (Eds.) *The Cambridge handbook of intelligence* (pp. 485–503). New York: Cambridge University Press.

Davis-Kean, P. E. (2005). The influence of parent education and family income on child achievement: The indirect role of parental expectations and the home environment. *Journal of Family Psychology, 19*(2), 294–304.

Davison, T. E. & McCabe, M. P. (2006). Adolescent body image and psychosocial functioning. *The Journal of Social Psychology, 146*(1), 15–30.

Deary, I. J., Strand, S., Smith, P. & Fernandes, C. (2007). Intelligence and educational achievement. *Intelligence, 35*(1), 13–21.

De Corte, E. (2003). Transfer as the productive use of acquired knowledge, skills, and motivations. *Current Directions in Psychological Science, 12*(4), 142–146.

de Graaf-Peters, V. B. & Hadders-Algra, M. (2006). Ontogeny of the human central nervous system. What is happening when? *Early Human Development, 82*(4), 257–266.

Dennis, A. R., Minas, R. K. & Bhagwatwar, A. P. (2013). Sparking creativity: Improving electronic brainstorming with individual cognitive priming. *Journal of Management Information Systems, 29*(4), 195–216.

Dennis, W. (1973). *Children of the creche.* New York: Appleton-Century-Crofts.

Deoni, S. C., Mercure, E., Blasi, A., Gasston, D., Thomson, A., Johnson, M., ... & Murphy, D. G. (2011). Mapping infant brain myelination with magnetic resonance imaging. *The Journal of Neuroscience, 31*(2), 784–791.

Department for Education (2014). *Promoting fundamental British values as part of SMSC in schools: Departmental advice for maintained schools.* London: HMSO.

Department of Health (2014). *Preventing suicide in England: One year on.* London: HMSO.

De Ribaupierre, A. & Lecerf, T. (2006). Relationships between working memory and intelligence from a developmental perspective: Convergent evidence from a neo-Piagetian and a psychometric approach. *European Journal of Cognitive Psychology, 18*(1), 109–137.

Deslandes, R. & Bertrand, R. (2005). Motivation of parent involvement in secondary-level schooling. *The Journal of Educational Research, 98*(3), 164–175.

Devers, P. L., Cronister, A., Ormond, K. E., Facio, F., Bransington, C. K. & Flodman, P. (2013). Non-invasive prenatal testing/non-invasive prenatal diagnosis: The position of the national society of genetic counselors. *Journal of Genetic Counseling, 22*, 291–295.

DeWall, C. N., Anderson, C. A. & Bushman, B. J. (2011). The general aggression model: Theoretical extensions to violence. *Psychology of Violence, 1*(3), 245–258.

DfE (2014). *Preventing and tackling bullying: Advice for headteachers, staff and governing bodies.* London: HMSO.

Diamond, A. (2007). Interrelated and interdependent. *Developmental Science, 10*(1), 152–158.

Dignath, C. & Büttner, G. (2008). Components of fostering self-regulated learning among students.

A meta-analysis on intervention studies at primary and secondary school level. *Metacognition and Learning*, *3*(3), 231–264.

Dignath, C., Buettner, G. & Langfeldt, H. P. (2008). How can primary school students learn self-regulated learning strategies most effectively? A meta-analysis on self-regulation training programmes. *Educational Research Review*, *3*(2), 101–129.

Dinsmore, D. L., Alexander, P. A. & Loughlin, S. M. (2008). Focusing the conceptual lens on metacognition, self-regulation, and self-regulated learning. *Educational Psychology Review*, *20*(4), 391–409.

Dishion, T. J. & Tipsord, J. M. (2011). Peer contagion in child and adolescent social and emotional development. *Annual Review of Psychology*, *62*, 189.

Dohnt, H. K. & Tiggemann, M. (2005). Peer influences on body dissatisfaction and dieting awareness in young girls. *British Journal of Developmental Psychology*, *23*(1), 103–116.

Dolmans, D. H., De Grave, W., Wolfhagen, I. H. & Van Der Vleuten, C. P. (2005). Problem-based learning: Future challenges for educational practice and research. *Medical Education*, *39*(7), 732–741.

Donndelinger, S. J. (2005). Integrating comprehension and metacognitive reading strategies. In S. E. Israel, C. C. Block, K. L. Bauserman and K. Kinnucan-Welsh (Eds.) *Metacognition in literacy learning: Theory, assessment, instruction, and professional development* (pp. 241–261). Mahwah, NJ: Lawrence Erlbaum Associates.

Dorn, L. D. & Biro, F. M. (2011). Puberty and its measurement: A decade in review. *Journal of Research on Adolescence*, *21*(1), 180–195.

Dougherty, J. & Ray, D. (2007). Differential impact of play therapy on developmental levels of children. *International Journal of Play Therapy*, *16*, 2–19.

Driscoll, M. P. & Driscoll, M. P. (2005). *Psychology of learning for instruction*. Boston, MA: Pearson.

Due, P. & Holstein, B. E. (2008). Bullying victimization among 13 to 15 year old school children: Results from two comparative studies in 66 countries and regions. *International Journal of Adolescent Medicine and Health*, *20*(2), 209–222.

Due, P., Holstein, B. E., Lynch, J., Diderichsen, F., Gabhain, S. N., Scheidt, P. & Currie, C. (2005). Bullying and symptoms among school-aged children: International comparative cross sectional study in 28 countries. *The European Journal of Public Health*, *15*(2), 128–132.

Dufresne, T. (2005). *Killing Freud: 20th century culture and the death of psychoanalysis*. London: Bloomsbury.

Dunbar, K. (1997). How scientists think: On-line creativity and conceptual change in science. In T. B. Ward, S. M. Smith and J. Vaid (Eds.) *Conceptual structures and processes: Emergence, discovery, and change*. Washington, DC: American Psychological Association Press.

DuPaul, G. J., Weyandt, L. L. & Januisis, G. M. (2011). ADHD in the classroom: Effective intervention strategies. *Theory Into Practice*, *50*, 35–42.

Durlak, J. A., Weissberg, R. P., Dymnicki, A. B., Taylor, R. D. & Schellinger, K. B. (2011). The impact of enhancing students' social and emotional learning: A meta-analysis of school-based universal interventions. *Child Development*, *82*(1), 405–432.

Durlak, J. A., Weissberg, R. P. & Pachan, M. (2010). A meta-analysis of after-school programs that seek to promote personal and social skills in children and adolescents. *American Journal of Community Psychology*, *45*(3–4), 294–309.

Dutta, S. (2015). Human teratogens and their effects: A critical evaluation. *International Journal of Information Research and Review*, *2*, 525–536.

Eatough, V. (2012). Introduction to qualitative methods. In G. Breakwell, J. A. Smith and D. B. Wright (Eds.) *Research methods in psychology* (pp. 279–318). London: Sage.

Ebbeck, M. & Yim, H. Y. B. (2009). Rethinking attachment: Fostering positive relationships between infants, toddlers and their primary caregivers. *Early Child Development and Care*, *179*(7), 899–909.

Eccles, J. S. & Roeser, R. W. (2009). Schools, academic motivation, and stage-environment fit. In R. M. Lerner and L. Steinberg (Eds.) *Handbook of adolescent psychology third edition* (pp. 404–434). New York: Wiley.

Eccles, J. S. & Roeser, R. W. (2011). Schools as developmental contexts during adolescence. *Journal of Research on Adolescence*, *21*(1), 225–241.

Ecclestone, K. (2007). Resisting images of the 'diminished self': The implications of emotional well-being and emotional engagement in education policy. *Journal of Education Policy*, *22*(4), 455–470.

Eisenberg, M. E., Neumark-Sztainer, D., Story, M. & Perry, C. (2005). The role of social norms and friends' influences on unhealthy weight-control behaviors among adolescent girls. *Social Science & Medicine, 60*(6), 1165–1173.

Eldrid, L. & Chaisson, R. (1996). The clinical course of HIV infection in women. In R. R. Faden and N. E. Kass (Eds.) *HIV, AIDS, and childbearing.* New York: Oxford University Press.

Elias, M. J. (2009). Social-emotional and character development and academics as a dual focus of educational policy. *Educational Policy, 23*(6), 831–846.

Elliot, C. D. & Smith, P. (2011). *British ability scales* (3rd edn). London: GL Assessment.

Ellis, A., Abrams, M. & Abrams, L. (2008). *Personality theories: Critical perspectives.* Thousand Oaks, CA: Sage.

Ellis, A. A. & Shute, R. (2007). Teacher responses to bullying in relation to moral orientation and seriousness of bullying. *British Journal of Educational Psychology, 77*(3), 649–663.

Emery, N. J., Clayton, N. S. & Frith, C. D. (2007). Introduction. Social intelligence: From brain to culture. *Philosophical Transactions of the Royal Society B: Biological Sciences, 362*(1480), 485–488.

Endler, L. C. & Bond, T. G. (2008). Changing science outcomes: Cognitive acceleration in a US setting. *Research in Science Education, 38*(2), 149–166.

Engstrom, E. U. (2005). Reading, writing, and assistive technology: An integrated developmental curriculum for college students. *Journal of Adolescent & Adult Literacy, 49*(1), 30–39.

Eppler, M. J. (2006). A comparison between concept maps, mind maps, conceptual diagrams, and visual metaphors as complementary tools for knowledge construction and sharing. *Information visualization, 5*(3), 202–210.

Erikson, E. H. (1963). *Childhood and society.* New York: Norton.

Erikson, E. H. (1968). *Identity: Youth and crisis.* New York: Norton.

Erricson, K. A. (2006). Protocol analysis and expert thought: Concurrent verbalizations of thinking during experts' performance on representative tasks. In K. A. Ericsson, N. Charness, P. J. Feltovich and R. R. Hoffman (Eds.) *The Cambridge handbook of expertise and expert performance* (pp. 223–241). New York: Cambridge University Press.

Eschenbeck, H., Kohlmann, C. W. & Lohaus, A. (2007). Gender differences in coping strategies in children and adolescents. *Journal of Individual Differences, 28*(1), 18–26.

Evans, E., Hawton, K., Rodham, K., Psychol, C. & Deeks, J. (2005). The prevalence of suicidal phenomena in adolescents: A systematic review of population-based studies. *Suicide and Life-Threatening Behavior, 35*(3), 239–250.

Evans, G. W. (2006). Child development and the physical environment. *Annual. Review of Psychology, 57,* 423–451.

Evans, R. L. (2007). *Every good boy deserves fudge: The book of mnemonic devices.* New York: Penguin.

Eveleth, P. B. & Tanner, J. M. (1990). *Worldwide variation in human growth.* Cambridge: Cambridge University Press.

Fabricius, W. V. & Luecken, L. J. (2007). Postdivorce living arrangements, parent conflict, and long-term physical health correlates for children of divorce. *Journal of Family Psychology, 21*(2), 195–205.

Fan, W. & Williams, C. M. (2010). The effects of parental involvement on students' academic self-efficacy, engagement and intrinsic motivation. *Educational Psychology, 30*(1), 53–74.

Fancher, R. E. & Rutherford, A. (2012). *Pioneers of psychology.* New York: Norton & Company.

Fantuzzo, J. W., Bulotsky-Shearer, R., Fusco, R. A. & McWayne, C. (2005). An investigation of preschool classroom behavioral adjustment problems and social–emotional school readiness competencies. *Early Childhood Research Quarterly, 20*(3), 259–275.

Farmer, T. W., Lines, M. M. & Hamm, J. V. (2011). Revealing the invisible hand: The role of teachers in children's peer experiences. *Journal of Applied Developmental Psychology, 32*(5), 247–256.

Farrell, P. (2010). School psychology: Learning lessons from history and moving forward. *School Psychology International, 31*(6), 581–598.

Farrington, D. P. & Ttofi, M. M. (2011). Bullying as a predictor of offending, violence and later life outcomes. *Criminal Behaviour and Mental Health, 21*(2), 90–98.

Farrington, J. (2011). Seven plus or minus two. *Performance Improvement Quarterly, 23*(4), 113–116.

Farver, J. M. & Wimbarti. S. (1995). Indonesian toddlers' social play with their mothers and older siblings. *Child Development, 66,* 1493–1503.

Feder, K. P. & Majnemer, A. (2007). Handwriting development, competency, and intervention.

Developmental Medicine & Child Neurology, *49*(4), 312–317.

Feist, G. J. (2009). The function of personality in creativity. In J. C. Kauffman and R. J. Sternberg (Eds.) *The Cambridge handbook of creativity* (pp. 113–130). Cambridge: Cambridge University Press.

Feldman, D. H. (2004). Piaget's stages: The unfinished symphony of cognitive development. *New Ideas in Psychology*, *22*(3), 175–231.

Fergus, S. & Zimmerman, M. A. (2005). Adolescent resilience: A framework for understanding healthy development in the face of risk. *Annual Review of Public Health*, *26*, 399–419.

Field, A. (2013). *Discovering statistics using IBM SPSS*. London: Sage.

Fife-Shaw, C. (2012). Introduction to quantitative research. In G. Breakwell, J. A. Smith and D. B. Wright (Eds.) *Research methods in psychology* (pp. 17–38). London: Sage.

Findlay, L. C., Girardi, A. & Coplan, R. J. (2006). Links between empathy, social behavior, and social understanding in early childhood. *Early Childhood Research Quarterly*, *21*(3), 347–359.

Finnegan, L. P. & Kandal, S. R. (1997). Maternal and neonatal effects of alcohol and drugs. In J. H. Lowinson, P. Ruiz, R. B. Millman and J. G. Langrod (Eds.) *Substance abuse: A comprehensive textbook*. Baltimore, MD: Williams & Wilkins.

Fishman, E. J. (2014). With great control comes great responsibility: The relationship between perceived academic control, student responsibility, and self-regulation. *British Journal of Educational Psychology*, *84*(4), 685–702. doi: 10.1111/bjep.12057

Flynn, J. R. (2007). *What is intelligence?: Beyond the Flynn effect*. Cambridge: Cambridge University Press.

Fontana, D. (1986). *Teaching and personality*. Oxford: Basil Blackwell

Fontana, D. (1995). *Psychology for teachers*. London: Palgrave Macmillan.

Forbes, E. E. & Dahl, R. E. (2010). Pubertal development and behavior: Hormonal activation of social and motivational tendencies. *Brain and Cognition*, *72*(1), 66–72.

Ford, T., Goodman, R. & Meltzer, H. (2003). The British child and adolescent mental health survey 1999: The prevalence of DSM-IV disorders. *Journal of the*

American Academy of Child and Adolescent Psychiatry, *42*, 1203–1211.

Fosnot, C. T. (2013). *Constructivism: Theory, perspectives, and practice*. New York: Teachers College Press.

Fox, E. & Riconscente, M. (2008). Metacognition and self-regulation in James, Piaget, and Vygotsky. *Educational Psychology Review*, *20*(4), 373–389.

Fraser, B. J. (2012). Classroom learning environments: Retrospect, context and prospect. In B. Fraser, K. Tobin and C. J. McRobbie (Eds.) *Second international handbook of science education* (pp. 1191–1239). Dordrecht, The Netherlands: Springer.

Frederick, D. A., Buchanan, G. M., Sadehgi-Azar, L., Peplau, L. A., Haselton, M. G., Berezovskaya, A. & Lipinski, R. E. (2007). Desiring the muscular ideal: Men's body satisfaction in the United States, Ukraine, and Ghana. *Psychology of Men & Masculinity*, *8*(2), 103.

Frederickson, N., Osborne, L. A. & Reed, P. (2004). Judgments of successful inclusion by education service personnel. *Educational Psychology*, *24*, 263–290.

Freud, S. (1913). *The interpretation of dreams*. New York: Macmillan.

Freud, S. (1960). *Jokes and their relation to the unconscious*. New York: Norton.

Frisch, R. E. (1983). Fatness, puberty, and fertility: The effects of nutrition and physical training on menarche and ovulation. In J. Brooks-Gunn and A. C. Petersen (Eds.) *Girls at puberty. Biological and psychosocial perspectives*. New York: Plenum Press.

Fritz, C. O., Morris, P. E., Acton, M., Voelkel, A. R. & Etkind, R. (2007). Comparing and combining retrieval practice and the keyword mnemonic for foreign vocabulary learning. *Applied Cognitive Psychology*, *21*(4), 499–526.

Frost, J. L., Wortham, S. C. & Reifel, R. S. (2008). *Play and child development*. Upper Saddle River, NJ: Pearson/Merrill Prentice Hall.

Furnham, A. & Bachtiar, V. (2008). Personality and intelligence as predictors of creativity. *Personality and Individual Differences*, *45*(7), 613–617.

Furnham, A., Moutafi, J. & Chamorro-Premuzic, T. (2005). Personality and intelligence: Gender, the Big Five, self-estimated and psychometric intelligence. *International Journal of Selection and Assessment*, *13*(1), 11–24.

Fuson, K. C. (2009). Avoiding misinterpretations of Piaget and Vygotsky: Mathematical teaching without learning, learning without teaching, or helpful learning-path teaching? *Cognitive Development, 24*(4), 343–361.

Gabora, L. (2002). Cognitive mechanisms underlying the creative process. In T. T. Hewett and T. Kavanagh (Eds.) *Creativity & cognition: Proceedings of the fourth creativity & cognition conference* (pp. 126–133). New York: ACM Press.

Gainsburg, J. (2008). Real-world connections in secondary mathematics teaching. *Journal of Mathematics Teacher Education, 11*(3), 199–219.

Gardner, H. (1983). *Frames of mind: The theory of multiple intelligences.* New York: Basic Books.

Gardner, H. (1999). *Intelligence reframed. Multiple intelligences for the 21st century.* New York: Basic Books.

Garn, S. M. (1980). Continuities and change in maturational timing. In O. G. Brim and J. Kagan (Eds.) *Constancy and change in human development.* Cambridge, MA: Harvard University Press.

Garz, D. (2009). *Lawrence Kohlberg: An introduction.* Farmington Hills, MI: Budrich.

Gathercole, S. & Packiam-Alloway, T. (2007). *Understanding working memory: A classroom guide.* London: Harcourt Assessment.

Gelman, R. (2006). Young natural-number arithmeticians. *Current Directions in Psychological Science, 15*(4), 193–197.

Gendron, B. P., Williams, K. R. & Guerra, N. G. (2011). An analysis of bullying among students within schools: Estimating the effects of individual normative beliefs, self-esteem, and school climate. *Journal of School Violence, 10*(2), 150–164.

Georgieff, M. K. (2007). Nutrition and the developing brain: Nutrient priorities and measurement. *The American Journal of Clinical Nutrition, 85*(2), 614S–620S.

Gerhardstein, P., Schroff, G., Dickerson, K. & Adler, S. A. (2009). The development of object recognition through infancy. In B. C. Glenyn and R. P. Zini (Eds.) *New directions in developmental psychobiology* (pp. 79–115). Hauppauge, NY: Nova Science Publishers.

Gerner, B. & Wilson, P. H. (2005). The relationship between friendship factors and adolescent girls' body image concern, body dissatisfaction, and restrained eating. *International Journal of Eating Disorders, 37*(4), 313–320.

Gibbs, J. C. (2013). *Moral development and reality: Beyond the theories of Kohlberg, Hoffman, and Haidt* (3rd edn). New York: Oxford University Press.

Gibbs, J. C., Basinger, K. S., Grime, R. L. & Snarey, J. R. (2007). Moral judgment development across cultures: Revisiting Kohlberg's universality claims. *Developmental Review, 27*(4), 443–500.

Giles-Corti, B., Kelty, S. F., Zubrick, S. R. & Villanueva, K. P. (2009). Encouraging walking for transport and physical activity in children and adolescents. *Sports Medicine, 39*(12), 995–1009.

Gilligan, C. (1977). In a different voice: Women's conceptions of self and of morality. *Harvard Educational Review, 47*(4), 481–517.

Gilligan, C. (1993). *In a different voice.* Cambridge, MA: Harvard University Press.

Ginsburg, K. R. (2007). The importance of play in promoting healthy child development and maintaining strong parent-child bonds. *Pediatrics, 119*(1), 182–191.

Glascoe, F. P. (2005). Screening for developmental and behavioral problems. *Mental Retardation and Developmental Disabilities Research Reviews, 11*(3), 173–179.

Glaser, C. & Brunstein, J. C. (2007). Improving fourth-grade students' composition skills: Effects of strategy instruction and self-regulation procedures. *Journal of Educational Psychology, 99*(2), 297.

Gluckman, P. D. & Hanson, M. A. (2006). Evolution, development and timing of puberty. *Trends in Endocrinology & Metabolism, 17*(1), 7–12.

Gluckman, P. G. & Hanson, M. (2005). *The fetal matrix: Evolution, development and disease.* Cambridge: Cambridge University Press.

Gmitrova, V., Podhajecká, M. & Gmitrov, J. (2009). Children's play preferences: Implications for the preschool education. *Early Child Development and Care, 179*(3), 339–351.

Gobet, F. (2005). Chunking models of expertise: Implications for education. *Applied Cognitive Psychology, 19*(2), 183–204.

Goetghebuer, T., Haelterman, E., Le Chenadec, J., Dollfus, C., Gibb, D., Judd, A., ... & Warszawski, J. (2009). Effect of early antiretroviral therapy on the risk of AIDS/death in HIV-infected infants. *Aids, 23*(5), 597–604.

Goldin-Meadow, S. (2003). The resilience of language: What gesture creation in deaf children can tell us about how all children learn language. In J. Werker & H. Wellman (Eds.) *Essays in developmental psychology.* New York: Psychology Press.

Goldstein, S. E., Davis-Kean, P. E. & Eccles, J. S. (2005). Parents, peers, and problem behavior: A longitudinal investigation of the impact of relationship perceptions and characteristics on the development of adolescent problem behavior. *Developmental Psychology*, *41*(2), 401.

Goleman, D. (1995). *Emotional intelligence: Why it can matter more than IQ*. London: Bloomsbury.

Gonzalez-DeHass, A. R., Willems, P. P. & Holbein, M. F. D. (2005). Examining the relationship between parental involvement and student motivation. *Educational Psychology Review*, *17*(2), 99–123.

Gordon, M. (2009). The misuses and effective uses of constructivist teaching. *Teachers and Teaching: Theory and practice*, *15*(6), 737–746.

Gottlieb, G. (1991). Experiential canalisation of behavioral development: Theory. *Developmental Psychology*, *27*, 4–13.

Greenwood, D. & Loewenthal, D. (2005). The use of 'case study' in psychotherapeutic research and education. *Psychoanalytic Psychotherapy*, *19*(1), 35–47.

Grilo, C. M. (2006). *Eating and weight disorders*. Hove: Psychology Press.

Grissmer, D., Grimm, K. J., Aiyer, S. M., Murrah, W. M. & Steele, J. S. (2010). Fine motor skills and early comprehension of the world: Two new school readiness indicators. *Developmental Psychology*, *46*(5), 1008–1017.

Grossman, P. & McDonald, M. (2008). Back to the future: Directions for research in teaching and teacher education. *American Educational Research Journal*, *45*(1), 184–205.

Guay, F., Ratelle, C. F. & Chanal, J. (2008). Optimal learning in optimal contexts: The role of self-determination in education. *Canadian Psychology/ Psychologie Canadienne*, *49*(3), 233–240.

Guilford, J. P. (1950). Creativity. *The American Psychologist*, *5*, 444–454.

Guilford, J. P. (1967). *The nature of human intelligence*. New York: McGraw Hill.

Guilford, J. P. (1977). *Way beyond the IQ*. Buffalo, NY: Creative Education Foundation.

Guilford, J. P. (1987). Creativity research: Past, present and future. In S. G. Isaksen (Ed.) *Frontiers of creativity research: Beyond the basics* (pp. 33–65). Buffalo, NY: Bearly.

Günther, A. L., Karaolis-Danckert, N., Kroke, A., Remer, T. & Buyken, A. E. (2010). Dietary protein intake throughout childhood is associated with the timing of puberty. *The Journal of Nutrition*, *140*(3), 565–571.

Guo, Y., Piasta, S. B., Justice, L. M. & Kaderavek, J. N. (2010). Relations among preschool teachers' self-efficacy, classroom quality, and children's language and literacy gains. *Teaching and Teacher Education*, *26*(4), 1094–1103.

Gureasko-Moore, S., DuPaul, G. J. & White, G. P. (2007). Self-management of classroom preparedness and homework: Effects on school functioning of adolescents with attention deficit hyperactivity disorder. *School Psychology Review*, *36*, 647–664.

Hackshaw, A., Rodeck, C. & Boniface, S. (2011). Maternal smoking in pregnancy and birth defects: A systematic review based on 173,687 malformed cases and 11.7 million controls. *Human Reproduction Update*, *17*, 589–604.

Hadders-Algra, M. (2010). Variation and variability: Key words in human motor development. *Physical Therapy*, *90*(12), 1823–1837.

Haga, M. (2008). The relationship between physical fitness and motor competence in children. *Child: Care, Health and Development*, *34*(3), 329–334.

Hagell, A., Coleman, J. & Brooks, F. (2013). *Key data on adolescence 2013*. London: Association for Young People's Health.

Hager, P. & Hodkinson, P. (2009). Moving beyond the metaphor of transfer of learning. *British Educational Research Journal*, *35*(4), 619–638.

Hagwood, S. (2006). *Memory power: You can develop a great memory – America's grand master shows you how*. New York: Simon and Schuster.

Haidt, J. (2007). The new synthesis in moral psychology. *Science*, *316*, 998–1002.

Haidt, J. (2008). Morality. *Perspectives on Psychological Science*, *3*(1), 65–72.

Halliday, J. L., Watson, L. F., Lumley, J., Danks, D. M. & Sheffield, L. S. (1995). New estimates of Down syndrome risks of chorionic villus sampling, amniocentesis, and live birth in women of advanced maternal age from a uniquely defined population. *Prenatal Diagnosis*, *15*, 455–465.

Halpern, D. F. (2013). *Sex differences in cognitive abilities*. Hove: Psychology press.

Halpern, D. F., Benbow, C. P., Geary, D. C., Gur, R. C., Hyde, J. S. & Gernsbacher, M. A. (2007). The science of sex differences in science and mathematics. *Psychological Science in the Public Interest*, *8*(1), 1–51.

Han, S. S. & Weiss, B. (2005). Sustainability of teacher implementation of school-based mental health programs. *Journal of Abnormal Child Psychology, 33*(6), 665–679.

Harari, R. (2001). *Lacan's seminar on anxiety: An introduction.* New York: Other Press.

Hardy, S. A. (2006). Identity, reasoning, and emotion: An empirical comparison of three sources of moral motivation. *Motivation and Emotion, 30*(3), 205–213.

Hardy, S. A. & Carlo, G. (2011). Moral identity: What is it, how does it develop, and is it linked to moral action? *Child Development Perspectives, 5*(3), 212–218.

Haroutunian, S. (2012). *Equilibrium in the balance: A study of psychological explanation.* New York: Springer Science & Business Media.

Harry, B. & Klingner, J. (2006). *Why are so many minority students in special education?* New York: Teachers College Press.

Hart, D. & Carlo, G. (2005). Moral development in adolescence. *Journal of Research on Adolescence, 15*(3), 223–233.

Hasbrouck, J. & Tindal, G. A. (2006). Oral reading fluency norms: A valuable assessment tool for reading teachers. *The Reading Teacher, 59*(7), 636–644.

Hascher, T. & Hagenauer, G. (2010). Alienation from school. *International Journal of Educational Research, 49*(6), 220–232.

Haskell, R. E. (2000). *Transfer of learning: Cognition and instruction.* San Diego, CA: Academic Press.

Haste, H. & Abrahams, S. (2008). Morality, culture and the dialogic self: Taking cultural pluralism seriously. *Journal of Moral Education, 37*(3), 377–394.

Hattie, J. & Timperley, H. (2007). The power of feedback. *Review of Educational Research, 77*(1), 81–112.

Hau, K. T., Sung, R. Y. T., Yu, C. W., Marsh, H. W. & Lau, P. W. C. (2005). Factorial structure and comparison between obese and nonobese Chinese children's physical self-concept. In H. W. Marsh, R. G. Craven and D. M. McInerney (Eds.) *New frontiers of self research,* Vol. 2. Greenwich, CT: Information Age Publishing.

Haugaard, J. J. & Hazan, C. (2003). Adoption as a natural experiment. *Development and Psychopathology, 15,* 909–925.

Havighurst, R. J. (2013). History of developmental psychology: Socialization and personality development through the life span. In P. B. Bates and K. W. Schaie (Eds.) *Life-span developmental psychology: Personality*

and socialization (pp. 3–24). San Diego, CA: Academic Press.

Hawke, J. L., Olson, R. K., Willcut, E. G., Wadsworth, S. J. & DeFries, J. C. (2009). Gender ratios for reading difficulties. *Dyslexia, 15*(3), 239–242.

Haynes, R. L., Borenstein, N. S., Desilva, T. M., Folkerth, R. D., Liu, L. G., Volpe, J. J. & Kinney, H. C. (2005). Axonal development in the cerebral white matter of the human fetus and infant. *Journal of Comparative Neurology, 484*(2), 156–167.

Haynie, D. L. (2003). Contexts of risk? Explaining the link between girls' pubertal development and their delinquency involvement. *Social Forces, 82,* 355–397.

Haynie, D. L. & Osgood, D. W. (2005). Reconsidering peers and delinquency: How do peers matter? *Social Forces, 84*(2), 1109–1130.

Health and Social Care Information Centre (2014). National Child Measurement Programme: England, 2013/14 school year. Leeds: Health and Social Care Information Centre.

Hedegaard, M. (2005). 10 The zone of proximal development as basis for instruction. In H. Daniels (Ed.) *An introduction to Vygotsky* (pp. 227–252). Hove: Psychology Press.

Helle, L., Laakkonen, E., Tuijula, T. & Vermunt, J. D. (2013). The developmental trajectory of perceived self-regulation, personal interest, and general achievement throughout high school: A longitudinal study. *British Journal of Educational Psychology, 83*(2), 252–267. doi: 10.1111/bjep.12014

Helwig, C. C. & Turiel, E. (2011). Children's social and moral reasoning. In P. K. Smith and C. H. Hart (Eds.) *The Wiley-Blackwell handbook of childhood social development* (pp. 567–583). Madden, MA: Wiley-Blackwell.

Hergenhahn, B. & Henley, T. (2014). *An introduction to the history of psychology.* Belmont, CA: Cengage Learning.

Hermanussen, M., Largo, R. H. & Molinari, L. (2001). Canalisation in human growth: A widely accepted concept reconsidered. *European Journal of Pediatrics, 160*(3), 163–167.

Herpertz-Dahlmann, B. (2009). Adolescent eating disorders: Definitions, symptomatology, epidemiology and comorbidity. *Child and Adolescent Psychiatric Clinics of North America, 18*(1), 31–47.

Hill, B. V. (2010). What's 'open' about open education? In D. A. Nyberg (Ed.) *The philosophy of open education* (pp. 2–9). Oxon: Routledge.

Hill, N. E. & Tyson, D. F. (2009). Parental involvement in middle school: A meta-analytic assessment of the strategies that promote achievement. *Developmental Psychology*, *45*(3), 740–763.

Hills, L. A. (2006). Playing the field(s): An exploration of change, conformity and conflict in girls' understandings of gendered physicality in physical education. *Gender and Education*, *18*(5), 539–556.

Hodapp, R. M. (1996). Down syndrome: Developmental, psychiatric, and management issues. *Child and Adolescent Psychiatric Clinics of North America*, *5*, 881–894.

Hodges, J. & Tizard, B. (1989). Social and family relationships of ex-institutional adolescents. *Journal of Child Psychology and Psychiatry*, *30*, 77–97.

Hodgkinson, G. P. & Healey, M. P. (2008). Cognition in organizations. *Annual Review of Psychology*, *59*, 387–417.

Hoeve, M., Dubas, J. S., Eichelsheim, V. I., Van der Laan, P. H., Smeenk, W. & Gerris, J. R. (2009). The relationship between parenting and delinquency: A meta-analysis. *Journal of Abnormal Child Psychology*, *37*(6), 749–775.

Hoff, E. (2006). How social contexts support and shape language development. *Developmental Review*, *26*(1), 55–88.

Hole, G. (2012). Experimental design. In G. Breakwell, J. A. Smith and D. B. Wright (Eds.) *Research methods in psychology* (pp. 39–74). London: Sage.

Honeyford, M. A. & Boyd, K. (2015). Learning through play. *Journal of Adolescent & Adult Literacy*, *59*(1). 63–73.

Hoover-Dempsey, K. V., Walker, J. M., Sandler, H. M., Whetsel, D., Green, C. L., Wilkins, A. S. & Closson, K. (2005). Why do parents become involved? Research findings and implications. *The Elementary School Journal*, *106*(2), 105–130.

Hornby, G. & Lafaele, R. (2011). Barriers to parental involvement in education: An explanatory model. *Educational Review*, *63*(1), 37–52.

Horowitz, J. L. & Garber, J. (2006). The prevention of depressive symptoms in children and adolescents: A meta-analytic review. *Journal of Consulting and Clinical Psychology*, *74*(3), 401–415.

Howard, T. J., Culley, S. J. & Dekoninck, E. (2008). Describing the creative design process by the integration of engineering design and cognitive psychology literature. *Design studies*, *29*(2), 160–180.

Hughes, D. J., Furnham, A. & Batey, M. (2013). The structure and personality predictors of self-rated creativity. *Thinking Skills and Creativity*, *9*, 76–84.

Hughes, D., Rodriguez, J., Smith, E. P., Johnson, D. J., Stevenson, H. C. & Spicer, P. (2006). Parents' ethnic-racial socialization practices: A review of research and directions for future study. *Developmental Psychology*, *42*(5), 747.

Hughes, J. N. & Kwok, O. M. (2006). Classroom engagement mediates the effect of teacher–student support on elementary students' peer acceptance: A prospective analysis. *Journal of School Psychology*, *43*(6), 465–480.

Humphrey, N. (2013). *Social and emotional learning: A critical appraisal*. London: Sage.

Inagaki, K. & Hatano, G. (2006). Young children's conception of the biological world. *Current Directions in Psychological Science*, *15*(4), 177–181.

Isada, N. B. & Grossman, J. H., III. (1991). Perinatal infections. In S. G. Gabbe, J. R. Niebyl and J. L. Simpson (Eds.) *Obstetrics: Normal and problem pregnancies*. New York: Churchill Livingstone.

Iverson, J. M. (2010). Developing language in a developing body: The relationship between motor development and language development. *Journal of Child Language*, *37*(02), 229–261.

Jackson, L. A., Hunter, J. E. & Hodge, C. N. (1995). Physical attractiveness and intellectual competence: A meta-analytic review. *Social Psychology Quarterly*, *58*, 108–122.

Jairam, D., Kiewra, K. A., Rogers-Kasson, S., Patterson-Hazley, M. & Marxhausen, K. (2014). SOAR versus SQ3R: A test of two study systems. *Instructional Science*, *42*(3), 409–420.

Janzen, H., Obrzut, J. & Marusiak, C. (2004). Test review: Roid, G. H. (2003). Stanford–Binet intelligence scales (5th edn) (SB: V). *Canadian Journal of School Psychology*, *19*, 235–244.

Jarvis, M. (2004). *Psychodynamic psychology: Classical theory and contemporary research*. Derby: Thompson.

Jennings, P. A. & Greenberg, M. T. (2009). The prosocial classroom: Teacher social and emotional competence in relation to student and classroom outcomes. *Review of Educational Research*, *79*(1), 491–525.

Jensen, L. A. (2008). Through two lenses: A cultural–developmental approach to moral psychology. *Developmental Review*, *28*(3), 289–315.

Jeynes, W. H. (2007). The relationship between parental involvement and urban secondary school student academic achievement a meta-analysis. *Urban Education, 42*(1), 82–110.

Johansson, T. & Ritzén, E. (2005). Very long-term follow-up of girls with early and late menarche. In H. A. Delemarre-van de Waal (Ed.) *Abnormalities in puberty* (pp. 126–136). Basel: Karger.

Johnston, D. D. & Swanson, D. H. (2006). Constructing the 'good mother': The experience of mothering ideologies by work status. *Sex Roles, 54*(7–8), 509–519.

Jones, M. B. (1988). Autism: The child within. In K. L. Frieberg (Ed.) *Educating exceptional children* (6th edn). Guilford, CT: Duskin.

Jordan, A., Carlile, O. & Stack, A. (2008). *Approaches to learning: A guide for teachers: A guide for educators.* Maidenhead: McGraw-Hill Education.

Jorgensen, G. (2006). Kohlberg and Gilligan: Duet or duel? *Journal of Moral Education, 35*(2), 179–196.

Joseph, N. (2009). Metacognition needed: Teaching middle and high school students to develop strategic learning skills. *Preventing School Failure: Alternative Education for Children and Youth, 54*(2), 99–103.

Joussemet, M., Landry, R. & Koestner, R. (2008). A self-determination theory perspective on parenting. *Canadian Psychology, 49*(3), 194–200.

Junaid, K. A. & Fellowes, S. (2006). Gender differences in the attainment of motor skills on the movement assessment battery for children. *Physical & Occupational Therapy in Pediatrics, 26*(1–2), 5–11.

Jung, A. & Schuppe, H. C. (2007). Influence of genital heat stress on semen quality in humans. *Andrologia, 39*, 203–215.

Kaplan, R. M. & Saccuzzo, D. P. (2013). *Psychological testing: Principles, applications, and issues* (8th edn). Belmont, CA: Wadsworth.

Kaplowitz, P. (2006). Pubertal development in girls: Secular trends. *Current Opinion in Obstetrics and Gynecology, 18*(5), 487–491.

Karcher, M. J. (2005). The effects of developmental mentoring and high school mentors' attendance on their younger mentees' self-esteem, social skills, and connectedness. *Psychology in the Schools, 42*(1), 65–77.

Karpicke, J. D. (2012). Retrieval-based learning active retrieval promotes meaningful learning. *Current Directions in Psychological Science, 21*(3), 157–163.

Karpicke, J. D. & Blunt, J. R. (2011). Retrieval practice produces more learning than elaborative studying with concept mapping. *Science, 331*(6018), 772–775.

Karpicke, J. D. & Grimaldi, P. J. (2012). Retrieval-based learning: A perspective for enhancing meaningful learning. *Educational Psychology Review, 24*(3), 401–418.

Katz, J., Lee, A. C., Kozuki, N., Lawn, J. E., Cousens, S., Blencowe, H., ... & Adair, L. (2013). Mortality risk in preterm and small-for-gestational-age infants in low-income and middle-income countries: A pooled country analysis. *The Lancet, 382*, 417–425.

Kaufman, J. C. & Beghetto, R. A. (2009). Beyond big and little: The four c model of creativity. *Review of General Psychology, 13*(1), 1.

Kaufman, J. C., Waterstreet, M. A., Ailabouni, H. S., Whitcomb, H. J., Roe, A. K. & Riggs, M. (2010). Personality and self-perceptions of creativity across domains. *Imagination, Cognition and Personality, 29*(3), 193–209.

Kaufman, S. B. (2007). Sex differences in mental rotation and spatial visualization ability: Can they be accounted for by differences in working memory capacity? *Intelligence, 35*(3), 211–223.

Kearney, C. A. (2008). An interdisciplinary model of school absenteeism in youth to inform professional practice and public policy. *Educational Psychology Review, 20*(3), 257–282.

Kerns, K. A., Tomich, P. L. & Kim, P. (2006). Normative trends in children's perceptions of availability and utilization of attachment figures in middle childhood. *Social Development, 15*(1), 1–22.

Kesselring, T. & Müller, U. (2011). The concept of egocentrism in the context of Piaget's theory. *New Ideas in Psychology, 29*(3), 327–345.

Kessler, S. R. (2007). Turner syndrome. *Child and Adolescent Psychiatric Clinics, 16*, 709–722.

Kiernan, K. E. & Huerta, M. C. (2008). Economic deprivation, maternal depression, parenting and children's cognitive and emotional development during early childhood. *British Journal of Sociology, 59*, 783–806.

Killeya-Jones, L. A., Costanzo, P. R., Malone, P., Quinlan, N. P. & Miller-Johnson, S. (2007). Norm-narrowing and self-and other-perceived aggression in early-adolescent same-sex and mixed-sex cliques. *Journal of School Psychology, 45*(5), 549–565.

Kim, K. H. (2006). Can we trust creativity tests? A review of the Torrance Tests of Creative Thinking (TTCT). *Creativity Research Journal*, *18*(1), 3–14.

Kim, K. H. (2011). The creativity crisis: The decrease in creative thinking scores on the Torrance Tests of Creative Thinking. *Creativity Research Journal*, *23*(4), 285–295.

Kirschenbaum, H. (2007). *The life and work of Carl Rogers*. Ross-on-Wye: PCCS Books.

Kirschner, F., Paas, F. & Kirschner, P. A. (2009). A cognitive load approach to collaborative learning: United brains for complex tasks. *Educational Psychology Review*, *21*(1), 31–42.

Kirschner, P. A., Sweller, J. & Clark, R. E. (2006). Why minimal guidance during instruction does not work: An analysis of the failure of constructivist, discovery, problem-based, experiential, and inquiry-based teaching. *Educational Psychologist*, *41*(2), 75–86.

Kitsantas, A. & Chow, A. (2007). College students' perceived threat and preference for seeking help in traditional, distributed, and distance learning environments. *Computers & Education*, *48*(3), 383–395.

Kleine, P. (2000). *A psychometrics primer*. London: Free Association Books.

Klomsten, A. T., Marsh, H. W. & Skaalvik, E. M. (2005). Adolescents' perceptions of masculine and feminine values in sport and physical education: A study of gender differences. *Sex Roles*, *52*(9–10), 625–636.

Knollmann, M. & Wild, E. (2007). Quality of parental support and students' emotions during homework: Moderating effects of students' motivational orientations. *European Journal of Psychology of Education*, *22*(1), 63–76.

Knopik, V. S., Maccini, M. A., Francazio, S. & McGeary, J. E. (2012). The epigenetics of maternal cigarette smoking during pregnancy and their effects in child development. *Developmental Psychopathology*, *24*, 1377–1390.

Kobayashi, K. (2007). The influence of critical reading orientation on external strategy use during expository text reading. *Educational Psychology*, *27*(3), 363–375.

Kohlberg, L. (1976). Moral stages and moralization: The cognitive developmental approach. In T. Lickona (Ed.) *Moral development and behaviour: Theory, research and social issues* (pp. 31–53). New York: Holt, Reinhart and Winston.

Kohlberg, L. (1977). The implications of moral stages for adult education. *Religious Education*, *72*(2), 183–201.

Kohlberg, L. (1978). The cognitive-developmental approach to moral education. In P. Scharf (Ed.) *Readings in moral education* (pp. 36–51). Minneapolis, MN, Winston Press.

Kohlberg, L. (1981). *Essays on moral development, vol. I: The philosophy of moral development*. San Francisco, CA: Harper & Row.

Kohlberg, L., Levine, C. & Hewer, A. (1983). *Moral stages. A current formulation and response to critics*. Basel: Karger.

Kopp, C. B. & Kaler, S. R. (1989). Risk in infancy. *American Psychologist*, *44*, 224–230.

Koriat, A. & Ackerman, R. (2010). Metacognition and mindreading: Judgments of learning for self and other during self-paced study. *Consciousness and Cognition*, *19*(1), 251–264.

Korthagen, F. A. (2010). Situated learning theory and the pedagogy of teacher education: Towards an integrative view of teacher behavior and teacher learning. *Teaching and Teacher Education*, *26*(1), 98–106.

Košir, K. & Pečjak, S. (2005). Sociometry as a method for investigating peer relationships: What does it actually measure? *Educational Research*, *47*(1), 127–144.

Krebs, D. L. & Denton, K. (2005). Toward a more pragmatic approach to morality: A critical evaluation of Kohlberg's model. *Psychological Review*, *112*(3), 629.

Krebs, D. L. & Denton, K. (2006). Explanatory limitations of cognitive-developmental approaches to morality. *Psychological Review*, *113*(3), 672–675.

Kroger, J. (2004). Identity in formation. In K. Hoover (Ed.) *The future of identity: Centennial reflections on the legacy of Erik Erikson*. Lanham, MD: Lexington.

Kroger, J. (2007). *Identity development: Adolescence through adulthood*. Thousand Oaks, CA: Sage.

Kroger, J., Martinussen, M. & Marcia, J. E. (2010). Identity status change during adolescence and young adulthood: A meta-analysis. *Journal of Adolescence*, *33*(5), 683–698.

Kuhn, D. (2009). Adolescent thinking. In R. M. Lerner and L. Sternberg (Eds.) *Handbook of adolescent psychology* (pp. 152–186). Hoboken, NJ: Wiley.

Kutnick, P. (2011). Moral judgement and moral action. In S. Modgil and C. Modgil (Eds.) *Lawrence Kohlberg: Consensus and controversy* (pp. 125–149). Abingdon: Routledge.

Laible, D. (2007). Attachment with parents and peers in late adolescence: Links with emotional competence and social behavior. *Personality and Individual Differences, 43*(5), 1185–1197.

Lam, S., Wong, B. P. H., Yang, H. & Liu, Y. (2012). Understanding student engagement with a contextual model. In S. L. Chistenson, A. L. Reschly and C. Wylie (Eds.) *Research on Student Engagement* (pp. 403–419). New York: Springer.

Lane, A. (2008). Widening participation in education through open educational resources. In T. Iiyoshi and M. S. V. Kumar (Eds.) *Opening up education: The collective advancement of education through open technology, open content and open knowledge* (pp. 149–163). Cambridge, MA: MIT Press.

Langlois, J. H., Kalakanis, L., Rubenstein, A. J., Larson, A., Hallam, M. & Smoot, M. (2000). Maxims or myths of beauty. A meta-analytic and theoretical review. *Psychological Bulletin, 126*, 390–423.

Lansford, J. E. (2009). Parental divorce and children's adjustment. *Perspectives on Psychological Science, 4*(2), 140–152.

Lansford, J. E., Malone, P. S., Castellino, D. R., Dodge, K. A., Pettit, G. S. & Bates, J. E. (2006). Trajectories of internalizing, externalizing, and grades for children who have and have not experienced their parents' divorce or separation. *Journal of Family Psychology, 20*(2), 292–301.

Larsen, R. J. & Buss, D. M. (2013). *Personality psychology: Domains of knowledge about human nature.* New York: McGraw-Hill.

Laursen, B. & Collins, W. A. (2009). Parent-child relationships during adolescence. In R. M. Lerner and L. Sternberg (Eds.) *Handbook of adolescent psychology volume 2, third edition* (pp. 3–42). New York: Wiley.

Leary, M. R., Terry, M. L., Allen, A. B. & Tate, E. B. (2009). The concept of ego threat in social and personality psychology: Is ego threat a viable scientific construct? *Personality and Social Psychology Review, 13*(3), 151–164.

Lebel, C., Walker, L., Leemans, A., Phillips, L. & Beaulieu, C. (2008). Microstructural maturation of the human brain from childhood to adulthood. *Neurorimage, 40*(3), 1044–1055.

Lee, J. S. & Anderson, K. T. (2009). Negotiating linguistic and cultural identities: Theorizing and constructing opportunities and risks in education. *Review of Research in Education, 33*, 181–211.

Lee, J. S. & Bowen, N. K. (2006). Parent involvement, cultural capital, and the achievement gap among elementary school children. *American Educational Research Journal, 43*(2), 193–218.

Leopold, C., Sumfleth, E. & Leutner, D. (2013). Learning with summaries: Effects of representation mode and type of learning activity on comprehension and transfer. *Learning and Instruction, 27*, 40–49.

Levitt, J. M., Saka, N., Romanelli, L. H. & Hoagwood, K. (2007). Early identification of mental health problems in schools: The status of instrumentation. *Journal of School Psychology, 45*(2), 163–191.

Levykh, M. G. (2008). The affective establishment and maintenance of Vygotsky's zone of proximal development. *Educational Theory, 58*(1), 83–101.

Lewis, M. D. & Todd, R. M. (2007). The self-regulating brain: Cortical-subcortical feedback and the development of intelligent action. *Cognitive Development, 22*(4), 406–430.

Liem, G. A. D., Ginns, P., Martin, A. J., Stone, B. & Herrett, M. (2012). Personal best goals and academic and social functioning: A longitudinal perspective. *Learning and Instruction, 22*(3), 222–230.

Lilenfeld, L. R., Wonderlich, S., Riso, L. P., Crosby, R. & Mitchell, J. (2006). Eating disorders and personality: A methodological and empirical review. *Clinical Psychology Review, 26*(3), 299–320.

Lillard, A. S., Lerner, M. D., Hopkins, E. J., Dore, R. A., Smith, E. D. & Palmquist, C. M. (2013). The impact of pretend play on children's development: A review of the evidence. *Psychological Bulletin, 139*(1), 1.

Lillard, A. S., Pinkham, A. M. & Smith, E. (2011). Pretend play and cognitive development. In U. Goswami (Ed.) *The Wiley-Blackwell handbook of childhood cognitive development* (pp. 285–311). Chichester: Wiley.

Litta, A., Eliasmithb, C., Kroona, F. W., Weinsteinb, S. & Thagarda, P. (2006). Is the brain a quantum computer? *Cognitive Science, 30*, 593–603.

Locke, E. A. (2005). Why emotional intelligence is an invalid concept. *Journal of Organizational Behavior, 26*(4), 425.

Locke, E. A. & Latham, G. P. (2006). New directions in goal-setting theory. *Current Directions in Psychological Science, 15*(5), 265–268.

Lunce, L. M. (2006). Simulations: Bringing the benefits of situated learning to the traditional classroom. *Journal of Applied Educational Technology, 3*(1), 37–45.

Luyckx, K., Goossens, L., Soenens, B. & Beyers, W. (2006). Unpacking commitment and exploration: Preliminary validation of an integrative model of late adolescent identity formation. *Journal of Adolescence*, *29*(3), 361–378.

Maccoby, E. & Martin, J. (1983). Socialization in the context of the family: Parent–child interaction. In P. H. Mussen (Ed.) *Handbook of child psychology* (pp. 1–101). New York: Wiley.

Mackintosh, N. & Mackintosh, N. J. (2011). *IQ and human intelligence*. Oxford: Oxford University Press.

Mackintosh, N. J. (1998). *IQ and human intelligence*. London: Oxford University Press.

Magliaro, S. G., Lockee, B. B. & Burton, J. K. (2005). Direct instruction revisited: A key model for instructional technology. *Educational Technology Research and Development*, *53*(4), 41–55.

Malas, M. A., Dogan, S., Evcil, E. H. & Desdicioglu, K. (2006). Fetal development of the hand, digits and digit ratio (2D: 4D). *Early Human Development*, *82*(7), 469–475.

Malina, R. M. (1990). Physical growth and performance during the transitional years (9–16). In R. Montemayor, G. R. Adams and T. P. Gullotta (Eds.) *From childhood to adolescence. A transitional period?* Newbury Park, CA: Sage.

Marcason, W. (2014). Is there a standard meal plan for Phenylketonuria (PKU)? *Journal of the Academy of Nutrition and Dietetics*, *113*(8), 1124.

Marcia, J. E. (1966). Development and validation of ego identity status. *Journal of Personality and Social Psychology*, *3*(5), 551–558.

Marcia, J. E. (1967). Ego identity status: Relationship to change in self-esteem, "general maladjustment," and authoritarianism. *Journal of Personality*, *35*(1), 118–133.

Marcia, J. E. (1980). Identity in adolescence. In J. Adelson (Ed.) *Handbook of adolescent psychology* (pp. 159–187). New York: Wiley.

Marewski, J. N. & Schooler, L. J. (2011). Cognitive niches: An ecological model of strategy selection. *Psychological Review*, *118*(3), 393.

Marsh, H. W. (2002). A multidimensional physical self-concept: A construct validity approach to theory, measurement, and research. *Psychology: The Journal of the Hellenic Psychological Society*, *20*, 459–493.

Marsh, H. W. & Craven, R. (1997). Academic self-concept: Beyond the dustbowl. In G. Phye (Ed.) *Handbook of classroom assessment: Learning, adjustment and Achievement*. San Diego, CA: Academic Press.

Marsh, H. W. & Craven, R. G. (2006). Reciprocal effects of self-concept and performance from a multidimensional perspective: Beyond seductive pleasure and unidimensional perspectives. *Perspectives on Psychological Science*, *1*(2), 133–163.

Marsh, H. W., Hey, J., Roche, L. A. & Perry, C. (1997). The srtructure of physical self-concept: Elite athletes and physical education students. *Journal of Educational Psychology*, *89*, 369–380.

Marsh, H. W. & Martin, A. J. (2011). Academic self-concept and academic achievement: Relations and causal ordering. *British Journal of Educational Psychology*, *81*(1), 59–77.

Marsh, H. W. & O'Mara, A. (2008). Reciprocal effects between academic self-concept, self-esteem, achievement, and attainment over seven adolescent years: Unidimensional and multidimensional perspectives of self-concept. *Personality and Social Psychology Bulletin*, *34*(4), 542–552.

Marsh, H. W., Seaton, M., Trautwein, U., Lüdtke, O., Hau, K. T., O'Mara, A. J. & Craven, R. G. (2008). The big-fish–little-pond effect stands up to critical scrutiny: Implications for theory, methodology, and future research. *Educational Psychology Review*, *20*(3), 319–350.

Marsh, H. W., Trautwein, U., Lüdtke, O., Baumert, J. & Köller, O. (2007). The big-fish–little-pond effect: Persistent negative effects of selective high schools on self-concept after graduation. *American Educational Research Journal*, *44*(3), 631–669.

Marsh, H. W., Trautwein, U., Lüdtke, O., Köller, O. & Baumert, J. (2005). Academic self-concept, interest, grades, and standardized test scores: Reciprocal effects models of causal ordering. *Child Development*, *76*(2), 397–416.

Martens, R. (2012). *Successful coaching*. Champaign, IL: Human Kinasthetics.

Martin, A. J. (2015). Implicit theories about intelligence and growth (personal best) goals: Exploring reciprocal relationships. *British Journal of Educational Psychology*, *85*(2), 207–223.

Martin, E. H., Rudisill, M. E. & Hastie, P. A. (2009). Motivational climate and fundamental motor skill performance in a naturalistic physical education setting. *Physical Education and Sport Pedagogy*, *14*(3), 227–240.

Martin, J. H. (2005). The corticospinal system: From development to motor control. *The Neuroscientist, 11*(2), 161–173.

Masel, J. & Siegal, M. A. (2009). Robustness: Mechanisms and its consequences. *Trends in Genetics, 25,* 395–403.

Mashburn, A. J., Pianta, R. C., Hamre, B. K., Downer, J. T., Barbarin, O. A., Bryant, D., ... & Howes, C. (2008). Measures of classroom quality in prekindergarten and children's development of academic, language, and social skills. *Child Development, 79*(3), 732–749.

Maslow, A. H. (1968). *Motivation and personality* (2nd edn). New York: Harper.

Maslow, A. H. (1968). *Toward a psychology of being* (2nd edn). New York: Van Nostrand.

Maslow, A. H. (1976). *Religions, values and peak experiences* (2nd edn). New York: Penguin.

Masten, A. S., Roisman, G. I., Long, J. D., Burt, K. B., Obradović, J., Riley, J. R. ... & Tellegen, A. (2005). Developmental cascades: Linking academic achievement and externalizing and internalizing symptoms over 20 years. *Developmental Psychology, 41*(5), 733.

Matson, J. L., Beighley, J. & Tuygin, N. (2012). Autism diagnosis and screening: Factors to consider in differential diagnosis. *Research in Autism Spectrum Disorders, 1,* 19–24.

Maxwell, B. & DesRoches, S. (2010). Empathy and social-emotional learning: Pitfalls and touchstones for school-based programs. *New Directions for Child and Adolescent Development, 2010*(129), 33–53.

Mayer, J. D., Roberts, R. D. & Barsade, S. G. (2008a). Human abilities: Emotional intelligence. *Annual Review of Psychology, 59,* 507–536.

Mayer, J. D., Salovey, P. & Caruso, D. R. (2008b). Emotional intelligence: New ability or eclectic traits? *American Psychologist, 63*(6), 503.

Mayer, J. D., Salovey, P., Caruso, D. R. & Cherkasskiy, L. (2011). Emotional intelligence. In R. J. Sternberg and S. B Kaufman (Eds.) *The Cambridge handbook of intelligence* (pp. 528–549). New York: Cambridge University Press.

Mayer, R. E. (2008). Advances in applying the science of learning and instruction to education. *Psychological Science in the Public Interest, 9*(3), i–ii.

McAdams, D. P. & Pals, J. L. (2006). A new Big Five: Fundamental principles for an integrative science of personality. *American Psychologist, 61*(3), 204.

McCaslin, M. (2009). Co-regulation of student motivation and emergent identity. *Educational Psychologist, 44*(2), 137–146.

McCrudden, M. T., Schraw, G., Lehman, S. & Poliquin, A. (2007). The effect of causal diagrams on text learning. *Contemporary Educational Psychology, 32*(3), 367–388.

McDaniel, M. A., Howard, D. C. & Einstein, G. O. (2009). The read-recite-review study strategy effective and portable. *Psychological Science, 20*(4), 516–522.

McDonald, G., Le, H., Higgins, J. & Podmore, V. (2005). Artifacts, tools, and classrooms. *Mind, Culture, and Activity, 12*(2), 113–127.

McFarland, D. & Pals, H. (2005). Motives and contexts of identity change: A case for network effects. *Social Psychology Quarterly, 68*(4), 289–315.

McInerney, D. M. (2014). *Educational psychology: Constructing learning* (6th edn). Sydney: Pearson.

McKee, D., Rosen, R. S. & McKee, R. (2014). *Teaching and learning signed languages: International perspectives and practices.* Basingstoke: Palgrave Macmillan.

McKusick, V. A. (1998). *Mendelian inheritance in man: A catalog of human genes and genetic disorders.* Baltimore, MD: Johns Hopkins University Press.

McLean, K. C. (2005). Late adolescent identity development: Narrative meaning making and memory telling. *Developmental Psychology, 41*(4), 683–691.

McMonnies, C. W. (2009). Mechanisms of rubbing-related corneal trauma in keratoconus. *Cornea, 28*(6), 607–615.

McNeil, N. M. (2008). Limitations to teaching children 2 + 2 = 4: Typical arithmetic problems can hinder learning of mathematical equivalence. *Child Development, 79*(5), 1524–1537.

McNeil, N. M. & Alibali, M. W. (2005). Why won't you change your mind? Knowledge of operational patterns hinders learning and performance on equations. *Child Development, 76*(4), 883–899.

Meade, M. L., Nokes, T. J. & Morrow, D. G. (2009). Expertise promotes facilitation on a collaborative memory task. *Memory, 17*(1), 39–48.

Mearns, D., Thorne, B. & McLeod, J. (2013). *Person-centred counselling in action* (4th edn). London: Sage.

Meece, J. L., Anderman, E. M. & Anderman, L. H. (2006). Classroom goal structure, student motivation, and academic achievement. *Annual Review of Psychology, 57,* 487–503.

Mendle, J. (2014). Beyond pubertal timing new directions for studying individual differences in development. *Current Directions in Psychological Science, 23*(3), 215–219.

Mendle, J. & Ferrero, J. (2012). Detrimental psychological outcomes associated with pubertal timing in adolescent boys. *Developmental Review, 32*(1), 49–66.

Mendle, J., Turkheimer, E. & Emery, R. E. (2007). Detrimental psychological outcomes associated with early pubertal timing in adolescent girls. *Developmental Review, 27*(2), 151–171.

Mercer, N. (2013). The social brain, language, and goal-directed collective thinking: A social conception of cognition and its implications for understanding how we think, teach, and learn. *Educational Psychologist, 48*(3), 148–168.

Mercer, N. & Sams, C. (2006). Teaching children how to use language to solve maths problems. *Language and Education, 20*(6), 507–528.

Mercer, N., Dawes, L. & Staarman, J. K. (2009). Dialogic teaching in the primary science classroom. *Language and Education, 23*(4), 353–369.

Messerly, J. G. (2009). Piaget's Biology. In U. Müller, J. I. M. Carpendale and L. Smith (Eds.) *The Cambridge companion to Piaget* (pp. 94–109). Cambridge: Cambridge University Press.

Meyer, J. P. (2010). *Reliability: Understanding statistics measurement.* New York: Oxford University Press.

Meyers, C., Adam, R., Dungan, J. & Prenger, V. (1997). Aneuploidy in twin gestations: When is maternal age advanced? *Obstetrics and Gynecology, 89*, 248–251.

Micali, N., Hagberg, K. W., Petersen, I. & Treasure, J. L. (2013). The incidence of eating disorders in the UK in 2000–2009: Findings from the General Practice Research Database. *BMJ Open, 3*(5), e002646.

Michaud, P. A., Suris, J. C. & Deppen, A. (2006). Gender-related psychological and behavioural correlates of pubertal timing in a national sample of Swiss adolescents. *Molecular and Cellular Endocrinology, 254*, 172–178.

Michnick-Golinkoff, R., Hirsch-Pasek, K. & Singer, D. G. (2006). Why play = learning: A challenge for parents and educators. In D. G. Singer, R. M. Golinkoff and K. Hirsch-Pasek (Eds.) *Play = learning: How play motivates and enhances children's cognitive and social-emotional growth* (pp. 3–14). New York: Oxford University Press.

Miles, J. (2012). Correlation and regression. In G. Breakwell, J. A. Smith and D. B. Wright (Eds.) *Research methods in psychology* (pp. 243–278). London: Sage.

Miller, D. N., Eckert, T. L. & Mazza, J. J. (2009). Suicide prevention programs in the schools: A review and public health perspective. *School Psychology Review, 38*(2), 168–188.

Miller, E. & Kuhaneck, H. (2008). Children's perceptions of play experiences and play preferences: A qualitative study. *American Journal of Occupational Therapy, 62*(4), 407–415.

Miller, G. (1956). The magical number seven, plus or minus two: Some limits on our capacity for processing information. *The Psychological Review, 63*, 81–97.

Mills, C. (2008). Reproduction and transformation of inequalities in schooling: The transformative potential of the theoretical constructs of Bourdieu. *British Journal of Sociology of Education, 29*(1), 79–89.

Minick, N. (2005). The development of Vygotsky's thought: An introduction to thinking and speech. In H. Daniels (Ed.) *An introduction to Vygotsky* (pp. 32–56). Hove: Psychology Press.

Mitchell, A. A., Gilboa, S. M., Werler, M. M., Kelley, K. E., Louik, C. & Hernández-Díaz, S. (2011). Medication use during pregnancy, with particular focus on prescription drugs: 1976–2008. *American Journal of Obstetrics and Gynecology, 205*, 51.e1–51.e8.

Modecki, K. L., Minchin, J., Harbaugh, A. G., Guerra, N. G. & Runions, K. C. (2014). Bullying prevalence across contexts: A meta-analysis measuring cyber and traditional bullying. *Journal of Adolescent Health, 55*(5), 602–611.

Molden, D. C. & Dweck, C. S. (2006). Finding 'meaning' in psychology: A lay theories approach to self-regulation, social perception, and social development. *American Psychologist, 61*(3), 192.

Moline, J. M., Golden, A. J., Bar-Chama, N., Smith, E., Rauch, M. E., Chapin, R. E., Perreault, S. D., Schrader, S. M., Suk, W. A. & Landrigan, P. J. (2000). Exposure to hazardous substances and male reproductive health: A research framework. *Environmental Health Perspectives, 108*, 803–813.

Möller, J., Retelsdorf, J., Köller, O. & Marsh, H. W. (2011). The reciprocal internal/external frame of reference model an integration of models of relations between academic achievement and self-concept. *American Educational Research Journal, 48*(6), 1315–1346.

Monks, C. P. & Smith, P. K. (2006). Definitions of bullying: Age differences in understanding of the term, and the role of experience. *British Journal of Developmental Psychology, 24*(4), 801–821.

Montgomery, M. J. (2005). Psychosocial intimacy and identity from early adolescence to emerging adulthood. *Journal of Adolescent Research, 20*(3), 346–374.

Moonie, S. A., Sterling, D. A., Figgs, L. & Castro, M. (2006). Asthma status and severity affects missed school days. *Journal of School Health, 76*(1), 18.

Moore, K. L. & Persaud, T. V. N. (1993). *Before we are born* (4th edn). Philadephia, PA: Saunders.

Moore, S. & Rosenthal, D. (2006). *Sexuality in adolescence: Current trends.* New York: Routledge.

Morley, D., Bailey, R., Tan, J. & Cooke, B. (2005). Inclusive physical education: Teachers' views of including pupils with special educational needs and/ or disabilities in physical education. *European Physical Education Review, 11*, 84–107.

Morra, S., Gobbo, C., Marini, Z. & Sheese, R. (2012). *Cognitive development: Neo-Piagetian perspectives.* Hove: Psychology Press.

Morrison, R. G. (2005). Thinking in working memory. In K. J. Holyoak & R. G. Morrison (Eds.) *Cambridge handbook of thinking and reasoning* (pp. 457–473). Cambridge, MA: Cambridge University Press.

Morrison Gutman, L., McLoyd, V. C. & Tokoyawa, T. (2005). Financial strain, neighborhood stress, parenting behaviors, and adolescent adjustment in urban African American families. *Journal of Research on Adolescence, 15*(4), 425–449.

Moseley, B. (2005). Pre-service early childhood educators' perceptions of math-mediated language. *Early Education and Development, 16*(3), 385–398.

Moses, L. J. & Baldwin, D. A. (2005). What can the study of cognitive development reveal about children's ability to appreciate and cope with advertising? *Journal of Public Policy & Marketing, 24*(2), 186–201.

Moss, D. (2015). The roots and genealogy of humanistic psychology. In K. J. Schneider, J. F. Pierson and J. F. T. Bugental (Eds.) *The handbook of humanistic psychology: Theory, research, and practice* (pp. 3–18). Thousand Oaks, CA: Sage Publications.

Mrug, S. & Windle, M. (2008). Moderators of negative peer influence on early adolescent externalizing behaviors: Individual behavior, parenting, and school connectedness. *The Journal of Early Adolescence, 29*(4), 518–540.

Muijs, D. & Reynolds, D. (2011). *Effective teaching: Evidence and practice.* London: Sage.

Müller, U. (2009). Infancy. In U. Müller, J. I. M. Carpendale and L. Smith (Eds.) *The Cambridge companion to Piaget* (pp. 200–228). Cambridge: Cambridge University Press.

Murata, M. (2000). Secular trends in growth and changes in eating patterns of Japanese children. *The American Journal of Clinical Nutrition, 72*, 1379–1383.

Myyrya, L., Juujärvi, S. & Pesso, K. (2010). Empathy, perspective taking and personal values as predictors of moral schemas. *Journal of Moral Education, 39*(2), 213–233.

Narvaez, D. (2010). The embodied dynamism of moral becoming: Reply to Haidt (2010). *Perspectives on Psychological Science, 5*(2), 185–186.

Narvaez, D. (2014). Human flourishing and moral development: Cognitive and neurobiological perspectives of virtue development. In L. Nucci, T. Krettenauer and D. Narvaez (Eds.) *Handbook of moral and character education* (pp. 121–139). New York: Routledge.

Narvaez, D., Lapsley, D. K., Hagele, S. & Lasky, B. (2006). Moral chronicity and social information processing: Tests of a social cognitive approach to the moral personality. *Journal of Research in Personality, 40*(6), 966–985.

Negriff, S. & Susman, E. J. (2011). Pubertal timing, depression, and externalizing problems: A framework, review, and examination of gender differences. *Journal of Research on Adolescence, 21*(3), 717–746.

Nelson, R. M. & DeBacker, T. K. (2008). Achievement motivation in adolescents: The role of peer climate and best friends. *The Journal of Experimental Education, 76*(2), 170–189.

Nesbit, J. C. & Adesope, O. O. (2006). Learning with concept and knowledge maps: A meta-analysis. *Review of Educational Research, 76*(3), 413–448.

Ness, D. & Farenga, S. J. (2007). *Knowledge under construction: The importance of play in developing children's spatial and geometric thinking.* New York: Rowman & Littlefield Publishers.

Netley, C. T. (1986). Summary overview of behavioral development in individuals with neonatally identified X and Y aneuploidy. *Birth Defects, 22*, 293–306.

Newton, E. & Jenvey, V. (2011). Play and theory of mind: Associations with social competence in young children. *Early Child Development and Care, 181*(6), 761–773.

Newton, P. E. & Shaw, S. D. (2014). *Validity in educational and psychological assessment*. London: Sage.

Ng, K. Y. & Earley, P. C. (2006). Culture+ intelligence old constructs, new frontiers. *Group & Organization Management*, *31*(1), 4–19.

Nicholls, D. E., Lynn, R. & Viner, R. M. (2011). Childhood eating disorders: British national surveillance study. *The British Journal of Psychiatry*, *198*(4), 295–301.

Nicholson, J. M., McFarland, M. L. & Oldenburg, B. (1999). Detection of child mental health problems in the school setting. *The Australian Educational and Developmental Psychologist*, *16*, 66–77.

Nickerson, A. B. & Nagle, R. J. (2005). Parent and peer attachment in late childhood and early adolescence. *The Journal of Early Adolescence*, *25*(2), 223–249.

Nickerson, A. B., Mele, D. & Princiotta, D. (2008). Attachment and empathy as predictors of roles as defenders or outsiders in bullying interactions. *Journal of School Psychology*, *46*(6), 687–703.

Nicolaou, A. A. & Xistouri, X. (2011). Field dependence/ independence cognitive style and problem posing: An investigation with sixth grade students. *Educational Psychology*, *31*(5), 611–627.

Niebyl, J. R. (1991). Drugs in pregnancy and lactation. In S. G. Gabbe, J. R. Niebyl and J. L. Simpson (Eds.) *Obstetrics: Normal and problem pregnancies*. New York: Churchill Livingstone.

Nisbett, R. E., Aronson, J., Blair, C., Dickens, W., Flynn, J., Halpern, D. F. & Turkheimer, E. (2012). Intelligence: New findings and theoretical developments. *American Psychologist*, *67*(2), 130.

Nithiananthrajah, J. & Hannan, A. J. (2006). Enriched environments, experience-dependent plasticity and disorders of the nervous system. *Nature Reviews Neuroscience*, *7*, 697–709.

Nobes, G., Panagiotaki, G. & Pawson, C. (2009). The influence of negligence, intention, and outcome on children's moral judgments. *Journal of Experimental Child Psychology*, *104*(4), 382–397.

Nock, M. K. & Kessler, R. C. (2006). Prevalence of and risk factors for suicide attempts versus suicide gestures: Analysis of the National Comorbidity Survey. *Journal of Abnormal Psychology*, *115*(3), 616–623.

Noddings, N. (2005). Identifying and responding to needs in education. *Cambridge Journal of Education*, *35*(2), 147–159.

Noddings, N. (2006). *Critical lessons: What our schools should teach*. New York: Cambridge University Press.

Noddings, N. (2010). Moral education in an age of globalization. *Educational Philosophy and Theory*, *42*(4), 390–396.

Novak, J. D. (2010). *Learning, creating, and using knowledge: Concept maps as facilitative tools in schools and corporations*. Oxon: Routledge.

Novak, J. D. & Cañas, A. J. (2007). Theoretical origins of concept maps, how to construct them and uses in education. *Reflecting Education*, *3*(1), 29–42.

Nucci, L. & Turiel, E. (2009). Capturing the complexity of moral development and education. *Mind, Brain, and Education*, *3*(3), 151–159.

Nucci, L. P. & Powers, D. W. (2014). Social cognitive domain theory and moral education. In L. Nucci, T. Krettenauer and D. Narvaez (Eds.) *Handbook of moral and character education* (pp. 121–139). New York: Routledge.

Oesterdiekhoff, G. W. (2013). Relevance of Piagetian cross-cultural psychology to the humanities and social sciences. *The American Journal of Psychology*, *126*(4), 477–492.

Office for National Statistics (2004). *Mental health of children and young people in Great Britain, 2004*. London: HMSO.

Office for National Statistics (2015a). *Statistical bulletin: Families and households 2014*. London: HMSO.

Office for National Statistics (2015b). *Statistical update on suicide*. London: HMSO.

Ojose, B. (2008). Applying Piaget's theory of cognitive development to mathematics instruction. *The Mathematics Educator*, *18*, 26–30.

Olson, D. R. (2007). *Jerome Bruner: The cognitive revolution in educational theory*. London: Bloomsbury Publishing.

Olweus, D. (2010). Understanding and researching bullying. In S. R. Jimerson, S. M. Swearer, and D. L. Espelage (Eds.) *Handbook of bullying in schools: An international perspective* (pp. 9–33). New York: Routledge.

Olweus, D. (2011). Bullying at school and later criminality: Findings from three Swedish community samples of males. *Criminal Behaviour and Mental Health*, *21*(2), 151–156.

Olweus, D. & Limber, S. P. (2010). The Olweus bullying prevention program: Implementation and evaluation over two decades. In S. R. Jimerson, S. M. Swearer and D. L. Espelage (Eds.) *Handbook of bullying in schools: An international perspective* (pp. 377–402). New York: Routledge.

Ong, K. K., Ahmed, M. L. & Dunger, D. B. (2006). Lessons from large population studies on timing and tempo of puberty (secular trends and relation to body size): The European trend. *Molecular and Cellular Endocrinology, 254*, 8–12.

Onis, M. (2006). WHO motor development study: Windows of achievement for six gross motor development milestones. *Acta Paediatrica, 95*(S450), 86–95.

Otters, H., Schellevis, F. G., Damen, J., van der Wouden, J. C., van Suijlekom-Smit, L. W. & Koes, B. W. (2005). Epidemiology of unintentional injuries in childhood: A population-based survey in general practice. *British Journal of General Practice, 55*(517), 630–633.

Owens, L. M. & Ennis, C. D. (2005). The ethic of care in teaching: An overview of supportive literature. *Quest, 57*(4), 392–425.

Oyserman, D. (2013). Not just any path: Implications of identity-based motivation for disparities in school outcomes. *Economics of Education Review, 33*, 179–190.

Oyserman, D. & Lee, S. W. (2008). Does culture influence what and how we think? Effects of priming individualism and collectivism. *Psychological Bulletin, 134*(2), 311–342.

Pajares, F. (2008). Motivational role of self-efficacy beliefs in self-regulated learning. In D. H. Schunk and B. J. Zimmerman (Eds.) *Motivation and self-regulated learning: Theory, research, and applications* (pp. 111–139). New York: Lawrence Elrbaum.

Panzer, S., Wilde, H. & Shea, C. H. (2006). Learning of similar complex movement sequences: Proactive and retroactive effects on learning. *Journal of Motor Behavior, 38*(1), 60–70.

Parazzini, F., Marchini, M., Luchini, L., Tozzi, L., Mezzopane, R. & Fedele, L. (2008). Tight underpants and trousers and risk of dyspermia. *International Journal of Andrology, 18*, 137–140.

Parent, A. S., Teilmann, G., Juul, A., Skakkebaek, N. E., Toppari, J. & Bourguignon, J. P. (2003). The timing of normal puberty and the age limits of sexual precocity: Variations around the world, secular trends, and changes after migration. *Endocrinology Review, 24*, 668–693.

Patterson, D. & Costa, A. C. S. (2005). Down syndrome and genetics: A case of linked histories. *Nature Reviews Genetics, 6*, 137–147.

Patton, G. C. & Viner, R. (2007). Pubertal transitions in health. *Lancet, 369* (9567), 1130–1139. doi:10.1016/S0140-6736(07)60366-3

Paus, T. (2005). Mapping brain maturation and cognitive development during adolescence. *Trends in Cognitive Sciences, 9*(2), 60–68.

Paxton, S. J., Eisenberg, M. E. & Neumark-Sztainer, D. (2006). Prospective predictors of body dissatisfaction in adolescent girls and boys: A five-year longitudinal study. *Developmental Psychology, 42*(5), 888.

Payne, V. G. & Isaacs, L. D. (2012). *Human motor development: A lifespan approach*. New York: McGraw-Hill.

Pellegrini, A. D. & Bohn, C. M. (2005). The role of recess in children's cognitive performance and school adjustment. *Education and Educational Research, 34*(1), 13–19.

Pellegrini, A. D. & Bohn-Gettler, C. M. (2013). The benefits of recess in primary school. *Scholarpedia, 8*(2), 30448.

Pellegrini, A. D. & Horvat, M. (1995). A developmental contextualist critique of attention deficit hyperactivity disorder. *Educational Researcher, 24*, 13–19.

Pepler, D., Jiang, D., Craig, W. & Connolly, J. (2008). Developmental trajectories of bullying and associated factors. *Child Development, 79*(2), 325–338.

Perels, F., Gürtler, T. & Schmitz, B. (2005). Training of self-regulatory and problem-solving competence. *Learning and Instruction, 15*(2), 123–139.

Pérez-Pereira, M. & Conti-Ramsden, G. (1999). *Language development and social interaction in blind children*. Hove: Routledge.

Perry, D. G. & Pauletti, R. E. (2011). Gender and adolescent development. *Journal of Research on Adolescence, 21*(1), 61–74.

Peters, S. J. (2007). 'Education for all?' A historical analysis of international inclusive education policy and individuals with disabilities. *Journal of Disability Policy Studies, 18*, 98–108.

Peterson, C., Beck, K. & Rowell, G. (1992). *Psychology. An introduction for nurses and allied health professionals*. Sydney: Prentice Hall.

Petrill, S. A., Lipton, P. A., Hewitt, J. K., Plomin, R., Cherny, S. S., Corley, R. & DeFries, J. C. (2004). Genetic and environmental contributions to general cognitive ability through the first 16 years of life. *Developmental Psychology, 40*, 805–812.

Piaget, J. (1954, reprinted 2000). *The construction of reality in the child*. Oxon: Routledge.

Piaget, J. (1965). *The moral judgment of the child*. New York: Free Press.

Piaget, J. (1971, reprinted 2000). *Mental imagery in the child: A study of the development of imaginal representation*. Oxon: Routledge.

Piaget, J. (1973, reprinted 2015). *Memory and intelligence*. Oxon: Routledge.

Pianta, R. C., Hamre, B. K. & Allen, J. P. (2012). Teacher-student relationships and engagement: Conceptualizing, measuring, and improving the capacity of classroom interactions. In S. L. Chistenson, A. L. Reschly and C. Wylie (Eds.) *Research on Student Engagement* (pp. 365–401). New York: Springer.

Piek, J. P., Dawson, L., Smith, L. M. & Gasson, N. (2008). The role of early fine and gross motor coordination on later movement and cognitive ability. *Human Movement Science, 27*(5), 668–681.

Piffer, D. (2012). Can creativity be measured? An attempt to clarify the notion of creativity and general directions for future research. *Thinking Skills and Creativity, 7*(3), 258N264.

Pinker, S. & Jackendoff, R. (2005). The faculty of language: What's special about it? *Cognition, 95*, 201–236.

Pinkerton, J. & Dolan, P. (2007). Family support, social capital, resilience and adolescent coping. *Child & Family Social Work, 12*(3), 219–228.

Pinyerd, B. & Zipf, W. B. (2005). Puberty—Timing is everything! *Journal of Pediatric Nursing, 20*(2), 75–82.

Piquero, A. R., Farrington, D. P., Welsh, B. C., Tremblay, R. & Jennings, W. G. (2009). Effects of early family/parent training programs on antisocial behavior and delinquency. *Journal of Experimental Criminology, 5*(2), 83–120.

Pirrie, A., Macleod, G., Cullen, M. A. & McClusky, G. (2011). What happens to pupils permanently excluded from special schools and pupil referral units in England? *British Education Research Journal, 37*(3), 519–538. doi: 0.1080/01411926.2010.481724

Plomin, R. (1990). *Nature and nurture: An introduction to human behavioural genetics*. Pacific Grove, CA: Brooks/Cole.

Plomin, R. (1994a). *Genetics and experience: The interplay between nature and nurture*. Thousand Oaks, CA: Sage.

Plomin, R. (1994b). Nature, nurture, and social development. *Social Development, 3*, 37–53.

Plomin, R. (2004). Genetics and developmental psychology. *Merril-Palmer Quarterly, 50*, 341–352.

Plomin, R. & Petrill, S. A. (1997). Genetics and intelligence: What's new? *Intelligence, 24*, 53–77.

Plomin, R. & Rende, R. (1991). Human behavioral genetics. *Annual Review of Psychology, 42*, 161–190.

Plomin, R. & Spinath, F. M. (2004). Intelligence: Genetics, genes, and genomes. *Journal of Personality and Social Psychology, 86*, 112–129.

Plomin, R., Haworth, C. M. A. & Davis, O. S. P. (2009). Common disorders are quantitative traits. *Nature Reviews Genetics, 10*, 872–878.

Plucker, J. A. & Makel, M. C. (2009). Assessment of creativity. In J. C. Kauffman and R. J. Sternberg (Eds.) *The Cambridge handbook of creativity* (pp. 48–73). Cambridge: Cambridge University Press.

Polatajko, H. J. & Cantin, N. (2005). Developmental coordination disorder (dyspraxia): An overview of the state of the art. *Seminars in Pediatric Neurology, 12*(4), 250–258.

Polderman, T. J. C., Benyamin, B., de Leeuw, C. A., Sullivan, P. F., van Bochoven, A., Visscher, P. M. & Posthuma, D. (2015). Meta-analysis of the heritability of human traits based on fifty years of twin studies. *Nature Genetics, 47*, 702–709.

Pollastri, A. R., Cardemil, E. V. & O'Donnell, E. H. (2009). Self-esteem in pure bullies and bully/victims: A longitudinal analysis. *Journal of Interpersonal Violence, 28*(8), 1489–1502.

Pollit E. P. (1994). Poverty and child development: Relevance of research in developing countries to the United States. *Child Development, 65*, 283–295.

Pollit, E. P., Gorman, K. S., Engle, P. L., Martorell, R. & Rivera, J. (1993). Early supplemental feedings and cognition. *Monographs of the Society for Research in Child Development, 58*(7, Serial No. 235).

Pomerantz, E. M., Grolnick, W. S. & Price, C. E. (2005). The role of parents in how children approach achievement. In A. J. Elliot & C. Dweock (Eds.) *Handbook of competence and motivation* (pp. 259–278). New York: Guildford Press.

Pomerantz, E. M., Moorman, E. A. & Litwack, S. D. (2007). The how, whom, and why of parents' involvement in children's academic lives: More is not always better. *Review of Educational Research, 77*(3), 373–410.

Posner, R. B. (2006). Early menarche: A review of research on trends in timing, racial differences, etiology and psychosocial consequences. *Sex Roles, 54*(5–6), 315–322.

Postmes, T., Haslam, S. A. & Swaab, R. I. (2005). Social influence in small groups: An interactive model of social identity formation. *European Review of Social Psychology, 16*(1), 1–42.

Powell, K. C. & Kalina, C. J. (2009). Cognitive and social constructivism: Developing tools for an effective classroom. *Education, 130*(2), 241–250.

Powell, K. C. & Kalina, C. J. (2009). Cognitive and social constructivism: Developing tools for an effective classroom. *Education, 130*(2), 241.

Prabhu, V., Sutton, C. & Sauser, W. (2008). Creativity and certain personality traits: Understanding the mediating effect of intrinsic motivation. *Creativity Research Journal, 20*(1), 53–66.

Prater, C. D. & Zylstra, R. G. (2002). Autism: A medical primer. *American Family Physician, 66*, 1667.

Preckel, F., Holling, H. & Wiese, M. (2006). Relationship of intelligence and creativity in gifted and non-gifted students: An investigation of threshold theory. *Personality and individual differences, 40*(1), 159–170.

Proos, L. & Gustafsson, J. (2012). Is early puberty triggered by catch-up growth following undernutrition? *International Journal of Environmental Research and Public Health, 9*(5), 1791–1809.

Psaltis, C. & Duveen, G. (2007). Conservation and conversation types: Forms of recognition and cognitive development. *British Journal of Developmental Psychology, 25*(1), 79–102.

Pulter, S. (2010, February 10). Size zero diets 'ruining girls' health' warns watchdog over teenagers copying celebrity role models. The *Daily Mail*. Retrieved from http://dailymail.co.uk/health/article-1249683/Teenage-girls-starving-bodies-essential-nutrients-warns-food-watchdog.html

Purdie, N., Hattie, J. & Carroll, A. (2002). A review of the research on interventions for attention deficit hyperactivity disorder: What works best? *Review of Educational Research, 72*, 61–99.

Putnam, A. L. (2015). Mnemonics in education: Current research and applications. *Translational Issues in Psychological Science, 1*(2), 130–139.

Putnam, R. T. & Borko, H. (2000). What do new views of knowledge and thinking have to say about research on teacher learning? *Educational Researcher, 29*, 4–15.

Quintero, R. A., Puder, K. S. & Cotton, D. B. (1993). Embryoscopy and fetoscopy. *Obstetrics and Gynecology Clinics of North America, 20*, 563–581.

Raghubar, K. P., Barnes, M. A. & Hecht, S. A. (2010). Working memory and mathematics: A review of developmental, individual difference, and cognitive approaches. *Learning and Individual Differences, 20*(2), 110–122.

Rakoczy, H. (2007). Play, games, and the development of collective intentionality. *New Directions for Child and Adolescent Development*, (115), 53–67.

Ramstetter, C. L., Murray, R. & Garner, A. S. (2010). The crucial role of recess in schools. *Journal of School Health, 80*(11), 517–526.

Rapee, R. M., Kennedy, S., Ingram, M., Edwards, S. & Sweeney, L. (2005). Prevention and early intervention of anxiety disorders in inhibited preschool children. *Journal of Consulting and Clinical Psychology, 73*, 488.

Rayce, S. L., Holstein, B. E. & Kreiner, S. (2009). Aspects of alienation and symptom load among adolescents. *European Journal of Public Health, 19*(1), 79–84.

Ream, G. L. & Savin-Williams, R. C. (2005). Reciprocal associations between adolescent sexual activity and quality of youth-parent interactions. *Journal of Family Psychology, 19*(2), 171–179.

Reeve, C. L. & Bonaccio, S. (2011). The nature and structure of 'intelligence'. In T. Chamorro-Premuzic, A. Furnham and S. von Stumm (Eds.) *Handbook of individual differences* (pp. 187–216). Oxford: Wiley-Blackwell.

Reeve, J. (2012). A self-determination theory perspective on student engagement. In S. L. Chistenson, A. L. Reschly and C. Wylie (Eds.) *Handbook of research on student engagement* (pp. 149–172). New York: Springer.

Reid, K. (2005). The causes, views and traits of school absenteeism and truancy: An analytical review. *Research in Education, 74*(1), 59–82.

Reinke, W. M., Stormont, M., Herman, K. C., Puri, R. & Goel, N. (2011). Supporting children's mental health in schools: Teacher perceptions of needs, roles, and barriers. *School Psychology Quarterly, 26*(1), 1–13.

Rest, J. R., Bebeau, M. J. & Thoma, S. J. (1999). *Postconventional moral thinking: A neo-Kohlbergian approach*. Mahwah, NJ: Lawrence Erlbaum.

Reynolds, B. M. & Juvonen, J. (2011). The role of early maturation, perceived popularity, and rumors in the emergence of internalizing symptoms amoung adolescent girls. *Journal of Youth and Adolescence, 40,* 1407–1422.

Rietzschel, E. F., Nijstad, B. A. & Stroebe, W. (2006). Productivity is not enough: A comparison of interactive and nominal brainstorming groups on idea generation and selection. *Journal of Experimental Social Psychology, 42*(2), 244–251.

Rigby, K. (2005). Why do some children bully at school? The contributions of negative attitudes towards victims and the perceived expectations of friends, parents and teachers. *School Psychology International, 26*(2), 147–161.

Rigby, K. & Smith, P. K. (2011). Is school bullying really on the rise? *Social Psychology of Education, 14*(4), 441–455.

Riley, J. G. & Jones, R. B. (2010). Acknowledging learning through play in the primary grades. *Childhood Education, 86*(3), 146–149.

Ritts, V., Patterson, M. L. & Tubbs, M. E. (1992). Expectations, impressions, and judgements of physically attractive students: A review. *Review of Educational Research, 62,* 413–426.

Robbins, J. (2005). Contexts, Collaboration, and cultural tools: A sociocultural perspective on researching children's thinking. *Contemporary Issues in Early Childhood, 6*(2), 140–149.

Roberts, C. (2013). Early puberty, 'sexualization' and feminism. *European Journal of Women's Studies, 20*(2), 138–154.

Robins, R. W. & Trzesniewski, K. H. (2005). Self-esteem development across the lifespan. *Current Directions in Psychological Science, 14*(3), 158–162.

Robson, C. (2011). *Real world research*. London: Wiley.

Rogelberg, S. G. (2006). *Encyclopedia of industrial and organizational psychology*. Thousand Oaks, CA: Sage publications.

Rogers, C. (1951). *Client-centered therapy: Its current practice, implications and theory*. London: Constable.

Rogers, C. (1961). *On becoming a person: A therapist's view of psychotherapy*. London: Constable.

Roid, G. H. (2003). *Stanford-Binet intelligence scales* (5th edn). Itasca, IL: Riverside Publishing.

Roorda, D. L., Koomen, H. M., Spilt, J. L. & Oort, F. J. (2011). The influence of affective teacher–student relationships on students' school engagement and achievement a meta-analytic approach. *Review of Educational Research, 81*(4), 493–529.

Rose, A. J. & Rudolph, K. D. (2006). A review of sex differences in peer relationship processes: Potential trade-offs for the emotional and behavioral development of girls and boys. *Psychological Bulletin, 132*(1), 98.

Rosenberg, A. A. (1991). The neonate. In S. G. Gabbe, J. R. Niebyl and J. L. Simpson (Eds.) *Obstetrics: Normal & problem pregnancies* (2nd edn), pp. 697–752. New York: Churchill Livingstone.

Rosenblith, J. F. (1992). *In the beginning: Development from conception to age two*. Newbury Park, CA: Sage.

Roseth, C. J., Johnson, D. W. & Johnson, R. T. (2008). Promoting early adolescents' achievement and peer relationships: The effects of cooperative, competitive, and individualistic goal structures. *Psychological Bulletin, 134*(2), 223.

Roskos, K. A. & Neuman, S. B. (2005). Whatever happened to developmentally appropriate practice in early literacy? *Young Children, 60*(4), 22–26.

Roth, W. M. & Lee, Y. J. (2007). 'Vygotsky's neglected legacy': Cultural-historical activity theory. *Review of Educational Research, 77*(2), 186–232.

Rowbottom, D. P. & Aiston, S. J. (2011). The use and misuse of taxpayers' money: Publicly-funded educational research. *British Educational Research Journal, 37*(4), 631–655.

Rudd, M. D., Berman, A. L., Joiner, T. E., Nock, M. K., Silverman, M. M., Mandrusiak, M., ... & Witte, T. (2006). Warning signs for suicide: Theory, research, and clinical applications. *Suicide and Life-Threatening Behavior, 36*(3), 255–262.

Rudnytsky, P. L. (2008). Inventing Freud. *The American Journal of Psychoanalysis, 68*(2), 117–127.

Runco, M. A. (2005). Motivation, competence, and creativity. In A. J. Elliot & C. S. Dweck (Eds.) *Handbook of competence and motivation* (pp. 609–623). London: Guilford Press.

Rushton, J. P. & Jensen, A. R. (2010). The rise and fall of the Flynn effect as a reason to expect a narrowing of the Black–White IQ gap. *Intelligence, 38*(2), 213–219.

Rutter, M. L. (1997). Nature-nurture integration: The example of anti-social behavior. *American Psychologist*, 52, 390–398.

Rutter, M. L. (2015). Some of the complexities involved in gene-environment interplay. *International Journal of Epidemiology*, 44, 1128–1129.

Ryan, R. M. & Deci, E. L. (2006). Self-regulation and the problem of human autonomy: Does psychology need choice, self-determination, and will? *Journal of Personality*, 74(6), 1557–1586.

Sadler, T. D. (2009). Situated learning in science education: Socio-scientific issues as contexts for practice. *Studies in Science Education*, 45(1), 1–42.

Sale, A., Berardi, N. & Maffei, L. (2009). Enrich the environment to empower the brain. *Trends in Neurosciences*, 32(4), 233–239.

Salovey, P. & Grewal, D. (2005). The science of emotional intelligence. *Current Directions in Psychological Science*, 14(6), 281–285.

Saltmarsh, R., McDougall, S. & Downey, J. (2005). Attributions about child behaviour: Comparing attributions made by parents of children diagnosed with ADHD and those made by parents of children with behavioural difficulties. *Child and Educational Psychology*, 22, 108–126.

Sandberg, A. & Pramling-Samuelsson, I. (2005). An interview study of gender difference in preschool teachers' attitudes toward children's play. *Early Childhood Education Journal*, 32(5), 297–305.

Sandstrom, M. J. & Cillessen, A. H. (2006). Likeable versus popular: Distinct implications for adolescent adjustment. *International Journal of Behavioral Development*, 30(4), 305–314.

Santrock, J. W. (2009). *Life-span development*. Boston, MA: McGraw-Hill.

Sayal, K. (2006). Annotation: Pathways to care for children with mental health problems. *Journal of Child Psychology and Psychiatry*, 47(7), 649–659.

Scarr, S. & McCartney, K. (1983). How people make their own environments: A theory of genotype environment effects. *Child Development*, 54, 424–435.

Scheuerle, A. (2005). *Understanding genetics: A primer for couples and families*. Westport, CT: Praeger.

Schunk, D. H. (2008). Metacognition, self-regulation, and self-regulated learning: Research recommendations. *Educational Psychology Review*, 20(4), 463–467.

Schunk, D. H. & Mullen, C. A. (2012). Self-efficacy as an engaged learner. In S. L. Christenson, A. L. Reschly and C. Wylie (Eds.) *Handbook of research on student engagement* (pp. 219–236). London: Springer.

Schunk, D. H. & Pajares, F. (2005). Competence perceptions and academic functioning. In A. J. Elliot and C. S. Dweck (Eds.) *Handbook of competence and motivation* (pp. 85–104). New York: Guildford.

Schwartz, D. L., Bransford, J. D. & Sears, D. (2005). Efficiency and innovation in transfer. In J. P. Mstre (Ed.) *Transfer of learning from a modern multidisciplinary perspective* (pp. 1–51). Greenwich, CN: Information Age Publishing.

Schwartz, D., Gorman, A. H., Nakamoto, J. & Toblin, R. L. (2005). Victimization in the Peer Group and Children's Academic Functioning. *Journal of Educational Psychology*, 97(3), 425–435.

Schwartz, S. H. (2006). A theory of cultural value orientations: Explication and applications. *Comparative Sociology*, 5(2), 137–182.

Seabrook, R., Brown, G. D. & Solity, J. E. (2005). Distributed and massed practice: From laboratory to classroom. *Applied Cognitive Psychology*, 19(1), 107–122.

Sebastian, C., Burnett, S. & Blakemore, S. J. (2008). Development of the self-concept during adolescence. *Trends in Cognitive Sciences*, 12(11), 441–446.

Sederberg, P. B., Howard, M. W. & Kahana, M. J. (2008). A context-based theory of recency and contiguity in free recall. *Psychological Review*, 115(4), 893.

Seligman, M. E., Ernst, R. M., Gillham, J., Reivich, K. & Linkins, M. (2009). Positive education: Positive psychology and classroom interventions. *Oxford Review of Education*, 35(3), 293–311.

Selikowitz, M. (1997). *Down syndrome: The facts* (2nd edn). Oxford: Oxford University Press.

Sentenac, M., Ehlinger, V., Michelsen, S. I., Marcelli, M., Dickinson, H. O. & Arnaud, C. (2013). Determinants of inclusive education of 8–12 year-old children with cerebral palsy in 9 European regions. *Research in Developmental Disabilities*, 34, 588–595.

Serbin, L. & Karp, J. (2003). Intergenerational students of parenting and the transfer of risk from parent to child. *Current Directions in Psychological Science*, 12(4), 138–142.

Serrien, D. J., Ivry, R. B. & Swinnen, S. P. (2006). Dynamics of hemispheric specialization and integration in the context of motor control. *Nature Reviews Neuroscience*, *7*(2), 160–166.

Sfard, A. & Prusak, A. (2005). Telling identities: In search of an analytic tool for investigating learning as a culturally shaped activity. *Educational Researcher*, *34*(4), 14–22.

Shadish, W. R. (2002). Revisiting field experimentation: Field notes for the future. *Psychological Methods*, *7*(1), 3–18. doi:10.1037//1082-989X.7.1.3

Shadish, W. R., Cook, T. D. & Campbell, D. T. (2002). *Experimental and quasi-experimental designs for generalized causal inference*. Boston, MA: Houghton Mifflin.

Sharma, R., Agarwal, A., Rohra, V. K., Assidi, M., Abu-Elmagd, M. & Turki, R. F. (2015). Effects of increased paternal age on sperm quality, reproductive outcome and associated epigenetic risks to offspring. *Reproductive Biology and Endocrinology*, *13*(1), 35–21.

Shaw, S. K. & Dallos, R. (2005). Attachment and adolescent depression: The impact of early attachment experiences. *Attachment and Human Development*, *7*(4), 409–424.

Shayer, M. (2008). Intelligence for education: As described by Piaget and measured by psychometrics. *British Journal of Educational Psychology*, *78*(1), 1–29.

Shayer, M. & Adhami, M. (2007). Fostering cognitive development through the context of mathematics: Results of the CAME project. *Educational Studies in Mathematics*, *64*(3), 265–291.

Shayer, M., Ginsburg, D. & Coe, R. (2007). Thirty years on–a large anti-Flynn effect? The Piagetian test volume & heaviness norms 1975–2003. *British Journal of Educational Psychology*, *77*(1), 25–41.

Shearer, C. B. & Luzzo, D. A. (2009). Exploring the application of multiple intelligences theory to career counseling. *The Career Development Quarterly*, *58*(1), 3–13.

Sheldon, W. H. (1940). *The varieties of human physique: An introduction to constitutional psychology*. New York: Harper.

Sheldon, W. H. (1970). *Atlas of men: A guide for somatotyping the adult male at all ages*. Darien, CT: Hafner.

Sheldon, W. H. & Stevens, S. H. (1942). *The varieties of temperament*. New York: Harper & Row.

Shih, M. & Sanchez, D. T. (2005). Perspectives and research on the positive and negative implications of having multiple racial identities. *Psychological Bulletin*, *131*(4), 569.

Shweder, R. A., Mahapatra, M. & Miller, J. C. (1990). Culture and Moral Development. In J. W. Stigler, R. A. Shweder and E. G. Herdt (Eds.) *Cultural psychology: Essays on comparative human development* (pp. 130–204). Cambridge: Cambridge University Press.

Siegal, M. (1991). *Knowing children: Experiments in conversation and cognition*. Hillsdale, NJ: Lawrence Erlbaum.

Siegler, R. S. (1991). *Children's thinking* (2nd edn). Englewood Cliffs, NJ: Prentice Hall.

Silenzio, V. M., Pena, J. B., Duberstein, P. R., Cerel, J. & Knox, K. L. (2007). Sexual orientation and risk factors for suicidal ideation and suicide attempts among adolescents and young adults. *American Journal of Public Health*, *97*(11), 2017–2019.

Silva, M., Dorso, E., Azhar, A. & Renk, K. (2007). The relationship among parenting styles experienced during childhood, anxiety, motivation, and academic success in college students. *Journal of College Student Retention: Research, Theory & Practice*, *9*(2), 149–167.

Silvia, P. J. (2008). Another look at creativity and intelligence: Exploring higher-order models and probable confounds. *Personality and Individual differences*, *44*(4), 1012–1021.

Silvia, P. J., Wigert, B., Reiter-Palmon, R. & Kaufman, J. C. (2012). Assessing creativity with self-report scales: A review and empirical evaluation. *Psychology of Aesthetics, Creativity, and the Arts*, *6*(1), 19.

Sinclair, D. (1989). *Human growth after birth*. Oxford: Oxford University Press.

Skaalvik, S. & Skaalvik, E. M. (2005). Self-concept, motivational orientation, and help-seeking behavior in mathematics: A study of adults returning to high school. *Social Psychology of Education*, *8*(3), 285–302.

Skinner, B. F. (1938). *The behavior of organisms: An experimental analysis*. New York: Appleton-Century-Crofts.

Skinner, B. F. (1957). *Verbal behavior*. New York: Appleton-Century-Croft.

Slavin, R. E., Chamberlain, A. & Daniels, C. (2007). Preventing reading failure. *Educational Leadership*, *65*(2), 22–27.

Slavin, R. E., Chamberlain, A., Daniels, C. & Madden, N. A. (2009). The Reading Edge: A randomized evaluation of a middle school cooperative reading program. *Effective Education, 1*(1), 13–26.

Slyper, A. H. (2006). The pubertal timing controversy in the USA, and a review of possible causative factors for the advance in timing of onset of puberty. *Clinical Endocrinology, 65*(1), 1–8.

Smetana, J. G. (2005). Adolescent-parent conflict: Resistance and subversion as developmental process. In N. Larry (Ed.) *Conflict, contradiction, and contrarian elements in moral development and education* (pp. 69–91). Mahwah, NJ: Lawrence Erlbaum Associates.

Smetana, J. G. (2006). Social-cognitive domain theory: Consistencies and variations in children's moral and social judgments. In M. Killen and J. Smetana (Eds.) *Handbook of moral development* (pp. 119–153). Mahwah, NJ: Lawrence Erlbaum.

Smetana, J., Crean, H. F. & Campione-Barr, N. (2005). Adolescents' and parents' changing conceptions of parental authority. *New Directions for Child and Adolescent Development, 108*, 31–46.

Smetana, J. G., Campione-Barr, N. & Metzger, A. (2006). Adolescent development in interpersonal and societal contexts. *Annual Review of Psychology, 57*, 255–284.

Smetana, J. G. & Turiel, E. (2008). Moral Development during Adolescence. In G. R. Adams and M. D. Berzonsky (Eds.) *Blackwell handbook of adolescence* (pp. 247–268). Madden, MA: Blackwell.

Smetana, J., Jambon, M. & Ball, C. (2014). The social domain approach to children's moral and social judgements. In M. Killen and J. Smetana (Eds.) *Handbook of moral development* (pp. 23–45). New York: Psychology Press.

Smith, E. R. & Semin, G. R. (2007). Situated social cognition. *Current Directions in Psychological Science, 16*(3), 132–135.

Smith, J. A. (2015). *Qualitative psychology: A practical guide to research methods*. London: Sage.

Smith, L. (2009). Piaget's develeopmental epistemology. In U. Müller, J. I. M. Carpendale and L. Smith (Eds.) *The Cambridge companion to Piaget* (pp. 64–93). Cambridge: Cambridge University Press.

Smith, L. B. (2005). Cognition as a dynamic system: Principles from embodiment. *Developmental Review, 25*(3), 278–298.

Smith, M., Calam, R. & Bolton, C. (2009). Psychological factors linked to self-reported depression symptoms

in late adolescence. *Behavioural and Cognitive Psychotherapy, 37*(1), 73–85.

Smith, P. K. (2005). Social and pretend play in children. In A. D. Pellegrini and P. K. Smith (Eds.) *The Nature of play: Great apes and humans* (pp. 173–209). New York: Guilford Press.

Smith, P. K. (2011). Bullying in schools: Thirty years of research. In C. P. Monks and I. Coyne (Eds.) *Bullying in different contexts* (pp. 36–60). Cambridge: Cambridge University Press.

Smithers-Sheedy, H., Badawi, N., Blair, E., Cans, C., Himmelmann, K., Krägeloh-Mann, I. ... & Wilson, M. (2014). What constitutes cerebral palsy in the twenty-first century? *Developmental Medicine & Child Neurology, 56*, 323–328.

Smoll, F. L. & Schutz, R. W. (1990). Quantifying gender differences in physical performance: A developmental perspective. *Developmental Psychology, 26*(3), 360.

Smolucha, F. (1992). Social origins of private speech in pretend play. In R. M. Diaz and L. E. Berk (Eds.) Private speech: From social interaction to self-regulation. Hillsdale, NJ: Lawrence Erlbaum.

Snarey, J. & Samuelson, P. L. (2014). Lawrence Kohlberg's revolutionary ideas: Moral education in the cognitive-developmental tradition. In L. Nucci, T. Krettenauer and D. Narvaez (Eds.) *Handbook of moral and character education* (pp. 61–83). New York: Routledge.

Sober, S. J. & Sabes, P. N. (2005). Flexible strategies for sensory integration during motor planning. *Nature Neuroscience, 8*(4), 490–497.

Soenens, B. & Vansteenkiste, M. (2010). A theoretical upgrade of the concept of parental psychological control: Proposing new insights on the basis of self-determination theory. *Developmental Review, 30*(1), 74–99.

Soenens, B., Vansteenkiste, M., Lens, W., Luyckx, K., Goossens, L., Beyers, W. & Ryan, R. M. (2007). Conceptualizing parental autonomy support: Adolescent perceptions of promotion of independence versus promotion of volitional functioning. *Developmental Psychology, 43*(3), 633.

Spearman, C. (1927). *The abilities of man*. London: MacMillan.

Spelke, E. S. (2005). Sex differences in intrinsic aptitude for mathematics and science? A critical review. *American Psychologist, 60*(9), 950.

Spencer, J. P., Blumberg, M. S., McMurray, B., Robinson, S. R., Samuelson, L. K. & Tomblin, J. B. (2009). Short arms and talking eggs: Why we should no longer abide the nativist–empiricist debate. *Child Development Perspectives*, 3(2), 79–87.

Spera, C. (2005). A review of the relationship among parenting practices, parenting styles, and adolescent school achievement. *Educational Psychology Review*, 17(2), 125–146.

Spiel, C. (2009). Evidence-based practice: A challenge for European developmental psychology. *European Journal of Developmental Psychology*, 6(1), 11–33.

St Clair-Thompson, H. L. & Gathercole, S. E. (2006). Executive functions and achievements in school: Shifting, updating, inhibition, and working memory. *The Quarterly Journal of Experimental Psychology*, 59(4), 745–759.

Staffieri, J. R. (1967). A study of social stereotype of body image in children. *Journal of Personality and Social Psychology*, 7, 101–104.

Stanton-Salazar, R. D. & Spina, S. U. (2005). Adolescent peer networks as a context for social and emotional support. *Youth & Society*, 36(4), 379–417.

Steinberg, L. (2005). Cognitive and affective development in adolescence. *Trends in Cognitive Sciences*, 9(2), 69–74.

Steinberg, S. J., Davila, J. & Fincham, F. (2006). Adolescent marital expectations and romantic experiences: Associations with perceptions about parental conflict and adolescent attachment security. *Journal of Youth and Adolescence*, 35(3), 314–329.

Stern, W. (1914, original work published 1912). *The psychological methods of testing intelligence* (G. M. Whipple, Trans.). Baltimore, MD: Warwick & York.

Sternberg, R. J. (1985). *Beyond IQ: A triarchic theory of intelligence*. Cambridge: Cambridge University Press.

Sternberg, R. J. (1986). *Intelligence applied: Understanding and increasing your own intellectual skills*. New York: Harcourt Brace Jovanovich.

Sternberg, R. J. (1997). *Successful intelligence: How practical and creative intelligence determine success in life*. New York: Plume.

Sternberg, R. J. (1998a). Principles of teaching for successful intelligence. *Educational Psychologist*, 33, 65–72.

Sternberg, R. J. (1998b). Teaching triarchically improves school achievement. *Journal of Educational Psychology*, 33, 374–384.

Sternberg, R. J. (2000). *Handbook of intelligence*. New York: Cambridge University Press.

Sternberg, R. J. (2003). What is an "expert student?" *Educational Researcher*, 32, 5–9.

Sternberg, R. J. (2006). The nature of creativity. *Creativity Research Journal*, 18(1), 87–98.

Sternberg, R. J. (2012a). Intelligence. *Wiley Interdisciplinary Reviews: Cognitive Science*, 3(5), 501–511.

Sternberg, R. J. (2012b). The theory of successful intelligence. In R. J. Sternberg and S. B Kaufman (Eds.) *The Cambridge handbook of intelligence* (pp. 504–527). New York: Cambridge University Press.

Sternberg, R. J. & Grigorenko, E. L. (Eds.) (1997). *Intelligence, heredity and environment*. New York: Cambridge University Press.

Sternberg, R. J., Torff, B. & Grigorenko, E. L. (1998). Teaching triarchically improves school achievement. *Journal of Educational Psychology*, 3, 374–384.

Stewart, E. B. (2008). School structural characteristics, student effort, peer associations, and parental involvement the influence of school-and individual-level factors on academic Achievement. *Education and Urban Society*, 40(2), 179–204.

Stodden, D. F., Goodway, J. D., Langendorfer, S. J., Roberton, M. A., Rudisill, M. E., Garcia, C. & Garcia, L. E. (2008). A developmental perspective on the role of motor skill competence in physical activity: An emergent relationship. *Quest*, 60(2), 290–306.

Stokes, D. E. (1997). *Pasteur's quadrant: Basic science and technological innovation*. Washington, DC: Brookings Institution Press.

Strumia, R. (2005). Dermatologic signs in patients with eating disorders. *American Journal of Clinical Dermatology*, 6(3), 165–173.

Sugden, D. (2007). Current approaches to intervention in children with developmental coordination disorder. *Developmental Medicine and Child Neurology*, 49(6), 467–471.

Sullivan, A. L. (2011). Disproportionality in special education identification and placement of English language learners. *Exceptional Children*, 77, 317–334.

Sullivan, K. J., Kantak, S. S. & Burtner, P. A. (2008). Motor learning in children: Feedback effects on skill acquisition. *Physical Therapy*, 88(6), 720–732.

Sung, S. Y. & Choi, J. N. (2009). Do big five personality factors affect individual creativity? The moderating role of extrinsic motivation. *Social Behavior and Personality: An International Journal, 37*(7), 941–956.

Sutton, A. J., Kendrick, D. & Coupland, C. A. (2008). Meta-analysis of individual-and aggregate-level data. *Statistics in Medicine, 27*(5), 651–669.

Sutton, J., Harris, C. B., Keil, P. G. & Barnier, A. J. (2010). The psychology of memory, extended cognition, and socially distributed remembering. *Phenomenology and the Cognitive Sciences, 9*(4), 521–560.

Sweller, J. & Sweller, S. (2006). Natural information processing systems. *Evolutionary Psychology, 4*(2), 434–58.

Tanner, J. M. (1990). *Fetus into man: Physical growth from conception to maturity* (revised and enlarged). Cambridge, MA: Harvard University Press.

Taube, J. S. (2007). The head direction signal: Origins and sensory-motor integration. *Annual Review of Neuroscience, 30*, 181–207.

Terzi, L. (2005). Beyond the dilemma of difference: The capability approach to disability and special educational needs. *Journal of Philosophy of Education, 39*, 443–459.

Thapa, A., Cohen, J., Guffey, S. & Higgins-D'Alessandro, A. (2013). A review of school climate research. *Review of Educational Research, 83*(3), 357–385.

Thapar, A., Holmes, J., Poulton, K. et al. (1999). Genetic basis of attention deficit and hyperactivity. *British Journal of Psychiatry, 174*, 105–111.

Tharp, R. & Gallimore, R. (1988). *Rousing minds to life.* Cambridge: Cambridge University Press.

Thoma, S. J. (2006). Research on the defining issues test. In M. Killen and J. Smetana (Eds.) *Handbook of moral development* (pp. 67–91). New York: Psychology Press.

Thomas, J. R. & French, K. E. (1985). Gender differences across age in motor performance: A meta-analysis. *Psychological Bulletin, 98*(2), 260.

Thorkdike, E. L. (1911). *Animal intelligence: Experimental studies.* New York: Macmillan.

Thurstone, L. L. (1938). *Primary mental abilities.* Chicago, IL: University of Chicago Press.

Tiggemann, M. (2005). Body dissatisfaction and adolescent self-esteem: Prospective findings. *Body Image, 2*(2), 129–135.

Tobin, M. C., Drager, K. D. & Richardson, L. F. (2014). A systematic review of social participation for adults with autism spectrum disorders: Support, social functioning, and quality of life. *Research in Autism Spectrum Disorders, 8*, 214–229.

Tomasello, M. (2000). Culture and cognitive development. *Current Directions in Psychological Science, 9*(2), 37–40.

Tomasello, M. (2003). *Constructing a language: A usage-based theory of language acquisition.* Cambridge, MA: Harvard University Press.

Toppino, T. C., Cohen, M. S., Davis, M. L. & Moors, A. C. (2009). Metacognitive control over the distribution of practice: When is spacing preferred? *Journal of Experimental Psychology: Learning, Memory, and Cognition, 35*(5), 1352.

Torellio, H. V. & Meck, J. M. (2008). Statement on guidance for genetic counselling in advanced paternal age. *Genetics in Medicine, 10*, 457–460.

Torrance, E. P. (1962). *Guiding creative talent.* Englewood Cliffs, NJ: Prentice Hall.

Torrance, E. P. (1988). The nature of creativity as manifest in its testing. In R. J. Sternberg (Ed.) *The nature of creativity* (pp. 43–73). New York: Cambridge University Press.

Torres, S. J. & Nowson, C. A. (2007). Relationship between stress, eating behavior, and obesity. *Nutrition, 23*(11), 887–894.

Tryon, R. C. (1940). Genetic differences in maze learning in rats. *Yearbook of the National Society for the Study of Education, 39*, 111–119.

Tse, D., Langston, R. F., Kakeyama, M., Bethus, I., Spooner, P. A., Wood, E. R., ... & Morris, R. G. (2007). Schemas and memory consolidation. *Science, 316*, 76–82.

Turiel, E. (2008). Thought about actions in social domains: Morality, social conventions, and social interactions. *Cognitive Development, 23*(1), 136–154.

Turiel, E. (2014). Thought, emotions, and social interactional processes in moral development. In M. Killen and J. Smetana (Eds.) *Handbook of moral development* (pp. 3–22). New York: Psychology Press.

Turner, E. A., Chandler, M. & Heffer, R. W. (2009). The influence of parenting styles, achievement motivation, and self-efficacy on academic performance in college students. *Journal of College Student Development, 50*(3), 337–346.

Twidle, J. (2006). Is the concept of conservation of volume in solids really more difficult than for liquids, or is the way we test giving us an unfair comparison? *Educational Research*, *48*(1), 93–109.

Ulrich, B. (2007). Motor development: Core curricular concepts. *Quest*, *59*(1), 77–91.

Urdan, T. & Schoenfelder, E. (2006). Classroom effects on student motivation: Goal structures, social relationships, and competence beliefs. *Journal of School Psychology*, *44*(5), 331–349.

Uren, N. & Stagnitti, K. (2009). Pretend play, social competence and involvement in children aged 5–7 years: The concurrent validity of the Child-Initiated Pretend Play Assessment. *Australian Occupational Therapy Journal*, *56*(1), 33–40.

Usher, E. L. & Pajares, F. (2008). Sources of self-efficacy in school: Critical review of the literature and future directions. *Review of Educational Research*, *78*(4), 751–796.

Vaisey, S. (2009). Motivation and Justification: A Dual-Process Model of Culture in Action1. *American Journal of Sociology*, *114*(6), 1675–1715.

Van Haastert, I. C., De Vries, L. S., Helders, P. J. M. & Jongmans, M. J. (2006). Early gross motor development of preterm infants according to the Alberta Infant Motor Scale. *The Journal of Pediatrics*, *149*(5), 617–622.

Van IJzendoorn, M. H., Bakermans-Kranburg, M. J. & Juffer, F. (2007). Plasticity of growth in height, weight, and head circumference: Meta-analytic evidence of massive catch-up after international adoption. *Journal of Developmental & Behavioral Pediatrics*, *28*, 334–343.

Van Merrienboer, J. J. & Sweller, J. (2005). Cognitive load theory and complex learning: Recent developments and future directions. *Educational Psychology Review*, *17*(2), 147–177.

Van Merriënboer, J. J., Kester, L. & Paas, F. (2006). Teaching complex rather than simple tasks: Balancing intrinsic and germane load to enhance transfer of learning. *Applied Cognitive Psychology*, *20*(3), 343–352.

Vass, E. & Littleton, K. (2010). Peer collaboration and learning in the classroom. In K. Littleton, C. Wood and J. Kleine-Starman (Eds.) *International handbook of psychology in education* (pp. 105–135). Bingley: Emerald.

Veenman, M. V. & Spaans, M. A. (2005). Relation between intellectual and metacognitive skills: Age and task differences. *Learning and Individual Differences*, *15*(2), 159–176.

Veenman, M. V., Van Hout-Wolters, B. H. & Afflerbach, P. (2006). Metacognition and learning: Conceptual and methodological considerations. *Metacognition and Learning*, *1*(1), 3–14.

Venetsanou, F. & Kambas, A. (2010). Environmental factors affecting preschoolers' motor development. *Early Childhood Education Journal*, *37*, 319–327.

Verdonschot, M. M. L., De Witte, L. P., Reichrath, E., Buntix, W. H. E. & Curfs, L. M. G. (2009). Impact of environmental factors on community participation of persons with an intellectual disability: A systematic review. *Journal of Intellectual Disability Research*, *53*, 54–64.

Vianna, E. & Stetsenko, A. (2006). Embracing history through transforming it contrasting Piagetian versus Vygotskian (activity) theories of learning and development to expand constructivism within a dialectical view of history. *Theory & Psychology*, *16*, 81–108.

Vicari, S. (2006). Motor development and neuropsychological patterns in persons with Down syndrome. *Behavior Genetics*, *36*(3), 355–364.

Villavicencio, F. T. & Baernardo, A. B. I. (2013). Positive academic emotions moderate the relationship between self-regulation and academic achievement. *British Journal of Educational Psychology*, *83*(2), 329–340. doi: 10.1111/j.2044-8279.2012.02064.x

Vincent, C. & Ball, S. J. (2007). Making up the middle-class child: Families, activities and class dispositions. *Sociology*, *41*(6), 1061–1077.

Visootsak, J. & Graham, J. M. Jr. (2006). Klinefelter syndrome and other sex chromosomal aneuploidies. *Orphanet Journal of Rare Diseases*, *1*(42), 1–5.

Vitaro, F., Pedersen, S. & Brendgen, M. (2007). Children's disruptiveness, peer rejection, friends' deviancy, and delinquent behaviors: A process-oriented approach. *Development and Psychopathology*, *19*(02), 433–453.

Voyer, D. & Voyer, S. D. (2014). Gender differences in scholastic achievement: A meta-analysis. *Psychological Bulletin*, *140*(4), 1174–1204.

Vygotsky, L. S. (1962). *Thought and language*. Cambridge, MA: MIT Press.

Vygotsky, L. S. (1978). *Mind in society: The development of higher psychological processes*. Cambridge, MA: Harvard University Press.

Vygotsky, L., Hanfmann, E. & Vakar, G. (2012). *Thought and language*. Massachusetts: MIT Press.

Waddington, C. H. (1957). *The strategy of the genes.* London: Allen & Unwin.

Wagemans, J., Elder, J. H., Kubovy, M., Palmer, S. E., Peterson, M. A., Singh, M. & von der Heydt, R. (2012). A century of Gestalt psychology in visual perception: I. Perceptual grouping and figure–ground organization. *Psychological Bulletin, 138*(6), 1172.

Wagner, A. D., Maril, A. & Schacter, D. L. (2000). Interactions between forms of memory: When priming hinders new episodic learning. *Journal of Cognitive Neuroscience, 12*(2), 52–60.

Wahlsten, D. (1999). Single-gene influences on brain and behavior. *Annual Review of Psychology, 50,* 599–624.

Waldorf, K. M. A. & McAdams, R. M. (2013). The influence of infection during pregnancy on fetal development. *Reproduction, 1,* 151–162.

Waldrip, A. M., Malcolm, K. T. & Jensen-Campbell, L. A. (2008). With a little help from your friends: The importance of high-quality friendships on early adolescent adjustment. *Social Development, 17*(4), 832–852.

Walker, L. J. (2006). Gender and morality. In M. Killen and J. Smetana (Eds.) *Handbook of moral development* (pp. 93–115). New York: Psychology Press.

Wallas, G. (1926). *The art of thought.* New York: Harcourt Brace.

Waller, G. & Sheffield, A. (2008). Causes of bulimic disorders. *Psychiatry, 7*(4), 152–155.

Wang, J., Iannotti, R. J. & Nansel, T. R. (2009). School bullying among adolescents in the United States: Physical, verbal, relational, and cyber. *Journal of Adolescent Health, 45*(4), 368–375.

Wang, M. & Holcombe, R. (2010). Adolescents' perceptions of school environment, engagement, and academic achievement in middle school. *American Educational Research Journal, 47*(3), 633–662.

Wardle, J., Brodersen, N. H., Cole, T. J., Jarvis, M. J. & Boniface, D. R. (2006). Development of adiposity in adolescence: Five year longitudinal study of an ethnically and socioeconomically diverse sample of young people in Britain. *British Medical Journal, 332*(7550), 1130–1135.

Watson, J. B. (1913). Psychology as the behaviorists view it. *Psychological Review, 20,* 157–158.

Watson, M. & Battistich, V. (2006). Building and sustaining caring communities. In C. M. Evertson and C. S. Weinstein (Eds.) *Handbook of classroom management: Research, practice, and contemporary issues* (pp. 253–279). Mahwah: Erlbaum.

Way, N. & Greene, M. L. (2006). Trajectories of perceived friendship quality during adolescence: The patterns and contextual predictors. *Journal of Research on Adolescence, 16*(2), 293–320.

Webb, N. M. (1980). A process-outcome analysis of learners in group and individual settings. *Educational Psychology, 15,* 69–83.

Wechsler, D. (2002). *Wechsler preschool and primary scale of intelligence* (3rd edn). San Antonio, TX: Psychological Corporation.

Wechsler, D. (2004). *The Wechsler intelligence scale for children* (4th edn). San Antonio, TX: Pearson.

Wechsler, D. (2008). *Wechsler adult intelligence scale* (4th edn). San Antonio, TX: Pearson.

Weigold, A., Weigold, I. K. & Russell, E. J. (2013). Examination of the equivalence of self-report survey-based paper-and-pencil and Internet data collection methods. *Psychological Methods, 18*(1), 53.

Weiten, W. (2001). *Psychology: Themes and variations* (5th edn). Belmont, CA: Wadsworth/Thomson Learning.

Wellman, H. M. (2011). Reinvigorating explanations for the study of early cognitive development. *Child Development Perspectives, 5*(1), 33–38.

Wells, B. W. P. (1983). *Body and personality.* London: Longman.

Welsh, M. C., Pennington, B. F., Ozonoff, S., Rouse, B. & McCabe, E. R. B. (1990). Neuropsychology of early-treated phenylketonuria: Specific executive function deficits. *Child Development, 61,* 1697–1713.

Wentzel, K. R. (2005). Peer relationships, motivation, and academic performance at school. In A. J. Elliot and C. S. Dweck (Eds.) *Handbook of competence and motivation* (pp. 279–296). New York: Guildford.

Wentzel, K. R. (2012). Socio-cultural contexts, social competence and engagement at school. In S. L. Chistenson, A. L. Reschly and C. Wylie (Eds.) *Research on Student Engagement* (pp. 479–488). New York: Springer.

Wertsch, J. V. (2009). Mediation. In H. Daniels, M. Cole and J. V. Wertsch (Eds.) *The Cambridge companion to Vygotsky* (pp. 178–192). Cambridge: Cambridge University Press.

Westerberg-Jacobson, J., Edlund, B. & Ghaderi, A. (2010). A 5-year longitudinal study of the relationship between the wish to be thinner, lifestyle behaviours and disturbed eating in 9–20-year old girls. *European Eating Disorders Review*, *18*(3), 207–219.

White, S. J., Boldt, K. L., Holditch, S. J., Poland, G. A. & Jacobson, R. A. (2012). Measles, mumps and rubella. *Clinical Obstertrics and Gynacology*, *55*, 550–559.

Whitebread, D., et al. (2009). The development of two observational tools for assessing metacognition and self-regulated learning in young children. *Metacognition and Learning*, *4*(1), 63–85.

Wigfield, A. & Wagner, A. L. (2005). Competence, motivation, and identity development during adolescence. In A. J. Elliot and C. S. Dweck (Eds.) *Handbook of competence and motivation* (pp. 222–239). New York: Guildford.

Wigfield, A., Byrnes, J. P. & Eccles, J. S. (2006). Development during early and middle adolescence. In P. Alexander and P. H. Winne (Eds.) *Handbook of educational psychology second edition* (pp. 87–113). New York: Routledge.

Willig, C. (2013). *Introducing qualitative research in psychology*. Maidenhead: McGraw-Hill.

Wilson, C. J. (2007). When and how do young people seek professional help for mental health problems? *The Medical Journal of Australia*, *187*(Supplement), S35–S39.

Winsberg, B. G. & Comings, D. E. (1999). Association of the dopamine transporter gene (DAT1) with poor methylphenidate response. *Journal of the American Academy of Child and Adolescent Psychiatry*, *38*, 1474–1477.

Woods, S., Done, J. & Kalsi, H. (2009). Peer victimisation and internalising difficulties: The moderating role of friendship quality. *Journal of Adolescence*, *32*(2), 293–308.

World Health Organisation Multicentre Growth Reference Study Group & de Onis, M. (2006). Relationship between physical growth and motor development in the WHO Child Growth Standards. *Acta Paediatrica*, *95*(S450), 96–101.

Worthington-Roberts, B. S. & Klerman, L. V. (1990). Maternal nutrition. In I. R. Merkatz & J. E. Thompson (Eds.) *New perspectives on prenatal care*. New York: Elsevier.

Wright, S. M. & Aronne, L. J. (2012). Causes of obesity. *Abdominal Imaging*, *37*(5), 730–732.

Wuang, Y. P., Wang, C. C., Huang, M. H. & Su, C. Y. (2008). Profiles and cognitive predictors of motor functions among early school-age children with mild intellectual disabilities. *Journal of Intellectual Disability Research*, *52*(12), 1048–1060.

Wyra, M., Lawson, M. J. & Hungi, N. (2007). The mnemonic keyword method: The effects of bidirectional retrieval training and of ability to image on foreign language vocabulary recall. *Learning and instruction*, *17*(3), 360–371.

Yeates, K. O., Bigler, E. D., Dennis, M., Gerhardt, C. A., Rubin, K. H., Stancin, T., Taylor, G. H. & Vannatta, K. (2007). Social outcomes in childhood brain disorder: A heuristic integration of social neuroscience and developmental psychology. *Psychological bulletin*, *133*(3), 535–556.

Yeung, A. S. & McInerney, D. M. (2005). Students' school motivation and aspiration over high school years. *Educational Psychology*, *25*(5), 537–554.

Yilmaz, K. (2011). The cognitive perspective on learning: Its theoretical underpinnings and implications for classroom practices. *The Clearing House: A Journal of Educational Strategies, Issues and Ideas*, *84*(5), 204–212.

Yin, Y., Vanides, J., Ruiz-Primo, M. A., Ayala, C. C. & Shavelson, R. J. (2005). Comparison of two concept-mapping techniques: Implications for scoring, interpretation, and use. *Journal of Research in Science teaching*, *42*(2), 166–184.

Zhang, J. & Patel, V. L. (2006). Distributed cognition, representation, and affordance. *Pragmatics & Cognition*, *14*(2), 333–341.

Zimmerman, B. J. (2008). Investigating self-regulation and motivation: Historical background, methodological developments, and future prospects. *American Educational Research Journal*, *45*(1), 166–183. doi: 10.3102/0002831207312909

Zimmerman, B. J. & Cleary, T. J. (2009). Motives to self-regulate learning: A social cognitive account. In K. R. Wentzel & A. Wigfield (Eds.) *Handbook of motivation at school* (pp. 247–264). Oxon: Routledge.

Zimmerman, B. J. & Kitsantas, A. (2005). Homework practices and academic achievement: The mediating role of self-efficacy and perceived responsibility beliefs. *Contemporary Educational Psychology*, *30*(4), 397–417.

Index

Taylor & Francis eBooks

Helping you to choose the right eBooks for your Library

Add Routledge titles to your library's digital collection today. Taylor and Francis ebooks contains over 50,000 titles in the Humanities, Social Sciences, Behavioural Sciences, Built Environment and Law.

Choose from a range of subject packages or create your own!

Benefits for you

>> Free MARC records
>> COUNTER-compliant usage statistics
>> Flexible purchase and pricing options
>> All titles DRM-free.

Benefits for your user

>> Off-site, anytime access via Athens or referring URL
>> Print or copy pages or chapters
>> Full content search
>> Bookmark, highlight and annotate text
>> Access to thousands of pages of quality research at the click of a button.

REQUEST YOUR **FREE** INSTITUTIONAL TRIAL TODAY | **Free Trials Available** We offer free trials to qualifying academic, corporate and government customers.

eCollections – Choose from over 30 subject eCollections, including:

Archaeology	Language Learning
Architecture	Law
Asian Studies	Literature
Business & Management	Media & Communication
Classical Studies	Middle East Studies
Construction	Music
Creative & Media Arts	Philosophy
Criminology & Criminal Justice	Planning
Economics	Politics
Education	Psychology & Mental Health
Energy	Religion
Engineering	Security
English Language & Linguistics	Social Work
Environment & Sustainability	Sociology
Geography	Sport
Health Studies	Theatre & Performance
History	Tourism, Hospitality & Events

For more information, pricing enquiries or to order a free trial, please contact your local sales team:
www.tandfebooks.com/page/sales

Routledge
Taylor & Francis Group

The home of Routledge books

www.tandfebooks.com